HISTORY OF BENTON COUNTY

BY J. DICKSON BLACK

Table of Contents

Author's Dedication iv
Introduction vii
Chapter 1   Naming of the County 1
         2   Benton County 4
         3   Lovely's Purchase 15
         4   Early Settlers 18
         5   Court Houses and Jails 25
         6   Early Documents 32
         7   Post Offices 41
         8   Newspapers 43
         9   Railroads 53
        10   Interurban 60
        11   Minerals and Mining 64
        12   Agriculture 75
        13   Schools 102
        14   Crimes and Criminals 116
        15   Benton County Industry 130
        16   Coin Harvey 140
        17   The Liberty Party 149
        18   People of Interest 154
        19   Places of Interest 173
        20   Items of Interest 191
        21   Civil War in Benton County 217
        22   Unveiling the Monument 264
        23   Bella Vista Resort 268
        24   Towns and Villages 276
        25   Benton County's Last Pioneer 324
        26   Small Talk 329
        27   Pictures from the Past 349

DEDICATION

This book is dedicated to the people that I wrote about and the lives they lived. If they hadn't lived and worked hard in Benton County, I would not have been able to write this book.

In writing this history I relied a lot on the old newspapers of the county. Those in my files, the ones on film at the Bentonville Library, and ones in newspaper offices in the county. So, I owe a big thank you to many newspaper editors who have been forgotten for many years.

Thanks go to the Benton County Historical Society, the Siloam Springs Museum and the libraries in the county. Here I found historic facts and also pictures that I copied to use.

Over the years I have copied many old photographs that belonged to so many people that it would take too much space to list them all, even if I could remember who they were. So, I just say thanks to them. I also owe thanks to those who told me of the days gone by; this was a big help to me.

Special thanks must go to the Library of the University of Arkansas at Fayetteville, and the members of the staff there who helped me find the old books that gave me the date and happenings that I could not have found otherwise. They have a vast historical file that I have used many times.

INTRODUCTION

In writing this history of Benton County, I haven't tried to write a scholarly book. Instead, I have tried to make it an easy to read and enjoyable history.

As much as possible, the happenings have been told as short stories in a newspaper feature article style. Some of the articles have been copied from newspapers, using the wording of the old editors who had a far different way of writing than we have today.

I have used pictures with as many articles as I could. There is a picture section of 200 pictures with which I have tried to show life as it was in past years. A section of old newspaper ads shows prices and items used from 1887 to 1936.

I have left out almost all talk of politics and the standard family history section. I feel these pages can be used for more interesting articles.

People keep talking about the good old days in the past, when things could be bought for what today seems so little. You must remember that in those days 50 cents to a dollar was standard day's wages. As you read this book, if a price seems cheap, remember people worked many more hours to buy that item than you do today.

J. Dickson Black

Chapter One
Naming of the County

Benton County and Bentonville were named in honor of Senator Thomas Hart Benton of Missouri, who was one of Arkansas' best friends in Congress both before and after Statehood.

Thomas Hart Benton was born March 14, 1782, at Hillsboro, N. C., he was the son of Jesse Benton. Upon the death of his father, Thomas became the head of his family at the age of eight. After some preliminary study with a friend of his father, a short term in grammar school, and a partial course at the University of North Carolina, he undertook the supervision of the "Widow Benton's Settlement," a farm of 3,000 acres with a claim to some 40,000 acres near Nashville, Tennessee. In 1809, he was a state senator in Tennessee, and took much interest in land issues.

During camp life in the War of 1812, he won the permanent friendship of Sam Houston and the temporary enmity of Andrew Jackson. The trouble with the latter grew out of a tavern brawl in which Thomas supported his brother, Jesse, in a melee of knives, pistols, and clubs. Jackson long carried a bullet fired by Jesse or perhaps by Thomas. Notwithstanding his excellent prospects in Tennessee at the close of the war, Benton moved in 1815 to St. Louis, where, as editor of the Missouri Enquirer and also having built a large law practice, he speedily identified himself with his adopted state.

He was nominated by the son of Daniel Boone, and with the support of David Barton, his co-senator, Benton was first elected to the United States Senate in 1820, and took his seat in 1821. In the Senate, he became involved almost immediately in his lifelong legislative effort, the defense of sound money. He favored settlers and discouraged land speculators.

After he went to Washington, as Senator, he renewed his friendship with Andrew Jackson and later helped him in his campaign for President.

Benton was the Senate Floor Leader in the war upon the

Thomas Hart Benton; this was copied from a painting of Benton that hangs in the Benton County Court House.

National Bank. He was a hard money man and favored gold and silver coinage, but no "bank of issue" with its paper currency.

He favored reduction in the cash price for land and advocated the grant of free homesteads of 160 acres based on five years settlement and improvement. He was said of, by many to be, "the father of cheap land."

Benton worked hard for several years on his land law, but it was President Jackson who saw the good in the law and personally recommended its passage.

It was due to Benton's hard work behind the scenes, and his long talks from the floor, that Arkansas was admitted in 1836. Without his help, the bill would have been tabled.

Benton was not a man to hold back or beat around the bush. What he thought, he said, then backed it all the way.

The following few words he used on the floor of the Senate in 1850, shows the kind of man he had always been.

"Mr. President, Sir, I never quarrel, Sir, but sometimes I fight, Sir, and when I fight, Sir, a funeral follows, Sir."

Thomas Hart Benton was the first man to serve 30 years in the Senate.

Chapter Two
Benton County

I would not try to say how old the hills and valleys are that make up Benton County or how many changes have taken place in all of these years.

Even the scientists are unable to put any date on the age of the land, or dates as to when anything would have happened. They talk of hundreds of millions of years, they tell of times when all of Northwest Arkansas was under deep water, it was just a large sea. Then other times when just parts of it were under shallow water.

Benton County has many large fossil beds where almost all of the rocks will have some type of fossil. If you will watch whenever you are in a rocky area of the county, you may pick up the fossil of some long forgotten sea life that lived 200 to 350 million years ago.

These fossils show up wherever there are rocks. Many have been found by people working up their gardens. The fossils are the records which enable scientists to look back at Northwest Arkansas and see what it was like millions of years ago.

Some of the most common fossils found in the county are snails or brachiopods, which resemble clams and crinoids (related to sea lilies), which are animals having a plant like shape with segmented joints, that separately look like buttons; Bryozoans, which were a lacy like animal life, and lots of Tabulate coral are found.

I am sure that the early settlers found the prairie grass and wooded hillsides much more to their liking than they would have the sea life of 300,000,000 years before.

A soil scientist said that grass and trees of some kind started growing here about 135,000 years ago. By 70,000 years ago, they would have been very similar to what we have today, they think. But due to the fact that there are no fossils of this first grass and trees, it would be hard to say for sure what they were like.

Many changes would have taken place in the vegetation as

1 - Brachiopod

2 - Tabulate Coral

3 - Bryozoans

4 - Bryozoans

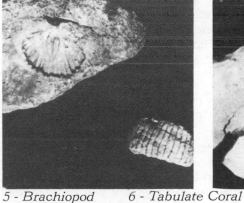

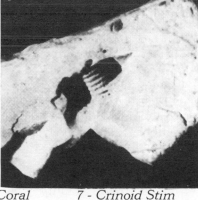

5 - Brachiopod   6 - Tabulate Coral   7 - Crinoid Stim

All of these rocks are from the Boome Formation and lived here when Benton County was covered with water the second time. This was about 325 million years ago.

5

the ice age moved south. After all, we know that just 18,000 years ago there were glaciers as far south as St. Louis, Missouri. They were only a few inches thick at the most, but the weather would have been cold here the year around. As the glacier melted and moved north, the weather warmed and a new type of grass and trees would have come up.

Chances are this was some different from the first trees and grasses.

Most scientists feel that the trees and grasses we have now have been very much the same for the past 2,000 years. But, as with any growing thing, there have been small changes taking place all the time. We can read the letters and notes of the first settlers and know that there have been several changes here in the last 150 years.

The Area as Part of Arkansas Territory

Benton County is part of the Louisiana Purchase which was bought from France, October 31, 1803. In 1805, President Jefferson appointed Gen. James Wilkerson, Governor of the Louisiana Territory. The first territorial legislature convened at St. Louis, June 26, 1806, and created the District of Arkansas, which took in all of the present State of Arkansas and most of Oklahoma.

Congress changed the name from Louisiana Territory to Missouri Territory on June 12, 1812, and in October of that year Governor Howard changed the five districts of Missouri to counties. So Arkansas County became, with Arkansas Post as its seat of Government.

It remained the Missouri Territory until 1819 when it became Arkansas Territory. The north boundary was set by the act making the State of Missouri, the Mississippi River had been the east boundary from the start, the south boundary had been set in the early days. But the west boundary was not set until 1824. This by an act of Congress, and was 40 miles west of today's boundary. This line was later changed because of a treaty with the Cherokee Indians in 1828.

Part of what is now Benton County was for a few years part of Crawford County. Then, on October 13, 1827, the territorial assembly created Lovely County, which took in most of Benton County. In 1828, when the President made a treaty with the Cherokees, Arkansas lost most of the land that had made up Lovely County. (Check article on Lovely County.)

Washington County was organized by a territorial act of October 17, 1828, and it embraced all of what is Benton, part of Madison, and about one-fourth of Carroll County, and all of what is Washington County today.

Benton County has no real territorial history, as what few

happenings there were here before statehood were written into Washington County's law books and history.

When the first white men came to what is now Benton County they were not allowed to stay. At that time the army was under orders to run out any white men who tried to settle here. The army order was to kill off their crops and burn any building they had put up. At that time this was Indian hunting ground.

Then the Arkansas Territorial Government tried to take it over by settling up Lovely County. So, in 1828, the President made a treaty with the Cherokees and after this white men could settle in the area.

The settlers who came in to the county between 1828 and 1836 had to go up into Missouri to find a store or to Fayetteville, where they also had a post office. There is said to have been a territorial post office at Osage Springs, but I have no date on this at all.

On March 3, 1819, President James Monroe gave the post of Territorial Governor of Arkansas to James Miller. This was a three year term. Miller was the first Territorial Governor.

Most of what he did had little bearing on Northwest Arkansas, but there was one unusual happening that I feel we should tell. In December of 1822, President Monroe discovered that he had forgotten to have Miller reappointed during the previous session of Congress.

This meant that everything Miller had done from March 3, 1822, to December that year was not legal. Monroe renominated Miller on December 16, and requested that this be dated from March 3, 1822. But the Senate set it to start January 3, 1823.

Then he asked for a law to legalize Miller's official acts from March 3, 1822, to January 3, 1823. This was passed on April 9, 1824.

As far as I know, Arkansas was the only territory to have an illegal governor for nine months.

Benton County Starts with Statehood

Arkansas was admitted as a State on September 30, 1836. The same day Benton County was admitted as the 34th county by an act of the General Assembly. Bentonville was the first town, followed by Maysville. As more settlers came to the county more towns started and new roads were opened. As time went on, post offices were opened all over the county. Most of these small post offices have been closed, and it is hard to prove where many of them were.

The county was named in honor of Missouri Senator Thomas Hart Benton, a man who worked very hard to have Arkansas admitted as a State. Without his help, it would have been several years before we would have reached this stage.

The first slate of county officers were appointed by the governor to serve until election could be held for officers. Those picked were George P. Wallace, county judge; John B. Dickson, county clerk; Gideon G. Pace, sheriff; Henry C. Hastings, treasurer; Henry Ford, coroner; and A. McKissick, surveyor.

The first meetings of the county officers and the first several terms of court were held in the home of Judge Wallace, just a mile and one-half east of Bentonville. Most of the county business was done here until the May term of court in 1838. At this time they moved all of the county records into the county's first courthouse, and held that term of court there.

This first set of county officers had a large size job cut out for them as they had to set up the running of the county from scratch. There was no one around to say we done it like this last year, or was there any books to look back on and follow someone else's mistakes.

Judge Wallace was almost as big a man as was his job. He is said to have been almost seven feet tall, so everyone in the county had to look up to him. It would be hard now to say if people saw things his way because of his size or because he was a much smarter man than most. But anyhow, several people writing of the setting up of the county have said that it was for the most part done his way.

Up until this time, all of the legal matters were taken care of at Fayetteville, as were tax matters. So, these men had to set up the law and order on a county level. Record keeping had to be started for the county, as well as a county tax set up. One big job was picking a county seat.

One of the early acts was the holding of an election to select three commissioners to pick a site for the county seat. These commissioners were Robert Cowen, Robert Weaver and Thomas Swaggerty.

On the 7th of November, 1837, they filed with the county clerk a report of their proceedings, to wit:

"We, the undersigned commissioners elected under an act of the General Assembly of the State of Arkansas, after having been duly qualified, and giving the notice required by law, and having duly examined the various situations, donations and conveniences, beg leave to report that we have selected a site to-wit: The south half of the southeast quarter of Section 30, in Township 20 north, Range 30 west of the fifth principal meridian, as presenting to your commissioners, duly considering its situation, the donations offered, and its eligibility for a county seat, more advantages and conveniences than any other situation which was presented for the consideration of your commissioners. They have, after selecting the same, in accordance with the powers vested in them as commissioners, proceeded to lay off a town thereon, leaving a square and 136 lots, and have named and called said town Bentonville; all of which is respectfully submitted to the court."

(Signed)   Robert Cowen
Robert Weaver
Thomas Swaggerty

The report was addressed to the circuit court, to which tribunal the law required it to be made, and on the second day of the first term of that court, which was held in November 1837, the report was presented to the judge thereof, and the following entry was ordered to be made of record:

"And now on this day comes the commissioners elected to locate a county seat for the county of Benton, and present their report, which is approved by the court and ordered to be filed and recorded. And it appearing to the court here that a court house will be prepared for the reception and use of the court by the next term thereof, it is therefore ordered by the court that the clerk of the Benton Circuit Court do move all the files, records and papers of his office to the town of Bentonville, the county seat so selected by said commissioners, or within one mile thereof, at least thirty days before the next term of this court. And that the town so selected be established as the seat of Justice for said county, and be called and known by the name of Bentonville in Honor to the Hon. Thomas Hart Benton, and that all writs and process hereafter issued from this office, shall bear test and be made returnable at the court-house in the town of Bentonville, County of Benton."

So, in May of 1838, the Benton County Circuit Court met for the first time in a building of their own.

The first general election was held in Benton County in August 1838. This was a general election for governor, legislature and county officers. There were 272 votes cast and the winners of this election were all Democrats. Right from the start Benton County has been a Democratic county.

For a short period following the Civil War, Republicans were voted into office. This was because too many Democrats had been disenfranchised for taking part in the war. After this period passed, it went back as a Democratic county. Now and then a Republican won office, but we never have had a full slate of Republicans officeholders.

The first Federal survey of Benton County date not known gave the total area as 900 square miles, or 576,000 acres. Broken down, it listed 86,000 unmodified prairie; 175,000 acres oak barrens or modified prairies; 200,000 acres wooded mountains or ridges; and 86,000 acres river and creek valley lands.

At first there were but two roads across Benton County, one the Line Road running down the western side of the county through what later were the towns of Maysville, Cherokee City and Silvan. This road was built by the Army and ran from Fort Smith to Fort Scott, in Kansas.

The other road, a state road, was built by the State to take travelers across the county in a northeast route. It ran close to what is the Frisco railroad track today. This route was used by cattleherders to take herds of cattle from Texas to St. Louis before the days of the railroads.

As more people came in to the county, new roads were built and before long the whole county was crossed with roads. Some of these could only be used part of the year. Many of them crossed creeks that could not be forded when the water was high. So you had to know a little about the roads if you were crossing the county.

Trail of Tears

It is said that several groups of Cherokee Indians crossed the county as they were moving from their old homes in Georgia and Tennessee to a new home in the Indian Territory. I have checked many articles on these movements and can find just two records that were made at the time of the trips that showed them going through Benton County.

One small group came down out of Missouri and crossed the Northwest corner of the county as they went into the Territory. There was not a date on this movement.

Then, in the summer of 1838, a large group of Cherokees came into the county at about Gateway and moved along or near to the state road through the county and on to Fayetteville where they camped a day or so.

Judge A. B. Greemwood was appointed commissary to travel with one detachment of Indians. He came as far as Nashville, Tennessee, with them. Then he went back to Georgia and got his family and moved on to Bentonville in the spring of 1838. It is said that he later that year visited with this same group of Indians as they went through Bentonville.

Yet, in his writings, he didn't say that he met them in Bentonville, but just that he had met them. So, I have wondered if he could have rode down near what is Rogers today and met the Cherokees there. This would have been the group that went on that route.

Happenings in the County

As the first roads stayed away from the White River, it would be hard to say when the first ferry was needed on the river in the county.

The records show that the first license for a ferry on the

White River was issued to Abner Jenning in January, 1857. This ferry crossed the White River at the Blackburn Mill Road. His fees were as follows: "Footman 5 cents; man and horse 10 cents; one horse carriage 20 cents; two horse carriages 25 cents; four horse carriages or wagons 35 cents; three yoke of oxen, or six horse wagons 50 cents; each head of loose stock of all kinds 2 cents each." He paid the county $1.00 license fee per year. For some years there was also a post office at Jennings Ferry, and so named.

That year in October William Early was granted a license to keep a ferry on the White River at the crossing of the Bentonville to Huntsville road. His price was somewhat higher than the other ferry.

In 1840 or there about Enoch Trott built a dram shop and general store along the State Road at where Brightwater later was. Other stage stops along this road were at Callahan Spring, Cross Hollows and Mudtown. The main business at these places was the sale of whiskey.

When the Butterfield Overland Mail came through Benton County, they followed the Springfield to Fayetteville road. They made just one stop in the county and that was at Callahan's Tavern. Their first trip got in there on Saturday morning, September 18, 1858. This stop was used until the line folded at the outbreak of the Civil War.

This road that Butterfield used later became known as the Wire Road when a military telegraph line was erected in 1860 from Springfield, Mo. to Ft. Smith, Arkansas.

The Frisco line was the first railroad in the county. They started building in 1880. By late 1881 the road was across the county and the towns of Garfield, Avoca, Rogers and Lowell were started.

In 1882 the Bentonville Railroad built track to Rogers to connect with the Frisco there. In 1898, it was extended to Grove, Oklahoma.

The town of Hico was started in 1840 and in 1880 the name was changed to Siloam City, then to Siloam Springs. Sulphur Springs was platted in December 1885, and Gravette was founded in 1894. It was just a short ways from the old town of Nebo. Gentry was laid out in 1894.

Pea Ridge got its start somewhere about 1850, and Decatur about 1870. Several other towns started between 1895 and 1908. They would all grow fast for a few years, and then just faded out.

The first Masonic Lodge in the county was organized at Hico in 1847.

Electric lights first came to Benton County in 1895 and Rural Free Delivery by the Post office started in 1904. Motion pictures showed in Rogers at a carnival in 1906, that was the first show in the county.

Benton County placed first in many fields over the years, and several of our people have won worldwide fame for the jobs they have done.

Benton County Census

The first census that covered what is now Benton County was the one made in 1835 for Washington County, the Territory of Arkansas.

This showed 6,724 white people, 504 slaves, 4 free negroes.

The 1860 census for Benton County gave a total population of 9,285, of which 8,905 white, 385 negro, and 16 Indian.

In 1880, the census listed 20,157 white, 128 negro, 35 Indians.

Later Benton County populations were:

1900 - 31,389; 1920 - 36,253; 1930 - 35,253

Benton County Census 1850

An analysis of the census for Benton County in 1850 showed 950 families. They came from 22 states, not a one from Texas. Tennessee led with a total of 521 families. Foreign born pioneers were rare in the county with 14 families from Germany, Ireland 5, Scotland 3, and England and Denmark each one.

The largest family was Jacob Roller with 24 children; J. Horton 13. Several had 12 and a great number had eight or nine.

Under occupations we find listed 36 blacksmiths, 21 carpenters, 12 clergymen, 11 merchants, 9 wagonmakers, 8 teachers, 7 physicians, 7 cabinetmakers, 6 shoemakers, 6 stone masons, 5 coopers, 4 bricklayers, 4 tanners, 4 wheelwrights, 4 clerks, 4 millwrights, 2 saddlers, and 2 lawyers.

The following had just one person to each occupation: carriagemaker, tavernkeeper, tailor, surveyor, hatter, gunsmith, miller, mechanic, and painter.

A few men were listed as holding offices for the county and the rest were listed as farmers or laborers.

U. S. Farm Census Benton County 1860

Improved Farms	41,183 acres
Unimproved Farms	150,019 acres
Cash Value of Farms	$1,411,920.00
Farm Tool Value	$70,544.00
Horses	3,205
Mules	625
Cows Milk	3,391
Working Ox	1,748
Other Cattle	4,883
Sheep	10,410

Hogs	22,044
Total Value of Livestock	$494,380
Wheat	76,701 bu. 2nd in State
Rye	6,356 bu.
Indian Corn	426,495 bu.
Oats	35,447 bu. 3rd in State
Tobacco	37,725 lb.
Pea and Beans	17,147 lb.
Irish Potatoes	10,858 bu.
Sweet Potatoes	10,437 bu.
Value of Orchard Crop Sold	$440.00
Butter	77,191 lb.
Cheese	531 lb.
Hay Sold	173 tons
Grass Seed	386 bu.
Hops	50 lb., 1st in State
Hemp	75 tons, 2nd in State
Flax	153 lb.
Sorghum Molasses	10,484 Gallons
Beeswax	239 lb.
Honey	6,089 lb.
Value of things made at home and sold	$18,761.00
Slave Owners	107
They owned	384 Slaves

U. S. Farm Census of Benton County 1880

Number of Farms	2,725
Number of Acres	307,605
Total Value of Farms	$2,256,424
Cost Fertilizer Used	$1,272
Hay	2,346 tons, from 2,814 A.
Hens and Fryers	83,000 birds
Eggs sold	236,875 eggs
Honey	24,671 lb.
Bee wax	581 lb.
Tobacco	395,982 lb. from 547 acres
Irish Potatoes	28,165 bu.
Sweet Potatoes	14,058 bu.
Value of Orchard crops sold	$4,265
Value of Timber sold	$47,878
Wool	35,764 lb.
Horses	5,864
Mules	2,233
Working Ox	69
Milk Cows	5,397

13

Other Cattle	6,307
Sheep	12,919
Swine	46,516
Milk Sold	452 Gal.
Butter Sold	298,346 lb.
Cheese	700 lb.
Cotton	125 Bales from 286 acres
Sorghum Molasses	55,120 Gal.
Barley	200 bu. from 6 A.
Corn	1,119,834 bu. from 49,135 A.
Oats	249,382 bu. from 13,912 A
Rye	1,360 bu. from 177 A
Wheat	156,087 bu. from 21,461 A

Agriculture Report 1887

This agriculture report for Benton County for the year 1887 was taken from the Benton County Democrat, June of 1888. It listed 2,725 farms—all but 41 of these were farmed by the owners.

Grain raised in the county: Corn 1,679,751 bu.; Oats 378,073 bu.; Wheat 234,000 bu.

Amounts and values of other crops raised:

Orchard Products	$900,000.00
Tobacco	400,000 pounds
Wool shipped	31,480 pounds
Potatoes sold	42,247 pounds
Eggs marketed	485,000 dozen
Tons hay baled for sale	3,519

Livestock on hand in the county was valued at $630,000 and listed as,

Horses	7,774	Val. $298,854.00
Mules	3,184	Val. $151,072.00
Cattle	18,123	Val. $144,290.00
Sheep	10,123	Val. $ 6,806.00
Hogs	31,643	Val. $ 29,043.00

Chapter Three
Lovely's Purchase

Lovely's Purchase and Lovely County

Lovely County was a short-lived county of the Territory of Arkansas. For twelve years this land changed from Indian land to White man's land several times, and its boundary changed as many times.

It all started in 1816. At that time all of what is Arkansas today was a part of the Missouri Territory. This was three years before the starting of the Territory of Arkansas.

Early in July of that year, Major William Lovely, Cherokee agent in the Missouri Territory, met with representatives of the Osage and Cherokee tribes. He made an offer to buy part of the Osage hunting land and give it to the Cherokees in order to bring about peace between the two tribes. Both tribes agreed to Lovely's plan and this block of approximately three million acres then became known as the Lovely Purchase.

Then the Government said that Lovely didn't have the authority to make the purchase, so for two years they wouldn't approve his bargain. On September 25, 1818, the Chiefs of the Osage and the Cherokee made a treaty with President James Monroe whereby the Cherokees got the land that had been the Lovely Purchase.

Both Indian tribes had felt that they had made a deal with Lovely, and took this new treaty as just a confirmation of the older transaction.

See map number one for the Lovely Purchase. As soon as this treaty was made, the Secretary of War, J. C. Calhoun, ordered all of the white people living on this land to move out except Mrs. Persis Lovely, who could live there till her death. The army moved in and made a short job of moving these few people out.

This purchase was to give the Cherokees a western outlet, yet the Cherokee thought of it as a tribal possession. The government was careful to avoid such a commitment.

Secretary of War, John C. Calhoun, stated in his letter to the Cherokees on October 8, 1821: "It is to be always understood that in removing the White Settlers from Lovely's purchase for the purpose of giving the outlet promised you to the West, you acquire thereby no right to the soil but merely to an outlet, of which you appear to be already apprized, and that the government reserves to itself the right of making such disposition as it may think proper with regard to the Salt Springs upon that tract of county."

As white men came into the Territory of Arkansas and saw the beautiful tract of land called the Lovely Purchase, they wanted it. After all, "This land was too good to give to Indians." So, acting Governor Robert Crittenden started writing to Washington to get an order to settle the purchase. He called it the "Garden Spot of the Territory".

Then on October 13, 1827, the Territorial Assembly, believing that they had jurisdiction over this land, created Lovely County. It took in all of the Lovely purchase except that laying in Crawford County. And went West and North to the boundary lines they had set for Arkansas Territory in 1824.

The act for Lovely County set the following lines: "Beginning at the upper Cherokee boundary line on the north bank of the Arkansas River, thence running up and with the meanders of said river to the mouth of the Canadian Fork, thence up said Canadian Fork to the western limits of the Territory of Arkansas, thence north with that line to the northwest corner of the territory, thence east to the southwest corner of Missouri, thence east with the line between Missouri and Arkansas, to the Fiery prairie or Brown's line, thence south with Brown's line to the Cherokee line, and thence with the Cherokee line to the place of beginning."

The Indians did not like this new attempt to take away their land and sent a delegation to Washington to stop this act. Of course, Arkansas sent her best talkers to defend their side.

The outcome of all this took place in the spring of 1828, when Secretary of War, James Barbour negotiated a treaty with the Cherokee delegation. Under this the present west boundary line for the state was set. All of the Cherokees east of this line moved west and the white settlers west of the line moved east of it. Congress gave the white settlers a very generous exchange for their land. This kept them happy. The Indians got more land to the west to make up for what they had lost.

Senator Thomas Hart Benton worked very hard against this treaty, as he said that this land had all been given to the Territory of Arkansas by an act of Congress in May 1824. He claimed that a treaty could not overrule an act of Congress. But he lost this battle, and Arkansas lost the land.

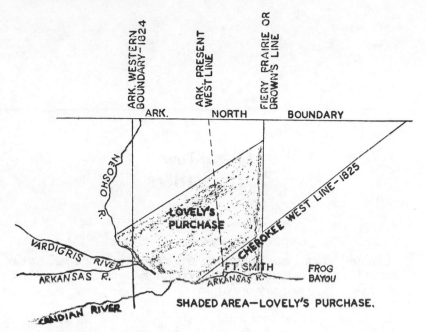

SHADED AREA—LOVELY'S PURCHASE.

Note map number two the Lovely County in shaded area is superimposed on present day counties. After this treaty of 1828, all that Arkansas had left of Lovely County was given to Washington County.

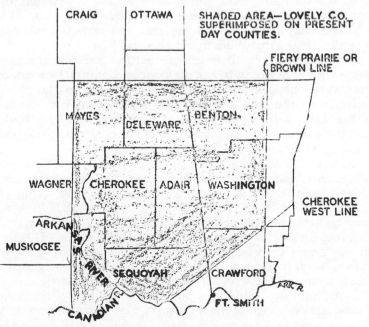

17

Chapter Four
Early Settlers

Benton County's Early Settlers

When Adam Batie settled on the prairie on the west side of Benton County that now bears his name, he was living in Washington County, Territory of Arkansas. His closest post office was at Fayetteville.

It is said that he first came to this prairie maybe as early as 1824, but was run out by the army, as at that time this was still Indian land, and the army wouldn't let any white men stay. Due to changes in Indian land, Batie was able to stay when he came back in 1828.

In the spring of 1830, John McPhail and his father settled nearby, giving Batie his first neighbors. They were followed soon by Martin Mays, who settled the site that now is the town of Maysville. Next came William Bird Keith.

It was late in 1838 before more settlers came to the prairie. They were Judge Engligh, Robert Cooper, Lemuel Tynnon. Soon others were following until the prairie was full of people.

Early in the 1830's, William Reddick and his son-in-law Samuel Burks settled near what is known as Elk Horn. Reddick became a prominent citizen and politician, controlling the politics of the sugar creek settlement for many years.

About 1830-32, Jacob Roller settled on Roller's Ridge. This ridge lies northeast of Garfield. It is about four miles long running east and west. Other Roller families were already living here. Jacob Roller, for years, ran a whiskey distillery that he erected where he lived. He was married thrice and had 24 children.

James Jackson settled near the site of Garfield in 1829. Daniel Ash was a very early settler near the state line north of Garfield. In 1849, Jacob R. Forgey settled in the same neighborhood. The Pascals were early settlers southeast of the site of Garfield.

Henning Pace settled on Sugar Creek north of Bentonville before statehood. Two of his sons settled on this same creek. One

These are logs from one of the first log cabins built near Benton-ville.

Chris C. Pace settled south of Bentonville. Henry Ford and other Fords were also early settlers on Sugar Creek.

The Woods settlement started when Samuel and William Woods settled three miles east of Bentonville in 1832. They both raised large families, who in time settled here close by. George P. Wallace and his son-in-law, James S. Black, settled one-and-a-half miles east of Bentonville. It was at Wallace's house that Benton County was organized at the beginning of statehood. He was a large and powerful man, being nearly seven feet tall. He had a lot to do with the picking and laying out of Bentonville. It is said that most men went along with his thinking because of his size.

John B. Dickson, the first county clerk, settled in what became Bentonville. He later moved to Osage Springs, then on to Texas. Thomas K. Blacke and John Breaithwaite, came about the same time as Dickson.

James Jackson and his son and Samuel Williams, his father-in-law, settled one mile west of Bentonville. Robert Dickson and his son, Joseph, settled one-half mile west of Bentonville; and Uncle Ezekiel Dickson, settled eight miles west of Bentonville.

James, Joseph and David McKissick settled five to eight miles west of Bentonville, around what is now Centerton. David McKissick brought the first apple seeds here, they were from Tennessee.

Edward Cunningham settled at a big spring six miles from Bentonville. William Pelham settled a mile south of him.

Rev. James Harris, a Cumberland Presbyterian minister and probably the first preacher in the county, settled three-fourths of a mile west of Bentonville. In 1828, Col. Hugh A. Anderson brought his family here and settled nine miles southwest of Bentonville.

Phineas Holmes settled about five miles southwest of Bentonville, and John Kinchelve settled near the same place on Osage Creek. Kinchelve took an active part in the organization of the county and was a justice of the peace for his township for many years.

The Graham settlement was a few miles southeast of Bentonville, having been settled by George and Joseph Graham. One early settler said there was a host of Grahams there.

Robert and James Cowan settled about eight miles south of Bentonville. A brother-in-law of the Cowans, by the name of Colville, settled here too. Colville township was named for him. In 1850 he went to the gold fields of the west and was killed there.

Robert Hubbard, the first representative of Benton County, settled near the Cowans, and Benjamin and Jefferson Hubbard settled lower down on the Osage. The Maxwells were also settlers here.

Isaac Horton settled near the site of Lowell in 1830, followed by Seth Thomas and Lafayette Kendrick. Most of the foregoing people were living in the county before statehood and all of them were here before Judge Alfred B. Greenwood came to Bentonville in 1838. Greenwood became the county's first attorney.

In 1833, Feli. O. Lindsey settled three miles west of Sulphur Springs. In 1835, Christopher C. Pace and his son, J. H. Pace, settled about six miles east of Maysville. Then, in 1840, Solomon Phillips and his son, Pleasant, settled about a mile-and-a-half north of Maysville.

The first child born in Benton County was John Keith in 1834, about three miles south of Maysville. Then his brother, Elijah, in 1836.

A. T. Hedges located one-and-a-half miles southeast of Maysville in 1844. Henry R. Austin and his mother Ellen Austin settled west of Nebo near his son, Elijah Austin.

In 1839, Richard Burgess and his family, including W. W. Burgess, settled on Lick Branch near the Osage. The same year Walter Thornberry and his son-in-law, David Brickey, and John Edwards settled on the same branch. At the same time, Joseph Neal and Charles Kincheloe settled on Brush Creek. In the fall of 1840, Areney Wilson and his brother Samuel settled in the Burgess neighborhood.

The day after he arrived, David Brickey and W. W. Burgess

went hunting and Brickey killed six turkeys. This proves there was plenty of free meat here at that time.

The first settlers on Flint Creek in the vicinity of Springtown were as follows: Isaac and Hasting Dial, the latter settling about a mile east where John Reynolds later lived. In 1850, Robert Duckworth, Matthew Vaughn, Parminter Morgan, Wiley Jones and Maj. Jack Russell settled in the same vicinity.

A year later Robert Hall and his sons, Jesse and Young, Rolly Hood, Joseph Thomas and his son, Joseph. Hiram Thomason and his sons, John and Sanford, and others settled along Flint Creek.

At this time, William Addington settled in Coon Hollow.

Simon Sager, a German, built the first cabin in the area of Siloam Springs in 1837 on a creek that bears his name. In 1851 he sold to John DeArmand and moved his family to Box Springs. From there he and his sons drove cattle to Kansas City, where his brother operated a butcher shop.

About 1844 Dr. Henry Powell settled with his family on Flint Creek four miles north of Siloam Springs. At the same time, James Riddle settled nearby.

John Quinton was the first settler on the place later occupied by Col. D. Gunter at Hico, who came in 1844. Daniel Copeland was a very early settler near Hico.

P. M. Phillips came to Benton County in 1838 and in 1847 settled on Round Prairie. Col. Henry Hastings settled seven miles west of Bentonville in 1836. He later moved to Corner Springs, today Decatur.

Thomas Quarles settled on the northeast part of Round Prairie about 1840. In 1844 Col. John Phagan settled at Double Springs on the Line Road. In 1846 David Chandler settled one-and-a-fourth miles southwest of Bloomfield.

Rev. John Givens, a Baptist minister, was an early settler on Butler Creek. About the year 1846, Z. M. Winnery settled near the site of Sulphur Springs. About the same time, Frank Lauderdale, James Thomason and Daniel Tittle settled nearby.

The first settlers on War Eagle Creek in Benton County were John B. and Julium Kirk. They were known as bear hunters. They came in the spring of 1832, and each raised three acres of corn that first year.

The following fall, Absalom Thomas, Henry Taber, Lewis Russell, Robert Taber, William Brazeel and a Mr. Nelson all settled with their families in the neighborhood. In December 1832, Sylvanus Blackburn, Josiah Blackburn, and Matthew Brewer and their families settled nearby. They first stopped at the home of John Fitzgerald at the site of Lowell.

They left their families here and the men went and selected a home. Sylvanus Blackburn located on the place where the mill is today, and Matthew Brewer about three-fourths of a mile above it.

Home In 1889—This picture was made on a glass plate negative. The house was somewhere in Benton County. It was typical of the farm homes at that date.

A year later, John David and Abram Matthews and Daniel Flannery came here and soon after George Crabaugh and Oliver Miller settled here.

Early settlers on the White River were two famous hunters, Stephen Coose and John Scennett.

Samuel Allen Jefferson came to Bentonville in 1841 as did David Walker. Walker was a brick mason and he erected the first brick courthouse the county had, that was 1842.

In 1849 M. R. Blevins settled north of Bentonville and David Edwards settled five miles southwest of there in 1850. The same year, Ozias D. Maxwell settled in Bentonville, A. J. Callis west of town, William A. Duncan near Centerton, and Joseph R. Rutherford was at Highfill in 1851.

Adam C. Gann settled near Garfield in 1849. Hopkins Douglas between Highfill and Osage in 1852. The same year Elijah L. Allen settled at Cave Springs, where he built a large mill.

The following all came to Bentonville in 1854: Capt. Whitefield C. LeFors, William Oakes, Thomas Nichols, Ardell Wright, Dr. Talliaferro, Charles W. Rice in 1855 and A. H. Alfrey in 1858.

EARLY SETTLERS

Rev. Wyatt Coffelt settled west of Bentonville in 1854; he had one of the first large orchards and nurseries. Robert A. Hickman settled on Pea Ridge in 1857, James C. Knott south of Bentonville in 1859. In 1860 John H. Burns settled in Bentonville.

C. Milt Henderson settled west of Bentonville in 1860 and about that time Mrs. Anna B. Patton settled near Pea Ridge.

About 1848 William Wells settled a mile south of Sulphur Springs. In 1851 G. W. Mitchell settled on the site of the village of Bloomfield. H. T. Gillespie settled on the Line Road, two miles south of Cherokee City at the same time.

In 1855 Jesse Benton settled on Honey Creek, eight miles west of Sulphur Springs.

Early settlers in the upper Pea Ridge neighborhood were Enoch Trott, James Wardlaw, Mat Caveness, George Miser, Lewis Pratt, Rev. Jasper Reddick, Wiley Foster and two brothers and Granville Medlin J. Wade Sikes and his father and family came in 1853.

H. H. Patterson and his two brothers, William Marsh, John Lee and the Morgans were early settlers in the Pea Ridge vicinity.

In 1851 Young Abercrombie and his sons, James, William, John, Samuel, Hiram, LaFayette and Floyd settled on Round Prairie.

Most of the first settlers of Benton County came from Tennessee. Several also came from the following: Georgia, North Carolina, Virginia, and Kentucky. A few came from the northern Free states.

They were mostly descendents of pioneers, so a new frontier and the hard life that went with it was not too much for them. They just set in to make a new home like their parents before them had. Most of them were farmers and hunters without much education or polish, and with moderate ambitions. Their wants were easily satisfied.

Very few of these early settlers brought cash money with them. The few that did also had slaves to do part of their work. There were no gentlemen of leisure in Benton County at that date. Very few of these people ever became rich. Most made a living and that was all they wanted.

The few doctors, lawyers and businessmen in the county were looked up to as the leaders in the county.

Few newcomers came to Benton County during the Civil War, but many came just after it was over. Those coming from 1865 to 1870 were: D. M. Young, W. T. Cook, Dan Maples, Samuel W. Peel, James H. Berry, Rev. Peter Carnahan, W. P. A. Britt, Releford Easley, Goldsmith Davis, Pierce Frank Paul, and Thomas Anderson Watson. All of these settled in or near to Bentonville.

William Horsley settled near Rogers in 1867; John R. Wooten

at Burgin Valley in 1868, John R. McKinney near Siloam Springs, Hugh Middleton southwest of Bentonville, and H. H. Campbell on the White River. The above all in 1868.

Hezekial Highfill settled at Highfill in 1869. James Haney, a brick mason and builder from Ireland, came to Bentonville in 1871.

William A. Terry came to Bentonville in 1874 and Edgar H. Looney in 1875. W. Y. Oakley settled south of Bentonville the same year. L. H. and J. T. McGill settled in Bentonville in 1878. Rev. F. M. Seamster to Pea Ridge in 1879.

J. E. and A. R. Applegate came to Rogers in 1881. With the coming of the railroad to the county many people moved in to all parts of the county from this date on.

Many of the people coming into Benton County after the war were men with money and they opened businesses soon and built large homes that were new to the county. Several new doctors and lawyers came to the county at this time.

I was unable to list all the early comers to the county but have tried to show the growth as best I could for the early years.

Chapter Five
Court Houses and Jails

Benton County Courthouses and Jails

Benton County has been very hard on courthouses over the years. They have held court in one home as a temporary courthouse, and have had five different permanent courthouses to date.

The county was organized in the home of George P. Wallace, who became the first County Judge. The first term of court was also held here as a temporary courthouse in April of 1837.

At this meeting they voted to build a small log courthouse and a log jail. The courthouse which sat on the north side of the square was finished in time for the spring term of court, 1838. The jail more than likely was done before this time.

As the first courthouse was used for just a few years, one can find out very little about it. I would say that it would have been about 18 foot square and been made of hewed logs. It sat someplace on the north side of the square.

The first jail was built some time in the spring of 1837. It stood on the north side of the east and west street, about sixty yards east of the northeast corner of the public square in Bentonville.

It was a small building consisting of a double wall of squared logs, with a cavity of several inches of space between the walls. In this cavity poles were stood upon end, thus making what might be called a third or interior wall. There is no record of windows in this building. But, if it was loosely chinked, they would have had more than enough air.

Some time late in 1841 a contract was given to John and William Walker to build a two-story brick courthouse in the center of the square. It was 50 by 50 feet and many of the bricks had the date 1842 pressed in them.

The courtroom was on the first floor and the second floor had the county offices and the jury room. It was reported that the Walkers lost money on this building.

In August, 1848, there was a meeting of the Benton County Grand Jury to consider the condition of the jail in Bentonville, which was badly in need of repair. The jury foreman, John B. Dickson, recommended that the jail be thrown down, with the unsound timbers thrown out, and the jail rebuilt.

The jury said the jail was to be rebuilt as follows:

"The foundation must be laid with two tiers of timbers, laid across each other; the foundation to be 18 inches from the ground; with two walls built with space between them for poles; the second floor of double timber, with a door in the middle, and the upper wall to be single.

The third floor, the record said, must be of timber hewed ten inches thick, and all well pinned together with wooden pins or iron bolts, and a good shingle roof." It was said that part of the jail must be lined with one and one half inch oak plank, and spiked with double ten-penny nails within an inch of each other.

The brick courthouse in the center of the square was burned some time in December of 1862 by Union troops. Most of the court records had been moved from the building in the spring of the year when the first Union troops came into the county.

Court House

There was no Court or other business taken care of during the Civil War. Just after the war the county rented some space for their offices for a few months, by which time they had a new two-story frame building put up just east of the County jail.

On January 4, 1870, the county court appointed William W. Reynolds commissioner of public buildings within and for the county. His first job was to find a proper piece of ground in the town of Bentonville on which to build a courthouse and jail. He later filed the following with the county court:

Hon. County Court of the County of Benton, State of Arkansas;

The undersigned commissioner of public buildings, instructed by order of your honorable court to purchase a suitable lot of ground for the erection of a court-house and jail thereon, beg leave to submit the following report; That he has (subject to your approval) purchased, of Joseph R. Rutherford's estate, Lots No's 90, 91, 94, 95 of the town of Bentonville, Benton Co. Ark. In arriving at the consideration for the purchased, the kind of payment was considered, and from the fact that such payment would be made in county warrants, the sum of $1,250 was agreed upon as the consideration for said lots. These lots could have been purchased with greenbacks for the sum of $1,000. The deed for said lots to the county of Benton, in fee simple, is herewith submitted and asked to be taken as a part of this report. As confirmation of the contrack of your commissioner, he would ask your honorable court that county warrants to the amount of $1,250 be issued to the said Joseph R. Rutherford in consideration of said property. Most respectfully submitted. Signed, W. W. Reynolds, Comm. of Public Buildings.

The report was accepted and approved by the court, and county warrants for $1,250 were drawn in favor of J. R. Rutherford. The commissioner was then ordered to submit plans and an estimate of the probable cost of a courthouse and jail to the court at its next term.

At that time, Commissioner Reynolds submitted plans drawn by W. T. Ritter, architect, with an estimate of its cost at $35,000. The court accepted the plans and ordered the Commissioner to take sealed bids from any and all parties until 12 o'clock of the first day of May, 1871. On that day all bids were to be opened by the court.

The court also ordered that bonds be issued not to exceed

Benton County Courthouse built in 1874. Picture made some time in 1890's.

$50,000, for the purpose of raising funds for the construction of the buildings. It was set up for the county to redeem $10,000 worth of the bonds each year for five years. They were all to pay 10 per cent interest.

The bids were opened just after noon on May 1, and were as follows: A. H. Leady, of Springfield, Mo. $36,575; M. A. Rowles, of Illinois, $36,500; W. T. Ritter & Co. of Springfield, Mo., $34,735; J. H. Neely and Samuel H. Kelton, of Bentonville, $33,000; J. Oliver, of Springfield, Mo., $31,910.

After examination of the bids, and much talk, the contract was awarded to John H. Neely and Samuel H. Kelton at $33,000. Work was started the next week.

Due to the fact that very few people had gold money to buy with the county was unable to sell the bonds. By May of 1872, they had sold $20,000 worth of bonds for which they had received a little over $14,500. In this time several ways had been tried in selling the bonds, but none worked.

In May, 1872, the following report of the work and costs was filed with the county court:

"Excavation, $150.00; stone wall, $1,500; cut stone, $800; guion corners, $1,000, door sills, $50.00, brick in wall, $8,500; cut stone window sills, $300; well and pump, $100; rods and anchors, $350.00; carpenter work, $1,700; material ready for use, cut stone, $500; cut post, $150; iron cornice, $1,400; vault doors, iron columns, $500; ceiling joists, $160; oil and paints, $300; 35,000 feet lumber, $1,050; 5,000 feet walnut, $160.00."

In January of 1873 the county court ruled that since Neely and Kelton had failed to complete the courthouse by the 1st of September, 1872, they must forfeit their contract. On the 15th of February, Commissioner Reynolds resigned and S. G. Elliott was appointed his successor.

In April, 1873, the court ordered more bonds printed and sold. This time it was forty-six one hundred dollar interest bearing bonds. They were to be sold at no less than 75 cents on the dollar. In July of that year the building was all done. It is said to have cost the people of the county as much as $60,000 for the three-story courthouse and jail. The jail, being on the third floor. The way the bonds were sold and discounted they could not say for sure what the cost was.

In January, 1888, a contract was let to build a new jail on the north side of the courthouse grounds. It was to be one story 42 x 32 feet. The cells were all in the center with walks around them so that no cells had access to an outside wall. This was in use by late fall.

This building was used until March 4th, 1905, when it was badly burned. A temporary jail was used until 1911 when a new modern jail was built.

Benton County Jailhouse built 1911.

The county court met in January of 1911, with County Judge W. A. O. Jones and voted to build a new county jail. The new jail would have rooms for the jailer's family to live in so there would always be someone there to open the jail in case of a fire.

They were still remembering the jailhouse fire of a few years before when two men burned to death because the jailer couldn't be found with the keys.

They named J. M. Jackson and W. T. Maxwell as commissioners. The March 9, 1911 Benton County Democrat carried a story saying that contracts had been let for the new county jail. They gave no date, but it would have to have been some days before this work had been started.

The jail building was to be two story of brick and cut stone. It had rooms for the jailer's family, jailer's office, a kitchen, women's ward, and other rooms they felt they needed. The main cellblock took up a large amount of the upstairs. There were to be six cells built to hold four prisoners each.

Lon A. Pace, a local builder, had the contract to build the building and do all inside work except the steel work. For this he was to be paid $11,200.

Steward Iron Works Co. of Cincinnati, Ohio was paid $3,100

29

for the steel and work on the cells, jail room doors and steel guards for the windows.

The plans were all made by Mathews and Clark, architects of St. Louis and Rogers.

I found no date as to when they moved in, but it must have been late that year. This building is still standing on north main street, just one block off the square.

Benton County's last courthouse, which is still in use, was opened and dedicated on Nov. 12, 1928. County Judge W. R. Edwards was master of ceremonies for the program. At this time he praised Ernest Patton, Joe Beasley and Kit Phillips who were the commissioners for the job.

The contractors had been Messenger and Dalton who had done an excellent job on the whole building. The architect was A. O. Clarke, who prepared all the plans and superintended its construction.

The cost of the building was $200,000. The lighting and furniture was about $10,000. It has two floors and a full basement. There are 36 rooms with a total of 75 windows. Back in that day windows were a main item. The courtroom and courtroom balcony could seat 750 people.

The list of materials used in the building is very interesting; it is all based on railroad carloads.

There were 12 carloads of cut stone, 30 cars of bricks, 40 cars of crushed stone, 4 cars of lumber, 4 cars of reinforcing steel, 12 cars of cement, 16 cars of sand, and several cars of miscellaneous material.

One of the interesting out of town visitors at the dedication was Mr. Charles McCarty of Gravette. He had also been at the dedication at the old court house 54 years before. He was the only one the papers wrote of having this honor.

Over the years the county has owned other buildings such as the poorhouses of which they have had several. But I feel that the courthouses and jails are the main buildings.

County Vault

For years this building was known as the Courthouse Office building. At one time it housed the Circuit Clerk, Treasurer and Sheriff and County Clerk's offices.

It was on north main street, just north of where the old courthouse used to set. The contract was let on Jan. 22, 1898 to James Haney of Bentonville. One of the offices was to have a big walk-in vault. Because of this the county listed it as the County Vault on the record books and all payments made for the building were listed on the Vault.

Haney put up a performance bond for $4935.70. This was also

This was a late picture of the old County Vault after it was being rented for private business.

the amount he was to be paid for the Vault building. He signed this on Jan. 22, 1898. But the contract and bond was not recorded until Jan. of 1899. At that time there was a note added to that saying the clerk had overlooked the recording, and to keep the record straight he was recording the paper late.

The Circuit Clerk, Treasurer, Sheriff and County Clerk moved in to the new office on June 15, 1899. The stone and brick building was said to be the nicest office building in the county at that date.

In later years rooms were added on the back of this building for the Sheriff or jailer to live in. The old county jail was right behind this building and they were connected.

In the north end of the front wall was a small elevation marker. The elevation is 1302.032. This was put up by the U. S. Geological department in 1904.

Some old timers say it was put up by Ex-President H. Hoover. He had worked on the survey, but that was in 1892. At that time he stayed for a few days at the Blake House. A small but good hotel.

When the county moved in to their new courthouse in 1928 they ordered the old one and the office building sold. At a sale on November 5, 1928, Seth B. Bates bought the office building and lot for $3250.

This building holds fond memories for many of the older people of Benton county, as the marriage licenses were all sold here from 1899 to 1928.

Chapter Six
Early Documents

First Note Recorded in Benton County

On or before the 25th day of December next I promise to pay James M. Dickson, one hundred & eighteen dollars, with interest thereon from the first day of July 1836, value received witness my hand & seal this 7th day of February 1837.

Jas. McKisick   Ezekiel Dickson (L.S.)
Filed 26th of May 1837   Recorded 1st. day of August 1837

Jno. B. Dickson Clerk and Ex Officio Recorder

Know all men by these presents that for and in consideration of the sum of one hundred & eighteen dollars the receipt of which I hereby acknowledge Ezekiel Dickson of the County of Benton in the State of Arkansas do hereby bargain, sell and convey unto James M. Dickson, six feather beds & furniture on the following terms, that is to say. That whereas I executed my note to the said James M. Dickson for the sum of one hundred & eighteen dollars due & payable on the 25th day of December 1837 which note bears interest from and after the 1st day of July 1836; Now therefore if the said above described note should not be fully paid up & discharged on or before the same falls due. Then & in that event the said James M. Dickson is hereby authorized & empowered to sell the six feather beds & furniture for cash or he is authorized to sell the same at any time he may think proper after said note falls due either at public or private sale as he may think proper & if there shall be any overplus in the hand of the said James M. Dickson arising from the sale of the said six beds & furniture after paying all expenses on said sale & the legal expense are this deed of trust the said James M. Dickson is to pay over said overplus into the hands of the said Ezekiel Dickson or to his order, & it is expressly agreed and understood that the said Ezekiel Dickson is to have the use & possession until said sale is made in witness whereof I the said Ezekiel Dickson have hereunto set my hand & affixed my seal this 7th day of February 1837.

Test; Jas. McKisick   Ezekiel Dickson (L.S.)
    Filed 26th day of May 1837 Recorded 1st of August 1837
        Jno. B. Dickson Clerk and Ex Officio Recorder
Benton County Deed Record Book A, page 1

First Will Probated in Benton County

This will was probated January 15th, 1838, being the first will filed for probate in Benton County.

"I, Samuel Tenan, of the County of Benton and State of Arkansas, being weak in body, but of strong mind and memory, thanks be to God for the same, do make and ordain this my last Will and Testament in the manner and form as follows;

First, I give my soul to God, who gave it to me, and my body to the earth, to be decently buried by the Executor herefore named.

Second; I request that my negro boy, Jack, be sold and that some of my connection buy him, and that the money be divided equally between my brother, L. Tenan, and my two sisters, Mary Allen and Zebe Yunt.

Third; I require my executors to take all my personal property, with notes and accounts, and pay all my just debts; and after all are paid, together with my funeral expenses, the balance to be divided equally between my brother and sisters as before named. I do hereby appoint Abner Allen my executor, and also request that my executor take my negro boy, Jack, and attend to selling him.

Given under my hand and seal this 20 day of August, 1837."

Attest; S. B. Woods   His
      William Reed   X
                       Mark (Samuel Tenan)

First Warranty Deed Record in County

Known all men by these presents, that for and in consideration of the sum of $400 to me in hand paid by James M. Dickson, the receipt of which is hereby acknowledged, I, Ezekiel Dickson, of the county of Benton, in the state of Arkansas, do hereby bargain and sell unto the said James M. Dickson, a Negro woman named Till about 45 years of age, also Negro boy child named Jack, about five years of age, which said Negroes I hereby sell and convey for life. And I do warrant and defend the title of said Negroes to the said James M. Dickson, his heirs and assigns forever.

In witness where of I have here unto set my hand and affixed my seal this the 7th day of February 1837.

Ezekiel Dickson
Witness James McKissick
From Benton County Deed Book A, page 1.

The First Circuit Court held in Benton County

At a Circuit Court began and held at the house of George P. Wallace (the temporary seat of justice for Benton County) for the county of Benton, State of Arkansas on the second Monday after the first Monday in October A. D. 1837. Present the honorable Joseph M. Hoge Judge of said court.

The Sheriff of Benton County returned into court here the following panel of good and lawful men of said county to serve as grand Jurors at this term of this court. To wit; Joseph McKisick, foreman, Philip Donaho, William Reddick, William Ford, Christopher S. Pace, George Graham, Joseph Dickson, Robert Cooper, John B. Robinson, Jonathan Duff, Samuel P. Woods, Dicolesian Jackson, Ezekial M. Dickson, Ambrose G. William, Thomas and Henry Ford who being duly sworn and charged retired to their duty.

Following is the first case they heard.

State of Arkansas
vs
Samuel Vaughn

And now on this day comes the said state by Evans her attorney and comes the said defendants in their proper person, and the said defendants move the court here to quash the indictment in this cause, which motion being by the court here heard and fully understood and after argument of counsel thereon had and it appearing to the satisfaction of the court here that said indictment and matters therein charged and set forth are insufficient in law to entitle said state to maintain her aforesaid action against said defendants, and that they the said defendants are not bound by the law of the land to answer there to. It is therefore considered by the court here that said Indictment be quashed set aside and held for nought, and that they, the said defendants, go hence, fully discharged therefrom and that they have and recover of said state their costs by them about their defense in this behalf expended.

From Benton County Circuit Court Record Book A, page 29. (the first page used in book).

EARLY DOCUMENTS

First Murder Trial in Benton County

The State
vs   Murder
Edward Welch

And now and on this day the prisoner was brought to the bar in custody of the Sheriff and being arraigned upon said indictment for plea says that he is not guilty in and manner and form as there in charged to which plea the attorney for the state issus and there upon came a jury of twelve good and lawful men to wit; William Hammock, Thomas Carls, Warrin Wight, Daniel Mays, John B. Walker, David McKissick, Joseph McKissick, James M. Pope, Alfred M. Wallace, Nicholas S. Kildern, Hampton Clark and Benjamin Hubbard, who being elected tried and sworn well and truly to try and a true deliverance make between the State of Arkansas and the prisoner at the bar according to law and evidence after having patiently heard the evidence, argument of counsel and instruction of the Court retired from the bar to consider of their verdict after mature deliberation returned into court the following verdict to wit; We the jury find the within named Edward Welch not guilty of murder but guilty of manslaughter in manner and form as charged in the withing bill of indictment and do say that he be punished by imprisonment for the term of seven years and that he be fined the sum of ten thousand dollars. Thomas Carls, foreman.

It is therefore considered adjudged and sentenced by the court that the said Edward Welch do pay unto the State of Arkansas the sum of ten thousand dollars as aforesaid assessed and that he be imprisoned in the common jail of the County of Benton and State of Arkansas for the term of seven years and ensuing from this date, this day to be computed as one day thereof and that he stand committed until the fine aforesaid and cost of this prosecution be fully satisfied and discharged the said defendant in mercy.

J. M. Hoge, Judge

May term of Circuit Court 1841. Benton County Circuit Court record Book A, page 109

First Divorce on Record in Benton County

David Mann   Complainant
vs   Bill for Divorce
Tainer Mann   Defendant

It appearing to the court from the affidavit of the complainant that the said Tainer Mann is a non resident of the State of Arkansas, and it also appearing to the court here that the substance and allegations of said complainant's bill is that on the first day of January 1843 the said complainant and the said defendant were intermarried with each other and that the said complainant did at times thereafter comfort and maintain the said defendant, and was in all respects a kind and dutiful husband, that the said defendant often threatened to take the life of the said complainant that some time in the month of August 1843 the said Tainer Mann took all her property and voluntarily abandoned said complainant and that for said causes the said complainant prays that the marriage contract be set aside and the said complainant be restored to all the rights and privileges of a single man.

It is therefore ordered by the court here that the said defendant appear here at the next term of this court to be holden in and for said County of Benton at the Court house in the County aforesaid on the third Monday in November AD 1844 and plead answer or demur or that said bill will be taken as confessed and a decree entered accordingly and this order be published in some newspapers printed in this State eight successive weeks the last insertion to be at least four weeks previous to the said term of this Court and that this case stand continued until the next term of this Court.

Judge J. M. Hoge
Benton County Chancery Court Book 1 page 4

First sale of land recorded in Benton County

We Samuel Whitehead and Martha Whitehead his wife have this day bargained and sold do here by transfer & convey to Singleton Lankston & his heirs for the consideration of Two Hundred Dollars to us in hand paid a tract of land in the State of Arkansas County of Benton containing eighty acres be the claim more or less bounded as follows (To Wit) the east half of the Northeast quarter of section no. thirty one in township no. Twenty North of range no. thirty west, to have & to hold the same to the said Singleton Lankston his heirs & assigns forever, we do covenant to the said Singleton Lankston that we are lawfully seized of said land have a good right to convey it & that the same is unencumbered. We do further covenant & bond ourselves our heirs representatives to warrant & forever defend the title to the said land & every part there of to the said Singleton Langston his heirs & assigns against the lawful claim of all persons whatever in testimony whereof we have here unto set our hands & affixed our seals this 27th day of February, one thousand eight hundred & thirty eight.

Signed sealed & delivered	His
in the presence of us	Samuel X Whitehead
Attest: Gideon G. Pace	mark
Joseph Dickson	Martha Whitehead

Benton County Deed Book A, Page 4.

A Lost Billfold Recorded

State of Arkansas

SS

County of Benton

And now and on this day came before me Jno. E. Dickson Clerk of the Circuit Court of Benton County, John Rose and made oath as follows to wit; I, John Rose do solemnly swear that on the 6th, day of November Inst. in the town of Bentonville or on the way from the said Town of Bentonville to the house of Christopher Pace I lost my Pocket Book containing the following papers & effects (Viz)

One Banknote on the Alabama & Mississippi Railroad Company for $25 and one three Dollar Bank Bill payable at Decater Alabama. One note of hand on James Strain for Seventy five Dollars due 25th day of December 1833. One note of hand for Twelve Dollars on Whitater Crabtree due first of November 1835 bearing ten percent interest. One note on hand on John Freeman for three dollars due first day of March 1835. One note of hand on Thomas Tyner for three dollars due 1st day of March 1835. One note of hand on John Elliot for twenty-four dollars due the first day of Oct. 1835. One note of hand on Martin Johnston for three dollars and fifty cents due the first day of August 1838. One note of hand on Pleasant Swagerty for ten dollars due the first day of February 1836. One note of hand on William Pace for Eleven dollars and fifty cents due the 1st day of October 1837. One note of hand on Alsa Pace for twenty one dollars due the first day of March 1837. One note of hand on William Offield for Ten dollars due the first day of April 1838. One note of hand on Edmund Cavness for eight dollars due the first day of May 1838. And one note of hand on Matthew Cavness for Fifty seven dollars due the 25th day of Dec. 1838. Also one Bank note for Ten dollars payable on Demand at Little Rock, Arkansas now due.

John Rose

Sworn to and subscribed before me this 19th day of Nov. 1838.

Filed 19th Nov. 1838, Recorded the 21st Nov. 1838 Jno. B. Dickson, Clerk of the Circuit Court of Benton County.

Jno. B. Dickson
Clerk & Ex Officio Recorder

Benton County Deed Record page 10, Book A

Bond for the First Benton County Sheriff

Know all men by these presents that we Gideon G. Pace, Samuel Burks, Philip Duneho, Samuel P. Woods and William H.

Woods are held and firmly bound unto James S. Conway Governor of the State of Arkansas & his successors in the Sum of Five Thousand Dollars of good and lawful money of the United States the payment of which well and truly to be made we bind ourselves our Heirs Executors & Administrators jointly by these presents sealed with our seal & dated this 10th day of March A. D. 1837.

The condition of the above obligation is such that whereas the above Gideon G. Pace has been duly elected & commissioned Sheriff of the County of Benton. Now if the said Gideon G. Pace shall well & truly execute all precepts which shall come to his hands & make due return of the same & shall collect & pay over to the proper persons all money by him collected and shall assess & collect all tax & pay over the same & do & perform all other required of him by law to do as Sheriff of said County then the above obligation to be void & of no effect otherwise to remain in full force & virtue, the date above written.

Filed 10th. March 1837

Gideon G. Pace (L.S.)
Samuel Burks (L.S.)
Philip Duneho (L.S.)
Samuel Woods (L.S.)
Wn. H. Woods (L.S.)

Recorded the 1st day of August A.D. 1837

Jno. B. Dickson
Clerk & Ex Officio Recorder

Benton County Deed Book A, page 3

First Papers for a Deacon Record in Benton County

Know all men by these present,

That I James Osgood Andrew one of the Bishops of the Methodist Episcopal Church in the United States of America under the protection of the Almighty God and with a single eye to his glory by the Imposition of my hands and Prayer have this day set apart Andrew Hunter for the Office of a Deacon in the Methodist Episcopal Church a man who in the Judgment of the Arkansas Annual Conference is well qualified for that work and he is hereby recommended to all to whom it may concern as a proper person to Administer the ordinance of Baptism, Marriage. And the Burial of the Dead in the absence of an Elder and to feed the flock of Christ so long as his Spirit and practice are such as become the Gospel of Christ and his continues to hold fast the form of sound words according to the Established Doctrines of the Gospel in Testimony whereof I have hereunto set my hand and seal this Tenth day of November in the year of our Lord one thousand Eight Hundred and thirty nine.

Fayetteville Arkansas James O. Andrew

Recorded the 4th day of May A. D. 1840

Jno. B. Dickson Clerk

Benton County Deed Record Book A, page 57

First recorded sale of a Store in Benton County

Beaty Township
Benton County Nov. 10th 1840
State of Arkansas

Know all men by these present that I Nehum Simons of Washington County and State aforesaid have this day sold Jeremish Robinson one house and half acre Lot that I purchased of John Scott in the Town of Maysville Benton in the State of Arkansas, I have also sold all my Liquors & Groceries that I have on hand at this place I also sell to the above Nineteen Barrels of Whiskey two Barrels of Sugar one sack of Coffee that is now in the hands of J. H. Herd & Co. at Fort Smith I sell in the same Bill Two Wagons & two Teams of Oxen (viz) 8 Yokes also three horses together with sundry Cattle runing in the range I also sell my Claim of all Cattle running in the Cherokee Nation that I lost during my contract at Fort Gibson I sell the above Liquors and all above mentioned for the sum of Two Thousand Dollars in hand paid as whereof I set my hand and seal as the year above written.

Teste;
Jno. Scott
Wesley Pogue (Signed in Italian)
(Signed in English Nathan Simons)

Filed for Record the 7th day of Dec. 1840
Recorded the same day filed this 7th day of Dec. 1840

Jno. B. Dickson
Clerk

Benton County Deed Record Book A page 81

A Slave Is Freed—A Slave Is Sold

This deed of Emancipation made and entered into in open court in the County of Benton and State of Arkansas, on this twentieth day of October in the year of Christ, Eighteen hundred and fifty three, between John H. May of the County and State afore said and Lewis, a negro man about six feet high, of yellow complexion, about forty-two years of age, formerly the property of Thomas Chisam and afterwards the property of Moses Fields, from which last owner the John H. May purchased said slave. The said John H. May for and in consideration of the long faithful service of said Lewis, do hereby manumit, emancipate, and set free from all his obligation of servitude as a slave as fully as if said Lewis had been born free, and the said John H. May, for himself and his heirs and assigns will forever defend the right and title to the said Lewis as a slave against the claim of all persons whatsoever in as full a manner as the title from Moses Fields will warrant.

In testimony whereof I, John H. May, have hereunto set my hand and affixed my seal this day and date above written.

John H. May

Attest: W. J. Howard
   J. K. Gibbetts

From the Benton County Court records, 1853

State of Arkansas)

County of Benton)

Received of William McDaniel, two hundred seventy-five dollars in full satisfaction for a negro woman slave for life named Lear, about forty-five of age, the title to said negro woman slave I warrant against myself, my heirs, and assigns and against the claim of all other persons whatsoever. I also warrant the said woman slave to be sound in mind.

In testimony whereof I have hereunto set my hand and affixed my seal this 26th, day of July, 1853.

John W. Phagan

Attest: Saml. Phagan
   John Harris

From the Benton County Court Records, 1853

Chapter Seven
Post Offices

I had a hard time running down the names of the post offices in the county. Many of the early day post offices were in private homes, as there were areas that needed a post office but there was no store or other business place close by to house them. A big part of the real early ones were in the grist mills in the county. As stores started they would be moved to these.

When a new postmaster was appointed he would move the office to his place of business, so many of them moved back and forth around town over the years.

I have listed every place that I could prove had been a post office at some time in the history of the county. There may have been some that I could not find or could not prove. I have not tried to put a starting date for any of them as I could find the dates of only a few.

Aldisson	Crump	Hico
Apple Orchard	Decatur	Highfill
Avoca	Dickson	Hiwasse
Beatty	Double Springs	Hoover
Bella Vista	Elk Horn	Herd
Bentonville	Equality	Ionia
Best	Falker	Jennings Ferry
Bloomfield	Flint	Kings Spur
Brightwater	Galitin	Key
Callis	Garfield	La Rue
Cannon	Garrett	Lime Dale
Cave Springs	Gateway	Linn Spring Hill
Centerton	Gentry	Logan
Cherokee City	Glade	Lowell
Cross Hollow	Gravette	Mason Valley
Clementine	Harmony Springs	Maysville
Colville	Healing Springs	Monte Ne
Creech	Hickory	Nebo

Pactoius
Parn
Pea Ridge
Pedro
Pippin
Pond
Puckett
Osage Mills
Orchard
Rago
Robinson

Rogers
Rollers Ridge
Round Top
Seba
Sedalia
Siloam Springs
Sliver Springs
Smiths Mill
Spavinaw
Spring Creek
Springtown

Spring Valley
Sulphur Springs
Trident
Trotts Mill
Twin Springs
Two Mills
Vaughn
Vinda
Wager
War Eagle

Places On The Maps

This list of names are places that have been listed on maps of the county at some time over the years. Some had just a small store, a river ford, railroad siding to load cars; a few came from county plot maps, and showed where someone had laid out a town that didn't go over. A few of the places I do not know why they were marked.

Apple Spur
Arlan Spur
Clantonville
Checks Corner
Corner Springs
Dorsey
Eldorado
Electric Springs
Frisco Springs
Hard Castle
Hazelwood
Hill Top
Jewell
Kenneth
Lee Town
Lincoln

Lookout
Lost Bridge
Miller Springs
Mountain Springs
Pine Top
Piney
Puckett Ford
Rhea
Rome City
Scravton
Silvan
Slick Rock Ford
Sugar Creek
Vagel
Van Winkle Ford

Chapter Eight
Newspapers

Benton County Newspapers

There have been many newspapers published in Benton county and a lot of them ran for just a few months, some a year or two. Most of them changed ownership many times over the years.

Because that Bentonville was the county seat the first paper was published there. That was 1857 when a newspaper moved from Madison county here. It was named the Northwest Appeal. Late in the year of 1857 "The Bentonville Appeal Independent" started in Bentonville. The first owners were J. P. Owen and B. T. Perkey, who published it for four or five months. They sold to Perkey and John R. Cox, who then sold to M. E. Harvey; it was closed in 1859.

Late in 1859, W. W. Reynolds started the "Bentonville Democart". He sold it to E. B. and W. D. Moore who moved the plant to Fayetteville in 1860, and started the "Fayetteville Democrat", which is now the Northwest Arkansas Times.

The "Theocrat" was a religious paper printed in the west part of the county at Harmony Springs by a religious group there. The date was about 1860 until near the end of the Civil War.

There were no newspapers printed in Benton County during the war.

In 1866 the "Beacon" was started in Bentonville, but it lasted just a few months. The "Arkansas Traveler" was started in 1868 by A. Caraloff who sold it to H. S. Cloeman, who later sold it to A. B. Cory. Someone renamed it "Bentonville Democrat" but it didn't have a long life.

In 1875, two papers closed their doors in Bentonville. They were the "Corner Stone" started in 1872 by T. Y. Reynolds and the "Bentonian" published by Gaston and Ham.

The "Bentonville Advance" started in 1873 by Col. R. S. Hynes was the first Bentonville paper to be known over the state. In 1877, one finds it edited by N. H. Biggers and Col. Pat Donan.

This was the Sun office building on South Main.

Roger's Champion - Roger's first newspaper was founded a few months after the start of the town. The building was at what is now 113 West Elm.

NEWSPAPERS

Donan left Bentonville for Deadwood, South Dakota in 1879 where he made fame as an editor on the frontier.

The "Benton County Journal" was started in 1885 by S. M. Dailey as the result of the consolidation of the "Advance" established in 1873 and his "Bentonian" started in 1881. This paper was first called the "New Bentonian", and was started by Ed. Porter Thompson. In 1883, I find it changed to "Bentonian", edited by S. D. McReynolds and S. W. Womack. There is no date for the ending of the "Journal", but Henry A. Cook and Mr. Hurd were publishers as late as 1900.

The "Benton County Democrat" was started in 1886, by D. W. Hamon and John W. Corley, who later that year sold to J. B. Thompson, who in turn sold to Mr. Henry A. Cook, Dec. 1887. He sold it to Joe Stevenson and Gus Hurley in 1888. After a few years Hurley left the paper and Mr. Stevenson ran the paper for some 25 years. It was one of the leading papers in Northwest Arkansas by 1912, when he sold it to Ben S. Terry. In April of 1923 Terry sold it to O. D. Stiles.

In 1890, Harvey L. Cross started the "Benton County Sun." For years this was a weekly like all the rest of the papers had been, but for a few months it went to a daily.

In 1916, W. H. Plank and his son Will Plank came to Bentonville and started the "Benton County Record". In 1921, they bought the Sun. In 1925, Will Plank bought the Benton County Democrat; he then named the paper the "Democrat and Record."

In 1926, Grover Lindsey, Jack Maxwell and J. L. McKeehen started the "Benton County Herald." This was a three-way partnership.

Some time in 1927, Curtice T. Boren, who moved to Bentonville from Pineville, Mo., bought out Mr. McKeehen's interest in the Herald. Mr. McKeehen then moved to Carthage, Mo., where he was manager of the job printing shop for the Ozark Wesleyan College.

It is not known just when Jack Maxwell left the paper, but in 1935 the Herald was owned by Lindsey and Boren; at this time they bought the Democrat and Record from Will Plank and changed the paper's name back to the Benton County Democrat.

Boren died in Dec. of 1936. Starting Jan. 1, 1937, his wife and three children, who retained his half interest in the paper with Lindsey, went on running it.

The "Benton County Democrat" is the only paper printed in Bentonville today. It is a weekly, and is made up of the following papers: Benton County Democrat, founded Jan. 1, 1886; Benton County Sun, founded Feb. 28, 1890; Benton County Record, founded April 25, 1916; Benton County Herald, founded July 29, 1926; Benton County Record and Democrat, founded Aug. 1, 1925.

The first paper printed in Rogers was the "Rogers Champion". It was started Sept. 1, 1881, just four months after the town really got under way. D. W. Hinman was owner, editor, but it faded out after six months.

Graham and Mason started the "Rogers New Era" in Oct. 1, 1881, and ran it until 1890. They sold it at that date. Some time between 1890 and Sept. 1, 1892, an unknown owner changed the name to the "Democrat". There are no records of the owners for those two years.

On Sept. 1, 1892, John P. Staford, publisher of the Springdale News, bought the "Democrat". He sold it to H. M. Butler early in 1893.

In connection with the weekly "Democrat", he began publishing the "Rogers Daily Democrat", the first daily paper Rogers had, on Nov. 1, 1894, and suspended publication Jan. 1, 1896. In Nov. of 1896, he sold the paper to E. M. Funk and son Erwin Funk.

The "Democrat", then just a weekly, was ran by Funk and Son until Aug. 11, 1919, when E. M. Funk retired and Erwin took over until he sold to E. W. Pate Nov. 1929.

In May of 1888, the "Rogers Republican" was started by Warner and Honeywell; they sold it to Roby and Cheynoweth Jan. 1889. On Jan. 1, 1892, Leo K. Fesler bought it.

For several years ownership of the "Republican" gave the Editor a first mortgage on the postmasters job.

In Jan. 1900, W. R. Cady bought the "Republican". His son Bryon Cady took over in the summer of 1903. In the fall of 1907, he sold it to A. J. Ward of Washington, D. C. Ward changed the name to "Rogers Free Press".

In 1908, J. M. McClelland leased the "Free Press" from the owner and bought the "Rogers Journal" from Christopher and Adams, and consolidated them to make the "Rogers Republican".

In 1912, he sold this paper to H. E. Brighton and started the "Rogers Co-operative Press".

Mr. Brighton sold the "Rogers Republican" to E. M. Fowler in June of 1915, and a few months later this newspaper went to the graveyard as so many others had.

The "Rogers Leader" founded in 1896 by Cain and Meritt, ran about a year.

In 1897, "Rogers Enterprise" started by Dr. W. L. Leister and sons Stanley and Lloyd lasted only a few months.

About 1900, Stanley Leister started the "Rogers Journal," which had many owner's until it was sold to J. M. McClelland in 1909.

The most unique paper printed in Benton County was the "People's Friend," edited by A. M. Merrill of Rogers. It was started on June 25, 1909. Its editorial columns were devoted to socialism and labor unionism. It ran about ten years. He was a crusader against all the political, religious, civic and economic edicts of the day, of which he found many.

On January 1, 1910, the "Rogers Daily Post" was started by John W. Nance and Ernest W. Vinson. They sold to P. M. Kokanour of Siloam Springs in Feb., 1912, who ran it until 1919.

From then until 1923 it had more owners than can be listed. In Aug., 1923, the plant was taken over by Guy Stafford and W. E. Runyan who called it the "Northwest Arkansas Times." He lasted just 13 days.

Next came C. E. Palmer for four years. In July, 1927, he sold to James P. Shofner, who changed the name to "Rogers Daily News" and moved it to the Whitlow building on Walnut St.

The first of Oct., 1929, he sold to E. W. Pate. In Nov., Pate bought the "Rogers Democrat" from Funk. Shofner acquired the commercial printing equipment of both the papers; Pate retained the two newspapers.

The "Rogers Daily News" is the only paper to survive the years. Pate ran it for a number of years.

Siloam Springs' first paper started the year the town was incorporated. In 1880, Thomas Gallagher started "The Siloam City Sun." In 1881, it became the Dispatch, but folded within a year. D. C. Bell published the "Globe" that year but it lasted only a few months.

S. Abernathy began the "Arkansas Herald" in 1882. In 1884, he sold to Grammer & Dameron. In 1889, Dameron sold to Alfred W. Perrine who changed the name to the "Herald Democrat." It has been in the Perrine family ever since.

In 1887, H. Milton Butler and J. Van Butler started the "Hummer." It quit humming around 1892.

The "Interstate American" under the sponsorship of John Brown College was started in 1934.

Gentry's first paper was the "Journal," started in 1894 by a Mr. Daker. He sold it to D. L. Host and Joe G. Bennett. In 1896, it was renamed the "Journal Advance." By 1900, Tallman Co. owned it; they sold to M. V. Crockett in 1921. From then until after 1936 it changed hands many times.

In 1894, A. C. Veach started the "Gravette Herald," which was the second paper of that town. All that is known of the first paper was that in one of his early papers Veach said he would be here more than three months like the last paper.

He sold to Herb P. Lewis in 1907, who changed the name to "News Herald." In the paper he said he was changing it just because he wanted to.

Veach also started another paper, the "Democrat," but it was very short-lived.

On May 26, 1926, Lewis sold to W. H. Plank, who the next

year sold to Mrs. Abbie Keeler. From then it changed hands many times until after 1936.

Sulphur Springs' first newspaper was the "Speaker," which was started in the fall of 1888 by John R. Huffman. It was printed on a homemade press. It was sold to Wn. Scott Stranahan in 1920, who changed the name to "Record." A. C. Veach started the "Echo" in 1921, but this was very short-lived. No date can be found for the ending of the "Record."

We find just one paper listed for Decatur, the "Decatur Herald" founded in 1896 by W. T. Gann, who later sold to Arthur Tallman. Later, John L. Buckner published it, but there are no dates as to when he bought it or when it stopped.

"The Advertiser," started by I. H. Baxter in 1905 at Pea Ridge, lasted but a short time. The "Pea Ridge Pod," founded by Wm. Beck in 1913, lasted a year or two.

At Monte Ne, Coin Harvey started the "Herald" in 1903 and it went under two years later.

Charley Bryson started the "Leader" at Lowell in 1903. It only lasted a year or so. He liked Lowell because it was close to the Cross Hollows distillery.

Cave Springs, as small as it was, had two tries at newspapers: the "Progress," started by Dotson Barnes in 1911, and the "Star," by C. Baker in 1912. They both folded soon after starting.

"The Centerton Times" was started by R. G. McLaren on July 2, 1914. At a time when the other papers in the county had upped their prices from the standard $1 a year to $1.50 or $2 a year, this paper started out for 50 cents a year. That may be why he didn't last long.

The second try at a paper in Centerton came in May, 1933, when J & R Kerns started printing "The Ad-Visor." It also was a short-lived paper, even at 25 cents a year.

Almost every town in the county had one or more newspapers. At one time there were 19 newspapers being printed in the county, a top for any county in the state.

As Mr. Erwin Funk, who gave me most of this county newspaper history of years ago said, "It would be hard to list all of the owners of the papers as many of them changed owners once or twice a year. There may even have been more newspapers started that didn't last long enough to get talked about so their names were lost."

From the Benton County Democrat, May 28, 1936. This was a special paper for the 100th anniversary of statehood.

Hit and Miss Memories
By Charles D. Haney

One of the earliest memories, the Hammond hanging. The

vast sordid and morbid crowd, Hammond sitting on his coffin going to the gallows. The gallows that stood for years after the hanging in what is now Scott's pasture, known then as the open Prairie. The "Hants" that were supposed to have their habitat around this place on Friday nights.

Ox teams hauling tobacco to the tobacco factory or to sell to the Reynolds Brothers buyers.

Deer and wild turkey hanging from the butchers rack. When everybody which included town people had hogs on the range and a registered mark.

Is there any one in the schools of the county who can tell what is meant by two under-bits in the left ear and a crop on the right.

The cordial greeting of "Alight friend," when one rode up to the home of a settler. Men borrowing money without written evidence of debt. No security except the spoken promise.

The backwash of the civil war, tattered Blue and Gray uniforms often to be seen. The intense feeling against carpetbaggers.

A hog cholera epidemic that kept people busy pulling carcasses out from under houses and barns and hauling them off.

Striped back long horn scrubby cows. W. R. Clark importing the first Jersey bull to the county, perhaps the most valuable animal it ever had.

Mack Rodgers selling to J. C. Knott two full wagon loads of cured bacon. Driving two teams of mules that would look like a million dollars today.

The suave and courteous Col. W. A. Terry selling merchandise and visiting with his trade.

The dignified and high minded A. W. Dinsmore with gray and silken beard. Among others Dave Woods and the Claypools, Craig and Sons, J. C. Pluck, R. W. Hansard, Uncle Johnnie Reed all honorable merchants selling honest goods at honest prices.

Pat Donan, the newspaperman who made an enviable and national reputation as a writer.

The fire that laid waste to the north side of the square. The saloon on the north side and one on the south. When the east side was the best business location and when D. J. Woods was still in the ring and Jim Vaughn opened the first five and ten.

When J. C. Knott opened a grocery store on the south side, where for nearly a half century he maintained a reputation for great business ability and unyielding honesty.

When Clint Crouch came to Bentonville a dapper young man to work at his trade. Calvin Coolidge and North Hampton, Mass., may have had its shoe shop and philosopher; lucky Bentonville has its "Backband and Gear Shop," and its Prof. Clinton Lycurgus Crouch.

Kit Campbell, little more than a mere boy coming to engage

in the barber business, in which he is still engaged. A pleasing personality, honest dealing and strict attention to business made his business a success and more, an institution for the town.

Joe S. Stevenson, an adventurous young Irishman, coming from the west driving a herd of broncs. He came to tarry a few days, lost his heart and found a home.

Judge R. W. Ellis, the orator and story teller, so kindly disposed he told all the stories on himself. Judge S. N. Elliott, the man with the great brain and the heart of a child.

Uncle John Black's reception of Gen. Franz Sigel, when he returned after an absence of years to finish his breakfast at the old Eagle Hotel that the Confederate vanguard forced him to abandon the day before the battle of Pea Ridge.

"I expected to be mit enemies but I see I'm mit gracious friends," said the Federal General.

First days of court. The valley under the town's spring stoped with camps and covered wagons, horse traders galore, patent rights exhibited, patent medicine shows, mule buyers in town, breeding stock cluttering the square and friends greeting friends in a hearty home spun way.

Old Bob Perry, the colored Confederate soldier, going down the street announcing, "They are here, Mister Vol and Wyth."

The Saturday night band concerts when dances were hops, girls wore sweeping skirts, leg mutton sleeves and Gibson coiffures.

The glamor of Harry Elliott when he returned from the west a successful miner.

Edward White, a boy about town, who went out in the world to make a great name for himself as a lawyer, author of law books, executive of a great railroad system and yet found time to become a renowned Shakesperian scholar.

The young man, ex-president Herbert Hoover, staying at the Blake Hotel, working on his first job assisting on the geodetic survey in the local area.

Memories come in battalions now, perhaps of no interest save to a few old cronies, and space for bids. The record is made closed but still, "The moving finger writes, and having writ, moves on nor all your piety nor wit can lure it back to cancel half a line, nor all your tears wash out a word of it."

From the Benton County Record and Democrat and the Benton County Sun Thursday Sept. 22, 1932.

Bentonville History In a Nutshell

Judge W. A. Dickson has written the following brief history of the town of Bentonville. His forebears being among the pioneers of the county, and having studied the question and given it much thought, he is an authority on the subject. We are grateful to Mr. Dickson for privilege of this article which we know will be interesting to our readers.

In the year 1830 a few families from Rutherford and Bedford Counties, Tennessee, after a long journey in ox-drawn wagons located in and around the present site of Bentonville. Then Arkansas was a territory and the present area of Benton County was embraced in Washington County. The nearest village, the post office and the seat of the county was at Fayetteville. It so remained until after statehood in 1836.

On September 30, 1836, Benton County was formed by Act of the first State Legislature, and named for Thomas H. Benton, United States Senator from Missouri. The temporary seat of Justice was by that act established at the house of George Wallace, about one and one half mile east of Bentonville as it now is. There the first county court was held in April 1837.

Pursuant to the act creating Benton County an election was held to elect three commissioners to select a site for the county seat. Robert Cowan, Robert Weaver and Thomas Swaggerty were elected.

On November 7, 1837, they reported to the Circuit Court that they had located the county seat upon the south half of the south east quarter of Section 30, Township 20, north range 30, West and had called the town Bentonville.

The report was confirmed and approved by the Circuit Court at its first term in November 1837. This court was held at the home of George Wallace referred to above. The first jury met under a spreading tree and was composed of Joseph McKissick, foreman, Philip Dumas, William Reddick, Wn. Ford, Christopher S. Pace, George Graham, Joseph Dickson, Robert Cooper, John B. Robinson, Jonathan Duff, Samuel P. Woods, Diolesian Jackson, Ezekiel M. Dickson, Ambrose C. Williams and Henry Ford. The grand jury returned one true bill.

The Petit Jury empanelled at the first term of court in 1837 was composed of; James Anderson, John Maxwell, Robert Hubbard, Geo. W. Ford, Samuel B. McClain, Ezekiel J. A. Dickson, Henry Hastings, Jas. Hammack, Nathan Coughman, Samuel Black, David Woods, and Samuel Woods.

It is remarkable how many of their Christian or given names are Bible names.

The Commissioners obtained from the United States a patent for a town site, and laid off a square and the balance there of into lots. There were 166 lots. Residence lots were 165 feet square and business lots 82½ feet square. The original town was bounded on the south by 13th street, on the west by the street running north and south on the west side of the public school building, on the north by tenth street, and on the east by a line drawn north and south near the foot of the hill on east 12th street.

The first general store in Bentonville was established about 1837 by Dr. Nicholas Spring. Twenty three years later in 1860 there were five general stores, a furniture store, a saddle and harness shop, two hotels or inns, and three mechanic shops.

The first church to be organized was the Cumberland Presbyterian church in the year 1830 or 1831. In 1850 there were two churches in Bentonville, the Cumberland Presbyterian and the South Methodist. Other denominations worshipped in these churches.

The Civil War left Bentonville in ruins. Both armies met and crossed the county here.

The battle of Pea Ridge began at the Clark Hotel in Bentonville when General Sigel was surprised while breakfasting with his officers there. This hotel occupied the site of the present Hotel Massey. (Today the Town House)

In 1880-1881, the first railroad was built in the county and missed Bentonville by six miles. At that time Bentonville citizens were under contract with another railroad, the Moffatt Road, which was never built. In 1882, the Bentonville railroad was built to connect with the Frisco railroad at Rogers and later this line was extended to Grove, Oklahoma, in 1898-1899.

Bentonville was incorporated as a town by the County Court in January 1873.

The first public school building was erected in 1872 on the site which the grammar school building occupied until the erection of the present building. The first building was of brick and stone and was burned in 1877. From then until 1882 school was taught in the churches and residence buildings. In 1882 another school building was erected on the same site, but it was torn down and a new building erected.

The Ouachita Baptist Academy was erected about 1896 was later acquired by the Bentonville School district and used for many years. It was torn down in 1929 when the new school building was erected on West Eleventh street.

Perhaps the most exciting day after the Civil War was the daylight robbery of the People's Bank by Henry Starr and his gang of outlaws in June 1893, when they successfully robbed the bank of $11,000.00. None were ever apprehended and tried for the offense.

Bentonville had a disastrous fire in the winter of 1880-81 when the entire north side of the Square except the building on the west end was destroyed with practically an entire loss of stocks.

Chapter Nine
Railroads

In 1860, Benton County didn't have too many roads...nor were the ones they had very good.

Yet that year the levying court appropriated $500.00 to assist in a survey to run a railroad from Van Buren to some place in Missouri to meet the Missouri Pacific Railroad. The Civil War started before the survey got under way so the money was returned to the county treasurer.

It was then 20 years before anything more was done about a railroad. In 1880, Benton county was assured of at least one railroad. It was that year that the Frisco line started grading and laying track across the south part of the county. This line missed Bentonville by several miles as did all the main lines that crossed the county.

The first passenger train ran through the county May 10, 1881. Several new towns were laid out along this line, Avoca, Garfield, Rogers and Lowell. Rogers has always used May 10 as their birthday because of this train.

Sometime in 1882 the people of Bentonville paid for a line from Bentonville to Rogers. This line was first named the Bentonville to Rogers line.

In 1889, the Kansas City, Fort Smith and Southern built a line in to Sulphur Springs. This line had been built from Kansas City down by buying out short lines and building what it took to add them together. They stopped at Sulphur Springs for several years. This was a big help to this one town in the county.

At this time many farmers in the west half of the county found that they could sell their crops for a better price by shipping them by rail to a bigger market.

Some changes took place in the K. C. F. S., and by 1893 it was known as the Kansas City, Pittsburg and Gulf, then in 1900 it became the Kansas City Southern which it is today.

In 1893, they started building again, going south out of

Sulphur Springs. They first came to Nebo, and a new town started which was Gravette. Then on to Decatur which then was a town of two or three stores and a post office. From here to Gentry which was a new town starting because of the railroad. Then on south and some what west and going out of the county in to Oklahoma, in to Adair county.

This line proved to be a big help to the apple growers and other farmers in the whole west half of the county.

One very interesting fact about this line was that most of it was financed by foreign investors, who were eager to invest in enterprises in growing America. A committee of Dutch stockholders came to Arkansas for firsthand information on the new road and were so favorably impressed by the time they got to the Gulf that they put up the money with some Americans and the line was completed in 1897.

In 1897, Rogers citizens subscribed $20,000 to help build a railroad from Harrison to Rogers, then Bentonville and on north west to McElhaney, Mo., where it would meet a main line going west. This line was never started, just lots of talk.

On April 7, 1898, a public meeting was held in Rogers and the people again pledged their $20,000 to help build a railroad. This one would run from Rogers to Gravette where it would meet the Pittsburg & Gulf line.

The line was incorporated in May 1898, with a capital of $200,000 and was named The Arkansas & Oklahoma Railroad company. They planned in time to run from Rogers to Grove, Oklahoma.

Those signing the papers were John M. Bayliss, E. J. Glascow, W. A. Miller, T. Mallen, W. K. Bayliss, W. R. Felker, J. A. Rice and D. H. Woods.

They secured control of the railroad between Rogers and Bentonville and laid a new roadbed and steel. The line was completed to Gravette by the fall of 1898.

The next year the line was finished and you could go from Rogers all the way to Grove, Oklahoma, by rail. The line was sold to the Frisco company in November of 1900. At this time Bayliss and Felker must have been the main stockholders as only their names were mentioned in the sale.

In Feb., 1904, W. F. Felker announced plans to build a railroad from Rogers to Siloam Springs where it would connect with the Kansas City Southern. This new line was to be the Rogers Southern.

In the summer of 1904, the Rogers city council granted them a 50-year franchise to a right-of-way up first street from the south edge of town to Cherry street then through the alley between First and Second street to Elm.

Surveying for the line started in the spring of 1905. That

54

John Lee, on his run from Rogers to Grove, Okla. At this time the line was owned by Frisco.

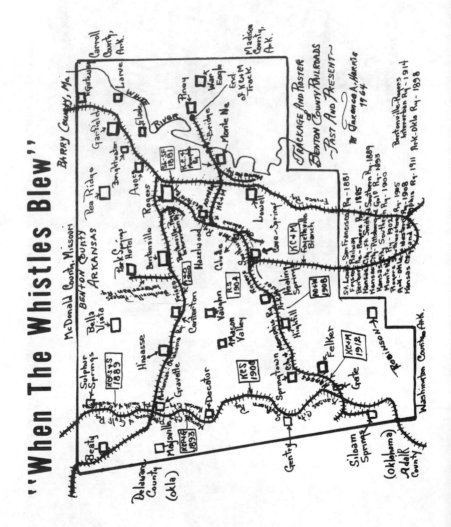

November, work began on the line with ten graders on the job under the supervision of J. H. G. Brown of Gravette. Ned Whitcomb was doing the surveying and establishing the grades. Grading in the McGaughey addition ran parallel with the Frisco then went southwest.

Laying of the track started April 18, 1906, when the first steel arrived in Rogers. By September the line had reached Springtown. On the 4th. of Sept., the first passenger train ran. They had a big celebration, with a picnic dinner, band concert, ball game, speeches and all the trimmings.

This line went through many changes as it was being built. On Feb. 13, 1907, it was taken over by the Arkansas, Oklahoma and Western Railroad. The officers were W. R. Felker, President; Alf Williams, Vice President; J. E. Felker, Treasurer; F. F. Freeman, Secretary. Locally the line was known as the A. O. & W.

It was granted a charter to build and operate a standard gauge railroad from Rogers east to Eureka Springs, and west through Siloam Springs to Pryor Creek. I. T. Capital stock was $3,000,000. Later this line became The Kansas City & Memphis Railroad.

It is not known for sure what day the line was finished to Siloam Springs, but there would have been a big celebration when the first train got there. The line stopped at Siloam Springs and never was built further west, or did they ever build east of Rogers.

The stations along this line were Hazelwood, which had just a cemetery, church and apple dryer, plus a couple of farm houses. Next was Colville Spur, which had a post office. Then came Cave Springs, Healing Springs, Highfill, Springtown, Felker, Siloam Springs. There were some other stops along where there were short sidings so the farmers could load out cars of fruit or other stuff they wanted to ship.

This line crossed the Kansas City Southern tracks two miles northwest of Siloam Springs; here there was a locked gate. The trains on the KC & M had to stop and the brakeman would unlock the gate as the train pulled through and crossed the other track and stopped for the brakeman who had then relocked the gate.

This was to keep the trains from crossing the Kansas City Southern line as one of their trains was coming. This gate was also the first stop sign in Benton County.

In 1902, the Monte Ne Railroad was built at a cost of $25,000. It had one depot, five miles of tracks, one passenger coach and one locomotive. It performed a shuttle service between Monte Ne and Lowell. Most people called it the Coin Harvey Train, in honor of the owner of the famous Monte Ne Resort that it serviced.

Runs were timed with those of the trains on the Frisco main line which ran through Lowell. The only ones who used this short line were tourists or visitors going to Monte Ne. Lots of young folks would take the train there just for a Sunday outing.

This line was in debt and having troubles right from the day it started. The men who backed it all lost money. In 1909, the AO & W took over this broken line and added it to their own line. To do this they ran a track east from Hazelwood to the Monte Ne line. To get there they had to tunnel under the Frisco railroad two miles north of Lowell.

They connected with the Monte Ne track at about midway; they then ran on to Monte Ne, but abandoned the part that ran back to Lowell.

In 1910, the Arkansas, Oklahoma and Western and the Monte Ne railroad became the Kansas City and Memphis Railroad. The slogan on the box cars was the "Fruit Belt Line," the emblem a big red apple.

The same year they continued the track from Monte Ne east two miles to the White River. Here they built a bridge across the river. It was a really big bridge for that day, being 1,000 feet long, and made to withstand the high water. The track then ran east four miles to Piney where this line could pick up the lumber from the sawmills in the east part of the county.

In 1911, this line built a track south from Cave Springs for 20 miles running in to Fayetteville. Here they connected with the Frisco line.

Before the east end of Monte Ne line was abandoned the trainmen got a notion that the bridge over the White River was not safe. So they would stop the train at the approach of the bridge.

A train on the Frisco Mail Line, south of Rogers. Picture made on a glass negative in 1889.

RAILROADS

Then two of the crew walked across the bridge to the opposite site. The train was started and the throttle set and the train crossed the bridge unmanned. The two men on the other side caught the engine and stopped the train and waited for the balance of the crew to walk across.

These train lines all filled a need of the day. Until the trains came in to the county, the farmers had very little market for anything they could grow. After the trains, they had markets for all their fruit, grain and cattle.

Then, because of the railroads, the canneries opened up all over the county; this gave a good market for the vegetables and small fruit.

By the beginning of World War One, part of the lines were losing money and when the Federal Government took over the railroads they closed the K. C. & M. As time went on other lines just dried up. It would be hard to say just what date the last train ran on any of the lines. By the late 1930's the only railroads left in the county were the Frisco and the Kansas City Southern.

The coming of trucks and going of the apples were the main reason that the railroads started losing money. Before the days of cars, the railroads all ran special trains to any big program that happened in the county. Some times there would be several carloads of people riding. But this all stopped after the car.

The railroad filled the need in their days, then when the need was gone the tracks were taken up and in a few years the trains were all but forgotten.

In the years of railroading in the county there were several wrecks and derailments. Three men were killed and a few hurt in these, all of them were railroad workers. In one wreck, four valuable show horses were killed. Some of the wrecks were very costly in money, some of the derailments were more of a loss in time than much money.

Chapter Ten
Interurban

Bentonville Interurban

In the good old summertime in the early 1900's, the highlight of entertainment was a trolley trip in the evening. Young and old alike would take a trip to the end of the line, visit, go to a show, or have an ice cream soda and go back home later that night.

Talk of the first trolley in Benton County began in 1912 when a charter was granted to the Arkansas Northwest Railroad Co. to run an interurban train between Rogers and Bentonville.

The company got a franchise from Rogers to operate its car down the center of second street from Cherry street north to the intersection with the Frisco track which ran to Bentonville.

In Bentonville they left the main Frisco line just west of the Bentonville station. The track curved off the main line and ran north down NW A street. This is now Highway 71, city route. They stopped at NW A and Central to let people out at the Massey Hotel, then went on out to the Park Springs Hotel on the north edge of town.

The work was halted several times by injunctions, once by Rogers Light and Water Company and the City of Bentonville, which owned the water system there. Both claimed that the train would disturb their water mains. The court ruled that inasmuch as neither complainant had complied with their own city ordinances in laying the mains at the required depth, and that they had no business to be in the middle of a street, the court would give them no relief.

On July 1, 1914, several hundred Bentonville citizens and a band went to Rogers on the first trips of the new motor car, and an informal reception was held. A little later Rogers returned the call and a dinner and picnic was held at Park Springs.

The fare was 15 cents at first and the car made several trips each day. The motor car was not always reliable and missed a good many trips. But this was a lot better than having just one run

The Bentonville Interurban Coach, stopped at Northwest A and Central. Note Massey Hotel in the background.

a day like the Frisco made with their train that ran from Rogers to Grove, Oklahoma.

The train was far different from any the people in Benton County had ever seen before. It was a big red coach trimmed in black and had gold lettering. The engine was built in one end of the long coach, and next to this was a small baggage room. The coach was 92 feet long inside. The passenger part seated about 130. Sometimes there would be standing room only.

The line was owned by J. D. Southerland, that is he owned both ends of it. Mr. Southerland came to Bentonville in the fall of 1913, and bought the Park Springs Hotel. At that time it was a large and beautiful summer resort. But it was hard for people to get from the main Frisco station in Rogers to it.

Mr. Southerland made a deal with the Frisco Railroad Line to run his train on their track from Rogers to Bentonville. The only trains they were running was a passenger train to Grove that went out in the morning and back at night. Then a few freight runs. Southerland made his runs between these.

Their Rogers' station was just a roofed-over platform a block from the Frisco station. There was a shop and shed at the Bentonville end of the line, and the train was kept here overnight. At that time the streets were all dirt, so when they laid the track they used short ties and built the track in the center of the road. The wagons and what few cars there were had to drive on both sides of the track.

"The Interurban filled a need at the time it was built," said Henry Cavness, one of the last men to die who had worked on this train. "I was the brakeman the whole time the train ran. There were several motormen, among them Ed. Largette, Ben Guol, Art Mayhall, and Jake Kohley. Bob Fowler and a man named Ketter were the conductors. We used just a three man crew to run the train."

"We hauled the mail between the two towns, and always met the trains that ran on the Frisco main line. The tourist going out to stay a month at Park Springs sure would have a lot of baggage, sometimes we would fill the little baggage compartment."

The first run left Bentonville at 6:15 in the morning and the last run got back to Bentonville at 11:30. They stopped at Cherry and Walnut streets in Rogers, then at Apple Spur, Arlan Spur, Massey Hotel and Park Springs Hotel in Bentonville.

In the evening there was always a good crowd riding. They could go to the show or visit in town. In the summer whenever there was a ball game, fair, or carnival in either of the towns, the coach would be full every trip.

The rate was raised to 40 cents for a round trip, one way 21 cents; 5 cents from the Massey Hotel to Park Springs. They had a ticket office in the Massey Hotel; this was also the business office. Most of the people just paid when they got on. This train stopped almost any place along the line to pick up or let off passengers.

"The only time we ever had any trouble was when we had a full load," said motor man Jake Kohley. "I remember one night in the summer of 1915, it was the last run and there had been a carnival in Rogers, and we had a load of about 150 people. Someone had opened the switch at the edge of Bentonville; when we hit that it knocked the wheels off the car. We were very lucky no one was hurt. But a lot of them had to walk home. We called the Taxi; there were two of them. They took a lot home. Every now and then someone would do something like this to us. Then we would have to get a crew of Frisco men out of Rogers to fix the car."

"The Auto took the place of the Trolley, but it seemed to me a lot of the fun of a trip went out when the trolley did," said Jake.

The motor car made its last trip June 11, 1916, when the Frisco railroad ordered it off their tracks for non-payment of lease dues.

At about this time Mr. Southerland lost or had to sell most of his holding here. Soon the track was taken up, the coach sold and the line was no more. But the oldtimers still talk about the trips to Bentonville or Rogers, or a trip to Park Springs for a picnic that was made on the Interurban.

The only one who ever talked of the bad parts of the line was a man who drove a team to a freight wagon. He said, "The ties stuck out so far that if you were not very careful a wheel would hit one and could throw you right off the wagon. But it had its place, just as the horse did, but they are both gone now."

Chapter Eleven
Minerals and Mining

Oil Drilling

It is not known for sure just when people in Benton county first started thinking of the easy money to be made in oil. Much of the early drilling was surrounded with secrecy.

I find listed in the book Arkansas Geological Survey that an oil well was drilled at Monte Ne in 1908 and 1909. They drilled to 1,212 feet but found no signs of oil or gas.

They also list a well drilled 5 miles southwest of Bentonville, no date given. It went down to 2,330 feet. In this well, gas was reported from sand at depths of 890, 955; 1,122; 1,342 and 2,225 feet as well as from limestone at 1,977 and 2,210 feet. A show of oil was reported in the sand at 2,365; 2,400 and 2,425 feet. This well was drilled by the Arkansas Publicity Bureau.

Several development companies were started in the county from 1916 until the mid-1920's. Most of their drilling was kept secret and the wells were capped or filled when they stopped drilling.

In 1916, when the Centerton Co-operative Development Company was formed at Centerton, the people all dreamed of a vast oil field and having more money than they could spend the rest of their lives. But their dreams never came true. To this day many of the people around there feel sure that there is a lake of gas and oil under their land.

When the company was formed they listed a capital stock of $100,000. In early 1919, their ad listed it as having a $250,000 capital stock. Over the next year or so the newspapers carried many articles about their drilling which began in 1919.

The Benton County Democrat, June 6, 1919, ran the following: "The so much talked of oil proposition at Centerton has become a fact. The drilling machinery and equipment has arrived and is being unloaded and hauled to the field, within a few days drilling will begin. Centerton truly enough started the work and

This is one of the few stocks left in the county from this Oil Company.

only a live wire town like Centerton will finish the bargain to determine if we are lucky enough to have oil in the vicinity.

The first well is to be drilled on the land of Marvin McGaugh, about one mile due south of Centerton. Every one is eagerly awaiting the results."

In an article August 1, 1919, it said that G. W. Webster the millionaire Tulsa oil man who owned the drilling machinery at the well south of Centerton, had ordered it all moved to Broken Arrow, Okla.

The article went on to say, "since beginning operation on the well about six weeks ago all their work has been closed in secrecy. But a little information has been allowed to leak out as to what progress was being made. For awhile they had to pierce a hard rock and made very slow headway. But since they have found easier drilling and had been making much better progress. The principal reason for suspending the operations is because of the great quantity of water that has been getting in the well. They were down to 1200 feet."

The Benton County Democrat ran the following letter on Aug. 22, 1919, from G. W. Webster: "Now as to the formation of the well it was as follows, about 38 feet of soil then very hard lime to 255 feet, then 60 feet of shale with sulphuric odor, then hard lime to 600 feet.

Then water sand to 612 feet, hard lime to 975 feet, then water sand to 990 feet, hard lime to 1,130 feet. Then salt water to 1,138 feet. Depth of well 1,138 feet. The cuttings which were saved from the well have been sent to Tulsa and then to the school of mines to be analyzed."

It was found out after Webster had removed all of his equipment from the well that he had also filled the hole so no one could use the hole he had drilled. The Centerton Company also had to bring suit in Chancery Court to get back the lease land from him. He lost this as he had not drilled as deep as his contract called for.

Also on Aug. 22, the paper stated that the Centerton Cooperative Development Company had formed plans in which they would again commence within 30 days using their own drilling outfit.

A contract with Collins, Culver and Manning had been made whereby these oil men agreed to put the drill down in the old hole to a depth of 1,200 feet for 5 leases on 500 acres of ground the company has under lease. Mr. Manning is an oil driller and will have charge of the work.

The Centerton Cooperative Development Company which some time ago put down a test well to a depth of 400 feet had to drill through 300 feet of hard rock. This was a very expensive proposition and enough money was spent to put down an ordinary well 2000 feet deep.

Nothing will be kept secret by the Centerton Company as in the case of Webster. The people will know at all times what is going on.

I couldn't find out just when the Centerton Company had bought their own drilling outfit. But they did some drilling of their own with it just south of Centerton at Mitchell's spring.

On September 26, we find the following: "Tuesday work resumed on the old hole of the Centerton Cooperative Development Company near Mitchell's spring, south of Centerton. John Manning who has been here from Michigan this summer looking over the field has taken charge of the work and will personally superintend it.

He is under a $3,600 bond contract with the Company to carry the well down a depth of 1,600 feet at which depth they feel sure they will be able to tell whether there is oil under the soil or not.

In consideration of the drilling, Mr. Manning and the Company he represents will receive 500 acres of leases. They agree to pay all expenses including labor and casings, but will use the Centerton Company's drill and outfit. A day and night shift will be employed and five men are on the job.

The Centerton Company had the test hole drilled down 400 feet at the time they were forced to quit for lack of funds and the contractors will go down 1,200 more."

Manning was associated with a well known oil man Judge Rush Culver.

We read on October 31, that "the Centerton oil well being drilled by the Development Company has been working steadily night and day until this week, and are now 1,145 feet deep. Tuesday they suspended drilling in order to pipe off the water. They will begin drilling again in a few days.

In November they slowed down because they ran out of coal. So they borrowed what they needed from the Vinegar plant in Centerton."

The news in the paper looked better December 12: "Whether they strike oil or not there certainly has been an abundant flow of water in the Centerton oil well. Due to the water pouring in to the well several hundred feet of casing has been pulled up. The casing was put back down the last of the week to a depth of 1,100 feet, but the water leak was still causing so much trouble that it will be pulled up again and cased to the bottom of the hole, a depth of 1400 feet.

Small quantities of oil have been encountered in the well and operators feel certain that a big strike will be made at only a few more feet."

Jan. 9, 1920: "Drillers at the Centerton oil well are having their full share of trouble these days. No sooner had the boiler been repaired last week and drilling was resumed, before another delay was caused by losing the tools in the well.

The rescuing tools they have were too big to be dropped to the bottom and they had to send for smaller ones to grab the lost drill and haul it out."

There was better news in the paper Jan. 31, 1920: "Drillers at the oil well are now encountering softer soil and are now able to make thirty feet a day. Monday morning they had passed the 1,600 foot mark and since then have been making steady progress.

It has been definitely decided to keep on going down further until they strike something or until hope has been abandoned. They have just received new and longer cables and now plan to drill 2,300 feet or more if necessary."

The big news came on May 11, 1920, when word went out to all the newspapers in the area that they had stopped drilling at 2,300 feet because they had reached oil sand. The well was plugged until they could get more casing, then they will shoot it.

For several days the well at Centerton was big news in the tri-state area. But it soon all blew over and no oil was hit. The well was plugged as were several others that were drilled in the County.

In the newspaper of Oct. 8, 1920: "The Inter-State Oil & Refining Co's light drill operated by Day Brothers, is drilling a shallow test well, seven miles northwest of Gravette on Wet Prairie and struck gas Wednesday at a depth of 222 feet.

Drillers are very optimistic over the strike which appears like a big one. The gas was struck after drilling through a shale formation of about 50 feet, and a few inches of sand. After striking the gas a driller touched a match and the flames leaped up 25 feet. Today the well has been plugged up and work was stopped.

The company plans to start their deep well test about a mile away and run the drill with the aid of gas. How large the gas pocket is cannot be estimated until the gas has been controlled and drilling goes deeper. The drill will be moved back to a safe distance and work started again.

The well is on the Rhoades farm. Once before a large gas pocket was struck on the prairie."

Jan. 8, 1921, Decatur Herald: "Decatur's first test well for oil was started Saturday, January 1, on W. S. McGaugh's farm 1 1/4 miles northwest of Decatur.

The operations are the result of the Decatur Development Company who secured enough leases to interest oil promoters to become interested here. A contract was let to Rush Culver of Fayetteville and calls for two 2,000-foot test wells and one 2,300 foot well.

The drill is now in operation daily in charge of competent drillers and was down 35 feet Monday when hard rock was encountered and the progress will be slower.

It is not yet known where the other test well will be located or the deep well drilled on the 4,000 acre leases.

Possess yourselves with patience and watch this community blossom like the proverbial 'Green Bay' tree."

No one can say today just how many wells were drilled to find oil in the county, but there was a lot of them and they covered most of the areas of the county.

Some gas has been found and a few wells have been piped in to houses for use. But for the most part this has been a loss of money for those who bought stock or paid to have a well drilled. Some of the wells that had been capped, have been opened and are now being used as water wells.

Mining

The early settlers were farmers and they didn't go around looking for minerals or trying to find mines of any kind. There is just one report of anyone looking for ore before the Civil War, and this was when a party of men spent some time along the White River looking for a silver mine. They gave up and left.

A few people left the county in the 1850's to go west and try their luck at finding gold. But they didn't waste their money or time looking for any here.

After the Civil War ended stories started going the rounds about caves or mines in the county where men had found almost pure lead ore during the war. Many people looked for these mines but no one found any.

The biggest interest in mining came in 1887. At this time they were working the Split Log mine northwest of Bentonville in the Indian Territory. The stories of the great wealth to come must have got to people for every week's newspaper would carry a new article on someone who had found some rich ore while digging a well, or just laying on top of the ground in their back 40.

The following news articles show how they were all year. "Mr. James Nees, who was digging a well in the northwest part of Bentonville last week, found some of the richest specimens of Jack or zinc ore we have ever seen. It would go 90 per cent zinc.

Col. Abert Peel of Avoca came by with a fine specimen of copper ore. He said there were strangers in his area locating mineral claims on Government land."

In the spring of 1887, W. A. Terry, C. R. Craig and S. F. Stahl formed the Bentonville Mining Company, with a capital stock of $1,000.

On May 7th, this article ran in the Bentonville paper. "The Bentonville Mining Co. struck ore in their mine on Pea Ridge that indicated exceeding richness. It is mineral of some kind, as it melts readily, and has every appearance of silver. Specimens have been sent to different points, and a report of its value is daily expected."

Then we find that James Holland had sent a rock to an assayer in Washington Territory. It was said to run $486 in Silver to the ton.

Someone writing in the newspaper late that summer about a big picnic at War Eagle, said that every man there had a piece of rock that had gold, silver, lead, zinc, or some other mineral too rare to talk about.

Late in the fall of 1887, the Benton County Democrat ran a story on some man who had sent off several rocks to an assayer in the west who said, "It was just like he had thought none of the rocks showed ore to make it pay to mine. Some did have a trace of ore but it was very small."

In the article, the editor would not say who sent the rock in. I somehow feel that he had as he had been writing as if maybe he didn't believe in the gold stories any more. So after a full year of big talk of mines and money it all blew over and people went back to hard work for a living.

In August of 1894, one F. C. Wilsey made a hard search for the old Spanish mine at Edens Bluff. He put down a 70-foot shaft. Each week the newspaper said he was coming very close to a rich vein of gold or silver. But all he ever found was a large stack of rocks.

Over the years several people have looked for this so-called lost mine. Some had maps, but no one ever found any ore of any kind.

One group looking for the mine in 1900 did make a find, but not one they could spend at all. They found five skeletons at the base of the Bluff as they dug.

In the spring of 1900, copper was the big talk in the county. Frank Page bought a large acreage on White River east of Rogers. Soon he started the Page Copper Co., which was incorporated with a capital stock of $200,000.

Page had the railroad run a spur track from the White River bridge to LaRue. Then he built one big building for the men to live in who worked the mine, and several smaller ones for shops and other uses.

Several tunnels were dug in the rock bluffs. Some traces of copper were found, but they never found a pay lode. After working for over a year at a loss, the money ran out so Page closed down the only copper mine we ever had.

For several years in the 1920's the Lady-Lady Mining Company of Rogers did a lot of mining on a farm belonging to Dr. Schekles. The farm laid on the east side of Bentonville.

Mr. and Mrs. E. L. Lady, who were experienced geologists

and miners, were in charge of the mining. In a test run where 400 pounds of ore was run through a small smelter they got approximately 10 ounces of silver, so the newspapers reported.

Later they told of them setting up a 50 ton smelter, and steam drills. They had a work force of 25 men. Part of these were shaft men who know mining. Lots of work was done but they never found any ore that would pay for mining it.

Promoters also failed in their efforts to recover valuable minerals from a mine near Elk Horn Tavern at Pea Ridge. After finding no lead or tin in the ore they stopped work in January 1930.

A small five-ton smelter had been set up to test the ore, which the promoters had declared was rich in lead and tin.

The tests were unsuccessful, it was said, because the plant was too small to extract the metal. Before the smelter was dismantled, however, it made a test run on an ore found near War Eagle which was said to be rich in gold, silver and platinum.

As far as is known, however, no valuable metal of any kind was ever recovered from either of the ores.

As one can see there has been much time, money and work go into mining in Benton county. But it has all been a lost cause, as was the drilling for oil in the county.

Kruse Gold Mine

One of the most fantastic mining stories to have ever happened in Benton County was the Kruse Gold Mine in Rogers.

The Kruse Gold mine started with a "Vision", and was carried out by the Kruse family as the Vision told them to. In fact as strange as it sounds the Kruse family lived and ran their business for years as the Vision said for them to do.

So far as the people of Rogers were concerned the whole fantastic story started on Jan. 27, 1903. That day some fifty people in Rogers received telegrams from W. H. Kruse, in Chicago, saying, "Ten Million dollars for all the people of Rogers."

No one knew what it meant. They all knew W. H. Kruse and also his father who was living in Rogers.

W. H. Kruse was the oldest son of Henry W. Kruse, and had moved from Ohio to Rogers with his father and family in 1883. After he grew up, W. H. Kruse moved to Le Sueur, Minn., where he was living when our story started. He later moved to Minneapolis. He had a good business and was making a lot of money at that time.

Some time in 1900, W. H. Kruse started to have "Visions". At first they worried him for he thought he could be losing his mind. But as time went on he would set down at his desk, hold a pencil with his eyes closed, and write what the Vision made him write,

This drawing of the Kruse mine tower was made by the late Mrs. Elsie M. Sterling, of Rogers. There seems to be no pictures left of the Kruse Gold Mine or tower. It, like the Vision is all gone.

not seeing or knowing what it was saying, sometimes until he read it later.

In one of these so-called visits from the Vision, Kruse was told about the Gold Mine on his father's farm in Arkansas. It told him that under the roots of an old wild apple tree he would find a gold mine, so rich that he could reconstruct the economy of the world after the ravages of a great War that was coming.

Kruse wrote to members of his family about the tree; they all said there was no wild apple tree. The Vision then told Kruse to go to Arkansas and look, he would find the tree and under its roots the mine.

He went back to Rogers and the family farm, and after some looking he found a wild apple tree that was hidden by some underbrush. He dug at its roots, and found some ore; it was loose and crumbling, and easy to handle and there was an untold quantity.

Then followed two years of vain attempts to convince assayers of the value of the ore. They all said it had only the faintest trace of gold, not enough to give it commercial value.

The Vision later told Kruse they were not testing the gold ore right. It told him how to test it. The assayers refused to follow the directions of a Vision, and would not try the new test.

Kruse made his own tests then, and the first ore he had taken out assayed at $425 worth of gold to the ton of ore. Later samples tested from $2,500 to $5,000 a ton. But that assayer was for the Vision only, as no one else would use that type of test.

The actual digging was started on Sept. 15, 1905. It started with a parade from in front of the Proctor Dry Goods Co. on the north side of Walnut Street in downtown Rogers. Mr. Proctor was a brother-in-law to Kruse, and a believer in the Vision.

The Rogers Cornet Band, playing "Silver Threads Among the Gold" and "In the Shade of the Old Apple Tree," led the way to the Kruse home. They were followed by 30 workers, seven two-horse scrapers, members of the Kruse family and many of Rogers' leading citizens.

The pay was really good for that day. The men received $1.50, and a man and team $3.00 for a six-hour day.

The plans were to put down a 125 foot shaft. There is no record of how deep they did go, but it was just a few feet. A rustic tower of logs and boards one hundred feet high was built. From here lanterns were hung at night and they could be seen for miles around.

The tower blew over in a high wind a few months later and was never rebuilt. The three crude smelters set here for many years to tell of a dead dream. That was all that was built for the mine.

On November 24, 1905, a carload of sacked ore was sent by the Frisco railroad to St. Louis. It is said that the ore was dumped in the river when demurrage charges went unpaid.

From time to time work was resumed at the mine as the Vision told Kruse to. The last work was done in 1912. No pay dirt was ever taken out of the mine, and it was left to grow back up in weeds and brush.

The Vision told Kruse of many other things beside the Gold Mine. Kruse published a small booklet to tell what the Vision told him. It was called "Sunshine and Truth." They printed 6,000 copies of each issue.

In the copy dated March 12, 1906, he said, "In the City of Minneapolis, Minn. and in the very near future, God will raise to life a man who has been dead for more than a year and a quarter. In the near future God will appear in Mid-air over the city of Rogers from which will come a loud voice."

On an inside page were a number of things listed that the vision had told Kruse of that had happened as it said they would. The Kansas City floods, the death of Queen Victoria, the Iroquois Theater fire, the earthquake at San Francisco, the eruption of Mt. Pelee in Martinique, the assasination of President McKinley, a tornado in Minneapolis and St. Paul, famine and floods in China, and a great war that must have been the first world war, but it didn't tell the date of the war.

Many of the other things happened almost on the same hour the Vision said. It was never off more than a day on any of these and many others. But some things like the coming of God and the Gold Mine it was way off.

When Ed Kruse wanted to buy a used printing press from Erwin Funk of the Rogers Newspaper, he had to wait a few days to see what the Vision said he should pay for the press. It said $150, and this was all right with Funk for he was more than willing to sell for $100. But he wouldn't go against the Vision, so he took the $150.

W. H. Kruse died on December 12, 1925, at the age of 65. He and his family had lived for many years doing what the Vision told them to. But in most things it lost them money.

There is nothing left today to show for this fantastic dream, and only a few newspaper stories to prove that it ever happened.

Chapter Twelve
Agriculture

Farming In Benton County

Almost from the beginning, Benton County has been a leading farm county in the state. They placed first in the amounts of many crops they grew and over the years have won many first place ribbons for their crops the world over.

Perhaps no other county in the state has made as many changes in the crops grown as cash crops as they have. At one time or another almost every known crop has been raised in the county.

Tobacco, cotton and hemp at one time were cash crops for Benton County. They gave way to small grains, herds of sheep, cattle, and large apple orchards. Then peaches tried to run out the apples. Other fruit took up hundreds of acres in the county just a few years ago. Next came the milk cows and broiler chickens.

When farmer Batie came to the county in 1828 he went out on the open prairie and plowed the land with an ox team, planted a big garden of the things that could be eaten green and those that could be dried for use in the winter.

He also planted wheat, oats, and Indian corn. These made his flour and corn meal, as well as feeding the cattle. He planted three or four rows of cotton which was worked up by his wife and wove into cloth for the family.

Most of the pioneers coming at that early date planted about the same crops. They also had a cow or two, for milk and butter; some hogs, horses, mules, ox, and sheep.

It is said that someone coming from Kentucky in about 1833 or 34 brought tobacco seed and started a bed. Soon almost everyone had a few rows of tobacco. At first it was raised just for home use. Later there was a market and tobacco became a big cash crop.

In 1840, an Indian woman near Maysville set the first apple trees in the county. She went on to build this small start into the first large orchard here. White men followed and by the end of

75

the Civil War there were several large orchards in the county. And almost everyone had a home orchard.

Tobacco became a cash crop as early as 1840. The quality grown here was better than that grown in Kentucky. It brought a good price sold on the farm, or the farmer could take the tobacco to the market at Bentonville.

Farming kept a good pace in the county from the very first. By the time the first farm census was recorded in 1860 there was 41,183 acres in improved farm lands.

The value of all the livestock in the county was $94,380. Benton County was second in the state on wheat with 76,701 bu. They grew 426,495 bu. of corn that year.

The county was 3rd. on oats with only 33,447 bu. They shipped 37,725 lb. of top grade tobacco that year. There was no record of the amount of low grade sold or that sold on the farm. Orchard crops sold listed at $440.

That same year they shipped 50 lb. of hops, and 75 tons of hemp. They were 2nd in the state on hemp produced and it was a top quality; 153 lb. of flax was shipped that year. Lots of people didn't report on what they bought or sold, so this is really just a part of the crops grown.

People sold $18,761 worth of homemade items that year. Half the field work was done with ox. There were 1,748 head of working ox listed.

From the spring of 1861 to 1864 very little farming was done in the county. Most of the men joined the army or left the county with their families until after the war.

It took several years to clean up the farms and get them back into crops after the war. At this time they went in for bigger fields and not as many different crops as before.

For some time a few farmers grew cotton; in 1869 there were 25 bales of Benton County cotton sold to the cotton gin at Eldorado, a town near Maysville. In 1880, 126 bales were sold; it was grown on 286 acres. Ten years later the cotton raising was about at an end.

By 1870, tobacco was becoming the big cash crop. They were growing Virginia Golden Leaf, White Burley, Yellow Pryor, and Hico Wrapper Leaf. At that time there were other counties in the state growing tobacco. But Benton County always had the best crop and quality.

In 1879, the cheaper tobacco was selling at an average of 4½ cents a pound. Bright and wrappers at an average of 12 cents a pound. Better tobacco went from 8 to 40 cents a pound.

It cost $43.50 for seed and labor to raise an acre of tobacco in 1879. This made a profit of from $28.00 to $100.00 an acre depending on the quality.

In 1880, there was 2,725 farms in Benton County. It was the

leading farm county in the state. That year the farmers only bought $1,272 worth of fertilizer. There was less than two milk cows for each farm. There were 46,516 swine in the county.

The 1880 census listed 69 working ox; 8,097 horses and mules. They grew 1,119,834 bu. of corn; 249,382 bu. of oats; and 156,087 bu. of wheat.

The sorghum molasses crop was 55,120 gal. A little over 5 times as much as was made in 1869.

In 1880, there were 83,000 hens and fryers in the county. In 1880, they cut 2,346 tons of hay.

By 1880, the orchards had just started to make a little money; $4,265 worth of fruit was sold. In 1918, it was well over the million dollar mark. Fruit was the first crop in the county to make that amount of money.

In Sept. of 1887, apples were selling for 50 to 65 cents a bu. Top grade Shannon Pippins brought 75 cents a bu. That was an apple year; full bearing orchards made from $350 to $500 an acre.

One Saturday of that month over fifty wagon loads of wheat were delivered at the mills in Rogers, just one of many places buying wheat then.

In July of 1887, W. A. Cash & Co. set a record while threshing for Alex Oakes of sugar creek. They threshed 200 bu. of wheat in two hours with a horse powered thresher. They had threshed 4,000 bu. by that time in the year.

Strawberries were selling for $4 for a 6 gal. crate in Benton County in 1887. There was a large acreage that year.

Arkansas was dropped from the list as a tobacco growing state in 1898. Most of the tobacco land went into grain and apples. The newspaper of 1892 said that ten acres of small fruit would make ten times as much money as wheat with less work.

Peaches were getting a real start in 1891. The Benton County Nursery Co. wanted to buy 300 bu. of peach seed that year.

The fall of 1897, corn was selling for 27 cents a bu. Irish potatoes 20 cents a bu.; eggs 9 to 11 cents a doz. They shipped 923 cars of apples out of the county that year.

For a number of years there were more plants to dry fruit in Benton County than any other county in the whole country and we had more acres of apples than any other state.

In 1919 5,000,000 bu. of apples were sold in Benton County at an average of one dollar a bu. That was the last really big apple year in yield and price both. By 1936, most of the apple trees were gone.

Milk production got off to a slow start in the county. It started with a few buyers of sour cream across the county. Then a cheese plant or two that bought whole milk part of the year.

For the most part, the cows in the county at first were not a very good grade of milkers or did the farmers understand the fine art of feeding to get more milk. At the peak of production most of these cows only gave a gallon or two of milk a day.

The first few tries at milk processing plants in the county just folded up and cost the investors and the farms thousands of dollars.

By the early 30's there was again some small cheese plants, but they only bought milk part time.

Many farm and business leaders saw the possibility of developing a major dairying enterprise, so for years they preached herd improvement, better cows and better feeding.

By 1935, Carnation had a plant in Rogers, and Pet was at Siloam Springs. A program was set up in the county to promote dairy herd improvement and from this slow start it was hoped they could make it a dairy county, in place of an apple county.

Ever since the beginning of the county every farmer or person living in town who had a place for them kept a few laying hens for eggs, and tried to always have a few chickens around to eat. This was the one meat they could have in the summer.

A young Cave Spring girl, the daughter of J. J. Glover, was the first person in Benton County to try growing broilers. She made some money on her first small flock in 1921.

The next year her father tried his luck at broilers. He put up what is said to be the first commercial broiler house in the county, and in the spring of 1922 he put in 328 chicks.

He used a kerosene brooder stove and carried the water and feed by hand. He would have fed them close to five months before selling. He sold 324 broilers on the market at an average of $1.20 each, his net profit was 55 cents per bird.

In time, people all over the county were raising broilers. This also fitted in well with other farm work.

The first broiler houses in the county were small and only held 300 to 500 birds. Some farmers put up as many as 20 of these small houses in rows on their farms. Then much later they started using the big houses.

A close study of newspapers and farm articles on Benton County for the past hundred years has shown a strange fact. Just as soon as a crop was beginning to make money for the farmers in the county, then they started looking for one that would make more money with less work.

In 1887, when tobacco was making a good return for the farmer, the newspaper was talking easy money with fruit, in 1919, when apples were at a peak, they talked of the easy money in small grain and sheep. When this got off to a start, the papers were talking about milking cows.

If this keeps up I wonder how many more changes will come in the next hundred years.

AGRICULTURE

Tobacco In Benton County

"How's your tobacco growing, Jake?"

"Doing just fine. Best crop of white burley I've ever had."

Today it would sound like make believe to hear men talking that way in Benton County. But in the 1880's, this was common talk here in the county.

Early settlers coming here from Kentucky are said to have brought the first tobacco seed into the county somewhere around 1833.

By 1840, tobacco was a cash crop on many farms in the county. The quality was much higher than that being grown in Kentucky at the time. When they took it to market it brought top prices. But most of the farmers could sell all they grew right on their farms, and still get a top price.

The tobacco raising increased as more people moved into Benton County. Most newcomers were surprised when they found the home grown tobacco here was of a better quality than most tobacco on the market at the time.

In 1860, 37,725 lb. of top grade tobacco was shipped out of Benton County. There was no records kept in those days as to how much was sold locally or how many pounds were sold to make plug, twist or smoking tobacco in the County.

Little is known of the tobacco industry in Benton County from 1860 until after the Civil War. More than likely due to the scarcity of hands to care for the crop, very little was grown in those years.

By 1868, there were a few reports of new tobacco barns being built in the county. In 1870, they were raising fields of Virginia Golden leaf, White Burley, Yellow Pryor, and Hico Wrapper Leaf over a large part of the county. All of these yielded heavily and were of a high quality.

Other counties in the State were growing tobacco at that time but none could come up to the quality of Benton county.

The two-story log tobacco drying barns were a common sight on farms throughout the county. In 1876, Oillie Anderson of Vaughn community says he helped raise ten tobacco barns in ten days within three miles of his home.

By 1870, there were many acres of tobacco grown in the county. There was over 200,000 lbs. shipped out of the county that year. The U. S. Farm Census of 1880 listed 395,982 lbs. of tobacco sold. This was raised on 547 acres. From then until 1887 the crop was listed as 400,000 lbs. Then the acres planted were cut and the tobacco industry started on a downhill run.

Firms from St. Louis, Neosho, and Pierce City, Mo., became interested in the Benton County tobacco in the 1870's. They ran ads in the weekly papers and also sent in buyers for several years.

At about this time several small tobacco factories were started

This is the inside of one of the Tobacco grading barns in Benton-ville. The picture was made about 1885.

in Bentonville to make cigars, smoking tobacco, plug and twist. At one time there were four of these plants.

Robert S. Hinds was one of the most prominent tobacco buyers in the area. He had a large warehouse in Bentonville where he bought tobacco of all grades for many years.

For years Trotter & Wilkes was the biggest tobacco company in Bentonville, and made a full line of tobacco goods which was sold over a six-state area.

In 1887, a group of local men bought them out and renamed it Arkansas Tobacco Co.

Col. J. J. Smiley, a Virginia tobacco man, was hired to manage the plant. He said that Benton County was one of the four places in the U. S. where white burley tobacco could be raised.

He also pointed out that our white hico wrapper, a favorite in cigar making, was tops and would bring 40 to 50 cents a pound on any market.

In a newspaper article in the spring of 1890, he stated that the tobacco grown in Benton County was superior to that grown anywhere in the U. S., and that we could produce two million pounds of tobacco a year in Benton County.

At that time the plant was said to be the busiest place in town. They hired thirty men and boys, and had a payroll of $500.00 a month.

The plant was enlarged in 1888. They added a large number of steam pipes in the drying rooms and an 8,000 gallon cistern, as well as more buildings for work rooms.

Their salesmen traveled over a seven state area selling their brands of plug, twist, and smoking tobacco. Their most popular brands were Golden Leaf, Old Honey, and Half Bushel Twist, Old Rip Plug and Ozark and Trotter smoking tobacco. They also sold packages of leaf tobacco for those who wanted to make their own.

This firm went out of business sometime in the 1890's.

The tobacco crops in Benton county were so outstanding that the U. S. Agricultural report of 1880 used over two pages in their book to report on them. The figures they used were for the 1879 crop, and read in part:

In 1879 the cheap tobaccos were selling on the market at an average of 4½¢ a pound, the bright wrappers at an average of 12¢ a pound. Prices for bright and high quality was from 8 to 10¢ a pound. The best market that year had been at St. Louis. It cost 2 cents a pound to barrel and ship the tobacco there from Bentonville.

The following is the average cost of planting and marketing an acre of tobacco in the spring of 1879 at a local market.

Fixing seed bed	$ 1.50
Rent on land	2.50
Preparing ground to plant	3.00
Setting plants	1.50
Care of crop and harvesting	33.00
Deliver crop to market	1.50
	$43.50

A crop with heavy leaves would grow about 1,600 lbs. per acre. It would be low grade bringing 4½¢ per lb. or $72.00 an acre, giving a profit of $28.50.

Some fields with smaller leaves would go about a thousand pounds per acre and bring an average of 12 cents or more per pound showing a profit of more than $75.00 an acre, which was big money in those years.

By 1888, many farmers were not taking good care of this valuable cash crop they were raising. That year there was 400,000 pounds sold in the county but it only brought an average of 5½ cents a pound. From then on the tobacco industry began to drift away. As growers cut down on the number of acres they put in, the buyers stopped coming. This put an end to the good market they had here.

One of the last ads in the county paper for tobacco was by Smiley and Handcock of Bentonville, makers of fine plug and

This is a double tobacco barn that was on a farm just west of Bentonville. Very few of the barns in the county were this big. It was built some time in the late 1870's.

twist tobaccos in 1893.

Benton county tobacco won first place in the Cotton Exchange Fair at New Orleans and at the trade exposition in Chicago in the early 1880's. It is also said to have won several first place awards in worldwide tobacco contests.

From The Benton County Democrat, Aug. 25th, 1898: "Arkansas has been dropped from the statistical report of Tobacco growing states. This should not be, as we have as favorable conditions for the culture of tobacco as any state in the Union, but the reason for its being dropped is the light acreage. Northwest Ark., especially Benton County has the soil and climatic influence necessary in the growth of all varieties of tobacco, especially bright wrappers. It had been thoroughly tested here."

From a tobacco growing county, Benton County changed to apples. Then many more changes came over the years. Now it is milk cows, beef cattle and broilers.

Benton County Democrat July 9, 1887
Prices Of Tobacco

Since our last report of June 1st there has been some improvement in the market as was then anticipated, and there is a good demand for all grades of tobacco. The amount of Burley on hand, the probable crop of this year, will make the amount available for the next two years, short of what it has been for several years; and, while prices appear high, there are many indications that they will go higher. Shipping leaf has also improved, and a few dealers in the country have sold at what we regard as very low prices for the present market, and prospects reasonable for an advance at an early day. Bright wrappers and smokers are very firm and holders believe there must be a heavy advance in all brights, of which there appear strong probabilities.

QUOTATIONS

Burley Lugs	$2.00 to $3.50
Burley Leaf, com. to med.	5.00 to 6.50
Burley Leaf good	7.00 to 10.00
Burley Wrappers	14.00 to 20.00
O. S. Lugs	1.75 to 2.50
O. S. Leaf com. to med.	4.00 to 5.00
O. S. Leaf good	5.00 to 7.00
Bright Wrappers	15.00 to 55.00

Boxes, light weight and out of condition packages, from 50¢ to $1.25 below these quotations.

Evans Bro. Tobacco Warehouse Co. St. Louis

Evans Brothers ran an ad the year around in the Democrat. It had a picture of their big warehouse in St. Louis and stated:

"The largest and oldest commission leaf tobacco warehouse in St. Louis. Mark and ship your tobacco to Evans Bros. Union Depot, St. Louis.

This is the only house in St. Louis which devotes its entire time and attention to the sale of Leaf Tobacco. We are prepared to handle leaf tobacco with more satisfaction and less cost to the farmer and shipper than any other house in St. Louis.

We have the largest warehouse, finest break floor, and the best light for the inspection and sale of leaf tobacco in the West. Railroad facilities unequaled. Commissions only $1.00 per. hogshead. Your liberal consignments respectfully solicited."

King Apple

For many years Benton county was known as the land of the big red apple. King apple had a long and profitable reign and he won us the distinction of being first in many ways.

We had more apple trees than any other county in the United States; we shipped more apples, both fresh and dryed; had more evaporators than any other county; we had the biggest apple brandy distillery and apple vinegar factory west of the Mississippi. Our apple growers won more awards at the St. Louis and San Francisco Exposition than any other county in the U. S.

Several of the early settlers bought apple seeds and set out a few trees for their own use, but it took a Cherokee Indian woman living near Maysville to see what could be done with a large orchard. Her timing was just a little bad when it came to making any money out of it.

She was very well to do and had been able to plant and care for the young orchard with slave labor. Just about the time she would have had fruit to sell, the Civil War started and she soon had to free her slaves. The orchard went uncared for then until 1866 when H. S. Mundell bought the farm and reworked the apple trees. He was the first white man in the county to have a large orchard.

Within two years he had a well producing orchard and was selling apples to freighters who hauled them in to Kansas and Texas. Texas was a good market for Arkansas apples as the people there had been buying a few freighted in from Washington county so they knew how good the apples were. A freighter could sell all he could get there with.

Mundell was paid 50 cents a bushel at the farm. Even at this low price, it is recorded that some of his trees made him $40 each. That would have been one lot of apples from a tree.

The freighters who made the long trips with apples could haul 40 to 50 bushels per wagon. They would leave here with wagon trains of from three to some times as many as 40 wagons. Many of their drivers were teenage boys, as they could hire them for less. At that time a boy would work for about half pay if he could go some place new.

Many of these young drivers saw their first railroad train as they freighted apples into Texas. Some of them were more scared of the train than the teams they were driving.

By 1870, there were just a few good sized orchards, but as other men saw these few making a big return for their labor, then they too set out trees. By 1880, there were several hundred acres of apple trees in the county. This was more than the local freighters could haul. Many farmers took their own apples into towns as far away as they felt they wanted to drive with them. But that many bushels of apple rotted in the fields as there was no market for them.

If a farmer went to Eurkea Springs with his apples, it would take three to four days for a round trip; if he went up in to Missouri, it would take a week or two. Most of the farmers here could only haul 30 bushels to the load, so it was hard for them to sell too many.

The coming of the railroad was one of the first big helps the

Spraying apples near Centerton.

apple industry got. When the Frisco built their line across the south part of the county, the apple growers had their first easy way to market. Now they had only to haul to Rogers; from there they could ship north or south, wherever they felt the best market would be.

In the next ten years, the apple acres jumped from hundreds of acres to thousands of acres.

The editor of the Gravette News, wrote in the paper in the fall of 1894 about the amount of apples that were going to waste that year because there was no ice or cold storage to take care of them, or the cars to ship them in. The Editor said he didn't think the way things were going that they could ship over six cars that year, and there would be at least 50 carloads go to waste in the Gravette area.

Within a few years most of this was taken care of and there was a market for all of the apples. As more railroad lines covered the county, there were more apple buyers and brokers. There were cold storage houses to hold apples in. Cull apples and tree runs could be sold to the evaporators, vinegar plants and the brandy distillery. By this time a grower could sell all of his apples somewhere.

Among the early and the bigger apple growers in the county were, Goldsmith Davis, Samuel H. Shelton, H. Highfill, Rev. Wyatt Coffelt, Mr. Britt, Thomas Brown, J. Alvin Dickson, Henry Woolsey, Lucien E. Griggs, Elbert Jennings, Joel Kimmins, H. W. Gipple, John Henry Kieth, Capt. George T. Lincoln, L. B. Lawton, John Breaithwaite, C. J. Eld, Jack Etris. W. E. Ammons, and Julius Giger.

The above list was in no order as to when the men started growing apples or how many acres they had. But almost all of them had at least one type of apple that they had bred and named.

This habit of each grower or nurseryman having several varieties of their own with their names made it very hard to ship apples out of the county. Most large buyers wanted a car of all one kind of apple, but it was almost impossible to ship that way.

Lots of cars going out were like one of summer apples shipped from Rogers in August 1896. It held 16 varieties, which were Buckinham, August Red, Mammoth Pippin, BellFlower, Golden Pippin, Shannon Pippin, 20 ounce Pippin, Smith Cider, Nickerjack, Red Streak, Blush Pippin, Baldwin, August Streak, Silver Pippin, Speepnose and Brightwater.

It is said that there were 300, most of the names have been long forgotten. From old papers I have found the following: Ada Red, Highfill Blue, Etris, Gano, Lady Pipton, Summer Champion, Lodi, Gano, Maiden Blush, Ben Davis, Gans Transparent, Stayman, Jonathan, Grimes Golden, Mammoth Black, Delicious, Arkansas Blacks, Winesap, Mammoth Black Twig, Red Bird, De

Luxe, Falawater, Horse Apple, Geniton. This is just a few of what there had been.

A lot of growers had a great number of varieties in their orchard, but those who had a few varieties and large acres of them made much more money, as it was easier for them to sell their crop.

A Rogers paper listed 287 cars of first class apples and 20 cars of dried apples being shipped in 1896. A year later 250 cars of first class apples, and 20 cars of dried apples were shipped. That year apples sold for 40 cents a bushel. Hundreds of bushels that were made into brandy were not included in these statistics nor were those shipped from other parts of the county.

The rain damaged the crop badly in 1898 and there were few apples to ship. The crop was better in 1899, and in 1900 they had a real big crop.

In 1901, the apple crop for Benton County was listed as two and a half million bushels. This was the largest apple yield in a single county in the history of the United States. Rogers shipped 375 carloads of first grade apples and 65 carloads of dried apples that year.

From then on Benton County was known as "THE LAND OF THE BIG RED APPLE." But every few years there would be a late frost or too much rain and there would be very few apples.

Arkansas apples won real fame in 1904 at the World's Fair in St. Louis when they captured all the major prizes offered in the horticultural division. Then in 1915 at the Panama Pacific Exposition in San Francisco they won 308 prizes for their apples. This was 11 more than they had won in St. Louis. Arkansas lost the grand sweepstakes because they didn't have their exhibit ready on the opening day.

John Henry Kieth won a gold medallion at the St. Louis World Fair in 1904 for a select and superior 24 barrels of Ben Davis No. 1 grade apples. He also received a large check for the apples.

He owned a 400-acre orchard which was said to be one of the biggest and best in the state. During 1919, they averaged 250 barrels a day from the well-tended trees. Fertilizer, a process relatively unknown then, was shipped in by railcar at an unheard of price of $25. per load. They set this as giving the quality and quantity of the Jonathan, Red Ada, Gano, and Ben Davis. They were paid a top price of $8.50 per barrel.

Harvey W. Gipple came to Benton County in 1896 and planted a large apple orchard and in time he was one of the bigger and better known growers. He planted mostly Jonathan, Ben Davis, Delicious Staymen, and Winesap. As well as shipping number one apples he also had his own apple evaporator and shipped dried apples.

In the spring of 1912, Gipple and Keith both ordered spray outfits. These were the first to come into the county. They were pulled by a team, and had a 2½ horse Bean engine. This had a 30-gallon water tank just to cool the engine. The spray tank was made of wood and held 200 gallons. In just a few years most all the orchards had them.

This short fact is from a souvenir book on Bentonville in 1910: H. W. Gipple has seventy acres of apple orchard, sent $3,000 in 1909 in care for the orchard, it produced 9,000 barrels of apples at $3 a barrel, making $27,000, netted $24,000, twelve crops in fifteen.

In 1919, Benton county growers marketed 5,000,000 bushels of apples, they sold for an average of $1 a bushel. This was the biggest year they had. From then on profits were not as high, the weather was not favorable for apples. There was an increase in diseases which attacked the orchards.

By the mid-20's people were having to spray the orchards a lot and as the years went on it became a costly program. In the early 30's, they were using nine different sprays a year.

In the fall or in the spring before the buds opened, a dormant spray was used. This was for San Jose scale. Then when the buds separate, but before the blossoms open, there was a spray for apple scab. There was a calyx spray applied when seven eighths of the petals have fallen. There was a first cover spray applied 21 days after the petals had fallen. Then there were six other cover sprays applied at intervals of about three weeks apart, clear until the fall months. These were used to fight the codling moth, curculio, blotch, black rot, bitter rot, Phoma spot.

Sometimes it would come up a hard rain just after they had sprayed and they would have to redo the job.

Not only did they have all these diseases to put up with, but the weather was going against them. There were late frosts, too much rain in the spring, or too dry in the summer. All of this cut into the crop bad.

Then came a time when the bugs became immune to all the sprays they had. In a few years, the trees were dying. At this time, the big apple growers were losing too much money, so they took out the orchard. This loss of apples in the county also broke many other businessmen in the county who sold to or bought from the apple growers. By the late 30's, the apples were no longer King of the county.

Apple evaporators or drying plants were a big sideline of the apple industry. Every town in the county had from one to three of these plants. There were evaporators on all the loading siding, and many of the bigger growers had their own plants.

Some writers have said there were over one hundred in the county at one time. But it would be too hard today to prove how many there were as they kept no records on these. Also, no one could even guess how many millions of bushels of apples were dried in the county.

Most of the plants had ten peelers. It took two girls to run a peeler. Then others slide them. Most of the work here was done by young girls. The men had the job of carrying the apples to the peelers, then taking them to the drying room after they were bleached. They dried for 24 hours and had to be turned over several times as they dried. It took 30 to 40 people to run a plant of this size, and they ran three or four months a year.

There were a few really big evaporators in the county that hired around a hundred people in all. This was all part-time work, but it did give many people a little spending money.

As you can tell by this clipping from the Gentry paper, they were not overpaid. "Sept. 26, 1907 — Girls strike at Gentry. Sixteen ladies who operate the peeling machines at the Gentry fruit growers association evaporator struck Monday for a raise of a cent a bushel. They had been receiving 3 cents per bushel up to that time. The managers of the evaporator have since offered them 3½ cents; the girls are still contending for 4 cents."

As far as I know, this was the first strike in Benton County.

Apple cider vinegar manufacture was a leading industry in the county since 1906. Here again, no one could tell us how many apples went into vinegar over the years. They could use just any size apple for this and a lot of what would have been culls were also used.

In 1905, O. L. Gregory built a vinegar plant at Rogers. This was the first one in the county and it cost about $20,000. He didn't get it done in time for the Benton County apples that year, but he had five carloads of cider shipped in from Massachusetts that winter so he could make and sell some vinegar.

He also built a plant at Siloam Springs and one in Centerton. He ran into financial troubles and by 1907 we find the Southern Fruit Products Company had taken over his plants. Later this outfit sold to Jones Brothers, who in 1914 were thrown into bankruptcy.

At this time, Mr. Gregory came back from Texas and bought out the plants. This time he was able to make money out of them and in time he bought out all of the vinegar plants in northwest Arkansas.

The plant in Rogers was the only one where they made vinegar. The other plants just ground the apples and made juice. At Centerton they had large holding tanks which were filled. Then after that their juice was loaded in tank cars and shipped to Rogers.

These tank cars each had four tubs that held 1,800 gallons each. Many days they sent a car a day from the Centerton plant into Rogers.

In 1914, the vinegar company bought the Macon & Carson Brandy Distillery in Bentonville. Here, too, they just made juice which was shipped to Rogers.

The plant at Bentonville had to lay a pipeline from the plant to the rail siding as to load their juice.

From a newspaper clipping in October 15, 1920, I find that one day the Bentonville plant of the Ozark Cider & Vinegar Plant (a new name for this old company) had bought 138,000 pounds of apples in one day. They were buying from 50,000 to 150,000 pounds a day. One day they paid out $3,750. At that time they had made 100,000 gallons of juice.

The Centerton plant had their tanks full 400,000 and had shipped 300,000 gallons. They were paying from 60 to 75 cents per hundred for apples.

By this time almost all of the evaporators were closed, so the only market for low grade apples were the vinegar plants.

As the apples went out so did the vinegar plants, until there was just one left.

Apple Blossom Festival

The Rogers Apple Blossom Festival was held for just a few years, and in this time it became known as the biggest program put on in the State. The weather was against it too many times, so it came to an early end.

The idea got started in the fall of 1923 when W. R. Cady told of the Peach Festival he had attended in Georgia. By the spring of 1924, a mass meeting was held in the old Opera house and plans were made to hold an Apple Blossom Festival April 25 and 26.

A steering committee was made up of R. H. Whitlow, W. R. Cady, J. W. Stroud, W. F. D. Batjer, J. S. Elder and E. C. Lone. It was their job to make all the plans and set up the various committees to see their plans worked out. The chairmen of these were: decorations, Mrs. R. H. Whitlow; entertainment, George W. Holand; publicity, Erwin Funk; automobiles, E. B. Howard; invitations, Morgan McMichael; orchard trips, Arch E. Owens; finances, Edwin Jackson; music, Lou Smith; railroad transportation, P. H. Welborn.

This first festival was purely a local affair; the floats were all sponsored by the civic organizations, clubs, schools and business houses.

It rained so hard the morning of the first day that they canceled the trips to the orchards.

The second day, they crowned Ruby Robinson of Rogers Queen of the Apple Blossom Festival. This part of the program was held on the Rogers Academy campus. The attractively decorated floats and many maids of honor made this a very colorful affair.

In spite of the rain they had a very good turn out and the festival made a local hit, that everyone thought should be opened to more people.

One newspaper stated that as a rain getting program the 1924 Apple Blossom Festival was a real success. The big day was Friday, April 25. It had rained all of the night before and was raining so hard Friday morning that the parade planned for that morning was put off until afternoon.

By the time they were half way through the route, it started raining hard again. By the end of the parade they were almost floating for sure. Everyone who rode a float was covered with dye from the float and was soaking wet.

One outstanding float from Pea Ridge represented the Pea Ridge battle field and the background was a huge painting of the old Elkhorn Tavern. On the float were seated Capt. C. L. Pickens, a survivor of the battle, and Uncle Wade Sikes, a 94-year-old veteran of the Confederacy.

One from Bentonville had "Adam and Eve in the Shade of the Old Apple Tree." After the rain they resembled a couple of striped peppermint candy sticks.

The main program took place on the Academy campus and Dot Webb of Pea Ridge was crowned Queen in the rain by Senator Joe T. Robinson.

St. Louis was well represented that day by President Kern of the Frisco railroad, Vice Presidents Kuntz and Hamilton, many department heads of that organization; Dr. Travis, rector of the St. Peters Episcopal Church of St. Louis, and the Hon. Godfrey Hertzlet, British consul at St. Louis.

That evening a banquet was served by the girls of the domestic science department of Rogers High School under the supervision of Mrs. R. S. Haun. The banquet was for the Queen, her maids, and the prominent guests who were in town.

For the 1925 Apple Blossom Festival, Rogers asked all of the nearby towns to enter floats and girls. Every town in Benton County had from one to three floats and even Fayetteville and Lincoln sent floats.

In 1925, they changed the date of the Festival to April 8, hoping to out plan the rain. But this didn't help much. Rain fell all morning of that day. But at noon the sun came out and they had the parade, pageant and coronation ceremonies. But they had no more than got these out of the way, than it started raining again and rained out the program planned for that night.

Some 15 to 20,000 people were there for the afternoon program, even if it had rained all morning. The owners of the floats all had float insurance that year, so when the program was rained out at 11:00 they knew they would collect their insurance money.

There were thirty-four floats and several decorated cars in the parade. They represented Eureka Springs, Lincoln, Centerton, Siloam Springs, Garfield, Avoca, Pea Ridge (which featured a large replica of the old Pea Ridge academy) Lowell, Springdale, Gentry, Sulphur Springs, Gravette, Cane Hill, Bentonville, Hiwasse, Prairie Grove, Fayetteville. Cars were from Rotary, Lions, The Queen, Benton County Tuberculosis Association, Elks, Kiwanis, Rogers Banks, American Legion, Rogers schools, Woman's Study Club, Rogers Apple Growers Association and Community Club.

Many of the St. Louis people came back again this year. Also Governor and Mrs. Tom Terral of Little Rock, and Congressman J. N. Tilman of this district was here.

Queen of the Festival that year was Helen Duckworth of Siloam Springs.

Her maids of honor were: Avoca—Gladys Wyatt; Bentonville—Mildred Dickinson; Cave Springs—Clara Stroud; Centerton—Ruth Brown; Fayetteville—Alice Letch; Garfield—Izella Baker; Gentry-Gladys Shepherd; Gravette—Vina Russell; Hiwasse—Gladys Edwards; Lincoln—Delphina Rogers; Lowell—Frances Graham; Pea Ridge—Demma Paterson; Prairie Grove—Alice Basham; Rogers—Lois White; Springdale—Uarda McDonald; Sulphur Springs—Mary Eldred.

Governor Terral officiated at the official coronation of Queen Helen, whose attendants were Linere Cottingham and Bernice Johnson. There was a program of songs, dance and other entertainment for the people. Also, apple bearers brought boxes of fancy apples for President Coolidge, Governor Terral and Will Rogers.

That night at the banquet, Hon. J. N. Tilman gave Queen Helen and each maid a beautiful bar brooch suitably engraved as souvenirs of the occasion.

April 15, 1926 was the scene of the largest crowd ever to be gathered in northwest Arkansas. This was the fourth Apple Blossom Festival and by far the biggest one. It is said that at least 35,000 people were in Rogers for the program. It was just a one-day show and the only apple festival that was not rained on.

This year they went all out to get people to attend the festival. The railroad ran special trains from Springfield, Joplin, and Fort Smith. Prominent state officials, civic leaders and businessmen were invited from over the three-state area. These Frisco special trains were loaded to the limit, and every road to Rogers was choked by thousands of cars. It was a beautiful clear warm day, and complaints were few save for those who could find nothing to eat.

The float parade was the largest ever seen by many people.

Gravette

Lowell

Floats in the 1926 Apple Blossom Festival Parade

Berryville, won 2nd place

Eureka Springs

Floats in the 1926 Apple Blossom Festival Parade.

Prairie Grove

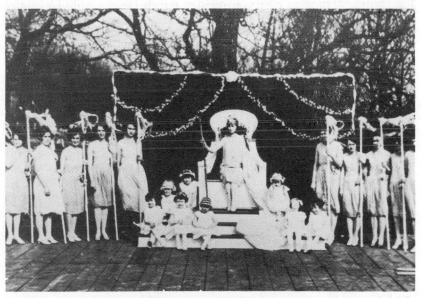

Queen and her court

Floats in the 1926 Apple Blossom Festival Parade.

Floats came from twenty towns and many of these had two or three. Rogers had a dozen or more. And there was a large number of bands in the parade, part of these were on floats, part marched.

Queen Lillian Ivy of Fayetteville was crowned at the amphitheater on the east side of town by Governor Tom Terrall. Her maids were: Avoca—Mildred Thurman; Bentonville—Lena Black; Centerton—Winnie Fields; Eureka Springs—Ruth Fuller; Garfield—Izella Baker; Gentry—Nina Austin; Green Forrest—Ruth Seitz; Harrison—Jewelle Fowler; Hiwassee—Velma Nichols; Lincoln—Elsie Snodgrass; Lowell—Dorothy Thomas; Pea Ridge—Meta Pierce; Prairie Grove—Marie Baggett: Rogers—Bertha Osborne; Siloam Springs—Mildred Shermer; Springdale—Virginia Owensby; Sulphur Springs—Helen Daniels.

Winners of prizes for the best floats were: Bentonville, first; Lincoln, second; Fayetteville, third; Pea Ridge, fourth.

The winners of the best window displays were: First, E. E. Adams Tin Shop; second, Bryant Hardware Company; third, Benton County Hardware Company; fourth, A. D. Callison Gift Shop.

The visiting bands were: Springfield Boy Scout band of 100 pieces; Springfield Girl Kilties, 27 who both sang and played; Springfield Frisco band of 25 pieces; Joplin High Girls drum corps, 24 pieces; Fort Smith Boy Scouts Bugle Corps, 55 pieces; Fayetteville U. of A. band, 40 pieces; Siloam Springs, John Brown College band, 20 pieces; Eureka Springs band; Bentonville DeMolay band, 25 pieces; Berryville band; Green Forest band; Junge's electric caliope from Joplin; Harrison sent Kirkham's Orchestra; Springdale sent professional performers on the harp and guitar; Fort Smith a mouth organ orchestra, and a noisy aggregation with bazoos.

Entertainment features were given at various points during the afternoon and evening. At one time a band concert was given by eight consolidated bands, directed by Lou Smith. Most of the visiting bands featured vocal and instrumental soloists among their members. There were solo and group dances and several vocal quartettes. Miss Julian Rogers of Prairie Grove, a professional outdoor singer, gave several popular songs of the day. In fact, there was something doing every minute of the day and evening in the downtown area.

This year's program was such a great success that they all felt the festivals could go on every year.

The uncertainty of April weather brought an end to the Apple Blossom Festival in 1927. The program was planned for April 14, but it rained so hard all day that the only part that they had was the banquet that night which was attended by Governor and Mrs. John E. Martineau as guests of honor.

Part of the special trains ran and the people who came on

them wished that they had stayed at home. The whole program was postponed until Sunday (Easter) afternoon, April 17. The crowd that day was estimated at 20,000. Some people writing of it, put it at a lot less. The Governor and many out of town people were unable to come back on this day.

Congressman John Tillman of Fayetteville crowned Dorothy Butt of Eureka Springs Queen.

Several of the towns were unable to get back that day with their floats. Huntsville's had been washed down the War Eagle River on the morning of the 14th. There were less floats, but many said they were more artistic and elaborate than other years.

Float winners were Springdale, first; Lincoln, second; Harrison, third; and Gravette, fourth. The bands in the parade were Pea Ridge, Harrison, and Fayetteville. The weather this day was really good. But having to have it four days late had hurt it bad.

The group putting on the apple blossom festival had become very disheartened over the weather, so when R. H. Whitlow declined to serve again as general manager that brought an end to what for a few years had been the biggest programs in the county. And also the best rain getting programs.

Apple Blossom Pilgrimage

The first Apple Blossom Pilgrimage was sponsored by the Southwest Times Record in 1934. They had hopes of bringing new interest to the then declining apple industry of northwest Arkansas.

The first pilgrimage, which was held on April 22, 1934, was such a great success that the following year the Fort Smith Chamber of Commerce, along with the Chambers from the towns in northwest Arkansas, all backed the pilgrimage.

The 1935 pilgrimage was held on April 14th. On that day between 3 and 4 PM, 1,080 cars passed a checkpoint at the Rogers Chamber of Commerce building. No one was able to say how many cars made the trip that day. It was known that 540 left Fort Smith by 10:30 that morning. A large number of cars were here from Missouri, Kansas, and Oklahoma.

The towns taking part in the program that year were Sulphur Springs, Decatur, Gravette, Gentry, Siloam Springs, Centerton, Lincoln, Summers, Farmington, Prairie Grove, Fayetteville, Rogers, Bentonville and Springdale.

U. S. Highway 71 was lined with cars throughout the day, but many motorists also made side trips to Bella Vista, the University of Arkansas campus and other points of interest off the main roads.

Early in 1936, the people planning the pilgrimage wanted something to use that would show who all were a part of the

Apple Blossom program. So that year they started using an official Apple Blossom flag.

The flag of pink, white and green was one that was designed by Miss Vera Key of Rogers and first used in the Apple Festival at Rogers in 1924.

The pink symbolizes the color of flowers and fruits of the Ozarks; the white, the clear streams; and the green, the mountains. Fort Smith and several other towns had their names on all the cars that came to the tour. The towns all flew large ones, as did many of the orchards that took part in the tour.

The towns taking part in the program had stopping points where people could get maps of the area orchards, and find out where to eat.

The eating and finding a place to get gas was a big thing to many of the people who had driven so far to get here. On that one big day most of the cafes had a hard time feeding everyone who came in. And many of the gas stations ran out of gas before night.

Bentonville was the only town to put on any entertainment for the people coming. They had a pageant, "The Spirit of the Ozarks at Apple Blossom Time." It was put on by the Bentonville school children.

Most of the people coming were here to see the apple trees, and much of their time was spent driving up and down the roads to see the trees.

The following is a list of part of the orchards that took part in the program that year: Everett Nail, Elbert Graham, south Rogers on Highway 71.

North of Rogers are the J. Frank Patterson, John Duty, Walter L. Hinton, Ed Perry and Garthside orchards which may be seen from Highway 62, and the Don and R. B. Patterson orchard near Pea Ridge.

Southeast of Rogers are the Penn orchards and east on the Monte Ne highway are the Kirkpatrick and Harris orchards; and Ed Adams, of the Halfway farm, and, at Avoca, Nathan Gordon.

Near Bentonville, Fagan, Lincoln, Breedlove, Puryear, Ivie, and owners of well known heavy bearing orchards. Continuing on Highway 71 are the Keith Brothers orchards near Hiwassee and the Curry-Anderson orchards near Centerton. Albert Boyle has one of the well kept orchards at Gravette.

At that time, for a week to ten days, no matter where you drove in the county you would see apple blossoms.

Mrs. Warren Writes on Apples

This interesting letter was written by Mrs. E. S. Warren of Rogers to her friend Mrs. Betsey Brown of Lowell, Mass., in the fall of 1907. At this time Mrs. Warren had just moved to Rogers.

AGRICULTURE

The letter was printed in the Rogers Daily News, July 1, 1950.

It shows how the apple industry looked at the time to a newcomer.

"Dear Old Friend; Well we had a good laugh at your last letter. You seem to think we people live on a rugged mountainside where we have room to put down only one foot at a time, and where we have to prop the pumpkins to keep them from rolling down hill.

This is a big country of ours, Betsey, and we don't know each other very well.

You ask how we manage to live on mountains without any factories? But it is not all mountainside, Betsey; quite the contrary. I know you all think there are no industries except those connected with shoe thread and pegging awls and I thought so, too once upon a time. But I've been seeing things lately and not in the dark either; but in broad day light and with eyes wide open and I want to tell you about it.

First with a friend I drove out the other day to see the orchards adjacent to Rogers and this country is nearly all orchard; a perfect forest of apple trees. Truly, it was a sight worth seeing. How I do wish you had been along. The trees are simply loaded; bending to the ground with their weight of big red apples.

The orchards here are not as they are with you, a few trees to each farm house, but acres of them in such long rows one can not see the end of them, just long streaks of vivid red and green. And to think that all these apples have to be picked one by one. The task seems impossible. They will surely bring to the farmers a mint of money. You remember our mothers used to say to we girls when reproving us for some extravagance, dollars don't grow on every bush, my dear. But dollars do grow on every apple tree in this county.

The question arises where do they go and what do they do with them. So following the apple wagons to town we first came to the cold storage plant and ice factory which is under the management of Mrs. H. Y. King. And the people who think a woman has no business capacity should come and see Mrs. King's management. She showed us the cold storage rooms with capacity of 16,000 barrels and told us application had been made for double that amount of room. Then she took us to the room where they store the ice for daily use, and when she turned on the electric lights the sight that met our eyes seemed most wonderful. There stood great blocks weighing from one to two hundred pounds each in long rows the full length of the room, and the ceiling and walls were encrusted thick with glittering ice. It seemed as though we had been transferred to fairyland.

This ice plant which is in connection with the cold storage has a capacity of 20 tons and a daily output of 15 tons; furnishes ice for Armour's refrigerator cars and ships ice both north and south. It is a very busy place, working ten men 18 hours out of every 24.

The next place to which we came had a big sign over the door, Farmer's Union, and here we found farmers and apples and apples and farmers, long rows of apple wagons waiting to unload. They were nearly snowed under here. Are setting on track two cars of first class apples and one of seconds daily and could ship more if they were prepared to handle them; are also sending 200 bushels daily to the canning factory. Are also handling evaporated apples and evaporated waste (cores and peeling) for the members. It reminds me of the story that used to be told, that the pork packing companies saved all of the pig but the squeal. The union this year shipped 30 cars of peaches and up to September 19, 30 cars of apples on track. Has its own cooper shop and makes its boxes and barrels.

The wood is cut round and round in one continuous piece, as we women cut potatoes for Saratoga chips, and then cut off the right length to make a barrel, the ends sawed in about a fourth and about the distance apart of a barrel stave so that they will bend in and shape the barrel. I am not advertising a barrel factory, Betsey, I don't know where they originated, perhaps in your country like the wooden nutmegs. Any way they are new to me. The barrels I mean, not the nutmegs.

Next in line is the Benton County Produce Company, which deals in fancy fruits and ships mostly by express. Also handles dried and evaporated fruit; up to date has sent out by express six cars and some by freight. Employs five men and one traveling salesman.

Then came the Hamilton Produce house, which has on hand 75,000 pounds of dried apples. Betsey, aren't you glad that you don't have to make them all into dried apple pies? These apples will all be packed in 50-pound boxes and quite a force of men and girls are employed for this work.

Teasdale Fruit and Nut Products company, which has its own evaporator with a capacity of 800 bushels daily, has shipped 20 cars of evaporated fruit which represents more than 100 of the green fruit. This firm employs 90 men and girls and it is a pleasant sight to see the long row of bright faced girls handing with nimble fingers the rosy red apples. No room here for loafers or lovers. In the packing house under the supervision of Miss Lizzie McFarlin, all were so busy and everything so nice and clean. The fruit is packed in 50 pound boxes, which are all nicely paperlined and carefully faced and made pretty by the use of lace paper. The apples certainly do look good enough to eat. Here and in fact all the places, the waste is carefully evaporated and sold.

Next we found J. W. Stroud, who has six crews working,

some packing in the orchards, some in the packing house. He has sold up to date more than 4,000 barrels of cold storage apples and of other apple stock 43 cars.

O. A. P. Oakley handles both green and dried fruit and has shipped 20 cars of green fruit and 12 of evaporated. This man deals also in hen fruit and has this season shipped 27 cars of eggs and seven of poultry.

Next we came to the Nelson Canning Company, which has a capacity of 1000 bushels per day. Shipped nine cars of peaches this season and has shipped up to date 50 cars canned apples. This factory furnishes a good market for all second grade apples and first grade culls. They employ 90 men, women and girls, mostly girls, and come to think of it, how would the business world get along without our girls. They have a weekly payroll of $850, the girls getting the bulk of it. Pays for apples an average of $2,500 per week.

The Rogers Canning Company comes next with a capacity of from eight to nine hundred bushels per day and have shipped up to date 45 cars, employs from 125 to 150 hands, mostly girls. Their payroll is from $600 to $1,000 per week and pays for fruit an average of $250 per day. This company also bought this season 6,000 bushels of peaches and paid for them nearly $6,000. And Betsey, just think of it, the peach pits bring 50 cents a bushel. Surely the fragments are all taken up that nothing be lost.

Next we visited the big vinegar plant of the Southern Fruit Products Company of which Rogers is justly proud. The factory is nearly as large as all out doors. Uses apples of all grades, large and small, and has a capacity of 3,500 bushels per day and then the bins get to running over though they work night and day. Last year it made 530,000 gallons of vinegar which finds its way to every section of the union. Sells by the train loads. Just think of that, Betsey, trainloads of vinegar. Really it makes me feel a little sour. When we came away each of us were presented with a 'Little Brown Jug' full of vinegar as a souvenir. Am saving mine for you.

So you see, Betsey, there are some real live industries here as well as there. And I haven't told you a word about the berries. Acres and acres of them which brought the farmers so much money they were in danger of becoming millionaires. Figures don't make very interesting matters for letters, Betsey, but I have given you these in response to your inquiry and hope it will enable others to see us as we see ourselves. Will send you this week our paper containing a picture of our new church. I expect it will surprise you to see it standing squarely on all fours either before or behind, like the pumpkins. Your Old Friend Martha A. Warren."

Chapter Thirteen
Schools

Benton County has had many grade schools, Academies, and small colleges. In the early days they were all subscription schools.

Most of the first schools in the county were held in one room of a private home and the teacher would be whoever could read, write and add. As time went on the people would build a one-room log house for the school and they would hire the best they could with what ever money they had.

These first schools were held for just three months a year, and it cost $1 per month for each child. There were no records kept of these schools, so no one knows today how many there were in the county or where they were.

It is thought that the first such school started at War Eagle in 1839. In 1840, one was taught near the home of Walter Thornberry, near Wager. Then a one-room log house was built in Bentonville in 1841. I have heard of several schools being held in homes in and near to Bentonville, but I can not find the dates of these.

In 1842, a Mr. Holstein taught in a small cabin at or near Hico; this is part of Siloam Springs today. Maysville built a building in 1844 or '45, to be used as both a school and church.

J. Wade Sikes taught school near Bentonville in 1853-54. His patrons boarded him and paid him $15 per month for his services.

There were no schools held during the Civil War. Some folks taught their children at home in those years, but many just didn't learn anything, outside of how to hunt, farm and put food on the table to eat.

It was the ruling opinion in Arkansas, as it was in all slave states, that every man should educate his own children, and that no man should be taxed to educate another's children.

The constitution that was adopted in 1868 set forth that a free school system should be set up for the state and every child

This was an early school class in Benton county at a time when there was no limit to how many students a teacher would have.

between the ages of five and twenty-one should go to school.

It also stated that a tax would be put on all taxable property to run such schools. But it was 1874 before this tax act became a law.

In 1874, Benton County set up 130 school districts to cover the county. The law stated that each district had to levy at least a two mill tax and no more than five mills. It also said they had to hold at least three months of school a year. But they could run as many months as their money would last.

In many cases the school districts didn't have the money to buy land for a school or to build one. In this case someone would give land off their farm. The neighborhood took up money to buy the material and then they all helped to put up the building. In many cases the schools would be named after whoever gave the land. In later years most of these names were changed.

The county school set-up had $25,619.50 to run on in 1886 from all the schools' income.

The first free school set up was for grade school only. When high school was first added it was for a two-year course. There were several high schools and academies opened in the county at this time. The student paid a tuition for the course he took; they could also room at the school.

Goodspeed's history lists a public and high school as having been started in Bentonville in 1872. It didn't say if the high school was free or if the students paid a tuition. I do know that for many years this was just a two-year high school. In 1888, they had a total enrollment of 326 pupils.

The Benton County Democrat ran the following ads for schools in the county, in the fall of 1887:

"Hico High School, Hico Benton Co. Ark. Non sectarian, open to both sexes. Unsurpassed advantages given in vocal and instrumental music. Boarding students under care of faculty. A preparatory school for the Teacher, the Business Man, and the Musician. Address for catalogue and other particulars. H. L. Stites Prin.

Osage Valley High School at Osage Mills, Benton County, Arkansas. Prof. A. W. Stark is Principal. It is an institution embracing all those studies properly belonging to a High School or Academy in addition to a common school branches. Being admirably suited to the wants of the young gentlemen and ladies of this practical age. Good board cost $1.50 to $2.00 per week with private families. Tuition from $1.00 to $2.00 per month. This is however a contingent fee for term, 25 cents due on entering.

Bentonville Academy began on Monday September 5, 1887, to continue Four Months. Rates of tuition, Primary, per month $1.50, Grammar School, $2.00; High School $3.00. Tuition due at the end of each month. Silas Dinsmoor, Principal.

Pea Ridge Academy, The eighth annual session of this institution opens on Monday, Oct. 3rd., and continues nine months. Tuition in Academic Department, $1.50 to $3.00 per month. Incidental fee, 50 cents for each term of three months, or $1.00 for the entire session. Boarding, $2.00 to $2.50 per week. J. R. Roberts, Principal."

In 1894, the Mason Valley Academy was built in Mason Valley. The people of the community paid for the three story building. It was just a grade and high school. They had from 125 to 150 students each year. It only lasted five or six years.

Pea Ridge Academy

The first academy started in the county was in 1851, at Pea Ridge. It was known as the Shelton Academy and it was abandoned in 1858.

The Pea Ridge Academy was established by Prof. Roberts in 1874. Its first session was held in Buttram's Chapel, two and a half miles east of Pea Ridge, and classes were held there during the first five years of its existence.

After a suspension of one year, the school was reopened at Pea Ridge, where the first academy building was erected in 1880.

Pea Ridge Academy, this picture was made about 1890.

This building was 24x40 feet, two stories, with a classroom and workroom on each floor.

The school was chartered as an academy with a full course of instruction in 1884. In 1887 and 1888 an additional two-story 50x60 building was added to the original building increasing the number of classrooms to seven. The enlarged plant had seating facilities for 250 students.

An ad from the 1902 Benton County Democrat: Pea Ridge Normal College; the largest normal and business school in the state. Our departments are not surpassed by any business college. Bookkeeping business practice, business correspondence, penmanship, commercial law, and literary work all for $3.50 a month. Teachers course $2 a month, elocution $1 to $2 a month, music $2 to $3 a month.

Board, room, heat, and lights, with private families $6 to $8 a month.

Bring us three students and your tuition will cost you nothing as long as they are with us. Buy your ticket to Rogers, leave there on U. S. Hack at a cost of 25 cents."

Prof. Roberts left the school in 1894. There isn't too much written history about it from then until 1914. In that year they had their 40th Anniversary and Prof. Roberts came back for a visit. At that time the school was the Pea Ridge Masonic College. Shortly after that, it was sold to the Pea Ridge school district.

Miss Nannie Roberts, a sister of Prof. Roberts, was one of the early teachers at the Academy. She stayed right there and taught even after it was a public school. This made her a total of 50 years teaching in Pea Ridge.

Rogers Academy

The Rogers Academy was started in 1883 and was the first school that town had. Classes the first year were held in the Congregational Church, and the Methodist Episcopal Church south.

The first teachers were F. S. Van Epps, Principal, and Miss Mary E. Webb and Miss Jessie Durham. Alice Emery taught music. Tuition was Primary, $1 a month; Intermediate, $1.50; language and mathematics, $2.50; and music at a special rate.

A building for the Academy was started in the fall of 1883. The brick work was all done by James Haney of Bentonville, at a cost of $1,451. The building was paid for by the people of Rogers. By the time the building was done they had run out of money to run the school.

Then the American Missionary Society of the Congregational Church came to the rescue. They agreed to run the school and pay the bills. Mrs. Rogers, the wife of the man the town was named after, was a big help in getting the church to take over the school.

Rogers Academy, picture made in 1909.

Prof. J. W. Scroggs was elected principal and school started in the new building in Nov. of 1884.

In 1886, the public school directors agreed to pay the Academy $100 a month for the use of one room and teachers for the grade school.

Only the first two floors were finished when the school was moved into, and it was 1889 before the rest of the building was done. In 1892, they built a three story building for a dormitory. It was named Elizabeth Hall.

The tuition in 1891 was set at: Academic department, $7.50 per term of three months; intermediate, $4.50; primary, $3; and music, $10.00. In 1892, girls or boys could board at Elizabeth Hall for $1.50 a week. They had to furnish their own rooms; the school only put in the lights and stove. That way you took your bed to school with you.

In 1892, you could go to this Academy for only $94 for a full year complete with tuition, board and books. A common school course was set at $84. There were two set rules always: No one used any tobacco at all in or out of school. You had to go to Church at least once each Sunday.

In 1896, they played their first football game. It was against Bentonville and they lost. That was the first football played in Rogers. Very few people went to that game. It was 1901 before they played a regular schedule.

In 1902, under Prof. Albert's coaching, the Academy football team won the championship of the section. They were so good that the Bentonville, Springdale and Fayetteville teams wouldn't play against them.

A few days after a football game in 1908, a son of Alvin Dickson died of injuries he received in the game. The Rogers Academy then banned football for several years.

There were only two students graduated at the first service in 1887. The class of 1896 was one of the big ones with 8 girls and 15 boys. In all the years of the Academy, 235 students graduated.

By 1897, the primary and intermediate departments had been dropped, and they just had Academy classes.

Prof. Scroggs left in 1898 and Rev. Morrison Weiner took over.

A small brick building used as a Science Laboratory was built in 1902, a gift from the father of Rev. C. E. Fowler. The same year a dining hall was added. In 1903, a heating plant for the Academy and Elizabeth Hall was set up.

In 1906, Rev. M. E. Alling was made president of the Academy. Then it went to Rev. J. F. Eaton in 1909.

In 1911, the Congregational and Presbyterian Churches united and the Academy was placed under the Presbyterian Synod of Arkansas.

SCHOOLS

Many changes were made in the school and the presidents, but it was losing money and there was no way to save the Academy. In 1914, the building and grounds were sold to the Rogers Public School District.

The buildings are all gone, but the land is still a part of the Rogers school.

Bentonville Academy

Two Bentonville schools of higher learning were Bentonville Scientific and Normal School 1883 and the Bentonville Business School 1887. I have not been able to find out anything about these two, but have seen their ads in early newspapers.

The Bentonville Academy was built in 1895. James Haney, a local contractor, was the builder. It was paid for with money given by the people of Bentonville.

It was located at the south end of main street on what is now the fairgrounds. The dedication was held on Sept. 17th, 1895.

The 1897 brochures said, "Annual Catalogue, Bentonville Academy, non sectarian school, for both sexes." The faculty and classes were: Mrs. Alice Jelks Read and Miss Gray Taylor, Associate Presidents; Miss Gray Taylor, instructor in history, literature and science; Mrs. Alice Jelks Read, instructor in Mathematics, orthography and English; Mr. S. S. Breckenridge, instructor in mathematics, languages and science; Miss Nellie M. Clifford, instructor in elocution, del sarte; Mrs. J. C. Hennon, instructor in instrumental music; Mrs. S. B. McClinton, drawing and painting. That year they had 105 students.

Tuition charges per term was: Academy, $10.00; Teachers course, $10.00; Music-Piano lessons per term, $10.00; Violin, $10.00; Organ, $10.00; Guitar, $10.00; Drawing per term, $5.00; painting, $10.00; Elocution, $100.00; French and German per term, $7.00 each. Music term consists of ten weeks, 20 lessons. Board including furnished rooms, heat and light and good food, $10 to $12.50 per month.

Just after the start of the 1900's, the Academy was turned over to the Arkansas Baptists who built a two-story dormitory. They changed the name to Ouachita Baptist Academy. This was short-lived.

It was later sold to the Bentonville School District and was used as a high school for many years. The building was torn down in 1929.

The old brick building that is used for the women's building on the fairgrounds was one of the buildings for this Academy.

Orchard Hendrix Academy

In the fall of 1897 the Kansas City, Pittsburg and Gulf Railroad made a deal with Hendrix College at Conway to put an Acad-

Bentonville Academy, in about 1898. After the Academy closed, this building was used for many years as Bentonville High School.

The Arkansas Conference College in Siloam Springs, picture made about 1900.

emy in Orchard, now Gentry. The railroad company gave them a ten acre plot for the school and the income from the sale of 100 city lots in Orchard; these brought $10,000.

The campus was about one mile east of the business block. By fall, they had the main building done which was a two-story handsome brick. A two-story frame house was built for the principal's home. This had fourteen rooms, so some students could also live there.

The following is an ad they ran in the newspapers: "It is far more important for the welfare of the future man that he should find the right school than the right college. The Academy is located in a town with a record for healthfulness, no malaria, pure air and invigorating climate. There is a ten acre campus. The main building is brick, the large light study hall will seat 200 at single desks. We have $500 worth of apparatus for elementary science, 1,000 volume library. It is as well equipped as many celebrated schools east of the Mississippi. The fall term will begin September 21, 1898. Tuition and fees will cost from $30 to $50 a session. Board in the Principal's Home will cost $12 a month and in private families from $8 to $12. Other expenses will be very reasonable. Principal Rev. James M. Hughey."

I have not been able to find out just when this Academy closed, but do not think it lasted too long.

Arkansas Conference College

The Arkansas Conference College was opened in Siloam Springs in the fall of 1898. Prof. Thomas Mason was President. It was housed in a two-story brick building that was near where the high school is today. The College was closed and sold to the Siloam Springs School District in 1919.

State Normal College

The 1905 class of Valparaizo College, Valparaizo, Ind. wanted to start a new college in some small out-of-the-way place so as to help the people. They chose Sulphur Springs as their town.

They had found it very hard to raise the money that they needed and were unable to build the size school they had planned on. They built a large rock building on Dickies Heights in Sulphur Springs. It is not known now where they built or rented the smaller building they used.

The school opened in September of 1907 and they said they were teaching everything from common school to civil engineering. Scott Duff was the President. Their plans were to teach all the courses that were taught at Valparaizo.

They were unable to reach their goal and the school closed at the end of the term of 1909. The building later burned.

SCHOOLS

When the state started their free high school system it was for just two years, so a student still went a few years to an Academy. When they went to a four year program, then there was little need for the Academies and they started folding all over the place.

The small one-room school and the Academy both filled a need in their day. As the towns grew bigger, so did the schools; then smaller ones were taken in until now we have just a few very big school districts.

School Names

Names and numbers by which Benton County school districts have been known. I feel that this list was first made in about 1900. I have found many other names for schools that were used in past years; then these names would be changed by the county. Some of the names would be used for many years by the local people who didn't like the new change.

Accident	63	Cottage Grove	29
Alden	132	Cottage Hill	60
Apple Glen	142	Cross Lanes	13
Avoca	127	Cross Roads	122
Banks	21	Crown	52
Bates	95	Deason	37
Bayless	34	Decatur	17
Beaty	25	Donivan	5
Bellview	78	Douglas	71
Benton County	1	Droke	42
Bentonville	6	Duckworth	91
Bethel	66	Dug Hill	4
Black Jack	102	Eagle Corner	137
Bloomfield	13	Edgewood	44
Bozarth	51	Elm Springs (WC)	110
Brightwater	16	Evening Star	55
Britt	110	Fairmount	79
Bud Cowart	33	Fairview	57
Burgin Valley	45	Falling Springs	47
Butler Creek	7	Flatt	126
Cave Springs	14	Flint-Duckworth	91
Centerton	104	Fox Squirrel	86
Center Corner	65	Freedom	121
Central	136	Friendship	119
Chamber's Springs	87	Frisco Springs	134
Cherokee City	48	Garfield	114
Cloverdale	123	Gentry	19
Coats	49	Goad Springs	64
Coal Gap	105	Gravette	20
Corinth	2	Harmony Grove	99

Hall	143	Osage Valley	69
Hall School House	46	Ozark	15
Hurd Switch	34	Pace	25
Hickory Creek	62	Pea Ridge	109
Hico	77	Phagan	75
Highfill	71	Pine Creek	46
High Top	31	Pine Log	111
Hiwasse	108	Pleasant Grove	116
Hopewell	81	Pleasant Hill	37
Jay-Bird-Maysville	27	Pleasant Rodge	40
Jay Bird-Siloam	85	Pleasant Valley	94
Jefferson	35	Potts	2
Jennings Switch	105	Postoak	18
Kincheloe	83	Prairie Chapel	124
Lee	8	Prairie Creek	39
Liberty	14	Prairie View	110
Liberty Hall	11	Providence	125
Liberty Hill	11	Quaker	78
Little Flock	36	Rascal Flat	139
Logan	23	Robinson	82
Logan Special	23	Rock Chimney	52
Lone Cedar	93	Rocky Branch	38
Lone Star	133	Rocky Comfort	12
Lowell	107	Rocky Dell	22
Maple Grove	7	Rocky Grove	3
Marrs Hill	32	Rocky Valley	130
Martin	113	Rogers	30
Mason	84	Roundtop	7
Mason Valley	53	Sassafras	117
Maysville	26	Shady Grove	24
Meadow Brook	30	Sigmon	62
Miller	74	Silent Grove	120
Monte Ne	97	Siloam Springs	21
Morning Star	43	Spring Creek	67
Mountain View	53	Springdale (WC)	50
Mount Olove	141	Springtown	72
Mount Pleasant	21	Spring Valley	131
Mount Zion	115	Stanley	98
Mundell (CC)	68	Stoney Point	58
New Home	19	Sugar Grove	7
New Hope	103	Sulphur Springs	6
New Salem	135	Summit	138
Nicodemus	100	Sycamore	106
Norwood	88	Taylor Branch	125
Oak Grove	59	Trammel	50
Oak Hill	41	Tuck's Chapel	81
Oakley Chapel	42	Twelve Corners	129

SCHOOLS

Valley View	18	West Point	75
Vaughn	54	Wet Prairie	10
Wager	90	Wild Oat	49
Walnut Grove	17	Williams	29
Walnut Hill	101	Willow Springs	92
Wann	9	Wire Springs	31
War Eagle	61	Word	28

Part of these schools had two or three different numbers over the years, so I used just the first number listed. At times there were two schools by the same name at the same time in the county. I didn't list both of the schools, as in a short time this was changed. Fairview was one, but I am not sure of the others.

Elm Springs had a (WC) after it meaning that some students from Benton County went just over the line to this school in Washington County. Springdale (WC) was the same. Mundell (CC) meant the students went to Mundell school in Carroll county.

This list is names that were used for schools in the county at an early day, and the names were never on the county records.

Buzzard Flock	New Kirk
Bentonville Colored School	Opossum Trot
Cash	Phillips
Chapel	Ruddick
Cromwell	Skud
Dickson	Simpson
Do Little	Stick In The Mud
Head Of The Creek	Wild Hog
Hoover	

There were more than likely many more names that have been lost with time.

Chapter Fourteen
Crimes and Criminals

Trial For Stand Watie

One of the strangest murder trials ever held in Benton County was that for Stand Watie the Indian, who had killed James Foreman, also an Indian.

On June 22, 1839, Stand Watie killed James Foreman in a fight that took place near Maysville, Arkansas. This was inside the state by less than a mile.

Foreman was a member of the John Ross party and Watie was of the Ridge and Watie party. They were all Cherokees and the two parties had been fighting for some time over the leadership of the Cherokees.

Members of the Ross party had killed Major Ridge, his son John Ridge, and Elias Boudinot who was really Buck Watie, a brother of Stand Watie.

Law moved very slow in those days, and the killing of an Indian didn't hurry it up any. By late summer of 1842, a warrant was issued for Stand Watie.

The Sheriff was a man who didn't want to bother the Indians in the west part of the county, so he gave the warrant to Joseph McKissick, a well to do farmer who lived where Centerton is today. He asked McKissick to give it to Watie and asked him to come in for the fall term of court.

So it was that in November of 1842 Stand Watie came to Bentonville with several of his white friends to turn himself in at the fall term of court.

From the Benton County Court record, book A, page 201

Circuit Court, November Term A. D. 1842

State of Arkansas

State of Arkansas	Plaintiff
vs	Indictment for Murder
Stand Watie	Defendant

This picture of Stand Watie was made many years after this trial.

And now on this day comes the said defendant in custody of the Sheriff of Benton County as well as Joseph McKissick, John A. Bell, George M. Paschal, Mathias Hilburn, James I. Anderson, and William Howard (Paschal and Howard, attorneys by leave of the Court) as his securities and acknowledged themselves to owe and be indebted to the State of Arkansas, the defendant in the sum of Two Thousand dollars and the securities in the sum of Two Thousand dollars to be levied of their respective goods and chattels, land and tenements, but to be void upon the condition that he the said Stand Watie, the defendant does well and truly make his personal appearance here at the next term of this court as a Court to be holden at the Court House in the town of Bentonville, Benton County Arkansas, on the second Monday after the first Monday in April 1843, to answer an indictment for murder now pending in said Court, and that he the defendant will not depart the Court without leave thereof.

After the bond had been set by the Court, it was found that there were no more cases for the Court to hear that term. Mr. Joseph McKissick asked the Judge if he couldn't have the trial for Stand Watie the next day, so they wouldn't have to come back in the spring.

"If you will go out and get enough men to serve on a jury we can have the trial in the morning," said the Judge. After this, he reset the trial date as follows:

From the Court records:

State of Arkansas   Plaintiff

    vs

Stand Watie   Defendant

At this time came the said plaintiff by her attorney Wilson who prosecuted on and in behalf of the State of Arkansas as well as the defendant in his own proper person in discharge of his bond, and being here arraigned on an indictment for murder, for plea says he is not guilty in manner and form charged in the said bill of indictment and puts himself upon the county for trial to which plea the State by her attorney joined issue, it was therefore ordered by the court here that a vebire issue returnable Wednesday morning at 8:00 o'clock.

From court records Wednesday morning. Criminal Docket book A, page 221.

State of Arkansas   Plaintiff

    vs

Stand Watie   Defendant

At this day the Sheriff returned into Court here the vebire issued in this case with the number of panneled thereto required to try the issue joined in the above entitled case out of whom were selected twelve good and lawful men of the County of Benton, with Joseph McKissick, James I. Anderson, John Burrow, Mason Phillips, Job R. Mound, Nicholas Spring, John Gilbreath, H. G. Bacomb, Mathew C. English, E. J. A. Dickson, James W. Dickson, and Henning E. Pace, who being duly elected and sworn to try the issue joined, after having heard the evidence, arguments of counsel and charge of the Court, retired from the bar to consider of their verdict and after mature deliberation returned into Court here the following verdict with,

"We the jury find the defendant not guilty," by N. Springs Foreman.

It is therefore considered by the Court here that said defendant be acquitted and discharged, and go hence without delay.

J. M. Hoge, Judge

Two of the men who came in with Stand Watie to go his bond sat on this jury, and one of them, Joseph McKissick, hand picked the jury. This could never happen in a Court today.

Stand Watie admitted that he had killed James Foreman because he had murdered his brother. He also said that in time he would get the rest of the Ross members that had been in that fight. But he would do it in the Indian Territory.

It would seem that the white men here felt that the Indians should deal with their own laws, to suit themselves or they wouldn't have turned Stand Watie free as they did.

But then most people felt that Stand Watie would make the best chief for the Cherokees. This may have helped. But just the same, there has never been another trial like it in Benton County.

Stand Watie later was made a Confederate Brigadier General during the Civil War; he was the only Indian to attain that rank. He fought at Pea Ridge, with his troop of Cherokee fighters. At one time three companies of Benton County men served under him in the Civil War. They were all white men. He also was the last Confederate Gen. to surrender after the war.

A Picnic At The Hanging

The last legal hanging held in Bentonville turned out to be the biggest get-together the county had ever had at that date. Many people started to town the day before, so they would be there to see the hanging. By daylight of Jan. 14th 1876, there was a big crowd in town. The stores all opened early and did a good business.

The excitement had all started on August 4th, 1875, when Columbus Handcock was found murdered near his home in White Hollow near White River in Benton county.

Sheriff J. H. McClinton soon arrested Cornelius Hammon and Girsham P. Hoytt. They were indicted for the murder of Handcock. They both pleaded not guilty. Hoytt asked for a change of venue and later was tried in Washington County and found not guilty.

Cornelius Hammon was tried in Bentonville in October 1875. The courthouse had been in use only about a year, and this was the first big trial to take place in it. People filled the courtroom and halls for the trial.

Col. Sam Peel was the prosecuting attorney and John M. Peel represented the defense for Hammon. They both were well known attorneys.

.During the argument at the trial, John M. Peel stated that from the kind of life and the clothing of the deceased Columbus Handcock the jury could judge that he would not have been murdered for money.

Col. Sam Peel, then looking over the courtroom, saw Uncle Hugh Middleton in the crowd and asked him to stand up. He stated that the clothing worn by Handcock was no worse than that worn by Mr. Middleton. And everyone knew that Mr. Middleton was one of the wealthiest men in the county.

The trial didn't last very long, and the jury was out a very short time. John W. Floyd was foreman of the jury. They returned a verdict saying, "We the jury find the defendant, Cornelius Hammon, guilty of murder in the first degree as charged in the indictment."

Hammon was sentenced by Judge J. M. Pitman to be hanged by the neck until dead, on the 14th day of Jan., 1876, between the hours of 10:00 in the morning and 2:00 in the afternoon, at some point selected by Sheriff J. H. McClinton within two miles of said courthouse.

The scaffold was erected just west of the Razorback Inn on the south side of the road on one of the knolls. This was south of Bentonville, about where the Highway 71 bypass leaves Highway 71.

Hammon was taken from the courthouse in a wagon, riding astride his coffin, at about 10:30 that morning to take his last ride. There was a big crowd at the courthouse, and they followed the wagon out to the scaffold.

As they made the trip out of town, people kept passing the wagon as they wanted to be sure they got there to see the whole show. Hammon called out to some of them saying, "There's no use to be in a hurry for nothing's going to happen until I get there."

His last words were, "You are hanging the wrong man," and afterwards some of the people got to thinking maybe they did. But it was too late.

Judge J. M. Pitman, the man who ordered the hanging. It is said that he didn't attend the picnic.

The story of this hanging has been told and retold by those who saw it. They all seemed to think it had been a day well spent. Many of them brought their lunch or bought food at one of the stores. It was one of those warm days in January, so a large number set down for a picnic lunch not far from the hanging. And many were still in sight of the scaffold on which Hammon still hung.

The scaffold stood for over fifty years as a reminder of what took place there on January 14th, 1876. But the scaffold and the old Razorback Inn are both gone and most of the people have forgotten that there ever was a hanging or a picnic here at one time. But to this day it is not known for sure if they hung the right man or not.

Peoples Bank in Bentonville Robbed

The clock in the Peoples Bank in Bentonville had just struck 2:30 on June 5th, 1893, when a rifle shot rang out. Then a loud and stern voice ordered everyone off the streets. The people all knew it was a bank robbery, and all they could think of right then was to get off the street and out of the way. After all, who wanted to get shot?

The bandits had entered through the west part of the town and left their horses in back of the Benton County Sun office, one of the weekly newspapers. The old Sun office faced South Main Street, just a block from the square and the bank.

As the bandits were tying their horses in the alley, they stopped Hollowell and Tom Barr, Wn. and E. E. Brock and F. F. Dumont, who were coming down the alley. They left one of their men to guard them.

Then five of the bandits went up the street toward the bank. They all acted as if they were drunk, and having a big time.

Three of the men went inside and stayed, one stayed outside to shoot at the people and see that no one got too close with a gun. The leader spent his time going back and forth between the man outside and the three sacking up the money.

When the robbers got inside they found A. D. Dinsmore, J. W. McAndrew, Geo. P. Jackson, and Rev. I. R. Hall, who were all very willing to put their hands up when told to.

J. W. McAndrew was the cashier, and Geo. Jackson was the assistant cashier. The rest of the men were stockholders in the bank. This made it very easy for the board to get a firsthand report on the robbery.

One of the bandits rushed behind the railing and made McAndrew open the vault, and ordered him to fill the sack he was holding with the bills. McAndrew filled it part way then stepped out of the vault and closed the door.

The robber cut at him with a knife and said, "None of that, I

This is how Bentonville looked in 1893. The tall building to the left in the picture is the Peoples Bank.

mean business."

"Then get it yourself," said McAndrew.

With that two of the robbers went into the vault. They put all the bills and gold into one sack and the silver into another.

As they came out of the bank, the four bank officials led the way. Then came Henry Starr and Kid Wilson, the leaders of the gang. Jackson followed them, and he was made to carry the sack of silver. He was followed by the other three robbers.

At the back end of the bank, the bank officials made a mad run up the alley and were let get away. The robbers kept up their march down South Main Street with Jackson still between them.

By this time there was a lot of shooting going on. Many of the citizens had got shotguns and pistols and were taking part in the show. The robbers had to keep shooting, and moving at the same time so no one could take too good an aim at them.

Just as Jackson got in front of the Benton County Sun Office, Miss Maggie Wood of the Sun force ran to the front door and opened it. When Jackson was even with the door, she called to him and he ran in. Before the bandits could do anything she locked the door.

With so much shooting going on, the robbers didn't have time to try to get back the silver held by Jackson. They ran around the building and into the alley to their horses.

Miss Maggie saved more than $900.00 for the bank, and was remembered the rest of her life as the bravest person that day.

Sheriff Galbreath was at the courthouse when the shooting started. He ordered his horse saddled and rode home to get his Winchester rifle. He then went to an open lot next to the hotel, from here he could see the robbers as they reached their horses. His rifle refused to fire, and he was unable to get off a single shot.

Starr rode west on Southwest Second Street, and the rest of the gang turned south at the Baptist Church, then west a few blocks from there. They met at the school and rode west out of town.

Will Buchanan was the first man in pursuit of the bandits, followed by the sheriff. Just as soon as they could get horses, others followed.

The gang met the Siloam Springs stage on its way to Bentonville, and sent word to the sheriff that he would die if he followed them.

At the Lark Wilson farm four miles west of town, the robbers met Lee McAllister in a wagon. They took one of his horses. He said that two of the men were wounded then. One very badly in the head.

It was at this stop that the posse first came close enough to shoot at the robbers. Wes Oaks, Will Buchanan and Jack Payne all took a few shots, but the bandits took off without being hit.

A few miles down the road the bandits forced a boy to trade horses with them, leaving him a very tired horse. When the sheriff caught up with him, he had him ride to Bud Wooten's with orders for Bud to cut across county and get ahead of the bandits and cut them off.

Henry Starr knew the road, too, and he had already made his plans. So just before they came to this place they left the road and went around the trap.

At Decatur the bandits stopped to get a little rest and plunder the stores. But the sheriff soon was there and off they rode again.

A few miles west of there the robbers set up an ambush for the posse. In the skirmish that followed, two of the bandits were wounded and they lost one horse. The posse was luckier. They didn't have any wounded here at all. But the bandits did get away.

Most of the posse turned around and went home as it neared dark. They of course wanted to know what was going on there and if anyone had been badly hurt in town.

Taylor Stone was the only man who was wounded badly. He was standing by the side of Craig's store taking aim with a shot-gun, when one of the bandits saw him. They shot him through the left groin, the ball went through his hip. He was able to drag himself back around the corner and into Wood and Hammel's Barbershop. Dr. T. W. and Chas. Hurley were called to take care of him. He had a bad limp the rest of his life.

Well over a 100 shots were fired that day, and if you look around you can still find the marks of them in the buildings.

Clint Croxdale, who was running a drugstore then, went out the back door and took a few shots at the bandits. But no hits. When he got back inside, he was asked if he hurt bad. He said why no, should he? Someone told him to look at the blood on his knee. He did and passed out.

When a close check was made, they found out that he had kneeled in some red paint outside. It was years before the men let him forget about this.

The next day was a busy day in Bentonville; everyone that could came to town to find out about the robbery.

President W. R. McIlroy and Cashier J. I. Dickson of the McIlroy Bank at Fayetteville came in by train with $8,000.00 in cash to loan the bank until they could get more money from the bank in St. Louis.

That same day the bank officers met and made up the loss of $11,001.53. They also placed an order for some rifles to be kept in the bank.

Word came back that the robbers had camped the first night near the store of Ward's and Wilmoth's by Cherokee City. They were said to have four men wounded. From there they went into Oklahoma. Then the sheriff and posse came home.

In July of 1893, Henry Starr and Kid Wilson were captured in Colorado Springs. At that time they had over $2,000.00 on them. L. H. McGill, attorney for the Bank, went there to try and recover this money as part of the money taken at Bentonville.

Starr and Wilson were returned to Fort Smith, Arkansas, and so was the money. Sheriff Galbreath and Jackson went to Fort Smith and identified the men as having been part of the gang that robbed this bank.

After a lot of court action, Henry Starr and Kid Wilson were sent to the pen for a murder at some other town. The bank got a part of the money the men had on them when arrested.

The Bank's part was $430.00. It was said to have cost them $1,000.00 to get this back.

To the people of Bentonville, this was the only big robbery there ever was. And for many years it was the big talk when old-timers got together.

Henry Starr one time said that if the people here could forget about the robbery, he would like to come back and visit some friends of his who lived here.

Many years later Starr was killed trying to rob the bank at Harrison, Arkansas.

Some say the Peoples Bank in Bentonville was Starr's first bank robbery. And the Harrison try sure was his last.

Bank Robbery In Benton County

The biggest and most colorful bank robbery in Benton County was when Henry Starr robbed the Peoples Bank in Bentonville in June 1893. This story was told in the chapter just ahead of this.

Several other bank robberies have taken place over the years. In checking the newspapers, I find the following ones.

This was not a bank robbery, but it fits in. Positive identification of a body found August 14, 1907, in a field near Hiwassee was never made but it was buried under the name of James Everett, this name having been found on a satchel near the body.

The man is supposed to have been fatally injured when a safe in the store of Mitchell & Sammons of Centerton was robbed on the night of August 9. So heavy a charge of explosive was used in the robbery, that the safe door was blown through the front of the store building. There were no gunshot wounds on the body, but it was covered with bruises and contusions.

Whether the man was carried to the spot where the body was found or whether he wandered there himself could not be determined as tracks had been washed away by rains. It cannot be definitely established that the man was one of the robbers, but there is no other plausible explanation for his death in that locality.

CRIMES AND CRIMINALS

It was a bloody scene that greeted officials of the Bank of Springtown when they opened for business on the morning of March 26, 1908. A few hours earlier, an attempt had been made by bandits to blast open the safe's vault. One of the men was almost decapitated by the force of the explosion, while two others escaped empty handed. Two suspects were arrested in Joplin the following day and they identified the dead man as J. L. Staley. They gave their names as Jim Wrenn and Harry Black.

Following World War I, many notorious outlaws were hiding in the Cookson hills in eastern Oklahoma. The banks of northwest Arkansas seemed to be an easy place for them to get their spending money. But it didn't always turn out so good for them.

At one time the Bank of Sulphur Springs was a prime target, having been robbed four times. The banks at Siloam Springs, Decatur, Gentry, and Gravette, were also hit at some time.

The notorious John Birchfield and four of his henchmen staged their first Sulphur Springs robbery on September 2, 1920. Within 12 hours, all of them were in jail and the money returned.

All were sentenced to the Arkansas penitentiary. Later Birchfield escaped and led a band of three others in a second robbery on June 11, 1925.

The late Storm O. Whaley, a cashier and a patron were in the bank when the bandits entered. Whaley and the customer were ordered into the vault. Miss Abercrombie, an assistant cashier, ran out a back door and gave the alarm.

As the robbers came out of the back, they were met by L. M. Stout, president of the bank. They opened fire on him and he died the next day in a Joplin hospital.

Birchfield and Boyd Jewell were wounded in the exchange of shots and were quickly captured by a citizen's posse. Tyrus Clark and Elva McDonald were trailed and captured the next day at Claremore. Most of the $1,000 taken was recovered.

Birchfield and Jewell made several attempts to escape from the state prison and were finally killed by guards on their last attempt.

The bank at Decatur was robbed on February 28, 1923, by Perry Ingram and Fred Martain, but they were captured four hours later by a posse led by Sheriff George Maples. The loot was recovered.

On March 23, 1923, a gang led by Al Spencer robbed the Gentry bank. With Spencer were Nick Lamar, Jesse Paul, and a man named White, who sometimes used the name Red. Those were the only names he would give the officers.

The men went in the front door and took about $2,000 in cash and an undetermined amount in Liberty bonds and travelers checks. They left the bank by the rear door and fled in a waiting car.

127

About four days later, White, Paul and Lamar were all captured and most of the loot was recovered. They were all convicted in Benton County Circuit Court and sent to the State Penitentiary.

Spencer later was killed by members of his own gang who dumped his body near Bartlesville, Okla.

For almost ten years the banks in the county had a little peace from the outlaws.

Then a group of five men drove into Gravette at about midnight on Sept. 20, 1932. They held up the night watchman, John Nitchman, and tied him up. This gave them the whole downtown to themselves.

They went into the Peoples Hardware, where they took all the tools they needed to break into the bank. There they drug the five-ton steel safe out. It was pulled outside town by their truck and then loaded.

It later was found, but it was badly broken up and very empty. They never did find out who pulled this job off.

This article ran in the Benton County Herald Nov. 17, 1932.

The safe is lifted at Decatur Bank.

Early bird bandits duplicated recent robbery at Gravette. They got away with about $3,500 cash.

The bank safe lifters who early Saturday morning at Decatur practically repeated in every essential detail the bank safe robbery of a few weeks ago at Gravette, have so far made a clean get away, as also have the Gravette bandits up to this date.

Arriving in Decatur around about one o'clock Saturday morning, the six unmasked men literally took possession of the town and all citizens and visitors who were up and around. Gurnie Wiles, night marshal, and Kenneth Hines, cafe owner, were the first captured by Decatur's uninvited morning callers. They were found and bound and gagged, and left in the Hines cafe. At the Kansas City Southern depot the early bird bandits added H. A. Robinson, railway employee, and two men awaiting the arrival of a train to their captives. Then they got busy on their real job.

They removed the large safe, said to have contained about $3,500 from the Bank of Decatur building and are believed to have dragged it behind their truck to beyond the outskirts of the town before loading it on the truck.

They were in town about four hours and when they left carried the railway employee and the two railroad customers to a point about two miles south of Decatur before releasing them. The marshal and cafe operator are said to have liberated themselves a few minutes after the safe lifters had left town.

The safe from the Decatur Bank was never found. And they

never found out anything at all about who pulled off these two robberies.

A few weeks after the bank robbery at Decatur the First National Bank of Gravett ran an ad saying, "The bank management now has installed a manganese safe encased in a solid block of concrete so as to make it literally a part of the concrete floor and walls. To haul away this safe it would be necessary, it seems, to carry away the entire building. And some resourceful American bandits may yet find a way to turn that very trick."

Some time after this the Decatur bank put in a new safe and it too was made a part of the building with concrete.

From the Nov. 24, 1932, issue of the Benton County Record and Democrat. "Gives Bank Robbers A Friendly Tip. Marion Wasson, president of the First National Bank of Gentry, in an advertisement in the Gentry paper gives prospective bank robbers a friendly tip that his institution does not keep enough cash on hand to make a robbery profitable.

He says, 'The bank robbers keep getting a little closer to us and some of these nights they may haul our safe off, or some day come in and hold us up again. That is when they are going to get a surprise, maybe more than that. But the biggest surprise is the small amount of money they will find in our bank.

It would surprise you what a small amount of money we keep on hand to do business with, just enough to make change. If any body wanted us to cash a big check, we would have to send it to the Federal Reserve Bank to get the money, and what little money we do have on hand is fully insured.'"

The three bandits who robbed The State Bank at Siloam Springs in 1933 lost most of their "loot" in a gun battle with officers and citizens, when a bystander knocked the sack containing several thousand dollars out of the hands of one of the robbers as he fled. The bandits escaped with the rest of the money, although a posse was in close pursuit.

Just $15 was taken from The Bank of Gravett in 1935 by a bandit who struck the cashier over the head and then escaped in a waiting car with two companions. A posse immediately started in pursuit, but the three escaped.

As far as I can find in reading later papers, no one was ever charged for either of the two above bank robberies.

I have found one old newspaper clipping that told of a robbery at both the Bank at Pea Ridge and the Bank of Hiwasse. The article told of the men being charged with these jobs. But there was no year date in the article.

I can't say that these are all of the bank robberies in the county, but these are all that I have found in looking over the old newspaper files.

Chapter Fifteen
Benton County Industry

Van Winkle Mill

Lumber from the Van Winkle Mill was used in the building of almost all the older towns in Northwest Arkansas. At one time this mill was the biggest industry in the county.

Peter Manalis Van Winkle was born in New York City on Feb. 25th, 1814. He moved to Washington County from Ill. in 1839. He lived on a farm three miles west of Fayetteville. On May 30, 1840, he married Temperce Miller of Fayetteville.

For 11 years he lived on the farm but worked at the building trade, making wagons, hacks, plows and any other pieces of machinery used at that time. He built the first spring wagon used by the 49ers leaving Washington County for the gold fields of California.

He was a natural mechanic and handy with tools. He was said to be the best at his trade in the county then.

In 1851, he decided to give up farming and after much prospecting, located, because of the heavy stand of oak and pine, on War Eagle River in Benton county. His first mill was run with oxen, the oxen being shod with iron shoes as were the horses to preserve their feet. They walked in a circle all day to turn the saws. The logs were dragged from the timber by oxen; they were swung under two wheel carts.

The first mill was located about one mile east of what was for many years known as the Van Winkle ferry on White River. In 1856, he moved four miles further east on what was called Little Clifty branch.

When the second mill was built, he imported a machinist from Baltimore, Md., to set up the machinery. This mill was powered by steam, and the logs hauled by six mule teams on heavy logging wagons built especially for that purpose.

Business was just getting well started when the Civil War started. This disrupted Van Winkle's plans. In the fall of 1862, he

Strange Scenes in the Ozarks —By M. E. Oliver

Van Winkle Mills

NOBODY KNOWS

EXACTLY WHAT THE FIRST SAW MILL BUILT IN 1850 OR 51, BY Peter Van Winkle LOOKED LIKE. WE DO KNOW IT WAS LOCATED 1 MI. E. OF THE VAN WINKLE FERRY UP IN DUTTON CANYON AND WAS POWERED BY OXEN. This PICTURE WAS DRAWN FROM INFORMATION GATHERED AND PLACED ON THE OLD MILL FOUNDATION USING THE SURROUNDING LANDSCAPE AS The BACKGROUND IN 1858 PETER VAN WINKLE MOVED 4 MI. E. OF THIS MILL SITE NEAR WAR EAGLE RIVER WHERE HE BUILT A STEAM POWERED MILL. TO THIS MILL HE ADDED A SHINGLE MACHINE, DOOR AND WINDOW FACTORY AND CABINET SHOP.

moved his family and 15 or 20 slaves to Texas, to get away from the invading Union Army. He could not bring himself to take a part in the war, as he felt both sides were wrong.

Just before going to Texas, Van Winkle buried $4,000.00 in gold to be available for a new start after the war. When the war was over, he freed his slaves, but most of them came back with him to work for him. He returned to War Eagle and found the mill burned to the ground and the gold missing. A small portion of the box in which the gold had been buried was the only reminder of its fate. Whether it was found by Union Soldiers, marauding outlaws or local residents was never known.

Undismayed, Van Winkle at once bought machinery for a new sawmill in St. Louis with borrowed money and began work on a new and bigger building. As there were no railroads in this part of Arkansas, the machinery was sent by steamboat down the Mississippi River to the mouth of the Arkansas river, then by river steamers up the Arkansas to Van Buren, Crawford County.

Dragging this heavy machinery, especially the two huge steam boilers, over mountain trails from Van Buren to War Eagle was a saga of those days. One of the men who drove an oxen team said of this journey it was a nightmare every foot of the way. Roads had to be chopped, bridges improvised, camps maintained and food for men, horses and oxen provided. The story of that trip would make a book in itself.

In addition to the sawmill, Van Winkle built a large flour mill, a planing and shingle machine, a door and window factory, and a cabinet shop. There is no estimate of the number of men employed in the mills, shops and logging operations, but it must have been a fair-sized community. It was by far Benton County's most important industry at that date.

In 1874, Van Winkle built a new home for his family. At that time it was one of the largest residences in the county and had ten rooms each 18 foot square, with ten foot ceilings.

In 1878, Van Winkle built the hotel in Fayetteville that bore his name and most of his later days were spent in that town.

On February 10, 1882, Peter Van Winkle dropped dead on the street in Rogers, the result of a stroke of apoplexy while he was there looking after business matters.

His son-in-law, J. A. C. Blackburn, took over the running of the mill after Peter's death. By 1890, the timber around War Eagle and Van Winkle mill began to play out, so for some years the mill was operated for short runs only.

At the writing of this book there are many houses still standing in Northwest Arkansas made out of lumber from the Van Winkle Mill.

Brick Making In Benton County

There were a few brick kilns in Benton county before the Civil War, but there is no record of these. The County Courthouse built in Bentonville in 1842 was built of brick, many of them were dated for that year. They are the only dated bricks that I have heard of in Benton county.

After the Civil War, several big brickyards were built in the county. One of the better known ones in Bentonville was Haney's

Peter Van Winkle, late in life.

This is the brick mill; the boy is holding one of the forms that were used to mold the bricks.

Brickyard. By the late 1880's there were at least three yards in Bentonville. Most of the other towns had yards at some time. The bricks for most of the brick farmhouses were fired right on the farms. No one seems to know for sure when the last brick kiln closed in the county.

Most of the brickyards were run about the same, so the article on the Haney Brickyard should cover the running of brickyards in the county.

"When I was 12 years old I was a offbare boy at the Haney Brick Mill," said Jake Scoggan, of Bentonville, "each of us had to carry 1,667 bricks from the mill to the kiln. We were paid 50 cents a day.

The Haney Brickyard was one of the best known brickyards in Benton county in its day. Jim Haney, owner of the yard, was well known as a brickmaker as well as a bricklayer and builder.

Jim was an Irishman who came to Bentonville in 1871. He had walked all the way here from Springfield, Mo. The first work he did here was to finish the brickwork on the courthouse.

He soon built the brickyard and started building brick build- ings all over town. It is said that he was the best bricklayer who ever layed bricks in Bentonville. Many of the brick buildings that are still standing on the square in Bentonville were built by

Men and boys filling a kiln. Note bricks in foreground sun drying.

Haney, with bricks he made.

Jake Scoggan went to work at the brickyard in the spring of 1892. At that time a days work was making 5,000 bricks. Some days it took 9 hours, other days 11 hours. But everyone had to stay and work until they had made the 5,000 bricks, or they all got short pay.

Haney's Brickyard, or mill as they called them then, was a block northeast of where the Bentonville cemetary is today. It was run much like any yard in northwest Arkansas at that time.

They had two brick mills, as they were called: they were really a mixer for clay. These were set down in the ground a bit and had a pit around them. The clay and top soil was put into the pit with water, then it was left standing overnight. The next day this mill was run.

One man worked at putting the clay and topsoil in the mill. A horse going around and around turned the mill. This mixed the clay and dirt inside the mill. A man stood on the other side, he was called the moulder. It was his job to fill the forms that held three bricks to each form. He packed as he filled and smoothed them off.

Next, Jake or one of the other two boys who also worked here would carry them over in front of the kiln and lay them out to sun dry. They layed them flat for one day, then they were turned edgeways for a day. After two days in the sun, they were put into the kiln.

135

This yard had two kilns. One was kept burning as one was filled. A kiln would hold about 50 to 60,000 bricks. The bricks were stacked in 20 feet wide, 20 feet long and 10 feet high.

As they filled a kiln, four eyes were left: these were holes 2 feet by 3 feet and running all the way through the kiln. Here was where the fire was built in a way to draw the heat through so it would be even on all the bricks. It took from 10 to 14 days to bake a kiln of bricks.

The old sand brick, as these first bricks were called, was 4 inches wide, 8 inches long, and 2 1/4 inches thick. They were made of red clay and just a little topsoil. The top bricks in the kiln would be a little soft; and these were used as inside bricks in the walls. The hard ones were used as outside brick.

These mills always had their own pond as they used so much water, and there was no city water at that time.

All the boys were paid 50 cents a day, the men $1.00 a day. "The pay wasn't as bad as it sounded," said Jake, "after all flour was 35 cents for 50 lb. and side meat 3 cents a pound."

The mill closed some time in 1908. By that time Jake was a bricklayer himself. They could ship better brick in then from Cherryvale and Coffeyville, Kansas, so there was no more need for local brick.

If you are around any of the old brick buildings in the county you might look close at the side walls. If you see some bricks that look as if they have hard glass on them, you will know that this building was made from the old sand bricks kilned in the county. This glass was here because the bricks sometimes got too hot.

Benton County Hardware Company

As far as I can find, the Benton County Hardware Company was the first chain store set up in the county. It also was the biggest business in the county at one time, yet like so many old businesses it is just a name we hear now and then.

In 1950, the Rogers Daily News ran a short but good article on the history of this company. Here is what they were able to find out about it.

Inasmuch as the Benton County Hardware company did not originate in Rogers, no date is available as to its founders. A reference is found that the first store of the company was opened in Bentonville about 1892. Later retail stores were opened in Siloam Springs and Rogers. The Rogers branch opened in 1909 and Morgan McMichael, from the Bentonville store, was the first local manager.

When the wholesale hardware business was established in Rogers in 1912, Mr. McMichael became its general manager, and Ellery B. Howard succeeded him as the local retail manager.

BENTON COUNTY INDUSTRY

By 1923, the capitalization of the company exceeded $700,000 and the officers at that time were Connelly Harrington, chairman of the board, Siloam Springs; W. J. Doke, Bentonville, president; Morgan McMichael, Rogers, first vice-president and general manager; Marshall Douglas, Fayetteville, second vice-president; W. J. McCarter, Siloam Springs, third vice-president and treasurer; L. P. Kemper, Siloam Springs, secretary.

Harrington and Doke came to Benton county from Plattsburg, Mo., and bought the stock of a bankrupt hardware store. A year later they bought a hardware store in Siloam Springs, Doke remaining in Bentonville and Harrington going to the new store. McMichael was a nephew of Doke and went to work for him in 1901. The Benton County Hardware Company was the successor of the Rogers Hardware Company.

In the year referred to in a previous paragraph, W. J. Doke was still manager of the Bentonville store; E. B. Howard was manager at Rogers and Walter Axtell, manager at Siloam Springs.

In addition to the three parent stores, the company had controlling interest in the following hardware companies:

Washington County Hardware Company, Springdale, L. M. Riggs, manager; capital $45,000.

Washington County Hardware Company, Fayetteville, W. M. Griffith, manager; capital $35,000.

Washington County Hardware Company, Lincoln, J. H. Hawn, manager; capital $25,000.

Carroll County Hardware Company, Berryville, D. L. Gleaves, manager; capital $30,000.

Boone County Hardware Company, Harrison, Fred J. Stewart, manager; capital $30,000.

Adair County Hardware Company, Westville, Okla., Fred Douglas, manager; capital $20,000.

Delaware County Hardware Company, Grove, Okla., W. H. Fergus, manager; capital $20,000.

Fletcher Hardware Company, Stillwell, Okla., capital $20,000.

McDonald County Hardware Company, Southwest City, Mo., A. G. Viles, manager; capital $25,000.

Platte-Clinton Hardware Company, Plattsburg, Mo., Joe O'Brien, manager.

Platte-Clinton Hardware Company, Edgerton, Mo., Cozine Boydstun, manager.

Platte-Clinton Hardware Company, Dearborn, Mo., W. A. Dooley, manager.

The Platte-Clinton companies were capitalized at $60,000 and were under the same general management.

The Benton County Hardware company controlled the output of the International Harvester company for their territory and mention is made of a single check for $156,000 in 1919 in settle-

Farm Wagons in Demand - Rogers was the principal center for farm wagons in Northwest Arkansas, and hundreds of such vehicles were distributed by the Benton County Hardware Company from its warehouses. The above shows eight new wagons loaded with merchandise sold to Madison County farmers in 1910. This warehouse was on West Elm street.

ment of the local account. In 1917, it was $77,000, and in 1918 $100,000.

The home of the wholesale department of the Benton County Hardware Company, built under the supervision of Mr. McMichael, was the two-story concrete block building on East Walnut street. The big frame warehouse just across the street south housed the implement section and the heavy hardware. They also had a building for their automobile business in the days when they were the general Ford distributors in this territory.

They had buildings for their automobile business in most of the towns in their chain. In 1912, when they first got to be Ford dealers, they told Ford they would sell 60 cars each year. There are no records to prove what they did sell.

Salesmen for the company in 1923 were Marshall Douglas, J. H. Martin, Lee Martin, George Lamberson, Lloyd Patterson and W. G. Deason. The general territory was from Monett south to Van Buren, east to Heber Springs, Ark., and west to Muskogee, Okla.

A year or two later the company opened a wholesale house in

Muskogee, with Eugene Doke as manager.

For a good many years the Benton County Hardware Company was the biggest business in the county, or the entire section of the state for that matter. In 1920, the company had occasion to issue stock to the amount of $250,000, most of it was taken right in the county.

But following the depression of 1930 and the failure of the Rogers and Bentonville banks, the company became bankrupt and ultimately paid only a few cents on the dollar of its liabilities.

This business, like many others in the county, had taken a bad loss due to the apple industry going out in the late 1920's and early 30's.

Chapter Sixteen
Coin Harvey

Coin Harvey the Sage of Monte Ne

The building of Beaver Lake was the beginning of the end for Monte Ne, but it was also the first thing to happen here that showed that the prophecy of William Hope (Coin) Harvey might come true. Will it all come true in time? Will the world and the people in it all be destroyed as he said?

It began with the flooding of the beautiful Monte Ne Valley. If Coin had finished building the pyramid as he had planned to, only a few feet of it could have been seen in a few years.

Coin Harvey was a financial wizard in his day. He was known the world over for his great understanding of financial affairs. As early as 1896 he warned the world that the bankers and investment syndicates would destroy all culture as they had in Egypt, Babylon and Rome.

His prophecy was that the bankers around the world would destroy the life as we know it today. People would almost all disappear from the face of the earth. It would be generations before the population would again reach Monte Ne.

There they would find his pyramid, and in it the secret of what had happened to this civilization. The figures he had showed that the valley would almost all be filled in by wash of land and rock. Only a few feet of the pyramid would be showing to these new people.

William Hope (Coin) Harvey was born in 1851 at Buffalo, West Virginia. He received his education at the Buffalo Academy and Marshall College. He gave his first lecture on financial affairs when he was eight years old. At 16 he started teaching school.

By the time he was twenty-one he had been admitted to the bar. For several years he practiced law at Cleveland and Chicago.

It is said that the murder of a wealthy client in Chicago started Coin on his mistrust of the bankers and people with money.

COIN HARVEY

The above is one of the last pictures made of William Hope (Coin) Harvey. It was made about the time he ran for President on the Liberty Party.

In 1884 he opened a real estate office in Denver and Pueblo, Colorado. He made a very dramatic career as a promoter in the west, and also a very great fortune for those days.

He returned to Chicago in 1893 and stepped right into the big talks for "free coinage of silver". One of his greatest triumphs was there in May of 1894 when he delivered lectures on six successive days on the subjects: Money, Trust, Imperialism.

These lectures were printed in a book called "Coin's Financial School". The book sold over a million copies in a very short time. It was from this book that he got the nickname of "Coin".

Coin was a close friend and advisor to William Jennings Bryan when he ran for President of the United States in 1896. It was at this time that Coin Harvey made his prediction of the downfall of the world if we didn't stop the money man.

For a short time after the defeat of Bryan, Harvey kept up his fight against the gold standard, and the people who backed it. But when people wouldn't go along with him and his thinking he became disgusted with civilization.

He retired to the seclusion in the Ozark hills in Benton County. He bought 320 acres at what was then called Silver Springs, getting the springs and all the land around it. It was just 5½ miles southeast of Rogers.

For some time he just wrote more books and pamphlets. This kept the money coming in.

Then Harvey became active again. He started the first summer resort in Northwest Arkansas. In the spring of 1901 the first hotel was opened. It was called the Frances. By that time the name of the town had been changed to Monte Ne. Harvey said the name was Spanish for Mountains of Water.

In 1902 the railroad was built from Lowell to Monte Ne. The station was built on the lagoon, and the visitors were transported from here to the hotels in bright colored Venitian gondolas. William Jennings Bryan was the speaker there the day the first train ran.

The Monte Ne Herald, with Tom Harvey and Tony Leblanc as editors, had its first issue on April 14, 1904. It told the plans for a big stone hotel and four rows of log and concrete cottages to be built soon. Later that year Harvey organized the Bank of Monte Ne. The shell of this old building was still standing when the lake was built.

Due to trouble with the labor union, the stone hotel was never built. Oklahoma Row and Missouri Row both were built, and were said to be the longest log buildings in the world. They were 300 feet long. Oklahoma Row was moved before the valley was flooded.

For the people who came to this vacation land there were many unusual things to see or do. They rode Harvey's special

Hotel Monte Ne—As it looked in the heyday of Monte Ne's fame. This motor launch or a Venetian Gondola was used to transport guests from the hotel across the lagoon to the railroad station. The hotel later was named the Frances Hotel.

Concrete Bridge,
Entrance to Indian Trail,
Monte Ne, Ark.

This concrete bridge was the entrance to the Indian Trail at Monte Ne.

train to the station on the lagoon. Here under the arched branches of giant trees they found gondolas awaiting them; and with the songs of the gondoliers, they were carried over the waters of the lagoon through the beautiful fairyland like natural scenery to the hotels.

A splendid golf course was among the entertainment features available to the guests. There was also an enclosed swimming pool, and a rustic pavillion. Many grand balls were held here, accompanied by imported music. The hospitality and beauty of Monte Ne was known far and wide in its day.

In 1913, Coin Harvey started promoting "The Ozark Trails." This association was trying to get better and more roads in the four state area, and to Monte Ne.

By 1920, the summer resort at Monte Ne was a past and lost dream to Coin. Along with that was gone the railroad, bank, and newspaper. There had been trouble with stockholders, and people just didn't come to Monte Ne as they once had.

Coin Harvey again went into retirement. He gave a lot of thought to the troubles of the world and a decaying civilization.

He had told himself and many other people that a pyramid should be built here to house the secrets of our civilization, so people a few thousand years from now would know about us. So, he took on the job of building it at Monte Ne.

Work was started on the stone and concrete foyer or amphi-

The Oklahoma building of the Club House Company. It was a log building 316 feet long.

theatre that was to be the base of the pyramid in 1925. It was built around the big spring. This is said to have had a seating capacity of 1,000 people.

This work was needed to keep the water from backing up to where the main base was to be built for the pyramid.

The following description of the pyramid as it was to have been built, was taken from a pamphlet Coin wrote in 1930. It said:

"The pyramid will begin 40 feet square and ten feet high, then reduced to 32 feet square and raising and perpendicularly 35 feet, then reduced to 22 feet square and rising in shaft-like formation 85 feet. Ending at the top six feet square. A total distance from the base of the top 130 feet. In the Pedestal there will be 300 square feet of room space.

In the part 32 feet square there will be a room 16 feet square surrounded by a wall eight feet thick. In the shaft-like formation there will be two vaults."

The pyramid was to be built to last two million years. It would take 18,000 sacks of cement; 30,000 cubic feet of sand; 60,000 cubic feet of gravel and tons of steel for reinforcement. The estimated cost was $100,000.00 for the pyramid and what was to go in it.

A metal plate on top of the pyramid was to read, "When this can be read, go below and find a record of and the cause of the death of a former civilization." Similar plates were to show where to get into the pyramid.

In the pyramid was to have been put a 400-page book telling of our civilization, and why it was falling apart. This was to be printed on very special paper to last for years. Also were to be many other books telling about the industry and scientific achievements to that date. Plus many pictures and articles in common use from a needle to an automobile.

A key to the English language was to be put in too, to aid in translation.

Coin Harvey had picked this part of the country because of the fact that the mountains are among the oldest in the world. There had never been any earthquakes or volcanos, therefore it would endure better for all times to come. He did think that the Monte Ne valley would some day fill up with rock and dirt.

At the same time he was working on the pyramid, Coin helped to launch the Liberty Party. He was the editor of their paper named the Liberty Bell. Their slogan was "Prosperity in Ninety Days."

In 1932 they held their national convention there at the amphitheater at Monte Ne. Coin Harvey was nominated as their candidate for the Presidency.

With a bad defeat in the fall election, the Liberty Party came to an end. And so did the active part of Coin's life. He was past 82

THE PYRAMID. As referred to in the Preface of this book and on page 34—60 feet square at the base and 136 feet high, to contain a history of this civilization and to admonish the people now living that prehistoric civilizations have perished and the life of this one is now threatened.

This picture shows what the Pyramid would have looked like if Coin could have built it.

at that time and this and so many other defeats were all he could take. The few years left to him were spent at home.

The pyramid was a great dream, but Coin had no money of his own left to build this and he was unable to raise the money. So the base and amphitheatre is all that was built. They still stand as a memorial to a great dream that didn't come true, but they are under water most of the year.

Until his last day, Coin said this civilization was doomed, because of the money man and taxes. He was sure, too, that the Monte Ne valley would also be destroyed and filled in.

William Hope (Coin) Harvey died in his sleep on the night of February 11, 1936. He was buried in a simple mausoleum, beside his long dead son, on the bank of the old lagoon at Monte Ne.

Before the lake was filled this mausoleum was moved to higher ground near Monte Ne. But what was left of the town Coin built was left and covered with water. In a few short years the silt from the lake will cover what he had built and a part of his prophecy will come true. Only time will tell for the rest of it.

Chapter Seventeen
The Liberty Party

Arkansas has had several unusual political meetings and campaigns. But one of the most unusual was the Presidential convention of the Liberty Party held at Monte Ne in the summer of 1931.

This was the only National party ever formed in Arkansas, and the only Presidential Convention ever held in this State. Also, Monte Ne is perhaps the smallest town in the world to host a National Presidential Convention.

William Hope (Coin) Harvey had been working on the forming of a new political party for several years. He called it a "Political Crusade," a party to save the country and the world from the rich money men, who were trying hard to destroy it for their own gain.

Plans had been in the working since early spring, and they expected 10,000 delegates from the 48 states to attend the convention. All the hotel space was held for it and Coin had rented tents and army cots from the State Guard to hold the delegates.

The advance guard delegates of 150 men met in Coin Harvey's office at Monte Ne, Monday, August 24, 1931. They outlined the major plank for the platform.

At 10:00 o'clock Tuesday morning Coin called the first meeting together. Mrs. Eugene Blandford of Rogers led the group in singing the Star Spangled Banner. The invocation was given by the Rev. Oscar Ingold of the First Christian Church in Rogers.

Homer Earl of Lincoln, Neb., introduced William Hope (Coin) Harvey, "As our great Leader and Saver of man kind." Harvey then gave his keynote speech.

In this he termed the new Political Party he had founded as a "Political Crusade" to serve the organism of government and civilization. He spoke out long and hard for free silver and putting

This is the Amphitheatre at Monte Ne as it looked when Coin built it. He charged 25 cents to go inside and look around. The signs on the wooden walls told some of the things he believed in. Part of the program for the Liberty Party was held here.

into practice the money ideas he had worked on for over 50 years.

He was received with loud and wild cheers as were the other speakers that day. But the crowds must have been a big disappointment to the Harvey backers. Less than 400 delegates came, and in all there were only about 600 or 700 people there.

Harvey's grandson, Dick Holliday, was there to cover the Convention for United Press Association. Even though he seemed a young man for the job, he became a key man of the Convention, and helped his grandfather in many ways.

Dr. John Brinkley of Milford, Kansas, of the goat rejuvenation fame, was one of the men who were working for the Presidential Nomination. The other was Alfalfa Bill Murray of Oklahoma.

Wednesday morning, Andrea Nordskog swept the delegates off their feet with an impressive plea for close harmony in the ranks of the new party. He pledged his every effort to the party's success, regardless of whether he was honored with a place on the ticket or not.

By this time there was so much unrest within the party that it seemed the party would fold before it got started.

After dinner that day, Coin Harvey, the 82 year-old sage of Monte Ne, was chosen as the Presidential Candidate by acclamation. Coin accepted the nomination rather than see the party disrupted.

Andrea Nordskog, Publisher of a Reform Paper in Los Angeles, Calif., was nominated vice president over Homer Earl of Lincoln, Neb. There were only 390 votes cast in all, the members coming from 28 states.

The nomination and voting was said to have been done under the wildest confusion that ever took place at a meeting in Arkansas. Jeers, catcalls, cries of steam roller tactics and similar remarks were made.

The crowd and delegates were made up with a sprinkling of Reformers, Socialists, Populists, and disgruntled Democrats and Republicans. Many of them were selling books and giving out tracts with their own beliefs.

Dr. Brinkley was late, because there was no airport at Rogers, and he had to land at Miami, Okla., and drive to Rogers. His name didn't get on the ballot at all. There was so much wrangling over a presidential candidate that Harvey was the only man who all the delegates would vote for; so he had to take it by acclamation.

The Platform Committee chairman was M. V. Harttranft of Los Angeles; and Henry J. Sutton of Utica, N. Y., was the secretary.

Sutton read the party platform on Thursday morning and was cheered loudly as he read each remedy.

Liberty Party Platform

A free coinage of silver as "Co-Ordinate Money" with paper currency issued by the Government demonetization of Gold and Silver coinage at its present fitness and weight regardless of any ratio of the value of gold.

Federal State and Municipal ownership of all Public Utilities.

The abolishment of taxes which be made up from the profits of Government utilities and the abolishing of tax collectors and assessors.

With all people owning their own homes and a large national road building program.

The immediate issuing by the government of enough moneys to put all the idle people at work on public improvements.

The Liberty party to pledge its presidential candidate to receive only one third of the present salary.

The abolishment of all private owned banks with government owned banks in their place. To prohibit paying interest on money, and repeal of all the present financial laws.

A moratorium on all mortgages, bonded debts and interest bearing debts for five years to give the people time to pay them, except debts due poor people who need the money to maintain them.

A big applause followed the reading.

Coin Harvey was to be the next speaker with his appreciation speech, but he was too tired and feeble to give it. The speech was read by Charles Murphy, who was editor of the Bugle Call, the national paper of the Liberty Party.

In this speech Coin put great stress on his money plans. He ran down the present banking system, claiming that if the banks were nationally owned there would be no bank failures.

After this speech a free-for-all discussion was held that gave vent to lots of steam but didn't change the program any.

In the platform debate, C. D. Lank of Wichita, Kan., took to the floor yelling at the Committee Chairman, "But there are several parts of the platform I would like to hear discussed. For instance the name, how would you like for us to be called 'Libertines' instead of Liberty Party."

"We went all over that in the committee," returned the chairman, "you know they call the Democrats Jackasses."

The last official act of the convention was picking the Liberty Party's National Committee. They were A. M. White, New Orleans; John L. Spiedell, Lincoln, Neb.; J. M. Smith, Rogers, Ark.; George W. House, Peru, Calif.; S. W. Wood, White Bear Lake, Minn.; J. M. Hughes, Edmund, Ark.; T. A. Entrekin, Birmingham, Ala.; William Tallackson, Crafton, N. D.; Charles Morrison, Coffeyville, Kan.; John J. Fella, Dayton, Ohio; P. A.

Spain, Paris, Texas; Roland E. Bruner, Kansas City, Mo.; Herman Eilers, Dell Rapid, S. D.; A. A. Hesperrus, Colorado; Miles Fosteen, West Frankfort, Ill.; and James G. Jackson, Dublin, Ind., who made chairman for the group.

The opening address of the campaign for the Liberty Party was made by Nordskog at the State Fair in Lincoln, Nebraska, on Sept. 8th, 1931.

On Nov. 2, 1932, Coin Harvey said, "I don't expect to win, but I do expect to advance my party to the position that in case the race between Gov. Roosevelt and President Hoover is close, my party will have the controlling votes of the electoral college. I'll run third."

Coin closed the Liberty Party campaign with a speech at Rogers on Monday, Nov. 7th. "I will carry Arkansas, Washington, Idaho, and Indiana," he stated, "By the next four years our crusade will sweep the U. S."

When the votes were all counted William Hope (Coin) Harvey had only 21,220 votes. This put the Liberty Party in fifth place. They had only 100 votes in the State of Arkansas. Most of his votes came from the western states.

Coin's comment on the outcome was, "The same destructive financial system is going on under Roosevelt as did under Hoover, confiscating the property of the people threatening the loss of free government and civilization."

The vote was so low that it put an end to the Liberty Party. Coin was too old to try and keep it going on. And the younger men could see it as a lost cause, and let it die.

Chapter Eighteen
People of Interest

Betty Blake and Will Rogers Married

It was on a Sunday afternoon, November 25, 1908, that Will Rogers and Betty Blake were married in the home of her mother, Mrs. Amelia Blake, 307 East Walnut St. in Rogers.

The wedding was a small and quiet affair with just members of the family and a few close friends of Betty's. Of course, there was a big cake and punch after the wedding and everyone there said it was a very fine wedding. And about time that Betty was getting married; after all, she was 28 years old.

It must be remembered that in those early days of the Blake-Rogers marriage, no special attention was paid to their affairs; for to local citizens, Will Rogers was only another vaudeville performer and most of the local interest was occasioned by the fact that Will's father was a ranch owner and a banker. Most people figured that when Betty and Will grew tired of rambling over the country, they would settle down on an Oklahoma ranch. That was their plans, too, at that time.

Betty had been in no hurry to get married. She started working when she was young and made all the money she needed. She worked as a typesetter in the local printing office over a period of years, but never would accept a steady job. She worked only when she felt that she needed a lot of money. She also clerked in Parks Dry Goods store part-time.

The work that Betty liked best was for the railroad. She met Will several years before their marriage while she was working with her brother Jim Blake, a Missouri Pacific agent in a small Oklahoma town. At the time of their courtship she was still working for the railroad in Oklahoma.

On their first visit to Bentonville, to see Betty's relatives, they stopped at the home of T. T. Blake. Here, Will said to Mrs. Blake, "I am so glad to meet you Antie, for I have heard so much about you."

"Well I have heard a lot about you too," she replied, "But I think that you are the homeliest man I ever saw." At this Will just laughed and said, "Antie, you are so honest."

Over the years, Will and Betty made many trips to Rogers. And after he became famous the people all looked up to him.

In 1910, this little article ran in the Rogers Democrat: "All the calves, colts, and dogs on the east side have taken to the tall timber for the summer. Will Rogers is here again and every small boy in the neighborhood is trying to emulate Will's skill in roping. They have just about worn out several hitching posts on east Walnut Street. No one worries about that. It is when the boys begin roping each other that the mothers protest. It means too much darning and repairing clothes and hides."

Betty was the daughter of Mr. and Mrs. J. W. Blake. When she was born, the family was living in a log and frame house at Silver Springs (later named Monte Ne). Her father ran a small mill there. Her father died when she was a little girl and her mother was left with the job of raising seven girls and two boys.

In the early days of Rogers, the Blake sisters were very active and attended most of the social affairs of the town. They also spent a lot of time at Monte Ne, in the heyday of that town.

When Betty and Will were married, they or no one else thought that Will was just before becoming very famous. They never forgot Rogers and came for visits when they had the time.

During World War One, Will gave one-third of all of his Red Cross donations to the Rogers branch. And many times he gave $50 or more to help with the street or other repairs in Rogers. But it was always given, only if they would tell no one. He did not like that kind of publicity.

Capt. Field E. Kindley, American Ace

Captain Kindley was born at Pea Ridge, and for many years made his home with an uncle at Gravette where he went to school. For a short time he was a traveling salesman out of Kansas City, and shortly before the opening of World War One opened a motion picture show at Coffeyville, Kansas.

He enlisted immediately after the United States entered the war, as a doughboy, and was slated for admission to an officer's training camp but was transferred to the aviation division.

Making good from the beginning, he was at first assigned to the flying corps in Italy, but was diverted to Scotland instead, and did much flying with the Royal Air Forces until he was finally transferred to the flying forces under General Pershing on the French front.

From a New York account published at the time of his return to the United States on June 27, 1919: "An American ace, Captain F. E. Kindley of Gravette, Ark., officially credited with shooting

Capt. Field Kindley and his mascot, "Folker". Picture made in the cockpit of a plane some place in Europe during World War I.

down twelve German airplanes, returned as a member of the One Hundred and Forty-First Air Squadron. He wore the Distinguished Service Cross with Oakleaf, the Distinguished Flying Cross of England and the Croix Deguerre of France.

Captain Kindley went overseas as an aviation cadet in September, 1917, and got into action May 22, 1918, in Flanders with the Sixty-fifth Royal Air Squadron. He fought twenty-seven air battles near Cambrai and Amiens as squadron flight leader.

One of the most thrilling of these, he said, occurred last September 28, near the Canal Du Nord after he had been transferred from the British squadron to the One Hundred Forty-eighth American Pursuit Squadron.

He started out with three other fliers in single-seated planes, and at an altitude of 5,000 feet near the German lines, the four aviators discovered that another American pursuit squadron was being attacked by twenty-five German machines. The quartet flew to their comrades aid. The fight lasted seven minutes, during which one of the Americans was shot down. Captain Kindley's machine was hit forty-seven times, his pilot cap pierced, goggles knocked off, and his leather jacket perforated but he escaped injury.

A machine gun bullet struck his gasoline tank, but the hole was above the fluid. Four of the Germans were sent down and the others flew back to their own lines, allowing the Americans to return to their hangars."

After his return home, he was soon sent to an Army air field at San Antonio. Then on Sunday, February 1, 1920, word of his death came back home and the papers ran the following.

"Capt. Field E. Kindley of Gravette, one of the best known of America's war aviators, was killed Sunday while flying at Kelly Field, San Antonio, Texas. General Pershing was to visit the famous flying field Monday, and Captain Kindly was assisting in preparing for the air maneuvers. It is stated that his plane fell only fifty feet, but he was caught under the engine and crushed and burned. No cause is known for the unexpected disaster and an army board has been appointed to investigate."

Captain Kindley's funeral was held in Gravette on Tuesday, Feb. 3rd. The body was brought to his home there from San Antonio under military escort and a full military funeral was given the aerial hero.

He was the son of Mr. George Kindley, and was just 23 years old and unmarried.

Captain Kindley was one of the two aces credited to the State of Arkansas. The other ace from Arkansas was Lieutenant Wendell A. Robertson of Fort Smith.

At the time of his sudden death, Capt. Kindley was in command of the 94th Aero Squadron stationed at San Antonio. He returned home from France last March a lieutenant but immediately afterwards was awarded a captain's commission for valiant services overseas. He visited his old home a few months ago and then left to assume command of the 94th Squadron."

This article was taken from the newspaper reports at the time of Capt. Kindley's death.

John Robinson, Revolutionary War Soldier

But a single soldier of the Revolutionary War rests in Benton County soil. This almost forgotten hero is John Robinson, one of the first pioneers to settle in Benton County. For years he has slept in the little cemetary at the old Thornbury camp ground near Wager. His descendants were all prominent citizens of the south part of the county.

John Robinson was a native of South Carolina and enlisted in the Continental Army when he was 17 years old. He served throughout the war.

Along with other neighbors, including the Yell families, he immigrated to the vast and little settled land west of the Mississippi and reached Benton County in about 1835. The colony settled on the fertile land along Osage river where fish were abundant in its waters and deer and turkey plentiful in the hills.

He died in 1842 and was one of the first to be buried in the Thornbury graveyard, which is said to be one of the oldest burial spots in the county.

According to Miss Clara B. Eno of Van Buren, a prominent officer in the Arkansas Daughters of the American Revolution, there are 70 Revolutionary soldiers buried in the State. That is less than one to a county.

If we just stop and think, John Robinson was about 75 years old when he made this long trip by covered wagon to Benton County. That was some trip for a man of his age.

Tom P. Morgan, Author

Benton County has had its share of writers over the years, but none were better known over the years than Tom P. Morgan of Rogers. His humorous quips, poems and stories at one time or another appeared in almost every publication in the country.

He moved to Rogers with his folks in 1890. He never married, and after the death of his mother in 1903 he lived with his father J. P. Morgan at their home on the corner of Walnut and Third Streets.

His varied experience in his younger days gave him the foundation for his later stories and tales. He traveled with an old-time dramatic company that played the smaller towns in the country. For a time he traveled with a circus and worked in various small town newspaper offices.

He wrote all kinds of stories for all kinds of magazines. He was responsible for many of the weird Kansas stories that used to delight eastern readers. He wrote a series of stories of Alkali Ike for an eastern syndicate.

Most of his later day quips appeared in Life, Judge, Puck and the Curtis publications. Publications on his early list were Golden Days, Leslie's Weekly, Saturday Night, Youths Companion. In his later years he was a special contributor to the Kansas City Star where his short stories of hillbilly life and daffy people appeared daily.

For more than 20 years Tom ran the Post Office Book Store. When there was no longer room in the post office for his shop, he moved to the corner of Elm and First, where he sold books and papers between writing until he died July 7, 1928.

Rev. Peter Carnahan

One of the best loved and most respected ministers who ever served in Benton County was Rev. Peter Carnahan. He served as pastor of the Cumberland Presbyterian Churches in the county for over 45 years. He was still marrying people and helping with the Lord's work at the time of his death.

Peter Carnahan was born on Oct. 9th, 1838, at Cane Hill, Washington County, Arkansas, the son of Rev. John Carnahan, who had organized the first Sunday School class in Arkansas.

He grew up there and went to school there. He was licensed to preach in 1861, and preached in Washington County. On June 19, 1862, he married Martha J. Buchanan, the daughter of a Cumberland Presbyterian minister in Cane Hill.

He served as Lieutenant in Company B, 34th Arkansas Infantry, in the Civil War and was in the battles of Oak Hill, Prairie Grove, Jenkins Ferry. Whenever he could, he preached to his comrades in arms.

Following the war he returned to Cane Hill and was ordained in the Cumberland Presbyterian Church in 1866. He farmed there and preached at Cincinnati and Pleasant Hill until 1870.

He preached his first sermon in Bentonville, on the second Sabbath in November, 1869. Rev. S. H. Buchanan asked him to preach this sermon, and later that day he was asked to meet with the board and they offered him the church, as Rev. Buchanan was leaving for a church at Little Rock.

At that time the Cumberland Presbyterian Church was the only church to have a building in Bentonville, and they had just rebuilt theirs. All the churches had been burned in the war. The Presbyterians, Methodists and Baptists all used this same house at special set times. Some people attended the services of all three for want of anything to do.

The population of Bentonville in the spring of 1870 was about 700. Most of the land that the town covers today was in corn, growing about 20 bushels to the acre. There were no school buildings at all. What school there was, was held in the church or a private home.

Land sold for from $5 to $20 an acre. The closest railroad was Springfield, Mo. All transportation from there to here was by wagons. There was not over a dozen buggys in the county then.

In 1877, Rev. Carnahan was employed by the American Bible Society to canvass the county and to place, if possible, a Bible or Testament in every home which didn't have one. They were sold at cost to those who had money to pay for them, and given as a gift to those who didn't. He was assisted by W. H. Patton, J. E. Dickson, Mr. Riley, Dr. J. L. Maxwell and M. B. Maxwell. They visited over 3,000 families, few of who refused to receive the books.

This canvass enabled him to preach in many communities that had no regular preacher. And he became acquainted with many of the splendid people of the county.

He preached over 5,000 times at regular appointments in Benton County. This didn't include weddings, funerals, and special meetings he held in his lifetime.

For 14 years he was the only Cumberland Presbyterian pastor in Benton County. He supplied Bentonville and Mt. Vernon (Pea Ridge) with regular services, and did missionary work in the county. He helped reorganize churches at Sulphur Springs, Hico (Siloam Springs), Old Union (Lowell), New Hope (Rogers) and Maysville.

He was retired in 1915 after 45 years of work as pastor in Benton County. He never made any big amount of money in his lifetime, but was always able to feed his family and help others he knew.

When he died, the newspapers of the county credited him with having married more couples than any other minister in this section. A few months before his death, a young couple came from New Mexico to be married at his home. He had performed the ceremony for the young lady's mother, Mrs. Harry Patton, and also for her grandmother.

It would take a large book to list all the good that Rev. Carnahan did in his lifetime, and all of it to help those around him, not himself. He was 88 years old when he died on November 9th, 1926. He was still taking part in the Lord's work, and helping those he could.

Senator James H. Berry

Senator James H. Berry was born on a farm in Jackson County, Alabama, on May 15, 1841. He was the son of James M.

Sen. James H. Berry.

and Isabella Jane Orr Berry.

He moved with his family to Carrollton in Carroll County, Arkansas in 1848. During the winter months he attended school at the village one room log school house. Here he received his rudimentary education. When he was 17 he entered the Berryville Academy, just 18 miles away. At that time this was the best school in the locality for miles around. Due to his mother's death, he dropped out of school after two months.

He then moved to Yellville with his father and went to work in a general merchandise store.

At the outbreak of the Civil War, he returned to Carrollton and enlisted in the Confederate Army. In Sept. of 1861 he was commissioned 2nd. Lieutenant in Company E, Sixteenth Arkansas Infantry.

He was in winter quarters at Elm Springs, Arkansas when Gen. Price's Army was retreating through there on the way to Fort Smith. His outfit moved south with them to the Boston Mt. Then, in March, he was at Pea Ridge for the battle there.

From here he went to Memphis, Tenn. and on to Corinth, Miss. He joined Gen. Beauregard's forces about April 15th, 1862. In May, he moved to Tupelo, Miss. On Sept. 19th he led his Company into Battle at Iuka, Miss., and on Oct. 3 and 4th was in the battle for Corinth, Miss.

It was in the battle of Corinth that Berry received a severe wound and lost his right leg. He was captured there by the Federal troops and sent to their hospital at Iuka.

Five months after he was wounded he returned to his outfit at Port Hudson, Louisiana. Following the fall of this town, he came back to Arkansas for a short visit with his sister, Mrs. Sam Peel.

He joined his outfit once more at Monticello and after several moves he was at Corsicana, Texas, with Gen. Cabell's forces when the war came to an end.

On June 10, 1865, he took a job as teacher in a school near Ozark, Ark., for three months. Here he met Miss Lizzie Quaile, and they were married in a few months. Her father was very much against the marriage. He said Mr. Berry more than likely couldn't make a living if he had two legs, but with just one he never could. Seventeen years later, when Berry was Governor of Arkansas, the old man made up with them.

In the spring of 1866 he went back to Carrollton where he started to read law. That fall he was elected to the State Legislature from Carroll County as well as being admitted to the Bar.

In 1869 he moved with his family to Bentonville. Here he practiced law with his brother-in-law, Col. Sam Peel.

In 1872 he was elected to the legislature from Benton County. At a special session during the Brooks Baxter War of 1874 he was elected speaker of the house. The constitutional convention was also held during this session.

Returning to Bentonville, he practiced law in partnership with Judge R. E. Ellis for four years. Then Berry was elected Circuit Judge in 1878, serving four years.

He was elected Governor of Arkansas in 1882, and was the only Governor ever elected from Benton County. He served in office from Jan., 1883 to Jan., 1885.

Refusing to run for a second term as Governor, he was appointed to the United States Senate to succeed Senator Augustus H. Garland, who resigned to become Attorney General under President Cleveland. Berry was sworn in to the Senate March 25, 1885, and served 22 years, until March 3, 1907.

He then returned to Bentonville to live and practice law.

On Oct. 17, 1910, he was appointed by the Secretary of War at the personal request of President Taft, as Commissioner to Mark the Graves of Confederate Soldiers who had died in Northern prisons during the war and who were buried near the place where they died. In December of 1912 he reported the job done.

Senator Berry died at his home in Bentonville on Jan. 30, 1913.

He was perhaps one of the most outstanding men in Arkansas history. In all of his long years in office he tried hard to vote for and work for the bills that would do the most good for the most people. He walked on crutches after losing his leg at Corinth.

Judge Alfred Burton Greenwood

Alfred Burton Greenwood was the first attorney to open a law office in Benton County. At the time he came to the county, an attorney would only have an office in the county seat town. So he chose Bentonville. At the time, Bentonville was the biggest town in the county. Most of his life he was known as Judge Greenwood.

Judge Alfred Burton Greenwood was born in Franklin County, Ga., in 1811, educated at Lawrenceville, Ga., and studied law under William Izzard. He was admitted to the bar at Monroe, Ga., in 1832, and opened an office in Decatur, Ga., where he practiced law a few years.

In 1837, young Greenwood was appointed as one of the Federal Commissary agents to accompany a group of one thousand Cherokee Indians on the Trail of Tears, when they were being transferred from Tennessee and Georgia to their new home in the Indian Territory.

He came as far as Nashville, Tennessee, with them. By this time he had heard so much about Arkansas as a new state that he returned to Georgia and got his family and moved to Benton-

Judge Alfred Burton Greenwood. Picture more than likely made when he was in Congress.

ville in the spring of 1838.

At this time they found Bentonville a town of thirty people, and one store. He opened a law office at once and made the town his home. He was a hard worker and helped in the growth of this frontier town, which it was at that time.

In 1846, Greenwood was elected by the State Legislature as Prosecuting Attorney and represented ten counties in Northwest Arkansas. In 1848 he was elected to this same office at the regular election and held it until 1852, at which time he was elected Circuit Judge of the Fourth Judicial District of Arkansas. He still had to cover the same ten counties. From this time on, he was called Judge Greenwood by everyone.

In 1852, he resigned as circuit Judge and was nominated to Congress from the First Congressional District, which was made up of all the territory north of the Arkansas River. There were only two congressional districts in the state at that time. At the election in November of that year, he was elected by a 10,000 vote majority. He served six years in Congress from this district.

In 1856, President Buchanan appointed Judge Greenwood Commissioner of Indian Affairs. He held that office during the remainder of Buchanan's administration.

When the Civil War started, he stayed with the South. Soon after the outbreak of the war, President Jefferson Davis of the Confederacy called upon Judge Greenwood to take the lead in enlisting the support of the Cherokee and Choctaw nations.

Greenwood was given credit for enlisting many thousands of Indians in the Confederate Army. He could get them into the army, but he couldn't make them fight like white men.

Later during the War he was made tax collector for the State of Arkansas. During the month of December, 1864, he collected over $2,000,000, being located at Washington, Hempstead County.

After the war he returned to his law practice, which he soon built to one of the largest in the county. At the time of his death in Bentonville, on Oct. 6, 1889, he was the oldest member of the Benton County Bar. He had been a big help in the growth and development of Bentonville and Benton County.

He was a Democrat in politics and gained a national reputation as one of the most influential men in Northwest Arkansas.

Greenwood, a town in Sebastian county, one time a county seat there, was named after Judge Greenwood, because he was the first Judge to hold Court there.

Hugh Anderson Dinsmore, Ambassador to Korea

Time and people have forgotten Hugh Anderson Dinsmore, who was one of the youngest foreign diplomats of his day. At the age of 35, he was the first American Minister to Korea. The one American who had been there before him was a military attache

Hugh Anderson Dinsmore - This photograph of Dinsmore was taken from a picture in the Benton County courthouse. It was made a few years after his return from Korea.

who did not hold the office of minister.

Hugh Anderson Dinsmore was born on December 24, 1850, at Cave Springs, the son of Alexander and Katherine Dinsmore. He received his education in Bentonville and at the Ozark Institute near Fayetteville.

After his formal study was finished, he studied law under Judge Samuel N. Elliott in Bentonville. Young Dinsmore served as clerk in the Benton County courthouse under "Uncle John Black" in 1873.

In 1874, he was admitted to the bar and in that same year he formed a partnership with U. S. Senator J. D. Walker in a law office in Fayetteville.

He was elected prosecuting attorney of the Fourth Judicial Circuit in 1878. He held that office for six years.

On May 25, 1883, Dinsmore married Miss Elizabeth LeGrand Fisher of St. Louis. She died on June 19, 1886, and Dinsmore never remarried. They had one son, Hamilton Atwood Dinsmore.

In 1886, Dinsmore was a presidential elector on the Democratic ticket. Later in that same year he was appointed as minister to Korea. At that time, Dinsmore's entire world had been in the area from Bentonville to St. Louis and back.

Edmond Penn Watson, Jr. of San Diego, Calif., a nephew of Hugh Anderson Dinsmore, has most of the letters that Dinsmore wrote to his father and sister from Korea.

On February 24, 1887, Hugh Anderson Dinsmore wrote a note to his father saying that he would be aboard an outward bound ship within the hour. His first letter from Seoul, Korea, was written April 18, 1887, to his father.

"The King having been ill for several days after my arrival, I did not get an audience until Wednesday of last week. On Tuesday I received a dispatch from the Foreign Office informing me that His Majesty had fixed Wednesday as the day and 10 A M as the hour. So I was on hand at the Palace Gate at that hour, accompanied by an interpreter, and the usual retinue of coolies, (chair bearers and soldiers).

In recognition of my being the bearer of a letter from the President, I was accorded the way of honor, which is the central of three parallel walks that go through the Palace Grounds and to the presence of the King. At every wall and entrance, and there are many, there are three gates, a large one flanked on either side by smaller ones to correspond with these walks. As soon as I was within the court in which the audience hall is situated, I came in full view of the King who stood on his feet, surrounded by his ministers and officials waiting to receive me. As soon as I came in view and while yet 100 feet from him, he gave me a cordial smile and I was received with warm greeting and cordiality. After making my little speech and delivering the letter, he entered into

Residence in Korea - Hugh A. Dinsmore shown at the right of his residence in Korea. The house is still being used by our legation.

conversation with me about American and Americans, said many pleasant things about us all and hoped that I would remain in Seoul a long time.

Before I left his presence he said, I shall take you more fully in to my counsel than any foreign representative, first because you are the highest diplomatic officer here and secondly because you are an American."

Letter to father, April 30, 1888 - "The three military officers who came out from the U. S. to organize and train the Korean Army have arrived and are quite an acquisition to our society. One of them, Maj. Lee, is my guest and has been for three weeks."

Letter to Sister, Sept. 16, 1888 - "We have been having a gay round in Social Affairs for tea. The Japanese Admiral was up with his staff and Band last week. A splendid band and they made it very pleasant for us. Now the Grand Duke of Russia (Alexander) is here, a very handsome and agreeable young gentleman. I had the honor of dinner with him night before last, quite informally and pleasantly at my friends, the Woebers, where he is stopping.

Inasmuch as our holidays have never been celebrated here, I sent to Japan and procured some fireworks and made the necessary preparations for a little celebration on July 4th. All the foreigners and a large number of Koreans were invited and I had about 100 guests. The grounds were illuminated with 500 lanterns, those upon the Legation building the American colors in flags painted on them. From the top of the flagstaff were suspended to the ground in different directions, three lines with lanterns attached at intervals, of red, white and blue, respectively. These could be seen from all parts of the city."

Letter to Sister Jan. 12, 1889 - Dinsmore said, "The Koreans have made frequent overtures to me to remain here in the service of the government but I declined to entertain them. I would rather go home and practice law.

The missionaries here live in the greatest comfort and every household has a coterie of servants numbering from three to a dozen. I often think that our poor people at home who give their money to foreign missions to support the missions in foreign lands bearing suffering and privation, would have wide eyes if they could see the luxuries surrounding them. To see for instance as I have seen then time and again, preachers rigged out in gay tennis suits going to a game with a servant carrying his bat. Never the less they are good people, some of them and with a good deal of harm, are doing some good."

This letter was the last one that Dinsmore wrote from Korea.

Dinsmore's last official letter to the Korean court was written on May 9, 1890, which announced arrival in Seoul of his successor, Augustine Heard.

The name of the Korean king at the time Dinsmore was there

was King ko-jong, father of the last king of the Yi Dynasty, Sun Jong.

The position offered to Dinsmore by the King of Korea before he left was that of Counselor of the Kingdom, at a salary of $25,000 per year. He turned it down to return to his home state.

The following article was taken from the Benton County Democrat, February 4, 1888. "Dr. Allen physician to the king of Korea, and attache to the Korean legation just arrived in Washington, was instructed by the King to tell the president that Minister Dinsmore is giving great satisfaction and that the Korean government makes the special request for his retention as minister as long as possible. His appointment was due to Senator James Berry of Bentonville. In Congress an effort will be made to advance his salary to $7,500 a year."

Hugh Dinsmore returned to Fayetteville in 1890, where he again took up his law practice. In 1892, he was elected to Congress as a Democrat and served there for six years.

He then returned to his law practice in Fayetteville, until 1905 when he retired from public life and moved back to Benton County. He maintained a limited practice in his home, but spent most of his time looking after his farms.

He died on May 2, 1930, in Barnes Hospital in St. Louis. He had been in ill health for several years before his death.

He was a member of the Board of Regents of the Smithsonian Institute, and served under Governor Thomas C. McRae as a member of the Board of Trustees of the University of Arkansas.

Colonel Sam Peel

Col. Sam Peel was one of the early day prominent men of Bentonville and the State. He was born near Batesville in Independence County, Arkansas, on Sept. 13, 1831. When he was just a small boy his parents moved to Carroll County.

He went to school at Carrollton, Arkansas, and received his start in business training by clerking in a store there at an early age.

He started his political career by being elected clerk of Carroll County, in 1858 to 1860.

Sam Peel enlisted in the Confederate Army at the outbreak of the Civil War. He served with an Arkansas regiment. He was in the battle of Wilson Creek and Prairie Grove. He was made Colonel and was at Little Rock when the War ended.

He went home to Carrollton where he found out that he was penniless. His wife and children had gone hungry many days before the war was over.

Peel then studied law and was admitted to the Bar in 1865.

Colonel Sam Peel.

In the spring of 1866 he and his family moved to Hindsville, where he started his practice of law. A year later he moved to Bentonville, and made that town his home.

He opened his law office in Bentonville in the spring of 1867, and he became one of the most outstanding attorneys in the county for the rest of his life.

He was elected Prosecuting Attorney in 1873 and held this office until 1882.

In 1882, he was elected to Congress and held that office until 1893. He served as Chairman of the Committee on Indian Affairs, and was a great help to the Indians. He helped them get money from the government many times.

He came back to Bentonville and his law practice in 1893; most of this practice then was court claims in Washington D. C. and Federal Court in Oklahoma where he won many cases.

From the time Col. Sam Peel moved to Bentonville, he helped in many ways to make this a better place for people to live. He was on more committees here than any other one man.

His wife, Mary Berry Peel, was the older sister of Ex-Gov. James H. Berry, who had also moved to Bentonville from Carrollton.

Col. Sam Peel died on Dec. 18th, 1924, at the age of 93. He was living in Bentonville, where he had been retired for a few years.

He was the first native of Arkansas to be elected to the Congress.

Chapter Nineteen
Places of Interest

War Eagle House

When Sylvanus Blackburn built his home on the banks of War Eagle Creek in the spring of 1833, he must have been thinking of the bible saying, "Build your house on a sound foundation." For this large two story log house is standing today as a living monument to Sylvanus and Catherine Blackburn, who lived in it until their death in March, 1890.

This home at War Eagle, as the farm has been called for years, is one of the oldest houses in Benton County. It was built three years before Arkansas was admitted to the Union. William Jasper Blackburn was born here on Sept. 9, 1836, the month that Arkansas was admitted. He later became a minister and teacher.

Sylvanus Walker Blackburn was born in Hickman County, Tennessee. In 1827, he married Catherine Brewer when they were both just sixteen years old. They lived with his father until coming to Arkansas.

When Sylvanus was just past twenty, he started out to find a new home somewhere in the Ozark Mountains where there was good virgin land. He traveled along through Missouri and Arkansas before picking out the 160 acres of land in the curve of War Eagle Creek.

He then returned to Tennessee for his wife, his father and mother, three brothers and three sisters. They all moved to War Eagle and his father also took up a homestead there.

They arrived there in December of 1832. They had to live in tents until they had the house built, as there were very few people living in this part of Arkansas at that time. And none too close.

The first part of the house was started just as soon as they got their farm. They must have been able to move in some time in January of 1833. It was made of hand hewn pine logs cut from the virgin timber growing on the farm. It is 24 x 28 feet inside and is two story. The face of the logs are all over one foot across. As the

Sylvanus and Catherine Blackburn. This picture was taken a few years before they died.

family grew they added on more rooms.

Sylvanus and Catherine had six boys and three girls. After the Civil War they took in eight more children who had been made orphans by the war.

No one seems to know for sure what years the other rooms were added to the house.

This two-story house was big enough for the family at the beginning. And Sylvanus had a lot of work to do to clear up his land so he could grow grain and cattle. By 1838, Sylvanus not only had his farm going and raising good grain and cattle, he had erected a blacksmith shop, a sawmill and a grist mill.

The grist mill brought a lot of people to War Eagle Mill as they called it. Because of that the roads were built by his place.

Soon after they had the saw mill running, he built on to the log house. The big pine boards were cut from timber on the farm. They built a two-story porch on the front of the log home.

The big downstairs room in the log house was known as the prayer room. It was here that Sylvanus, who was a staunch Baptist Minister, always said prayer, before meals and before bedtime. The room was the living room as well as the girls' bedroom. In the east end there were four four-poster beds. At the west end was a fire place big enough to take whole rails.

From this living room you went back into a big hallway. On the left was the kitchen and dining room. This room was far bigger than the living room. There were two big fireplaces here where all the meals were cooked.

On the right hand side of the hall were three large rooms. The first was a guestroom, then the bedroom for the housemaids. At one time slaves slept here. Then came the loom room. It was a real big room with lots of windows. It held several types of looms, and spinning wheels. Someone was working here at all times. The cloth for all the family's clothing and bedding had to be handmade.

At the end of the hall was the master bedroom for Sylvanus and Catherine. The boys all slept upstairs over the prayer room.

In the loom room was the money box. It was big and sturdy and looked a lot like the old wooden icebox. Here was where Sylvanus kept all his money and papers. It was never locked, as he didn't believe in locking up a thing. As long as he lived there was never a lock on any door on the place.

A short ways from the house was a soap house where the ashes were kept to get lye to make soap. They also made the soap here.

There was also a carpenter shop where Sylvanus made the furniture for his home and made and sold furniture and coffins to the neighbors. They also made barrels which were much in demand then.

The primitive industries that Sylvanus ran brought settlers from miles around to trade here. In later years he built a merchandise store here. When he settled here, Cassville, Missouri was the closest store they could go to on good road. It was fifty miles away. About the only things they had to buy from the store then was salt, needles, gunpowder, or something made of metal that they couldn't make.

The gristmill and sawmill were burned down in the Civil War by orders of a Confederate General so the northern army could not get flour here. But the house was saved, as it was used for headquarters for this general and later it was used by the northern general.

Sylvanus and Catherine had a long and loving life in this backwoods home. Like all people they had their ups and downs, but never gave up, and lived in this house until they died.

Catherine Blackburn passed away on March 13, 1890. Sylvanus told his sons to dig the grave big, but not to close it until he was dead. He began to pray and in five days was buried in the same grave with his loving wife.

Since then the farm has changed hands several times. The back part of the house was rebuilt. But very little changes have been made in the log part, which is still very sound.

War Eagle Mill

In the middle of the night on August 24, 1924, fire was seen coming out the windows of the War Eagle mill at War Eagle. The cry went out, "The mill's on fire". The few people who lived close (that is, within four or five miles) came, but it was too late to save the mill. They had water enough to put out ten fires, but not a thing to pump it with.

This fire burned down the mill, and brought an end to one of the oldest and best known gristmills in Northwest Arkansas. But it didn't put an end to the memory of the War Eagle Mill. Even today if you should be talking to any of the older citizens of the county about fishing, chances are they will tell you some tale of a fish caught there or about some trip to War Eagle to fish.

The first mill was built here some time in 1835 by Sylvanus Blackburn. It must have been a very small and crude gristmill. All that is known about it is that it was used by all the early settlers who could get to it. They ran it only when there was enough grain for a day's grinding. It had just one set of stone burrs and they ground both wheat and corn the same way. The dam was a small one made of a few logs and stones.

In the spring of 1848, the mill and its small dam was washed out with the spring rains. Sylvanus ordered new milling equipment from St. Louis. This was shipped by river boat to Ft. Smith and then by wagon from there to War Eagle.

War Eagle Mill. This picture was made about 1900; the mill looked just as it did in 1872 when J. A. C. Blackburn rebuilt it.

This mill was a larger two-story mill. They built a dam of logs and rock with about a seven-foot fall. There were burrs for both flour and cornmeal. At this time it was one of the best mills in the State. And had a very good water supply.

They did a lot of grinding for the farmers, taking a part of the flour or meal for their pay. The mill was run full time the year around, unless the water was too low to turn the wheel.

At the beginning of the Civil War, they ground grain for the Confederate Army. But early in 1862, when the Union Army was coming into Arkansas, a Confederate General ordered the mill burned so the Union Army couldn't use it. All that was saved were the large stone burrs.

After the war was over and Capt. J. A. C. Blackburn of the Confederate Army came home, he took over and rebuilt the mill. Equipment was hard to find then, and it was the spring of 1872 before the mill was running again.

This was the mill building that is so well remembered today. It was four stories high, and very large. He built a new dam of timber and rock. From the day Blackburn rebuilt the mill he had a big business.

Goodspeed's History of Arkansas 1889 lists War Eagle Mill as having the best water supply in the State. They also had a phone line to Siloam Springs, Bentonville, and Rogers.

Blackburn also ran a large sawmill on water power from the mill dam.

Blackburn sold the mill some time in the late 1890's to James K. P. Stringfield who operated the mill for a few years. Then Abner and Powell ran it. In the spring of 1903, Mr. J. E. Crossman bought the mill.

At this time the mill had a reel sifting system to sift the flour as it came from the stone burrs where it was ground. This system gave just one grade of flour and bran. The cornmeal was ground on the stone burrs and was unbolted. This meal would keep better than bolted meal, and it had more food value.

Mr. Crossman made a lot of changes in the mill. He put in a roller system to grind the wheat, and a Barnum and Lee Plan sifting system. The wheat was ground through five sets of big rollers, then went through fifteen silk sifters. With this system they made two grades of flour and mill run bran. He also built the big cement dam that is still there today.

Crossman sold the mill to Dr. J. B. Kilgo in 1912. Then, in 1914, Kilgo sold the mill to his son, B. B. Kilgo, who ran it until it burned in 1924.

"I think as many people came to the mill to fish as did to have grain ground," said Kilgo, as he recalled the years he had ran the mill.

The only change that he made was taking out the center

This old turbine wheel was all that was left of the mill after the fire was over. It was pulled out of the water.

window on the first floor, and putting in a door. This opened out onto a porch out over the dam. It was about 6 x 8 feet, and had several chairs. Over three hundred different people signed the guest book one year as having fished from there.

Kilgo had his own brand name for flour and cornmeal. It sold so good that he kept the mill running ten to twelve hours a day. With the cement dam to hold water, they never had to shut down due to low water.

At one time the Queen of the Ozark Flour sold for $1.00 for a 50 lb. sack.

The mill had a grinding capacity of 40 barrels of flour in 24 hours. A barrel was 192 lbs. They could grind corn faster than this. The mill was fixed to grind corn and wheat at the same time, but it ran too slow that way, so they ran one at a time.

Most of the people who brought grain to be ground paid with part of their flour. Some would bring their grain and trade it for flour and meal that was ready. In a typical trade, if you took a bushel of corn that was 56 lbs. to the mill you got 48 lbs. of cornmeal. They took in very little money at the mill. Their cash came from the sales to stores in town.

The grinding stones used at the mill were like those used at all other mills. They were made from buhrstone, a form of silica like flint in hardness, but not so brittle. The rock is found only in the mineral basin of Paris. They were made up of a number of pieces of stone strongly cemented and bound together with iron hoops.

The ones used here were about 5½ feet across; the top one was 18-inches thick and the bottom one, twelve. They could be sharpened with a steel tool and a nidging hammer. They cut the sloped grooves deeper. This was done once a year.

"If you had a mill paid for, you were all right," said Kilgo. "As the water power was free and you had no over head. As the work was done by water power. The grain was lifted and carried through the mill by it."

At the time of the fire, the mill was doing a good business. But so many changes were coming that Mr. Kilgo didn't think it would go on making good money if he built it back. So he didn't.

Leetown

Leetown, like several other early day small towns in the county, had a very good start, but soon faded and was gone. But Leetown does hold the honor of having been the only town in the county that was killed by the Civil War.

Leetown was started by and named after John W. Lee, a first cousin of Gen. Robert E. Lee who came to Benton County in the 1840's. He and his wife Martha homesteaded a large acreage between Little Sugar Creek and Pea Ridge. The small creek that

PLACES OF INTEREST

The Lee home at Leetown - This picture was made some years after the Civil War and Mayfield's owned it. In the picture are Mrs. Mayfield, W. P. Mayfield and John Woodard, her father. This building was used as a hospital during the battle there.

ran through their farm was named for them.

Lee was a businessman as well as a farmer, and in a short time after his arrival he opened a general store. Soon a small town sprung up around his store.

The Lee house was a two-story building with five or six rooms that stood on the north side of the town. His store stood a short ways from the house.

At the beginning of the Civil War, Leetown was considered one of the leading small towns in the county. They had two general stores, one blacksmith shop, a tannery on the creek, a church and school. Plus the lodge.

In 1857, the Lee family sold half an acre of land to the Pea Ridge Masonic Lodge 119. They built a large hall there. This was one of the early lodges in the county.

Until the famed Civil War battle there, Leetown was a typical slow-going southern town. Mrs. Lee, Martha to all her friends, visited with everyone in town. The big place for a visit was at the spring where the town people came for water. On pretty days the women all gathered there to do their washing and visit.

Lee's raised a large family in their big house. But by the time of the battle they were all either married or in the army and away from home.

Most of the inhabitants of Leetown left several days before the battle there. But John and Martha stayed on to look after their store and home.

It was about 10:30 on the morning of March 7th, 1862, when Generals McCulloch and Pike arrived near Leetown, and the Union Army attacked soon after that.

Before the battle started Martha Lee brought her horse, a magnificent black animal, into the kitchen of her home. She could not think of letting this horse get hurt in the battle if she could help it.

During the battle, fire was set to all of the buildings in Leetown. The Confederate Army picked the Lee house as a hospital because it sat at an edge of the battlefield.

There is no record as to how many men were cared for in here or how long the building was used. The Lee's lived in the kitchen with the horse until a few days after the battle.

Leetown was never rebuilt after the war. When the residents came to find their homes gone, they drifted on to other farms in the area.

A few years after the war was over John Lee sold his home and farm to the Mayfield family. From then on it was known as the Mayfield place.

Sam Peel Home

Any one seeing the old Col. Samuel Peel home on the south edge of Bentonville will be reminded of the South of days gone by. In fact the house shows that many days have gone by since it was built. It is very hard to look at it today and think of it as having been the greatest showplace in northwest Arkansas at one time.

The house is actually a copy of one of the large plantation homes of the deep South, but is somewhat smaller than the one it was copied from.

Many people in Benton County think that the house was built with slave labor before the Civil War. This is due to the fact that in years gone by there was a row or two of small tenant houses behind the main house where colored laborers who worked on the farm lived.

The true fact is that Col. Samuel Peel had the house built in 1875. At that time it was well outside of Bentonville with just a country road running by. Today it is well within the city limits and Highway 71 bypass goes past its doors.

The house is built of red brick and native stone. The outside walls are 18-inches thick; the inside walls are one-foot thick. The timbers are all oversized rough sawed oak. The ceilings upstairs

The Peel house about 75 years after it was built. By this time the nice red bricks had been covered with stucco.

and down are all twelve and one-half feet high. Downstairs the floors are narrow oak; the second story features four-inch tongue and groove hard pine.

The double doors and large stained glass windows and the upstairs veranda all mark the style of the era when this house was built. Or should we say the era of the time the house was built that this one was copied from.

There are eight fireplaces in this fourteen room house. Each was built by the master craftsman, John C. Sheffield. He is said to have been the best builder of fireplaces at that time. All of the heating was done by fireplaces at first.

All of the bricks used in building this house were baked from clay dug on the farm, as was done for most farm homes at that date.

Col. Peel, who was in politics for many years, entertained most of the important people who came to Bentonville in this show house. They entered from the large veranda through huge double hardwood doors into a large vestibule with chandelier and winding black walnut staircase. To the left was the formal oak paneled parlor; on the right was the sitting room.

Continuing straight ahead, the visitor entered the dining room with counter and service windows through the partition into the serving or butler's pantry behind. Adjoining the butler's pantry in the rear of the house is the large kitchen. The upstairs rooms were all bedrooms.

There is a fine and large cellar under the house too. During the Civil War, Mrs. Peel had been hungry many times and she had asked to have a large space to store food.

A grandson said that she would have more food canned and fresh food stored in the cellar than the family and the hired help could eat all winter. Then she would give food to anyone she heard of that needed it.

The house was an answer to a lover's promise. When Samuel Peel married a girl from the deep South, he promised that some day he would build her a home like the ones she had known in the past.

At first they lived in Carrollton in Carroll County where he started his political career by being elected clerk of Carroll County in 1858 to 1860.

He entered the Confederate Army at the outbreak of the War. By the end of the war he held the rank of Colonel.

He went home to Carrollton where he found out that he was penniless. His wife and children had gone hungry many days before the war ended.

He then studied law and was admitted to the Bar in 1865. In the spring of 1867 he moved his family to Bentonville, where he opened a law office. He soon bought the land and started making plans for his home.

Although he lived until 1927, he didn't live his last days in this fine old home he had built. He moved into a smaller house in 1903. The farm was then put up for sale.

In the next seven years the house saw several would-be owners, but none of them were able to keep up their payments. In this time the house suffered much; many valuable fixtures were removed from the house.

In 1910, a cash sale was made to J. J. Jones, who three years later sold to Capt. Ammon. He had a lot of repairs and changes done to the house. One was covering the red brick with stucco.

A few years later he sold to W. L. English of Springfield, Mo., who was an Agricultural Agent for the Frisco Railroad. English and his family lived here for eight years. In 1920 he sold the farm to Lee A. Allen, the present owner.

Over the years this has also been a very profitable farm, and many were the crops grown here. At one time there was a large apple orchard, but like most of the larger apple orchards in the county the trees were taken out many years ago.

Meat Market of Early Days

Loin and round steak, 10 cents per pound; chuck steak, three pounds for 25 cents. These are the prices quoted on an 1899 hand-

Butcher Shop, 1905 - Pictured above is the interior of the D. S. Foster & Son Meat Market, about 1905, with (L to R) D. S. Foster, Charles Foster, Dot Ford and George Hutchinson, all of Bentonville. Note they gave trading stamps.

bill from D. S. Foster and Son Meat Market, Bentonville.

Mrs. Winnie Foster Senter, Bentonville, has a copy of the handbill which was distributed by her father. The old handbill also read; "On this same day we started on a cash business strictly. This does not mean one, but means all every body."

"My Dad, D. S. Foster, ran one of the early meat markets in Bentonville," said Mrs. Senter. "A meat market was a lot different in those days. All they sold was meat and bread."

Foster and H. B. Wright founded their meat market in 1896 in a building on the square which is now being used for an auto supply store.

In 1899, the meat market was moved to South Main Street, and Uncle Dave Foster, as he was called then, bought out Wright. Foster's son Charles came into the business and it was renamed Foster and Son.

The two ran the store in the same location until 1918. Then the meat market was closed and the equipment sold. In the early part of the century, butchers had to butcher their own cattle. The Fosters butchered late in the day or at night, then brought the meat to the shop and hung it on hooks on the wall in front of the market to cool.

The meat was left there until morning, then was put in the icebox.

"Three and one-half tons of ice is a lot," said Charles Foster, "But that is what we had to keep on hand at all times to fill our iceboxes. Back in those days ice was the only way we had to cool things."

Cutting meat was more difficult then, for there were no electric saws and meat grinders. It was all done by hand with a knife or handsaw. The meat grinder was turned by hand.

It kept three to four men busy cutting meat and waiting on the customers. The average week's sales were about six hogs, six beef and two mutton. Usually the Fosters paid from one and one-half to two cents a pound for the meat, live and on the foot."

The only time I know of that we lost money was the time we paid five cents a pound for our first hog. That was too high and we had to sell part of it for less than that after it was butchered." Foster said.

One handbill dated July 6, 1908, stated that free meat delivery would begin that day, twice daily. An Aug. 1st, 1908, handbill reads, "On account of the unsatisfactory results of selling meat on credit, and in order to sell for cash strictly, we have decided that on and after the first day of August we are going to reduce the prices of all meats from two to five cents per pound. And all parties who desire to purchase a coupon book we will allow a discount of 5 per cent for cash. Our delivery boy will be instructed to collect on all deliveries made."

There are copies of an old ad that carried a one-column picture and a verse to advertise the meat.

One which carried a picture of Mary and her little lamb, had this verse:

> "If Mary still has that little lamb
> She so long did keep
> We figure that little lamb ere this
> Has grown to be a sheep
> That Mary sold her lamb to us
> Need not be your fears
> The lamb and mutton purchased here
> Is all of tender years."

In pictures of the old meat market the only thing that resembles a meat market of today is a sign saying, "We Give Eagle Stamps." Even this is fast fading from our life.

The A. T. Still Park Springs Sanitarium

This sanitarium opened October 1, 1910, and is purely osteopathic. We have a modern, up-to-date institution, and one that can offer all the conveniences and necessities to be found in any well

Park Springs Hotel.

regulated sanitarium in the country.

The building is of pressed brick, modern in respect, has large verandas surrounding it; all rooms are conveniently located and well ventilated and will accommodate seventy-five patients.

The sanitarium is situated in a beautiful ten-acre park just outside of the corporate limits of the beautiful little city, thus securing that important factor in the treatment of all cases: Absolute Quiet. Throughout the park are several hundred beautiful trees and flower beds and over four thousand feet of granitoid walks.

In connection with the sanitarium are six two-room cottages and four never-failing springs, one of which is particularly efficacious in stomach and intestinal disorders, while another spring nearby contains properties of a diuretic nature.

The reason this site was selected is that the country lies from 1,200 to 1,800 feet above sea level; its winters are comparatively short and usually without excessive cold; the summers are long and delightful; the picturesque surroundings, invigorating climate, pure fresh air and the ideal water from the never failing Ozark Springs.

All the nurses employed will be graduates of the Osteopathic Hospital at Kirksville, Mo.

Dr. C. E. Still is president; Dr. G. M. Laughlin is Vice President; Dr. E. H. Laughlin, late of the Faculty of the American

School of Osteopathy at Kirksville, Mo., will be the Physician in charge; Dr. Z. T. Martin, General Superintendent.

Dr. A. T. Still, who the sanitarium was named after, was the founder of the American School of Osteopathy.

This sanitarium was another one of Bentonville's short-lived businesses.

Opera House

The old Opera House building which stood on the Northeast corner of the square in Bentonville, was taken down in 1962 to make way for the new building for the Bank of Bentonville.

The opera building, as it was called for years, was built a year or so after the bad fire of the winter of 1880-81, which burned most of the north side of the square. But there is no date as to when it was built.

The records at the courthouse show that T. M. Duckworth sold this lot to James Caldwell the 3rd of April, 1849. It was just a part of the deal in which Caldwell got several hundred acres.

In 1872, R. N. Corley sold this lot to J. D. Harston for $900.00. It would seem that there was some kind of a good building here then. A year later, J. T. and C. R. Craig bought the lot.

I have been unable to find out who had the opera house built, but in talking to Jim Craig of Bentonville in 1960 he said that he could remember his father talking about having rented it for plays or programs at the time he and Jim's grandfather owned the place.

Col. Sam Peel owned the building in the late 1880's. It changed hands many times over the years. And the value changed just as much—the sales are listed on the books all the way from $1.00 to $9,000.00. It just runs up and down a scale that way. In 1901, it was sold for back taxes for $40.16.

People in Bentonville saw all types of vaudeville and stage shows here. It is said that after the railroad came, some of the best acts in the country stopped and made a one-night show here.

Throughout the year there would be other programs. As on the night of Feb. 3rd, 1888, when there was a Band Benefit Concert by Alex Black's band, a local group with other short acts to fill in. Alex Black's cornet solo of the Lauterback Waltz and a violin solo, The Last Rose of Summer by Frank Hammell, were the highlights of the program that played to a full house.

On August 31, 1892, Richards and Pringle brought their famous minstrel show here for a one-night stand. The Famous Georgias, as it was called, was the only legitimate all-colored minstrel in the country.

The night of Jan. 2nd, 1893, was a benefit night. The program was put on by the children and parents of the colored school. They were raising money to repair the roof of the colored school.

PLACES OF INTEREST

Bentonville fire department and Black's band in front of the old opera house about 1889.

Price was 25 cents for adults and 15 cents for children, and this included a light lunch.

Another highlight in the entertainment world here at the opera house was the political speeches. If the weather was bad they would hold the rally here. The oldtimers say that these old time politicians had a lot more wind and they talked longer than a candidate does today.

In 1898, along came a new and different entertainment that was the Chautauqua era, and for a few years each summer you could hear a lecture, band music, singing, oratory, or maybe a little of each if you stayed for the whole program.

I found no one who could remember what the inside of the opera house was like at first. The building was two stories, and there were two business rooms in the front on the ground level. You went in from the front and upstairs. Some think that the inside was all balcony and it looked down at the stage that was in the back of the building just about ground level.

Sometime around 1900 the building was remodeled. The upstairs had a stage and seats; the downstairs was made into a store. At one time Jackson's grocery store was here.

In 1914, the Ozark Trails Garage moved in downstairs in

place of the store, and it stayed here until about 1921. It was run by Ed. Pace and Clyde Adams.

The Mo-Hawk Dance Club was held here upstairs every Saturday night from about 1911 to 1914. At that time there was a stairway on the outside of the east side of the building.

In 1914, the building was condemned and they stopped using the upstairs.

During World War One the Government used the upstairs as an armory. The 142nd Field Artillery was stationed here for some time. They slept upstairs and drilled in the street in front of the building.

About 1922, the building was bought by M. J. Kilburn who had it rebuilt for a movie picture house. The entrance was again moved to the front of the building. The inside had a stage downstairs, and seats down, as well as a balcony. There were two small rooms in the front that opened onto the street. These were rented for small cafes or real estate offices. The big outside balcony was taken down and a marquee put up. The building was used as a theater until a few years before it was taken down.

The last few years before the building was razed, it was used for storage only.

Only a few memories of the days of Vaudeville, Chautauquas and hometown entertainment put on by local people are left.

Chapter Twenty
Items of Interest

Who You Going To Shoot?

This story is told about Alfred Smartt, one time businessman in Maysville.

While he was running his store in Maysville, he made an Oklahoma man mad. The man was said to be a killer, and it was told around that he was going to kill Mr. Smartt.

The office in Smartt's store was built so he could see anyone who came in. One day he saw the man from Oklahoma come in. He picked up his .38 cal. Colt revolver and started to the front of the store just as the man asked, "Where's that no good so and so Smartt?"

The Oklahoma man was wearing two guns.

As Smartt walked up to the man, his hand with the gun was going up and down like a windmill plunger. The man stopped still, and just looked.

"I understand," Smartt said, his weaving motion making his gun touch the man's center with every swing, "that you are going to kill me."

"Now that ain't right," the burly gunman whined. "I just came to find out from you who the man was that started that damn lie. That's the man I'm going to kill."

From the Benton County Record and Democrat and the Benton County Sun. Thursday, November 3, 1932.

Several Rural Mail Routes To Be Extended

According to a report from Washington five rural mail routes in Benton County will be lengthened from one to three miles beginning December 1st. Two carriers from the Bentonville post office will be affected by the change and given increased compensation.

Route No. 1, which is served by Fred Phinney, carrier, will have its route lengthened from 40.4 miles to 41.9 miles, and he will receive an increase in salary from $2,280 to $2,340 yearly. Forest Brock, carrier on Route No. 5, will travel 35.77 miles instead of 34.87 miles and receive $2,160 in place of $2,130.

Luther Allen, carrier on Route 3 out of Gravette, who now travels 30.1 miles will have 2½ miles added to his route and will receive $2,070 instead of $1,980 annually.

Mail route No. 2 out of Lowell with Sam Cuppe as carrier, whose present route covers 25 and three-eighths miles will receive yearly $2,190 in place of his present salary of $1,010, owing to his route being extended to 30 miles.

Route 2 out of Rogers, for which Wn. L. Keith is carrier, will have his route extended from 27 miles to 30.3 miles and receive a salary increase from $1890 to $1980.

Death of Old Dart

We would not advocate the custom of writing obituaries to horses. But some of the noble animals seem to deserve a nice notice at their death.

If such there be, it is due the faithful horse of Dugan Heagerty, which passed over to greener pastures on the 4th of June, 1907, at the age of 25 years, 7 months.

Old Dart died literally in the harness. Mr. Heagerty had ploughed him all day and soon after he had turned him in to the lot for the night the old horse fell to his death suddenly with the colic.

Old Dart leaves a disconsolate mate, Charley, 23 years old, by whose side he worked faithfully for 20 years. The team was bequeathed to Dugan by the will of his father, who died eleven years ago, and were counted in value as one horse at that time, owing to age, and they have done noble service ever since at the old homestead for the new owner. Old Dart and Charley had made three trips to Texas and back in their day.

From Bentonville Sun June 7, 1907

High Prices In Benton County

Food prices in the Civil War were very high in Benton County. And the food for sale was almost as scarce as the money to buy it with.

In the early part of 1864, a barrel of flour cost $300.00 in Confederate money. A pair of shoes, $150.00; calico, $30.00 a yard; and coffee, $50.00 a pound.

Many people had to parch acorns and chinquapins to use in place of coffee. Salt was washed from the dirt in the floor of the old smokehouses.

One man is said to have bought a cow bell in Benton County for $60.00.

These were standard prices in Northwest Arkansas that year. No wonder people said it was a hard year, and that they couldn't afford to eat.

Likes Arkansas Apples

This letter was taken from the Benton County Sun, Jan. 15, 1912.

A. G. Boyle, Bentonville, Ark.

Dear Sir; During the Christmas holidays our Mr. Nolte forwarded to us a box of "Rome Beauty Apples" which were grown in your orchard and won first prize at the Bentonville Fruit Show.

We desire to compliment you on this splendid fruit, as it is some of the finest we have seen for a long time and the quality of it will long be remembered in this office. You may be justly proud of this fruit and we trust your reputation along this line will continue.

We wish you a prosperous New Year, and with best wishes remain.

Very truly yours,

The Sherwin-Williams Co.
F. B. Gaber, Manager.

Benton County Weather

Whenever we get a cold spell or snow then the oldtimers always say, "This isn't like it was in - - I remember." So here are a few official reports of what they could have remembered.

Nov. 16, 1880—16 below zero.

April 17, 1881—At Rogers a freeze killed the fruit crop and some trees.

February 21, 1885—26 inches of snow on the level in Bentonville.

1898—The wettest year, 71 inches of rain.

February 12, 1899—Rogers 24 below zero; 30 in some parts of the County.

February 12, 1905—Over one foot of snow and ice, then it dropped to 22 below zero at Bentonville; 19 at Rogers.

1909—a drouth year; July to Sept. 15 just 1.70 inches of rain fell. Temperature to 106.

February 22, 1912—24 inches of snow in most parts of the county.

January 12, 1918—18 below at Bentonville.

January 17, 1930—20 below at Rogers.

July 18, 1936—the hottest we found; it was 112 and stayed near there a few days.

Bentonville Had A Building Boom In 1887

Bentonville is enjoying a building boom that few towns in this country can equal. On every hand the spirit of improvement is evidenced by scores of neat cottages, interspersed with large and elegant residences, of which any city would justly feel proud. Not a street in town but has new buildings in course of construction or recently finished, and the work goes on with no prospect of a let up. But with all this it is difficult to supply the demand for homes of the vast throng of immigrants that is pouring into our "garden spot of the Ozarks."

Below we give a very incomplete list of the buildings that have been erected since January 1st, 1887, and those now in course of construction, together with the cost of same.

It listed 41 residences, 1 story, 1½ story and two-story frame homes and a few brick homes, with a cost of from $150.00 to $3,000.00. Three box houses were listed at a cost from $100.00 to $250.00 each.

In the way of business buildings was W. A. Terry, 2 story frame hotel, $2,000.00; Dr. J. M. Thompson, two brick offices, $800.00; Dunn & Henry, frame office, $250.00; Dr. W. R. Davis, 2 story brick business house, $3,000.00; James Haney, 2 story brick business house, $3,500.00; Dr. Davis, frame business house, $400.00; F. C. Hawkins, frame office and implement house, $500.00.

The Peoples Banking Co. is erecting on southwest corner of public square a two story brick which it is said will be the finest business house in Benton County. In the same block, I. B. Gilmore will build two 2-story bricks, and Davis & Haney one 2-story brick each to join these on the west, filling up the entire block. We understand these buildings will all be finished before cold weather sets in.

In addition to the above, there have been many small houses built—neat, comfortable ones, too, besides barns, outhouses and various other improvements that go to prove the thrift and enterprise of our town; to mention all of which would require too much space. These are enough, however, to give the outside world some idea of what is being done here.

Verily our town is booming.

1836 Territory Map

It would be hard to prove from the early maps of Arkansas just when any of the towns were started. The territory map of Arkansas by Augustus Mitchell, 1836, shows Washington County as fifty miles square taking in all of what today is Washington, Benton, and Madison counties and a part of Carroll County. The only towns shown were Fayetteville, Canehill and Vineyard. All were in what is Washington County today.

Tanner's Universal Atlas map of Arkansas, 1836, showed the three counties, but not with the same boundaries as today. Here, too, the only towns were Fayetteville, Canehill and Vineyard.

The first time there was a town listed in Benton County was 1842 on The Jeremish Greenleaf map of Arkansas. He listed Bentonville.

In 1855, Joseph Hutchins Colton's map of Arkansas was the first to show very many towns in Northwest Arkansas. For Benton County he listed Bentonville, Maysville, Osage Mill, Robinson, and Double Springs.

There were very few roads shown on this map, but it did show enough roads to get you across the county without getting lost.

Bill of Sale for Horses and Wagon

This bill of sale was from the papers of Dr. William G. Ball, who lived near the spring where Spavinaw creek heads. He was a minister for the Christ Union Church and a Doctor. He moved here in the early 1870's.

The copy was made as it was written. The few misspelled words were the way many oldtimers used them.

Bill of Sale

This agreement made this twenty-fifth of June one thousand eight hundred and seventy seven (1877) between Simpson C. Ball of Mongomery Co. Arkansas of the first part and William G. Ball of Benton Co. and state of Arkansas of the second part.

Witnets that said Simpson C. Ball hereby agress to sell to the said William G. Ball one bay mare known as Suse, one Gray horse fore yeurs old, one black yearlin colt and one waggon fore the sum of Two Hundred and Sixtyfive Dollars (265 $) in hand paid and I covenant fore my self my heirs executors and adminestrators with the said William G. Ball to warrent and defind the sale of said horses and waggon unto the said William G. Ball his executors administrators and asigns against all and every persons lawfully claiming one to claim same Whomesoever.

In witnefs whereof I have hereunto set my hand and seal this Twentyfifth day of June one Thousand and eight hundred and seventy seven.

Simpson C. Ball

This mixture to use for the Ague was also in the Dr. Ball papers.

Elix of Vitriol	1½ oz.
Elix of Lavender	1½ oz.

To one pint of water. Dose wine glass full three times a day for Ague.

Benton County Had Many Firsts

Benton County is not the largest or oldest county in the state, but over the years we have been first in many ways. Here is a list of ways in which we were first in 1905.

More Masonic lodges, 19. More Odd Fellows lodges, 17, and more members, over 600. More Sunday schools, 145, and more members, over 9,000. More members of the Baptist, Methodist, and Congregational churches.

More weekly newspapers, 11. More banks, 12, and more starting up. More rural free delivery routes, 31. Largest distillery in state. Largest evaporator in state. Largest vinegar factory in state. Shipped most lime in one year.

For several years had largest number of white children enrolled in its county schools.

In 1900, cast heaviest democratic vote of any county in state and gave the largest democratic majority.

Heard more addresses (18) in 1905 by Governor Jeff Davis than any other county in the state.

The Sun Supplement Aug. 5, 1893

Harman's "Dish-Washer" a Success

Rogers Democrat

On yesterday, after enjoying a sumptuous dinner, we had the pleasure of witnessing Mr. S. W. Harman's Dish-Washer put to a practical test. To say that it met the test satisfactorily would be placing it none too strongly. Thirty pieces, besides knives and forks, were placed in the machine and in just two minutes by our best watch they were taken out nice and clean. They were inspected by the entire company, consisting of several ladies and gentlemen, and all pronounced it a decided success. Our best two thirds was there and she was so well pleased that she gave us a piece of her mind, which being interpreted, means that she had us place an order for one of the machines before leaving the room. This machine is calculated to revolutionize the monotony of culinary work. The machine is also very handy as a sprayer and has many good points which want of time and space compels us to omit. The ladies, God bless them, should thank Mr. Harman for this labor saving machine. The patent for this valuable invention is owned by our citizens Messrs. S. W. Harman and W. A. Mundell.

ITEMS OF INTEREST

Taken from True Tales from the Hills, by Nolen Bulloch in the Benton County Democrat May 23, 1936.

Jeff Davis against Senator Berry

For twenty-two years James H. Berry served Arkansas in the United States Senate. Then announced Governor Jeff Davis for the place.

Gov. Davis was on his way to Bentonville to make a campaign speech. Word reached the hills that the governor was accompanied by a bodyguard.

A group of native sons was discussing this. Jeff Davis had injected a new color into the graceful art of running for the high office in the state.

"Well we got to do something," a Berry supporter exclaimed.

"And that we will," one of the group spoke up. He spoke with a quiet authority. He was Alfred Smartt, son-in-law of Senator Berry.

The day before Jeff Davis was to speak, Smartt called a group of friends. He outlined his plan.

The afternoon of the speaking, Smartt led his group onto the platform. The Davis party had not arrived. Shortly afterwards Davis arrived, surrounded by his bodyguard.

Smartt arose from his chair, walked over to Davis.

"Governor," he said quietly. "You can say anything you like, all you want about your platform, but if you mention Senator Berry by name, I'll shoot hell out of you."

He turned to the bodyguard.

"And you men are going to sit through the speech with your hands on your knees. Just like my men are doing."

Members of the Davis party twisted their heads to look at Smartt's men.

They were sitting quietly, their hands on their knees. But each was holding a revolver in his right hand.

Gov. Davis, the papers of the day recalled without comment, made an unusually dignified and serious campaign address at Bentonville.

Congress 1886

From the Washington letter of April 17, 1886, of the Rogers New Era, one learns that the problems of that day facing Congress were not too different from those of the present day.

The defeat of a bill by Senator Logan to increase the strength of the army was largely due to the argument that the military forces of this country would be used to aid capital in its struggles with labor. Every Democratic Senator opposed the bill.

Bills just passed included one to give pensions to the survivors of the Mexican War, and another to provide for the erection of a Congressional Library building.

It was urged that voters contact their Congressman to insist upon opening of the Indian lands in the Territory of Oklahoma to settlement.

The Gould railroad system was in violent argument with the Knights of Labor and a strike was threatened. Blood was said to have been shed in fights at Little Rock, Fort Worth and East St. Louis.

A small army of men and women were busy in Washington mailing out the annual Congressional seed allotments. Each got 6,000 packages of vegetable seeds; 500 of flower seed; 300 packages of tobacco seed; 20 of seed corn; 50 of grass seed; 28 quarts of sugar beet seed.

Pioneer Homes

When a new family moved into the county in the early days they either stayed with a nearby family or camped in their covered wagon by some good spring until they could get their own home built.

As soon as they located the land they wanted and picked the spot for their house, men would come from far and near to help them build. This was called a house raising, and they also had barn raising.

Axes were used in cutting and preparing logs, froes to rive the clapboards, augers to bore holes for the pins and to prepare wooden hinges for the doors were the only tools needed.

If help was plentiful, the logs would be hewed, otherwise they were put up round. Ridge poles would be placed in order, the clapboards placed thereon and weighted down with poles; and the cabin would be covered. A big fireplace cribbed with logs and lined with stone and mud was put at one end of the house. It was topped out with a stick and mud chimney. Floor and doors would be made of puncheons and the door hung with wooden hinges. Bedsteads were made of small poles in the corners of the building. The boards for the roof were six or eight inches wide, two or three feet long. Some had earthen floors and some were of puncheon.

Pioneer Mill

A large tree was felled, leaving a tall stump with level surface. A fire was started in the center of the top and the outer portion or rim kept wet to prevent its burning. The hole would be of a depth for a good bowl; the fire was taken out and the bowl cleaned of charred wood in order to be clean and hold a quantity of corn. Then a pole with one end hinged to a forked post was set near the stump and extended horizontally over the stump. A maul was suspended to the pole over the bowl of the stump, completing the early settler's gristmill.

The corn would be placed in the bowl and one or two persons would take hold of the loose end of the pole or "sweep" and move it up and down to pound the corn into meal. Bread or hoe cakes baked in the hearth of the fireplace, together with wild fruits, greens, and wild meat which was plentiful, and perhaps a little coffee and sugar was the pioneer's diet until he could plant a crop and garden.

Turkey For Dinner

It was the day before Christmas so Mr. Bob Rucker told his wife that he would go out and kill a wild turkey for Christmas dinner. The year was 1881; Bob was hunting with a cap and ball rifle. He had walked all day and it was just about night and he still had no turkey. But all at once he saw one not too far off. He took very careful aim and shot. Down went Mr. Tom Turkey.

Bob sure felt happy as he walked over to the turkey. He was thinking how good it would taste. But just as he got close, that turkey jumped up and ran. Bob looked at his dinner running off; then down at the ground to see what had happened. There, not far from where the turkey fell, was a ball of feathers, so Bob picked them up. His rifle ball had hit the end of the turkey's chest bone and took off some feathers and a little meat.

He took this home to show his wife how close he had come to getting the turkey. She cooked the little bit of meat and they ate it on Christmas day along with a ham she had cooked that night.

The next year Bob tried his luck again. This time he did better, for he shot his turkey within an hour or so and took it home.

His wife was in the kitchen cleaning the fowl when she discovered a large scar on its chest. Also, just a small part of the bone was missing. She called her husband in to see the turkey. Then he knew that this year he would eat the turkey he had sampled the year before.

To Break An Egg

One warm summer day in 1906 Bill walked into Tanner's Grocery store. He was a bit drunk, as was Mr. Tanner. They talked for a little. And Bill kept looking at the big wooden tub that the eggs were in. Bill said he would bet a dollar that he could jump in the tub without breaking an egg. Mr. Tanner took him up on it.

So in jumped Bill. He turned around in the broken eggs and

gave Mr. Tanner a dollar. Then stepped out and walked out of the store dripping egg all over the place. Outside, he told the men that it sure was worth the dollar just to see the look on Mr. Tanner's face.

A Nickel's Worth of Cheese

One afternoon back about 1888 a salesman, or drummer as they were called then, was calling at the general store run by Mr. George Bates in Bentonville.

He had all his samples laid out on the counter and was giving George a real sales talk. George, who was just a little drunker than usual, was having a time with the samples. When in came a man who wanted a nickel's worth of cheese and crackers.

George got the crackers without any help. But he couldn't get the cheese to stay still to be cut. So he reached down under the counter and got out a .44 Colt. He would just shoot off a piece of cheese. So he waved the gun around his head a few times and then shot. He missed the cheese and shot a hole through the wall.

As he looked around to see why he had missed the cheese, he also looked to see what the drummer was doing. He was gone. As George was getting ready to shoot, he had grabbed up what samples he could and made.a run for the door. He hastily threw his samples into the buggy and took off.

This had been his first call on Mr. Bates and it also was his last.

What Market Best

Sometimes the market at home is best, even if it is the lowest. To prove this, we have the story of Mrs. Rucker's carload of peaches.

That was back in 1880. The peach crop in Benton County was very good that year. But the price here was way under the New York price.

So Mrs. Rucker made up her mind to ship a carload of fancy packed peaches to New York City. This way she could get in on this high market.

The cost ran very high. The peaches had to be packed by hand, boxes had to be bought, the car loaded; then the freight to be paid. When they got to the city she had to pay a broker to sell them.

Her profit on all this? There wasn't any. It cost $168.16 more for all this than the peaches brought.

Mrs. Rucker sold the rest of the crop in Bentonville and made more money clear. Even the culls made more. But then Mrs. Rucker was able to say she had sold a carload of peaches in New York City.

ITEMS OF INTEREST

Rogers Hub and Spoke Factory

Early in 1900, work was started on the Rogers Hub and Spoke factory. By late that year it was in full operation.

William Burke was made manager and Dan Cahill, foreman. Clint Deason and Cal Van Winkle were among the first employees.

Because of the difficulty in securing materials in sufficient quantity to run the plant full-time, a portion of the machinery was moved to Fayetteville in the spring of 1901.

Then, because of a water shortage in Fayetteville, the machinery was again installed in the Rogers plant. When a report was made public around the first of 1902, the plant was working 20 men, had a payroll of $250.00 a week, and had manufactured 80,000 wagon spokes and 350,000 buggy spokes.

Lack of material was again responsible in a year or so for the removal of the machinery to Fayetteville and other points. When the factory was located in Rogers it was with expectation that a railroad would be built east from Rogers into the hardwood territory.

Trott's Tavern: Beginning of Brightwater

Some time in 1840, Enoch Trott built a tavern and wagonyard on the road that later became the wire road. This was a good stop for the few travelers on this early road.

He also had a line of groceries, but the leading staple in that line at that time was in a liquid form.

At the outbreak of the Civil War it was owned and operated by Judge Long and it is said that most of the buildings, along with the tavern, were burned during or just after the battle of Pea Ridge.

After the war, the land was bought by Albert Peel, who erected a store and home here. Soon others followed and it became a flourishing little village until the Frisco located Avoca a few miles south. Peel and others moved their stores to the new town.

Early in the 1900's the postoffice department officially changed the name to Bestwater. But the people never took to the new name. So, when a rural route went in, Bestwater was forgotten.

Pea Ridge Lodge No. 119 F&A.M. was long located at Brightwater and was one of the first in this section.

Brightwater came to an end the night of April 29, 1947, when almost all of the remaining buildings were destroyed in a cyclone that also killed nine people.

Bentonville Grade and High School

The following outline of courses was taken from an ad for the Bentonville Grade and High School in 1889. The school had three terms of 12 weeks each. Grade school tuition was $6.00 per term; and high school $9.00 per term.

Grade School

1st year, Chart and first Reader, Reading and writing Numbers to 1000, Combination to 10.

2nd year, Second Reader, Local Geography, Felter's Primary Arithmetic to page 95, Language.

3rd year, Third Reader Geography of North America and U. S., Felter's Primary Arithmetic finished, Language.

4th year, Fourth Reader, Geography of S. A. and Review of U. S., Grammer, Ray's Arithmetic, 3rd part to Fractions.

5th. Fifth Reader, Ray's Arithmetic finished, Geography of Europe and Asia with General Review, Grammar.

High School

1st year, Algebra, Latin, U. S. History, English, Elocution, Botany, Bookkeeping, Stenography, Higher Arithmetic, Zoology.

2nd year, Geometry, Latin Rhetoric, Physiology, Bookkeeping, Stenography, General History.

3rd year, Trigonometry, Surveying, Latin, Physics, Astronomy, Geology, English, Literature, Chemistry, Civil Government.

County Home For The Poor First Operated Under Contract

One of the pet peeves of the editor of the Rogers Democrat in his early years in Arkansas was calling the State Hospital the "Insane Asylum," and the Benton County Home the "Poor Farm." These were official titles at the time.

By a special act of the 1907 session of the general assembly the name was changed to the "Benton County Home." The last home we had in the county was first occupied in November, 1905. The inmates were cared for by contract at so much per day. In the fall of 1906, W. R. Ford was awarded the contract at 30 cents a day, which included board, clothing and medical treatment.

That was not the lowest bid, which was 15 cents a day. A year or two later, Benton County abandoned the contract system and elected a superintendent for the county home, paying him a salary. It cost the county more money, but the inmates of the home were not at the mercy of a contractor, and the home was under the direction of the County Judge.

It was along about this time that the insane asylum officially became the Arkansas State Hospital.

ITEMS OF INTEREST

Teacher's Grade Certificate

It is hereby certified that E. H. Dickson has this day been examined in the branches required to be taught in the Public Schools of this State, and having furnished evidence of good moral character and ability to govern, is entitled to a First Grade Certificate for the Counties of Benton, Washington, Crawford, Sebastian and Scott.

This certificate shall be valid for two years unless sooner revoked.

Dated at Bentonville, the 11th day of August, 1871.

Signed E. E. Henderson
Circuit Supt., Fifth District

Teacher's Oath

I, E. H. Dickson, do solemnly swear (or Affirm) that I will honestly and faithfully support the Constitution and Laws of the State of Arkansas, and that I will encourage other persons so to do; that I will never countenance or aid in the secession of this State from the United States; that I will endeavor to inculcate in the minds of youth sentiments of patriotism and loyalty, and will fully, faithfully and impartially perform the duties of the office of Teacher according to the best of my ability, so help me God.

Sworn and subscribed to before me this 30th. day July, 1872.

H. A. Pierce, Circuit Superintendent, 5th Judicial Dist.

Claim Jumping In Benton County

In the Spring of 1936, J. Vince Lee was plowing up a patch of new land to put in a strawberry bed on his farm near Pea Ridge.

He found a bottle that appeared to be covered with a mixture of tar and beeswax. When it was opened, he found a note written on the blank portion of the last page of the Book of the Apocrypha, torn from an old Bible. It had been written with a quill pen and homemade ink.

It was hard to read the note, but the following is the text of it.

"To the one that finds this, my name is John Calayhand, was borned in Nashville in 1811. Came here in 1851. Was drove from my house by some men, by the name of Redick, and Burks and Lasaters. There is lots of game here. I have killed one elk, one panther and 15 deers in one year. If I have to go from here I will come again. I am ordered away in 10 days. Clame that this is Burkes clame. I will leave this so it will be found. Yours, John Calayhand."

Mr. Lee's grandfather was an early comer to Northwest Arkansas, as were the three men named in this note. And so he knew about them, but not this act.

This letter is from the Benton County Democrat, Jan. 8, 1887.

Sulphur Springs, Ark.
Jan. 4th, 1887

Dear Editor:
One of the most remarkable cures of total blindness that was ever effected at any place or by any agency whatever occurred here recently. Mr. Arch Click, a farmer who lives near the springs, dreamed that he gathered up the sediment that settles from the White Sulphur Springs of this place and bound it on the eyes of a little blind girl that lives at his home. It was a part of his dream which he says was most real and made a lasting impression that the child speedily recovered from her affliction and was soon able to read, a pleasure she had not enjoyed for five years.

Mr. Click related his dream to his wife and a number of others, all of them thought it a singular dream but attached no special importance to it. Mr. Click is not a believer in dreams in general but was so impressed with this one that he resolved to test the experiment.

A few days ago he came over to the springs, collected the sediment, and returning home bound it to the little girl's eyes. From the very first a decided improvement began. All inflamation and pain disappeared from the first application. The process was kept up for a few days when, lo and behold, the little blind girl opened her eyes and did see.

Gradually her sight has grown stronger and now, for the first time in five years, she is able to read from a book. Mr. Click is a prosperous Benton County farmer and lives on his farm about one mile north west of the Springs. This is the daughter of Mr. Elvin Mattison, a widower, and was raised in this county. She is here to be seen or consulted by the incredulous. This is given for the benefit of those suffering in like manner and is the truth, the whole truth, and nothing but the truth, as any of the citizens here will attest. No little excitement has grown out of this most wonderful cure and others will try the experiment. Many and great have been the cures effected here of different diseases, but none, we dare say, has created more intense interest.

(An editor's note following the letter says, "The above comes to us authenticated by two gentlemen of high standing. It is worthy of consideration by those similarly affected.")

Benton County's First Circus

It was a new town and a new entertainment when the first circus came into Benton County and played in Rogers. That was the fall of 1881.

ITEMS OF INTEREST

The Rogers Champion, the newspaper of that day, devoted a large share of its space for that edition to the circus advertisement.

A circus was a novel experience for most of the hill people, and spectators began arriving in town on the day before the show, camping in wagon yards or sleeping in their wagons to be sure to be on hand when the big show arrived.

Most of the crowd remained until the last tent stake had been pulled and the circus again loaded aboard its special train, before starting for home. Some of the spectators were disappointed because the show did not include everything depicted on the gaudy posters.

One newspaper later recalled that drunks were so numerous that the town's calaboose soon was filled to capacity. And two boxcars were borrowed from the Frisco railroad to serve as temporary jails.

It's hard to say just why, but there was a record crowd for the Haggenback and Wallace Circus on October 11, 1916. At the time it was the largest crowd to ever be in Rogers.

The people came early to see the afternoon performance. But due to track trouble in Missouri, the circus was real late. So there was no afternoon performance.

This big crowd just milled around town all day and ate everything that was eatable. One local vendor of popcorn took in over $100. Food was rushed here from Bentonville, Springdale and nearby farms, but it seemed no one was willing to go home without seeing the big show.

The night attendance was estimated at over 10,000 and it required scores of special police to keep the crowd back so tents could be raised.

The showgrounds were between Oak and Pine street and between Sixth and the present Highway 71, east of the cemetery. Thousands of people watched the unloading, saw the performances, and remained to see the circus reload. For once they really got the worth of their money and for many years October 11, 1916, was the big circus day and was talked over many times.

Fox Hunters

The Northwest Arkansas Fox Hunters Association is the oldest fox hunting association west of the Mississippi River. It was formed in Bentonville at the fall term of court, 1893.

The fox hunts in Northwest Arkansas go back long before the starting of the association. At first, they were called camp hunts, when a group of farmers would get together and hunt for a week. They went in their wagons or horseback and cooked their food over an open fire. One of the oldest pictures of a hunt to be found today is the one made in 1891 at Hearter Springs near

Part of the hunters who attended the meet in 1893.

Gravette. And how many camp hunts there were before this no one knows.

The association was started at the fall term of court in the old Courthouse at Bentonville, 1893. It seems that in the spring of that year Bill Young, who was running for Circuit Clerk, said that if he was elected he would buy a good set of hounds and let the boys hunt with them. He was elected and so he sent off to Tennessee and bought the best set of hounds he could. That October the group met at the Courthouse and Bill, who was also a lawyer, drew up the bylaws for the association.

But due to business, Bill was unable to attend this first meet. It was held that October at McNelly Springs near Bentonville. A few who did attend were Milt and Arthur Henderson, Taylor Stone, Joe Ford, Marshall Morrison, John Scott, and Bailey Jones. The sons and grandsons of most of these men are in the association today.

Many of the hounds in the races today are descendants of the hounds that Bill Young bought.

Bentonville Weather Bureau

Some time in the spring of 1906, Bentonville became the smallest town in the United States to have a First Order Weather Bureau.

The weather bureau was obtained for Northwest Arkansas by the Horticultural Society and Sen. James Berry of Bentonville.

Bentonville Weather Bureau as it looked in 1906.

At the time it was brought here, the bureau was badly needed because of the apple and fruit industry. At that time, Benton County was the leading apple growing county in the United States.

Very little history of the bureau has been kept by anyone. The newspaper didn't even carry a story about the bureau at the time it was opened. The building was a two-story brick with a full basement.

Capt. Orin Parker was the first person in charge of the bureau.

The Captain is said to have had a very good sense of humor, and that was proven by a report of the Horticultural Society, meeting on May 10th, 1906, at which time he was introduced to the members of the society.

The strawberry grower called on Captain Parker for better weather, as it was nearing time for the berries to bloom.

"My plans are to use up all of the cold wet weather I have before the berries start to bloom," he answered them, "Then I will give you the very best weather that I have in stock."

The report went on to say that most of the members tried to tell Parker what kind of weather they wanted, and this left him very uncertain as to what weather they really needed.

Captain Parker had a very interesting life. He joined the Union Army as a boy in the last year of the Civil War. He served as a powder monkey. When the war ended he reenlisted and within a short time was transferred to the Army Weather Bureau. From there he went on to the U. S. Weather Bureau.

He came to Bentonville in 1906 from Dubuque, Iowa. On Aug. 20, 1920, he retired as head of the Bureau. Mrs. Parker was appointed to take his place and he served as her assistant until Jan., 1928, at which time they both retired.

At the time of his death in 1929, Capt. Parker held the record as having been in the Weather Bureau longer than any other man, and being the oldest man in the service. He was 84-years-old and had served 63 years with the Weather Bureau. He had never lost a day's work due to sickness in all that time.

When the Parkers retired, Mrs. J. T. Gibson was appointed to their job. She had worked under the Parkers for many years. It is not known for sure when Mrs. Gibson left the Weather Bureau, but in 1942 when the office was closed, Verda Neeley was running the Bureau.

It opened as a First Class Weather Bureau in a special building that stood where the post office does today. There were rooms for the weather equipment, offices and living quarters for the Parkers. There was also several rooms that were used by a fruit specialist, who worked under the Department of Agriculture.

As a first class office, they put out a full weather report and forecast each morning and reported any storms moving in later in the day. Anyone could telephone any time of the day to get the latest report. The weather report was also given out to all of the newspapers in the area.

Among special services of the office was sending out cards to every box holder each day with the weather forecast, cards to the fruit farmers telling them to spray and what for. Large cards were put in stores and other places around town with the forecast.

The Bureau did such a good job without the radio, it was easy for people to find out what the forecast was.

After Capt. Parker and his wife retired, the office was changed to a cooperative Bureau. Under that set-up, readings were taken early in the morning from all of the instruments. These readings were telegraphed to New Orleans.

There the weather specialist using the readings made up the forecast and sent it back in time for the office help to print up the cards and mail them out.

Some time in the summer of 1934, the lot that the station was built on was sold so they could build a post office building. The Weather Bureau building was taken down.

The station was moved then to a room in the County Courthouse until the post office building was done in 1935. There is a special room in the upstairs in the post office that was built for the Weather Bureau. They moved right in when the new post office opened.

Some time in the spring of 1942, the equipment from the Bentonville Weather Bureau was moved to an Army Air Field. That ended Bentonville's record of being the smallest town to have a Weather Bureau.

At the time Sen. Berry was working so hard to obtain the Weather Bureau for Northwest Ark., it was badly needed. It will never be known how many thousands of dollars worth of fruit was saved in Northwest Ark. because of this station.

It is a shame that the history of the Weather Bureau was not kept better so we could know all of the people who worked there over the years and the amount of good that they did.

Even the Weather Bureau at Little Rock has no records of the station here. They have said that we didn't have a Weather Bureau building. But we do have several pictures left to prove this.

Though most of the fruit has been gone from Northwest Arkansas for many years, we still have a need for the Weather Bureau. A true weather forecast is just as badly needed by the farmers today as it was by the fruit growers 60 years ago. And I'll bet they did a better job then with less equipment than the bureaus do today.

The Big Snow of 1912

History of the county shows several 18-inch snows over the years of record keeping. But the 24-inch snow of Feb. 22, 1912, was the biggest one ever recorded in the county.

It was one of those storms that moved in out of the west. It started snowing early in the day in Oklahoma. By noon, it was snowing hard in Bentonville.

The Grove to Bentonville train that was due in Bentonville at 4:30 in the afternoon didn't make it until 12:30 the next morning. Then it had to go on to Rogers to meet a southbound Frisco with the mail.

The train had got hung up in an eight-foot snow drift a few miles east of Grove and had to be dug out by hand. Then it had a hard time pushing its way through the drifts all the way in. But the train on the main line of the Frisco was so late that they met at Rogers.

On the return trip to Bentonville, the Grove to Bentonville train got stuck in a deep drift at the ice plant and they just let it set for a day.

The next morning, several drummers staying at the Massie Hotel called for a taxi, that was run by Fred Cunningham. He told them that they could just plan to spend the day and maybe

Snow bound train near Grove Oklahoma. Feb. 22, 1912.

two of them here for he couldn't get to his barn. The taxi was a team and buggy.

A few people walked downtown that day, but there was very little going on. It snowed off and on for two days. By then, there was two feet on the level and drifts up to ten feet all over town and the county.

The Grove train didn't run for three days. And several of the trains on the Frisco main line didn't get through either. Many of them had to be dug out of drifts in the cuts along the line.

It was ten days before the snow all left the ground and then there was so much water around that it was hard to get anywhere for that many more days.

In that day, people didn't have to get out too much in the bad weather as they kept enough food and wood on hand to take care of a bad storm.

One bit of good came from this storm, many men were hired to shovel snow from the train tracks and other places in the county.

Benton County Fair

The first Benton County fair was held in Rogers in October of 1888. Like most happenings of that time, they put a big name on it. Calling it The Benton County Horticultural Agricultural and Mechanical Fair.

Officers at the time were Joshua Huffman, president; W. R. Felker, treasurer; W. J. Todd, secretary. Directors were W. A. Miller, Charles Warbritten, J. A. C. Blackburn, J. S. Miser, J. W. Scroggs, and G. F. Kennan.

The grounds were south of Oak Street and east of First Street. Little is known of this first fair, but it was said that they had a good crowd every day. The main program that day was horse races and many people came for them.

The fair was held each year for the next eight years, but for the most part it lost money. In 1896, one of the attractions was a $5 prize for the most graceful lady bicycle rider. First honors went to Anna Blake; second, Jessie Morgan; third, Grace Adams. Other entrants were Anna Stroud, Betty Blake, Eva Blackburn, Grace Adams and Edna Wunder.

Bicycle races were a regular feature of the early fairs.

After this fair, the association was so badly in debt that they sold the land and buildings to pay off the mortgages.

By September of 1903, a new group of Rogers businessmen had bought back the old fairgrounds and put up new buildings and had a fair that month. Gov. Jeff Davis was the guest speaker the opening day, and it rained all day.

Racing was the highlight of the fair, and much local interest was placed in the trotting races and centered on the county trot, in which all the horses were local and driven by their owners.

Gail McMahon, driven by Dr. A. M. Buckley, won first place in 2:56. The papers each year carried more on the races than other programs. In 1906, the silver cup for trotters was won by Senator Boy, 14 years-old, in 1:18. He was owned by Miss Adlyn Morris.

When the bills were all in for the 1906 fair, the stockholders found they had lost $700, making them over $5,000 in the red. So, the Rogers fair came to an end and the land and buildings were sold.

Harmonial Vegetarian Society

The Harmonial Vegetarian Society came to the northwest part of Benton County in the spring of 1859. They have been referred to as a communist group and as a religious colony, but neither is known for a fact.

The Society was incorporated and the members bought 520 acres of land east of Maysville. Their plans were to build their own town and grow whatever they needed. They didn't want to mix with other people.

Before the first year was passed, they had built a three-story building with 90 rooms that was their home and hospital. They also had built a large bath house, machine shop, blacksmith shop, print shop, sawmill, gristmill, and a general store.

A big spring house was built at the spring and the water was piped to the different buildings. Each of the 90 rooms in the big house had running water. This was undoubtedly the first house in the county with running water.

Most of the land was put into cultivation. They kept only milk cows and work horses. The society made good farmers and they were noted for always having the best and biggest crops.

For about a year they printed a paper named "The Theocrat." It was used to advocate the theory of living as the society did.

They held all things in common. When anyone joined the society, they turned all that they had over to the society for the common use of everyone.

Married couples were required to renounce their marriage vows and contracts. Then they could go on living with their mate or pick a mate by lot. It was understood that children born of members were to be considered the off-springs of the society.

They lived on a purely vegetable diet, with milk or water to drink. They had very little to do with the outside world, and lived to themselves and their social ways.

They did, however, carry on a commercial trade with others. The mill was kept busy most of the time doing work for the out-side world, for cash. They did do some for trade in things they needed or could sell.

They ground a lot of grain for the Confederates in the first part of the War. The Confederate Camp Walker was very close to them.

The men all dressed in the attire of quakers and the women wore bloomers, of the bloomer girl type.

The buildings were all burned near the end of the Civil War. The society then sold the land and left.

As far as is known, this was the only group like this ever to settle in Northwest Arkansas.

The Shooting Of Deputy U. S. Marshal Maples

This short article is taken from the May 14, 1887, Benton County Democrat, and is just as they ran it.

Death of Dan Maples—An account of the killing of Deputy U. S. Marshal Maples was published last week, but no particulars were given. We learn from Geo. H. Jefferson, the only eye witness, the following particulars.

Mr. Maples and his posse, consisting of J. M. Peel, G. H. Jefferson and M's brother and son Sammuel, had encamped near Tahlequah, at a spring west of town. Messrs. Maples and Jefferson were returning to their camp from the town, and just as they started to cross a ravine on a foot-log, they discovered a man on the opposite side behind a tree, with a pistol pointed at them.

Jefferson says, "Don't shoot here." Dan laughingly said, "He won't shoot." Just then the assassin fired, and Maples fell, shot through the right breast. He drew his pistol, however, and fired four shots at random. Jefferson drew his pistol and commenced work, firing six shots in rapid succession. The assassin fired eleven shots at Jefferson, and then ran. Mr. Maples was conscious for only 20 minutes. He said as he fell, "George, I am killed." He sent his son home with a message for his mother saying, "Tell her I am willing to die."

His remains were brought in a hack to Bentonville, arriving here at 2 p.m. Friday. His funeral took place immediately after at the M. E. Church South, of which he was a member. Rev. T. J. Reynolds preached a touching and appropriate discourse, then the remains were taken in charge by the Masonic brethren and buried in the Odd Fellow's cemetery. A committee of the Tahlequah lodge escorted the remains to this place and were in the procession.

Mr. Maples had many friends, and was an energetic officer, unacquainted with fear. He distinguished himself for bravery in the Confederate army, and died while attempting to enforce the laws of the Government.

Sat. May 21, 1887—$500 Reward—By virtue of authority given me by the department of justice, I will pay the following reward. Five Hundred dollars for the arrest and conviction of the murderer of Deputy Marshal Dan Maples on the 4th day of May

1887, in the Indian Territory, Western District of Arkansas.

John Carroll, U. S. Marshal, Western Dist. Ark.

The man who killed Maples was later killed in a shootout with the law in the Indian Territory.

Benton County Jail House Fire

Tragedy hit the Benton County Jailhouse in the early morning hours of March 4th, 1905. At this time, it was seen that the jailhouse was on fire, a fire which took the lives of two inmates, Dar Reaves and Henry Crow, who were burned to death in their cells.

The Benton County Jail at the time was behind the Old Courthouse. The lot where it stood is now a parking lot.

It was a one-story brick structure with steel cells surrounded by a steel runway. There was no room for the jailer, Henry Williams, or the Sheriff, Taylor T. Blake, so they were not on hand to open up the jail, or turn in a fire alarm.

Reaves and Crow occupied a cell together, while four other inmates were shackeled in pairs and occupied cots in the corridor.

There is no doubt but that the fire was started by matches, used by either Reaves or Crow to light pipes or cigarettes. Their bedding caught fire and Crow, in his terror, clung to Reaves so desperately that the latter was unable to extinguish the flames. Neither was burned seriously enough to cause death, but smoke and flames were inhaled and both were quickly overcome.

It took some time for word to reach the jailer of the fire. By the time he got there, some people had broken out the windows and the firemen threw a stream of water in the cell. This saved the four men in the Corridor, but was too late to save Reaves and Crow.

Reaves, who was serving a sentence for petit larceny, was to have been released the following Saturday. He lived at Siloam Springs, and left a wife and four children.

Crow had first been arrested on a charge of insanity. He improved so much with a short stay in the jail, that the County Judge gave him 50 cents and sent him home. But he invested the money in files, which he gave to the prisoners in jail. For this he was back in jail and setting out a $100.00 fine.

For several years after the fire, a temporary jail was used. In 1911, a new and modern jail was built.

Some Firsts in Benton County Churches

Probably the first organized church in Benton County was the Cumberland Presbyterian, located two miles east of Bentonville and called Woods Church. This was in 1830.

The second, also Cumberland Presbyterian, was organized

Little Flock Primitive Baptist Church. This church was organized in April, 1843.

near Pea Ridge; and shortly afterwards, another was organized at Maysville. The Reverends Andrew and John Buchanan were among the early pastors in these churches.

The beginning of Methodism in the county was in 1831 in the home of Walter Thornsberry at Wager Mills. He organized the first Methodist church with seven members. Just after this he held a revival and organized a church at the present site of Bentonville.

In 1844-45, when the separation of the churches took place because of the slavery issue, nearly all the members transferred to the Methodist Church South, leaving the original church without an organization.

The first Baptist society in the county was known as "Twelve Corners." It was organized in 1842 in the log home of William Reddick, that was later to be called Elk Horn Tavern.

It was organized by Elders J. F. Mitchell and Charles B. Whiteley.

Whiteley, a year before his death, announced that if he lived to be 50 he would preach his own funeral sermon. Shortly before his death, he delivered the sermon. After his "Death Sermon," he gave a public dinner.

215

The Methodist Church South, after its organization in 1844-45, grew rapidly in Benton County. Many churches of this denomination sprang up in the county after that date.

The first organization of the Christian Church was on Spavinaw Creek in 1840.

An Elder Goodnight was the founder. In May, 1887, Elder Larkin Scott took into the church fellowship the celebrated "Uncle Dick Bennett," who at 109 years old decided to join the church.

The Presbyterian Church was organized in 1844 at the headwaters of the Osage, by the Rev. Cephas Washburn, who was a missionary, by appointment, for the Osage Indians.

Only a few churches held meetings during the Civil War. But right after that, they started to rebuild and many new churches were started all over the county.

Chapter Twenty One
Civil War in Benton County

Battle of Pea Ridge

The Battle of Pea Ridge, or Elkhorn Tavern as some have called it, was the Gettysburg of the West. If the Confederates had won this one battle, they might have won the Civil War. They would have at least changed the whereabouts and dates of most of the battles that followed it.

On August 10, 1861, the Confederate Army under General Sterling Price defeated the Union Army at Wilson Creek, Missouri. If the Confederates had gone on that fall, Price might have captured St. Louis and won the State of Missouri for the Confederates.

But both armies went into winter quarters until February, 1862. Then the Union Army drove General Price out of Missouri and into Arkansas.

Then, on March 6, 7 and 8, followed the battle that could have changed the outcome of the War.

The sun came out just a little on the morning of March 6, 1862, to see the tired, cold, ill-fed and ill-equipped men of Confederate Major General Earl Van Dorn's Army of the Trans-Mississippi West, called to order at Elm Springs, Arkansas.

Major General Van Dorn walked briskly from headquarters to his large black steed, mounted and rode to the side of Major General Sterling Price, then gave the order to march.

Destination was Bentonville, then Sugar Creek where the Federal Army of the West was camped and dug in for battle. The Confederates had defeated the Federal Army at Wilson Creek, Mo., in August 1861, so the Confederate soldiers knew this battle would not last long; then they would march all the way to St. Louis, at least General Van Dorn said they would.

The men were glad to start, as the morning was cold and a light snow had fallen the night before. It would be a little warmer, marching. By two o'clock in the afternoon of March 8, several

THE BATTLE OF PEA RIDGE, ARKANSAS—THE FINAL ADVANCE OF OUR TROOPS, MARCH 8, 1862.—[SEE PAGE 202.]

This picture ran in Harper's Weekly, March 29, 1862, titled The Battle of Pea Ridge, Arkansas — The final advance of our troops, March 8, 1862. This one was drawn from the writings of a northern newsman.

Battle of Pea Ridge - This reproduction of an 1889 print by Kurz and Allison shows a highly imaginative version of the Battle of Pea Ridge. Print shows Indians in full battledress charging into the fray with Southern forces. This charge was shown more or less from the Southern view.

Union Gen. Samuel Ryan Curtis, Federal Commander.

Gen. Earl Van Dorn, Confederate Commander.

Confederate Gen. Ben McCulloch was killed at about 10:30 near Lee Town the first day of the battle.

hundred of these marchers lay dead or wounded on the battle-fields of Lee Town and Elk Horn Tavern on Pea Ridge, with a like number of Federal troops. In that one battle, the Confederates lost three of their great generals.

The Battle of Pea Ridge, or Elkhorn Tavern, was the biggest and bloodiest battle west of the Mississippi. It can well be called the "Gettysburg of the West", because when Federal Major General Samuel Ryan Curtis won the battle of Pea Ridge, he saved the state of Missouri for the Union and made it possible for the Union Armies to capture Fort Henry and Fort Donaldson in Kentucky, and win the battle of Shiloh Church and Vicksburg. But on March 8th, he didn't know what a great victory he had won.

In January of 1862, the Confederate Army laid plans for one of the most daring moves of the war. It started when General Albert Sidney Johnson said to Major General Van Dorn, "Capture St. Louis, Missouri, at any cost."

If the Confederates had taken St. Louis they would have cut the supply line of Federal Generals Buell and Grant in Kentucky. Then the Federals couldn't have captured Fort Henry and Fort Donaldson in Kentucky. They couldn't have marched to the Mississippi River, and there couldn't have been a battle of Shiloh Church or Vicksburg.

Major General Van Dorn was one of the Confederate's most outstanding officers at that date, having been raised from a Colonel to Major General in less than a year. In Texas, he had forced the surrender of all the Union troops under Major Sibley and Colonel Reeve. This gave him a name of being able to get a job done. That is why Jeff Davis told General Johnson to give this command to him.

He made his headquarters at Pocahontas in Northeast Arkansas late in January, then started making plans to unite the forces of General Price in Springfield, Missouri; General Ben McCulloch in Arkansas, and General Pike in the Indian Territory.

The plan was for McCulloch and Pike to meet General Price at Springfield and turn east to St. Louis. Major General Van Dorn would march north from Arkansas, and meet them near Rolla, Missouri; and with this combined force he hoped to capture St. Louis with very little trouble.

Major General Curtis, Federal Commander in Missouri, had different plans. In February, he marched into Springfield and drove Major General Sterling Price and his Missouri State Guard, that had turned rebel and sided with the Confederates, out of Missouri and south of Fayetteville, Arkansas, to the Boston Mountains.

General Van Dorn, knowing that the troops of Generals

McCulloch and Price could not get along together, left for the Boston Mountains when he received word of Price's defeat in Missouri. General McCulloch felt that since his troops were regular army troops of the Confederates, he was above General Price and his men who were still Missouri State Guardsmen.

It was 250 miles to General McCulloch's headquarters in the Boston Mountains, and from Pocahontas, General Van Dorn made the trip in five days. When he arrived at the Confederate camp deep in the Boston Mountains on March 3rd, General McCulloch's artillery fired a 44 gun salute.

Van Dorn called a council meeting of the Generals and higher officers that afternoon. Van Dorn told Generals McCulloch and Price that he didn't want any more show of feeling between them. "We are all in the same army and we are going to fight together for the Confederate cause," he said. "And I don't want to lose a battle because my troops can't get along."

After studies of maps of the area and talks with the officers who had been in the area around Sugar Creek in Northwest Arkansas, he checked on the number of men, artillery guns, shells and food in the armies of Generals McCulloch, Price, and Pike. He had a total of 16,000 men, counting the Indian troops of General Pike.

He put out a march order for 6 a.m., March 4th. General Price's army was to lead, followed by McCulloch's. General Pike was to meet him at or about Elm Springs. Each man was to carry four day's rations.

By the evening of March 5th, the armies were at Elm Springs—a march of nearly 50 miles in two days. Over the rough mountains, where some of the roads were too bad to march on, they had to push through the woods. "You were either falling down a hill or being pushed up one," said a Missouri soldier of that march. It had been a very hard march with very little rest or food. What food they had was eaten cold, and the weather was cold with a light snow most of the time.

The afternoon of March 5th found Federal Major General Curtis hard at work in his camp at Cross Hollows. He was planning for the coming battle. At 2:30, he heard a horse coming up fast. Before the rider could knock, he yelled, "Come in, where in hell are they and how many."

"They will be at Elm Springs by dark," the rider said. "God, there must be 30 or 40 thousand of them and they will all gather there tonight. Those Indians look mean as hell to me. I fought some in the West a few years ago, and they were bad."

General Curtis cared very little for how they looked. He wanted to know how many, what guns they had, how much cavalry; and, most of all, where they would hit his line. He had only 10,500 men, and had to have a good position if he was to win

Major General Sigel as he looked in about 1863.

against the number of men he had heard was in the Confederate Army.

As soon as orders could be written, General Curtis sent for the rest of his command, Brig-General Franz Sigel at McKissick's farm, and Colonel Vandever near Huntsville, to gather their command at once and march at top speed to an area along Sugar Creek that had been picked as the best position for a battle.

Union General Sigel also was reminded that he was not to play around and hold back like he had at Wilson Creek the past summer. That blunder had lost many of his men, and Sigel himself was almost taken prisoner there.

By 6 o'clock that evening, General Curtis was marching with the divisions of Colonel Carr and Colonel Davis for Sugar Creek. They arrived there at 2 a.m. Curtis ordered the men to rest until daylight, but as soon as they could see, to start to dig in.

They had a good position on the hills overlooking Sugar Creek valley, where the telegraph road ran through from Springfield to Fayetteville. They were facing south and could also see a road that ran along the creek from Bentonville. Behind them was a high wooded ridge called Pea Ridge. Also, there was a good road into Missouri, if they should have to retreat.

The Federal army dug in, built up breastwork, and cut trees to fight from behind. They also cut trees across all the roads in the area that the rebels might use. Curtis was so sure that the rebel

Van Dorn would march his troops right up the Telegraph Road, that it was in this area that he planned and built his best defense. This he never used.

When Brig-General Sigel received the orders from General Curtis, he at once ordered his first division, under General Asboth, and the second division, under Colonel Osterhaus, to return to Bentonville and on to Sugar Creek.

By 8 o'clock on the morning of March 6th, all the Federal troops had passed through Bentonville and were on the way to the Sugar Creek camp, except General Sigel and his rear guard. This consisted of the 12th Missouri Volunteers under Major Hugo Wangelin, five companies of the Benton Hussars Missouri Cavalry, under Colonel Joseph Nemett, and two mounted companies of the Sixth Illinois Volunteers under Captains Albert Jenks and Henry A. Smith, with a total of 60 men, and five pieces of artillery.

Their rifles stacked, the men all rested while Sigel was having breakfast in the Eagle Hotel in Bentonville. This was the way that the rebel cavalry found them. The advance force was too small to make an attack, but they did set off the alarm.

Sigel ran from the hotel, yelling, "Bugler, sound the call to arms." He jumped on his horse and ordered his troop to the wooded area north of town. This was gained in a record time. Once into the timber, he stopped to be sure all of his men had made it. By this time, Lt. Shipper rode up. The rebels had been after him for over two miles, and he was glad to be back with a bigger force. Sigel had been waiting for him to come in from Osage Creek.

When Sigel turned east to go to Sugar Creek, he found that the rebels were almost around him. "Damn it, I'll be caught here worst then I was at Wilson Creek," he was heard to say," and all because I tried to have a good breakfast."

General Price's Confederate Cavalry under Colonel Gates was giving Sigel a hard time. He was forced to stop and fight every ten or fifteen minutes, to keep them from getting around him. As soon as General Asboth and Colonel Osterhaus heard of Sigel's plight, they came quickly to his aid with the First and Second divisions.

They were just in time, Price's Cavalry was closing the circle and almost had Sigel surrounded. When they came face to face with the two Federal divisions, they came to a fast halt. Soon both sides set up their artillery, and for half an hour they had a very fine artillery duel. Then they stopped for the night. The Federal troops all returned to Sugar Creek.

That night, with all of his forces united, Federal Major General Curtis posted his divisions in line for battle. General Asboth's division was on the right, next was Colonel Osterhaus' first division; then Colonel Davis' third division, with Colonel Carr's fourth making up the far left. The line was running east and west and facing the south.

That same evening, Rebel General Van Dorn bivouacked his army four miles west and a little south of the right wing of the Federal army. They were at a point where the Bentonville to Keetsville road crosses Sugar Creek.

At dark, the General called a staff meeting of his officers to plan the battle for the next day. On finding out that Generals McCulloch and McIntosh knew the county so well, he asked their advice. "Attack them from behind, is the only chance we have," said McCulloch.

"How are we to get behind them, when they have the road to the north cut off," Van Dorn demanded to know.

Then McCulloch showed Van Dorn on the map how they could go northeast on the Bentonville to Keetsville road and come in to the Telegraph Road four miles behind where the Federal Army was dug in, and two miles from Elk Horn Tavern where McCulloch was sure the Federal rear guard would be. This move would give the Confederates a high wooded area from which to fight.

Confederate Generals Van Dorn, McCulloch, McIntosh, Price and Pike spent the next hour making their plans. They would move out soon, General Van Dorn at the lead with General Price's army. They should be at Elk Horn by sunup and make a surprise attack on the Federal Army and wipe them out in a few hours.

General McCulloch's army and General Pike's Indians were to follow Price's army, but they had orders to leave the road north of Lee Town and go southeast until they found the right wing of the Federal Army, then attack. This gave Van Dorn a battle line with two fronts. General McCulloch was in command of his left and General Price was in command of his right.

Major General Van Dorn overlooked a great many things when he made his plans to detour around the Federal army on the Bentonville road. He had not sent out scouts to see what the road was like. He didn't know that the Federals had felled trees to block the road. The rebel army was slowed to a standstill many times that night. It was 10 o'clock in the morning before General Price's army was on the Telegraph Road. It also was that late in the day before General McCulloch was able to make his move south for Lee Town.

The Confederate Army was in no shape to go into battle on that March 7th. They had been marched too long and hard in the last three days. Better than half of the time was spent in the rough mountains, with no roads in places, and all the little streams had been up. The soldiers were wet a lot of the time. Most of the food they had to eat since March 4th had been cold. Most of them had

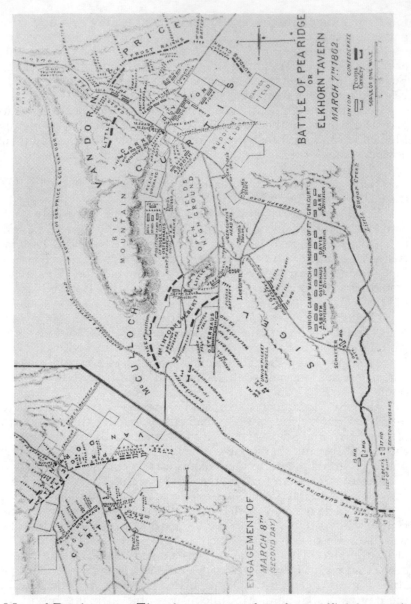

Map of Battle area—The above map, taken from official records of the United States Army, shows the disposition of troops during the last two days of the Battle of Pea Ridge. The battle opened with a clash at Leetown, which lies about a mile west of the area covered by the above map. The main fighting took place in the vicinity of Elkhorn Tavern, at the right center of the larger map.

done very little training since the past fall.

The troops they were going to fight were well trained and seasoned fighters. General Curtis, knowing the importance of a well fed and rested army, had seen that his men had hot meals and were well rested.

Just after daylight on March 7th, Major Eli Weston, who with his 24th Missouri Volunteers had pulled night guard for the Federal army at Elk Horn Tavern, detailed a troop of pickets to go and see if the rebels were coming from the north as he had been told by a lookout.

Soon they met General Price's pickets and had a short skirmish. They returned to the Major with word that the woods were full of Rebels.

Captain Barbour Lewis was dispatched at once, and rode at top speed to General Curtis' tent. "The whole rebel army is behind us in the woods at Elk Horn Tavern, Sir," he reported. A scout came in just then to report that McCulloch's army had been seen just north of Lee Town.

Curtis called his commanders together in General Asboth's tent at once. "I overestimated the enemy, gentlemen," he said, as he walked into the tent. "Turn your troops all about. Our left flank is now our right, and we are facing the enemy coming from the north and ready for battle." After looking over the maps and the reports, he ordered Colonel Carr to take his division to Elk Horn Tavern, and ordered Colonel Osterhaus to Lee Town. "Attack and attack hard and fast," was the order.

Generals Van Dorn and Price made the most of the short time they had before the Federal army would be upon them. Price posted his men in the best positions on the hills and ridges. His extreme right wing rested on the eastern slope of Pea Ridge, the left, far to the east of Telegraph Road. They were ready for battle in a very short time. Colonel Henry Little's brigade was west of the road and on the east slopes of Pea Ridge. Next was General William Y. Slack's division of Second Missouri Confederate Volunteers. The cavalry here was under Colonel John T. Hughes.

East of the road was the Missouri State Guard divisions. Running east from the road were General Price's division. Colonel James P. Saunder's fifth division, General D. M. Frost's seventh and ninth divisions and General S. Rain's eighth division. East of them were Colonel Green's Third Brigade Confederate Volunteers. The cavalry on this side of the road was all under Colonel Elijah Gates.

All of Price's artillery was placed just back of this line and in high and protected areas. Shortly after the artillery started firing, the Confederates made two hits on the Federal caissons near the tavern. This killed so many men and horses that the Federals had to withdraw, losing three guns (which they recaptured later

Confederate Gen. Y. W. Slack was mortally wounded on the morning of the first day of the battle. He was making an attack on the east side of the Telegraph Road.

that day).

Just after the battle started, Price ordered Slack and Little to move their divisions east of the Telegraph Road, and replaced them with all his artillery. This gave the artillery a higher and better position, on the high slopes of Pea Ridge.

As soon as this heavy artillery fire had stopped part of the Federal guns, he ordered Slack, Little and Gates to "Attack that damned outfit with everything you've got." But just as they reached the Federal line, Colonel Vandever came up with fresh troops, and in the battle that followed General Slack was mortally wounded. The Confederates were forced to pull back.

About the same time, at the other end of the Federal line, Dodge saw the advancing Confederate infantry under General Clark. He turned to his men, saying, "Lie flat along that rail fence. Let them come across the field, and come up shooting when they are within fifty feet to you."

The Federals didn't have to wait long. On a signal, the Confederate artillery stopped, and Clark moved his men across the field fast. Then up came the Federals wildly shooting. More than 100 rebels fell almost as one. They withdrew very fast. Dodge received a wounded hand, but lost only a few men.

Curtis showed his military ability that day. He was all over the field and seemed to always know where the men were needed worst.

"We'll have to hit them with all we have, if we are to run them off the battlefield by dark," said Van Dorn.

"I know sir," replied Price, "but my men are very tired. It will be hard for them to do, and tomorrow they will not be able to fight. The three days of marching was too much for them."

"Right now we must plan an attack forgetting who is tired," replied Van Dorn. So the plans were made.

Price was to take as many of his troops as could be spared from the line and make a flanking move on the right end of the Federal line, driving Dodge and his Illinois and Iowa infantry troops out into the open where Price's cavalry could cut them down.

Van Dorn had placed his batteries so well that when the order to increase fire was given, the Federal line was wilted with a terrible storm of shell, shot and grape. This was concentrated around the Elk Horn Tavern and aimed at the Federal artillery. The firing was so fierce, the Federals withdrew fast to save the guns and men.

Union Colonel Carr sent a rider with orders for Colonel Shunk to take his Eighth Indiana Infantry and three pieces of Klauss' First Indiana Battery, move to the right flank, and support Col. Dodge and the Fourth Iowa Infantry. The guns were ordered into battery, but before they took the first shot the rebels attacked and drove them all back.

Before Colonel Vandever could close the gap in the Federal line, made by moving Colonel Shunk, the Confederates attacked so hard that the whole Federal line was driven back.

Soon rebel General Frost and Colonel Little had taken Elk Horn Tavern and were talking to newspaper reporters who had spent the day there.

The Federals rallied when the rebel artillery fire stopped, so they could move the guns up to Elk Horn Tavern. Little's rebel infantry attacked and captured part of the Federal artillery. So many of the Federals were wounded, that Colonel Carr was forced to move back over a mile. The Colonel was wounded in the arm and hand. Lieutenant Colonel Harran, who commanded the Ninth Iowa Volunteers, had his horse shot from under him. He was wounded and captured.

Just before dark, Union General Asboth moved up with four companies of the Second Missouri Volunteers and four pieces of the Second Ohio Battery. They met Colonel Carr's battleworn and bleeding troops who shouted with joy. Part of his men went back into battle with the Missouri outfit, but most of them were walking wounded.

With the fresh troops, the Federals were able to drive back the rebels, gaining a good position for their artillery. Then started an artillery duel that lasted until dark. Both sides quit because they were either short or out of ammunition.

General Curtis was riding along his battle line when he met Colonel Dodge and his men retreating. "I am out of ammunition, sir," the Colonel reported.

"Then fix bayonets and charge the rebels. Dammit, how can you win a war if you run," was the General's reply. Charge they did. But, upon advancing, they found that the Confederates had withdrawn for the night. The men were very glad of that.

General Curtis ordered the Missouri Second Volunteers to stand guard that night. He drew the rest of the men back. They were fed, but slept that night on their arms.

All day March 7th, as the bloody battle raged at Elk Horn Tavern, another just as bloody was fought at Lee Town two and a half miles on the Federals' left flank.

By shortly after ten in the morning, Confederate General McCulloch had his army moving south toward Lee Town. The General's own troop was on the left, General McIntosh was on the right, with General Pike and his Indians just behind McIntosh, with orders to spread farther to the right as soon as he could. In this formation, they were moving through the wooded area and small fields, planning to attack the Federal's left flank.

At the same time, Union Colonel Osterhaus had been ordered to take his First division and go to Lee Town to attack the rebels.

Under his command were five companies of the Third Iowa Cavalry, under Lieutenant Colonel Henry H. Trimble; four companies of the Fifth Missouri Cavalry, the Benton Hussars, under Colonel Joseph Nemett; four companies of the First Missouri Cavalry, under Colonel C. A. Ellis; and the companies of the Fourth Missouri Cavalry Fremont Hussars, under Lieutenant O. P. Howe. Three pieces of Captain Elbert's battery of Missouri light artillery went with the cavalry. Commanding all of this cavalry was Colonel Cyrus Bussey of the Third Iowa Cavalry.

The infantry was under the command of Nicholas Greusel, of the 36th. Illinois Volunteers, consisting of his own regiment, Captain Hoffman's battery, Ohio Light Artillery and the 12th Missouri Infantry under Major Hugo Wangelin, three pieces of Captain Welfley's battery of Missouri Light Artillery, and the 22nd Indiana Infantry under Lieutenant Colonel Hendricks.

Colonel Osterhaus and Colonel Bussey were in front of the Federal Army as they rode into the little field north of Lee Town, and were first to see the enemy coming.

Colonel Osterhaus ordered up Captain Elbert's battery and two companies of the First Missouri Cavalry. As the guns were coming into battery, the cavalry units were formed in a battle line. This cavalry unit was armed with revolvers and revolving carbines. They were facing General Pike's division of Choctaw and Cherokee Indian Cavalry.

When the Federal artillery shelled the Indians with grape shot, they broke formation forthwith and took to the woods. Colonel Bussey ordered Lieutenant Colonel Trimble to take two companies of the Third Cavalry and attack before the Indians and rebel troops could regather. But, as the Cavalry reached the woods, they were met by the Confederate infantry. The fighting was so fierce that they retreated. Colonel Trimble was shot through the head.

Before Colonel Osterhaus could give more orders, General McIntosh and General Pike made one of the boldest cavalry attacks made in the whole battle. The attack was very fierce, and the Indians under Colonel Stand Watie gave out with hideous yells and war whoops. They ran the Federal cavalry off, taking three guns.

Colonel Osterhaus fell back to his infantry. As they were forming for battle, the Union cavalry came back with the rebels close on their heels.

Thinking fast, Captain Welfley shouted for his and Captain Hoffman's artillery to turn their guns on the rebel cavalry, thus saving the Federal cavalry.

"Ride as fast as you can, and tell General Curtis to send me all the men he can spare. There must be 20,000 Rebels out there," said Colonel Osterhaus to his aid. Then he ordered his men to stay in the woods and shoot as fast as they could to keep the rebels from crossing the field. The battle was very fierce, and neither side was able to gain any ground.

Just after 2 p.m., Colonel Jeff Davis arrived with his Third Division to support the federal drive. This was the turning point in the battle. The Confederates were losing ground.

Colonel Thomas Patterson, with his 18th Regiment Indiana Infantry and the 22nd Indiana Infantry, saved the day for the Federal army with a move that surprised even the planner. Patterson had moved his regiments to the right flank of the Union line. He planned to move to the foot of Little Mountain, then around the left end of the Confederate army. Just as he got there, Colonel Hebert had made a break through the Federal lines, captured White's guns and ran off his men.

Patterson moved in and closed this gap and attacked Hebert's command so hard from behind that they fell apart and retreated in all directions. Colonel Hebert and Colonel Mitchell of the 14th Arkansas Infantry were among the many Confederates captured. They also took back the artillery that had just been lost.

It was an hour since the reinforcements had arrived and the fighting had been very fierce with heavy losses on both sides. For the first time that day it looked as though the Federals might win.

"Colonel Hill, send two companies of your men out as skirmishers. Move south through the woods and into the field ahead.

231

Confederate Gen. James McIntosh, shot through the head in a field near Lee Town, at about 10:30 first day.

You follow with the rest of the 16th Arkansas Infantry and attack as soon as the Federals open fire," said Confederate General Ben McCulloch, and this was the last order he gave.

He moved out with the 16th Infantry and was following the skirmishers as they moved south across the field. In the Federal line on the north side of the field, according to congressional report, Peter Pelican of Company B 36th Illinois Infantry spotted the General riding out into the field from the south. He was dressed in a dove colored coat, sky blue pantaloons, patent leather high top boots, a large broad brimmed Texas hat, and had a Maynard rifle slung from his shoulder. Private Pelican took very careful aim and shot. The General fell from his horse. He was found by Lieutenant Joseph M. Bailey, face down and shot through the heart. At almost the same time, and not far away, General McIntosh was shot through the head. Both Generals were removed from the battlefield and sent back to Fort Smith in an ambulance, where they were buried.

The great losses of officers and men in the last hour had been too much for the Confederates. They retreated into the woods and stayed. The Union flag was raised over Lee Town and half the battle of Pea Ridge was won.

Most of the Indians had seen all the fighting they wanted, and left the battlefield. They went back to the Indian territory. There were more Indians in the battle here than in any other battle, but they failed to be as effective as they should have been, being too scared of the artillery fire. After the battle, General Clark reported that 18 of his men were scalped, but no one knows what group of Indians did it. Colonel Stand Watie and his Cherokee Indian cavalry made a good attack that day against the Union Army, showing what good soldiers the Indians could make.

After Lee Town was taken, Union General Sigel ordered Major Poten to take troops and capture General Martin Green and the Confederate supply train. It was camped at the crossing of Sugar Creek and the Bentonville road.

The Major moved out with the 17th Missouri Volunteers, two companies of the Fifteenth Missouri Volunteers under Major Landry, two companies of the Fifth Missouri Cavalry and two pieces of the Missouri Light Artillery under Captain Elbert. It was almost dark when Major Poten arrived. The rebels opened fire with artillery when they were about 600 yards away. There was a short artillery duel, then the Federal troops returned to their camp for the night.

General Green, knowing that he couldn't get through to General Van Dorn with the supplies, started back for the Boston Mountains. If he stayed where he was, he was sure that either the Federals would capture the train or he would be forced to burn the supplies.

By midnight, all of General Curtis' Union troops were in position facing the Confederate Army and ready for the battle at dawn.

After the death of the two Generals, the Confederate Army had taken to the hills; Colonel Greer and General Pike took over at different points and gathered as many men as they could. All of the Indians except Colonel Watie's regiment had left and were well on their way home.

General Pike reached Van Dorn at midnight with the remainder of the regiments of Colonels Churchill, Rector, and Hill, all Arkansas Infantry; Major Whitefield's battalion of Texas Infantry; Colonel Stand Watie's Cherokee Indian regiment, Captain Good's battery and some other men of General McCulloch's broken army.

Colonel Greer had what was left of Colonel Herbert's Louisiana Volunteers, Colonels McNair, McRae, and Mitchell; the regiments of Arkansas infantry of the Third, Fourth and 11th Texas Cavalry; Colonel W. P. Lane's regiment of Texas Cavalry; Colonel Embrey's Arkansas regiment, and Captain Hart's battery.

The Confederate Army had fought hard all day with nothing to eat. The only water they had was what they found in springs or mudholes on the battlefield. That night, they slept on their arms with still no food to eat.

That night there were command meetings held in both

camps. The meetings were for high-ranking officers only. "Gentlemen, where can we withdraw to," was General Curtis' opening remark. A long study of the maps failed to show a safe way to leave the battlefield. Curtis and his officers felt that they could not hold out through another day of fighting like this had been. If the Confederates were able to get their supply train through that night, they could not hope to win.

They didn't know for sure how many men the Confederates had lost. And they didn't know that Van Dorn's army was almost out of ammunition.

"You can all sit up and wait until daylight if you want to, but I am going to bed," said General Sigel. "To fight good, you have to be rested." With this, he went to his tent and to bed. The rest of the officers were up most of the night trying to think of something that would save the men. They still thought the rebels outnumbered them two or three to one.

In the Confederate camp the meeting was one of gloom. "May God take pity on those killed here today," said General Van Dorn, when what was left of his commanding officers were all gathered.

"There is very little we can do tomorrow, we are almost out of ammunition," said Van Dorn. "All we can do is fight until it is all gone then march south to Huntsville, and back to Fort Smith."

They didn't tell any of the men about the loss of the three Generals, as the men had enough to worry about.

The camps were so close together that night that they could see each other around their campfires.

March 8th dawned clear and cold. Federal Captain Davidson of the Peoria battery started the day by getting the first shot fired. He was answered by Teel's battery. Soon the artillery fire was so fast that it sounded like one shot going off and lasting.

General Sigel tried to make an advance on the rebel line, but the artillery all but cut him down.

About 10:00, the Confederate artillery was approaching the end of its ammunition. Van Dorn ordered them to advance down the Huntsville Road, and off the battlefield.

"We're out of shot, sir," said a rebel gunner. "Here's lots of shot, dammit. Shoot rocks at them," said Churchill S. Clark, as he started his battery shooting rocks at the Federal troops until they ran out of powder, too. Churchill S. Clark was not an officer. In fact, he was just a youth of about 17 years. When General Slack was wounded, Clark took over command of the artillery that had been under Slack. His was the last of the artillery to leave and he was killed in the last few minutes of the fighting.

As the Confederates withdrew, the Federal army took over the field, and soon it was all over. The Federals made camp and started to care for the wounded.

Van Dorn and his men moved down the Huntsville Road about two or three miles and made camp. They needed a rest.

It would be hard for anyone today to say for sure the number of men killed and wounded in the Battle of Pea Ridge. After the battle was over, each side listed the dead and wounded about 658 or 668.

Some of the generals, writing in later years about their outfit's service, had different reports to make on their killed and wounded than they did the day the battle ended. Thousands of walking wounded left the battlefield without reporting their wounds, only to contract infection and die, or go to the hospital at a later date.

One unexplained part of the battle of Pea Ridge was: Why didn't General Curtis follow the Confederate army and capture them when they made camp to rest after the battle?

Was it the fact that too many of the officers and men in both armies had fought together in the Union Army before this date?

Did General Curtis feel that a defeat on the battlefield was enough for his old friends without capturing them? The answer to this is lost for all time.

There were just two newspaper reporters at the battle of Pea Ridge. One was Thomas W. Knox, who was a war correspondent for the New York Herald. His article on the battle has been used many times.

But I feel that the last part of this article gives an insight to the battle that we should have in our history. So, here it is as he wrote it, the night of the 7th.

"Viewed in its best light the situation was somewhat gloomy. Mr. Fayel, of the (Missouri) Democrat, and myself were the only journalists with the army, and the cessation of the day's fighting found us deliberating on our best course in case of a disastrous result. We destroyed all documents that could give information to the enemy, retaining only our note-books, and such papers as pertained to our profession. With patience and resignation we awaited the events of the morrow.

I do not know that any of our officers expected we should be overpowered but there were many who thought such an occurrence probable. The enemy was nearly twice as strong as we, and lay directly between us and our base.

If he could hold out till our ammunition was exhausted, we should be compelled to lay down our arms. There was no retreat for us. We must be victorious or we must surrender.

In camp on that night, every thing was confusion. The troops that had been on the left during the day were being transferred to the front. The quartermaster was endeavoring to get his train in the least dangerous place.

The opposing lines were so near each other that our men could easily hear the conversation of the Rebels. The night was not severely cold; but the men, who were on the front, after a days fighting, found it quite uncomfortable. Only in the rear was it thought prudent to build fires.

The soldiers of German birth were musical. Throughout the night I repeatedly heard their songs. The soldiers of American parentage were generally profane and the few words I heard them utter were the reverse of musical. Those of Irish origin combined the peculiarities of both Germans and Americans, with their tendencies in favor of the latter.

I sought a quiet spot within the limits of the camp, but could not find it. Lying down in the best place available, I had just fallen asleep when a mounted orderly rode his horse directly over me. I made a mild remonstrance, but the man was out of hearing before I spoke.

Soon after, someone lighted a pipe and threw a coal upon my hand. This drew from me a gentle request for a discontinuance of that experiment. I believe it was not repeated. During the night Mr. Fayel's beard took fire and I was roused to assist in staying the conflagration."

Battle of Maysville

The second major battle of the Civil War in Benton County, Arkansas, was at Maysville on Oct. 22, 1862.

The guerrilla warfare in Northwest Arkansas and South Missouri had been bad all summer long. The Union Army under Gen. Schofield was unable to handle the rebels, so Gen. Curtis sent Gen. James G. Blunt to help clean up the area before all these small units joined forces with Confederate Gen. Hindman.

On Oct. 4th, 1862, Generals Blunt and Schofield routed the rebel troops out of Newtonia, Mo. Those who were under Cooper retreated to the Indian Territory where there were other Confederate troops. Blunt went on to Pea Ridge, from where he later made his attack.

Following is Gen. Blunt's report of the Battle of Maysville, taken from the New York Daily Tribune, Dec. 26, 1862. The report had the dateline November 28, 1862, Old Fort Wayne near Maysville.

"I left camp at Pea Ridge at about 7 o'clock Oct. 20th with the second and third Brigades of my command, consisting of the 2nd, 6th, 10th, and 11th Kansas, and that of the 1st and 3rd Cherokee Regiments, the 1st Kansas and the 2nd Indiana batteries and four mounted howitzers, leaving the first Brigade, Gen. Salamon to protect my rear and flank and supply train, meeting the command of Gen. Herron about midnight, which caused considerable delay.

I did not reach Bentonville until daylight of the 21st. At this

Union Gen. James G. Blunt.

latter place I halted until 5 o'clock p.m., at which hour my train, left behind at Pea Ridge, came up. Having learned from my scouts sent out during the day that Cooper and Stand Watie were at or near Maysville, with a force estimated at from 5 to 7,000, I determined if possible, to reach their camp and attack them by daybreak. The distance to march was thirty miles, and the road through a rough and wooded and hilly country.

Three miles west of Bentonville I directed my train to go into camp and follow, Gen. Cloud's brigade being in the advance.

At about 2 o'clock in the morning the advance was halted by Gen. Cloud with the view of letting the column close up. The men were weary and exhausted, and no sooner were they halted than they dropped down in the brush by the wayside and soon fast asleep.

After waiting half an hour at a halt, I took a portion of my body guard, went ahead to learn the cause of the delay, and ordered the command to be moved on, going myself with the advance guard. After proceeding on five miles farther, an open prairie (called Beattie's Prairie) lay before us of some five miles in extent, over which we had to pass to reach the Rebel camp.

At this point I went ahead of the advance guard, accompanied by Capt. Russell of the 2nd. Kansas Regiment, and two men, for the purpose of getting information. In this we succeeded admirably. Stopping at a large farmhouse at the edge of the prairie, and disguised as Rebel soldiers just escaped from the Unionists, and wishing to get with Cooper's command, I readily enlisted the sympathies of the lady, whose husband was a soldier in the Rebel camp. She informed me where their pickets stood, the location of their camp, and of their strength, which was near 7,000 men. Two Texas regiments having joined them the day before.

I now moved the advance across the prairie, and halted a quarter of a mile from their outpost, which was at the edge of the timber, on a little wooded stream, near the town of Maysville. From this point I sent Companies B and I, of the Second Kansas, under command of Capt. Hopkins, by a circuitous route to enter the town in the rear of the enemy's pickets for the purpose, if possible, of capturing them without alarming their camp.

This however proved fruitless from the fact, as I afterward learned, that they heard us advancing across the prairie and ran in, alarming the town as they went. All of the male inhabitants speedily decamped to seek Rebel protection.

It was now near 5 o'clock. My desire was to attack at daylight. While waiting to give Capt. Hopkins time to get in the rear of their pickets, on going back to ascertain if the column was closed up, I learned, much to my surprise and disappointment, that during the last two or three hours march, the only troops with me had been three companies of the Kansas 2nd. Two of which had already been sent ahead under Capt. Hopkins.

The main column was back seven miles where it was first halted. After sending a messenger back to order it up I proceeded with the one company remaining with me to the town, and reached there at the same time with Capt. Hopkins.

There I learned that intelligence of an approach had gone ahead of us. Fearing that the enemy would retreat, I sent Col. Cloud, who had come up with me in the advance back to move his brigade forward as rapidly as possible, while with the three companies, I determined to push ahead, attack the enemy and endeavor to hold them until re-inforcements could arrive.

Finding an intelligent contraband, whose master was in the Rebel camp, with the locality of which he was well acquainted, I had no difficulty, by promising him his freedom, in engaging his service as a guide.

The route from Maysville to the timber where the Rebels were posted lay across the prairie in a northwesterly direction, about three and a half miles distant. Dashing on rapidly we drove the pickets from the open ground under cover of the timber.

The remainder of the 2nd Kansas with the two mountain howitzers attached, now came galloping up, and the whole regiment was quickly formed in line, and under command of Lieut. Col. Bassett, was ordered to skirmish the woods on foot to ascertain the position of the enemy.

At this point five of my body guard captured ten armed

Rebels who had been out of camp and were endeavoring to get to their command. Lt. Col. Bassett, not being able to ascertain the whereabouts of the Rebel forces, was ordered to withdraw his men from the woods and have them mount.

Advancing through an opening in the timber about a quarter of a mile in width, I discovered the enemy in force. Their line extending across the open ground in front, and occupying the road.

Between the point I occupied and their line was a pasture of open ground, some two hundred yards, and two fences intervening. Believing that the enemy were contemplating a retreat, I determined to lose no time in trying the effect of a few shells upon their ranks from the two little mountain howitzers.

The 2nd Kansas was accordingly moved forward in line to the first fence and the two howitzers under command of Leiut. Stover, supported by Co. A of the 2nd Kansas under Lieut. Johnson, were ordered to advance through the fence to within two hundred yards of the enemy's battery, from which position Lieut. Stover opened upon them with shells, and with much animation.

The fire was returned by the enemy's guns and in a few minutes the entire line engaged the small force I had opposing them. I then dismounted the entire regiment. The Kansas 2nd formed them on foot, and I ordered them to advance through the fence to within short range of the enemy's position, which order was obeyed with alacrity, then opened upon the Rebel lines a terrific fire with their Harper's Ferry rifles. The enemy observing our small force upon the field, the main column not yet having come in sight, attempted to overwhelm us by superior numbers and by flank movements to obtain possession of the protecting woods on my right and left.

Fortunately, at this juncture the Kansas 6th and the 3rd Cherokee Regiment under Col. Phillips came upon the field. The former was ordered to advance upon the right, and the latter on the left, which they did by rapid movements, throwing back the flanking columns of the enemy.

At the same time Company B, Capt. Hopkins; Company D. Lieut. Moore; Company E, Capt. Gardner; Company H, Lieut. Ball and Company K, Capt. Russell, of the 2nd Kansas, all under command of Capt. S. J. Crawford, made a gallant charge driving in their center, capturing their artillery and bringing it in triumph from the field.

The battle was now won. The enemy began flying in disorder before our victorious troops. The 2nd Indiana Battery, Lieut. Robb, came up in time to pay its respects to the rear of the flying enemy with excellent effects. Col. Judson of the 6th Kansas and Col. Phillips of the 3rd Cherokee Regiment pursued them in their retreat for a distance of seven miles, skirmishing with their rear.

The Rebels, as I have since learned, did not halt in their retreat until they had reached the Arkansas River, where they arrived thirty hours after their rout at old Fort Gibson, seventy miles from the battleground.

The casualties in my command were one killed on the battle field, and nine wounded, four mortally who since have died.

I have heard a report that the enemy's losses were 150 men killed and wounded. The battery we captured consists of three six-pound brass guns, and one twelve-pound brass field-howitzer, with horses, harness and caissons complete. We also captured quite a large number of horses and a portion of their transportation and camp and garrison equipment.

It was my intention to have surprised and attacked them at day break and had it not been for the unfortunate occurrence of the night, the neglect of the column to move forward as ordered, I have no doubt I should have succeeded in destroying or capturing the entire Rebel force.

Too much praise cannot be awarded to the gallant Second under command of Lieut. Col. Bassett, which took a prominent part in the affair of the morning. Truly they have added new luster to their laurels won at Wilson's Creek. With less than 600 men, outnumbered, and with guns without bayonets, they charged the enemy's line and artillery, and drove them from the field."

In closing the report, Brig. Gen. Blunt listed many men and officers who proved their gallantry on the field of battle that day.

Army Camps In Benton County

During the Civil War, there were many small army camps in Benton County. They were all started by the Confederate Army, but most were used by the Union Army before the war was over. None of them were very big, as we think of army camps today.

Camp Walker

This camp was established by Gen. Nicholas Bart Pearce, a Benton County man who had been a West Pointer, and the first Brig. Gen. in Western Arkansas. The camp was located one and one-half miles NE of Maysville. It was named for a member of Pres. Davis' Cabinet. It was here that soldiers from Arkansas, Missouri and the Indian Territory trained before the Battle of Wilson Creek and after the return from the battle. Then there were troops from Texas and Louisiana too.

Brig. Gen. N. B. Pearce trained the first soldiers from Benton County with others from all over the western part of the State. The camp was located on the Old Military Road, established by the federal government as a communication line from Fort Scott, Kansas, to Fort Smith, Arkansas, in the late 1820's.

This camp was training ground, not only for northwest

Arkansas, but for southwest Missouri and the eastern part of the Indian Territory. Gen. Stand Watie, the famous Cherokee general, trained his regiment there, which consisted of two companies from Benton County, under Captains Hugh Tinnin and W. H. Hendren with his Cherokees and Creeks.

There, also, the companies of Captains T. T. Hays and Daniel McKissick were trained and went direct to Wilson Creek, near Springfield, Mo., for the first battle in which any Arkansas troops were engaged, August 10th, 1861.

Seven other companies were raised in Benton County under Captains J. N. Hoobs, Cyrus L. Pickens, John Miser, Tom Jefferson, James Ingram, and Bill Brown. All of these trained at Camp Walker.

Camp Walker had long been an object of search among historians. But, on Sunday, February 28th, 1953, in company with several of the descendants of the soldiers who trained there, Alvin Seamster was able to establish the position of the camp by the springs and creeks, also the remains of the old mill at Pactolus, where the soldiers ground their flour and meal. The mill was operated at that time by members of the Harmonial Vegetarian Society, which was organized in 1860, owning 520 acres of land. The group flourished for a few years on a strictly vegetable diet.

Camp Jackson

Camp Jackson was located 4 miles East of Maysville, or two miles from Camp Walker, on the 520 acre plot that had been occupied by the Harmonial Vegetarian Society. It was here that the 4th Ark-Reg, 3rd Louisiana, McRea's, Good's and Reid's were established on the 5th of September, 1861. They left Oct. 12th.

Camp Stephens

This camp was named for Alexander H. Stephens and was established in July, 1861, by the 3rd. Louisiana troops. It was located on Sugar Creek, east of the old Robbins farm, and reached below the Kinley place. Headquarters for the officers was up Brush Creek. By the old road at that time, the camp was about 7 miles NE from Bentonville. This was where the first main skirmish was fought with Sigel, when he was forced from Bentonville on March 6th by the Confederate forces.

Camp McCulloch

This camp was established by McCulloch forces in July, 1861, and was located on the farms that were then occupied by the Wallace and Black families, just one mile NE of the square in Bentonville. On the 27th of October, 1861, this camp was occupied by the 4th Ark-Reg. And, according to Dr. Gammage, it was here that by eating good beef and plenty of red apples, the sick of the regiment were thoroughly recovered in a few weeks.

Camp Cross Hollows

This camp was south and east of Rogers, at the crossroads where the east ravine leads to Monte Ne. At one time, this was thought to be the best place for a battle because of its strategic position. The buildings for the soldiers had been built in a 24 x 24 foot square with a fireplace through the center. This is where part of the Confederates spent the few months before the battle of Pea Ridge. When forced to retreat by the Union army under Gen. Curtis, most of the camp was burned. It was used by the Union army for some time after that.

Camp Benjamin

This was two miles east of the Cross Hollows camp. It was established by the 4th Ark-Regiment under McNair, and the 3rd Louisiana under Hebert. It was occupied on the 29th of Nov., 1861, until forced to retreat before the Union army in Feb. 1862.

They had several building here as the soldiers got lumber at a nearby sawmill.

Camp At Smith's Mill

This was the home of Gen. Nicholas Bart Pearce. He and his father-in-law were running a store, post office and mill here before the war started. The mill was used by both armies during the war.

Camp At Osage Springs

Confederate troops were camped here before the Battle of Pea Ridge; then, on or about the 20th of February, 1862, this camp was used by the Union army until after the Battle of Pea Ridge.

Camp On Osage Prairie

This was headquarters for the 4th Ark-Regiment when they first came to the county. It was about 2½ miles SE of Bentonville and was used as an enlistment center.

Camp At Walnut Springs

The camp was about 2½ miles NE of Cave Springs, where the Tom Vickery farm was later located and was common campground for both armies on account of the good springs. It was here in 1863 that 5 Union soldiers were killed by enraged citizens who they claimed had been terrorized by the soldiers.

Camp On Lindsey's Prairie

This camp was between Siloam Springs and Flint Creek.

Soldiers were trained here during much of the war and several skirmishes were here and along the old line road north of Siloam Springs.

Camp On McKissick's Farm

This was a very large farm south and east of Centerton and both armies had camped there. Gen. Sigel was camped here when he was ordered back to Sugar Creek by Gen. Curtis, the day before the Battle of Pea Ridge.

Camp At Bentonville

Many Confederate troops were stationed here before Bentonville was captured at 12:20 on the 18th day of February, 1862. After the battle of Pea Ridge, Dr. Gammage moved several of the wounded from that battle to Bentonville, where a Dr. Moore cared for them. Many of them were cared for in the jail. The Union army camped along the Town branch.

Camp At Elkhorn Tavern

Soldiers camped here all during the war. First, the Confederates; then the Union army after the battle and until April. Later, Gen. Blunt camped here before the battles of Maysville and Prairie Grove.

Camp At War Eagle Mill

Both armies camped here to use this mill to grind grain for their armies. Early in 1862 the mill was burned by the Confederates, to stop the Union from using it.

Camp At Mud Town

This camp was much used by both armies. It was just east of Lowell, and the headquarters was the old stage stop.

Battle of Dunagin Farm

Although it was not a very big battle, and lasted for only a few minutes, the battle of Dunagin's farm on Feb. 17, 1862, was an important one.

This was the first battle in Arkansas in the Civil War where both sides had fatalities. It also was one which taught the Yankees something new about fighting a war.

Union General Samuel Curtis had attacked Confederate General Stirling Price at Springfield, Missouri. Price, knowing that he was outnumbered, ordered a withdrawal of his troops into Arkansas. There, they would join forces with Gen. McCulloch's army.

The Confederate troops entered Arkansas on the old Wire

Road. The army was so ill-equipped and tired out, that they were moving slow over the frozen ground.

General Asboth's cavalry was leading the Union advance. Several times that day he had been close enough to the moving Confederate army to fire at their rear guard.

Confederate General James Rains, who was bringing up the rear of the Confederate army, became very annoyed by this sniping at his troops. Even though the Union soldiers were still too far away to make any hits.

He knew that if something wasn't done to stop the advancing Union forces, that they could make a flank movement on Gen. Price's army as they moved across the level land between Sugar creek and Callahan's spring. The Confederate Army could not afford to have a major battle there.

General Rains decided it was time to set up an ambush for the advancing Union troops. He felt sure that if he hit them hard enough, they would pull back and wait for the full army to catch up with them.

They were about a half mile northeast of the town of Avoca on the farm of Rev. J. Dunagin. Here, he placed a battery of his horse artillery in what looked to be an unprotected position on the road.

Then he had the rest of his troop dismount and take up positions in the woods and brush along both sides of the road. This would make a deadly crossfire on the enemy, and at so close a range they couldn't miss.

The Union army was new at waging war and they didn't take any precaution of sending out skirmishers when they saw the unprotected guns in front of them.

Their cavalry charged ahead to take the Confederate artillery, with the glee as if going to a party. By the time they knew what had happened, it was too late.

When Gen. Rain's men opened fire, they were trapped. Horses and men alike fell all over the road. The troops tried to turn on the narrow road, but had so much trouble because of the dead men and horses that littered the ground.

As Rains was sure would happen, the Union army fell back and waited for their full strength before they moved after the Confederate army.

The Union loss was twenty men and six horses. The Confederate's was about half a dozen.

The small battle at Dunagin farm was just what the Confederate army needed to slow up the Union army so they could get away. And they did, only to meet again at Pea Ridge in March of that year.

When the Union army moved back down the road to Dunagin farm, they were still looking for revenge of some kind for

This picture was made just a few weeks after Pvt. Charles S. Squires went into the army.

the ambush that had cost them so many men.

They stopped at the farm house and put the Dunagin family out and burned the house. This was the first of several hundred houses and buildings that were burned in Benton County during the Civil War by troops of both sides, and the bushwhackers.

Civil War Diary

A roll of old brown wrapping paper, that was stained and broken, proved to have a very interesting diary of the travels of a Union soldier in the Civil War.

Just a few years ago, the late Charles C. Squires, of near Pea Ridge, was looking in an old trunk that had been his father's. Down near the bottom, he found the old roll of brown paper. It looked like something that should be thrown away.

But when it was opened up, it proved to be a travel log of all the places his father, Pvt. Charles S. Squires, had been to in the Civil War. It showed the miles traveled and whether by rail, boat or on foot. It also listed the battles and skirmishes he had been in.

Pvt. Squires didn't list any dates, except the date when he started from Chicago, and the dates of the battles he fought in.

The paper must have been written after the war and taken from notes that he made on marches. It showed that his outfit spent most of their time going back and forth from one town to another and back again.

Pvt. Squires' handwriting was like many people of his day. It was a little fancy, very neat, and easy to read; and some today would call it beautiful writing.

Also with the diary was a map of the Pea Ridge battlefield that Squires drew after the war was over.

He started out of Chicago on Sept. 19, 1861. The trips and happenings are listed as follows.

	MILES BY		
	Water	Rail	Foot
Chicago, Ill. to St. Louis, Mo.		280	
St. Louis to Boonville, Mo.	300		
(Transport Gray Eagle Via Otterville)			
Boonville, to Springfield, Mo.			155
Springfield to Syracuse, Mo.			110
Syracuse to Otterville, Mo.			6
Otterville, to Sedalia, Mo. and back			40
Otterville, to Springfield, Mo.			125
(This move was dated Jan. 25th. 1862)			
Springfield, to Pea Ridge, Ark.			75
Pea Ridge, to Camp Halleck, Ark. and back			24
(note after this, he had fought the battle of Pea Ridge)			
Pea Ridge, to Camp Steavens, Ark.			12
Camp Steavens to Cassville, Mo.			20
Cassville, to Newtona, Mo. and back			70
(in thirty-six hours)			
Cassville, to Springfield, Mo.			35
(dated June 27th, 1862)			
Springfield, to Ozark, Mo., and back three times			84
Springfield, to McCullocks, Mo. and back			70
Springfield, to Marshfield, Mo.			30
Marshfield, to Hartsville, Mo.			35
Hartsville, to Springfield, Mo.			65
Springfield, to Foryth and back			172
Springfield to Newtona, M.			75
(Dated Sept. 28th, 1862)			
Newtona, to Cassville, Mo.			35
Cassville, to Mt. Vernon, Mo. and back			60
Cassville, to Huntsville, Ark.			65
Huntsville, to Fayetteville, Ark.			40
Fayetteville, to Marionsville, Mo.			90
Marionsville, to Ozark, Mo.			35
(in one day)			

	MILES BY		
	Water	Rail	Foot
Ozark, to Camp Syon, Mo.			48
Camp Syon, to Prairie Grove, Ark.			110
(in three days)			
Prairie Grove, to Van Buren, Ark.			50
(dated Dec. 27th, 1862)			
Van Buren, to Fayetteville, Ark.			60
(via Prairie Grove)			
Fayetteville, to Camp Rosencranse, Ark.			30
Camp Rosencranse, to Huntsville, Ark.			20
Huntsville, to Camp Bliss, Mo.			85
Camp Bliss, to Ozark, Mo.			45
Ozark, to Bloomington, Mo.			30
Bloomington, to Camp Totton, Mo.			50
Camp Totten, to Rolla, Mo.			10
Rolla, to St. Louis, Mo.		113	
St. Louis, to Cape Girardeau, Mo.	150		
(to beat Fisher)			
Cape Girardeau, to Chalk Bluffs and back			202
(in six days and nights)			
Cape Girardeau, to St. Louis, Mo.	150		
(Transport J. W. Sroure)			
St. Louis, to Pilot Knob, Mo.		86	
Pilot Knob, to St. Genevieve, Mo.			60
St. Geneivie, to Vicksburg, Miss.	700		
(Transport Hannibal)			
Vicksburg, to Yazoo City, Miss.	125		
(Transport Istan)			
Yazoo City, to Big Black and back			64
Yazoo City, to Vicksburg, Miss.	125		
Vicksburg, to Port Hudson, La.	260		
(Transport Thomas)			
Port Hudson, to New Orleans, La.	150		
(Transport Arago)			
New Orleans, to Morganya, La.	155		
(Transport D. G. Taylor)			
Morganya, to Atchafalaya, La. and back twice			132
Morganya, to Scout and return			45
Morganya, to New Orleans, La.	155		
(Transport D. G. Taylor)			
New Orleans, to Southwest Pass, La.	125		
(Transport Steamer Geo. P. Body)			
Southwest Pass, to Brayos De Santiago, Tex.	675		
(Transport Steamer Geo. P. Body)			
Brayos De Santiago, to Brownsville, Tex.			37
(24 hours with out drinking water)			

	MILES BY		
	Water	Rail	Foot
Brownsville, to Rio Grand City, Tex.	180		
(Transport Mustang)			
Rio Grand City, to Brownsville, Tex.	180		
(Transport Mustang)			
Brownsville, to Point Isabell, Tex.			37
Point Isabell, to New Orleans, La.	800		
(Steam ship St. Mary)			
New Orleans, to St. Louis, Mo.	1200		
St. Louis, to Chicago, Ill.		280	

Walked 2622 miles. By rail 932 miles. By water 6238 miles.

Grand Total Miles Traveled 9792 miles.

Battles Fought

Pea Ridge, Arkansas	Fought March 6,7,8, 1862
Prairie Grove, Ark.	Fought Dec. 7th, 1862
Chalk Bluffs, Mo.	Fought March 2nd, 1863

Siege of Vicksburg, Miss. from June 11th to July 4th, 1863.

Skirmishes

Sugar Creek, Arkansas, Springfield, Mo., Cowskin Prairie, Indian Nation, Newtone, Mo., Neosho, Mo. three times, Kings River Ark., Van Buren, Ark., Cape Girardeau, Mo., Yazoo City, Miss., Atchafalaya, La., Huntsville, Ark.

Battles Three   Seige One   Skirmishes 13   Total 17

There is numerous scouts and marches not in this record there being some of the accounts lost the Exact account of our marchs and travels is at Springfield, Ill. and the total of miles is some over (13,000) miles.

Charles S. Squires
Co. C 37th. Regt. Ill. Vols. Inft.

The General Came Back For Breakfast

A tall, elderly man sat at a table in the Eagle Hotel at Bentonville, carefully studying a menu. It was the spring of 1887.

After selecting his meal, the man told the maid who waited on him that it didn't matter how long it took to prepare his order. He could wait this time.

When at last the maid carried his breakfast to the table, the man looked up and said aloud: "This is the same as the last breakfast I tried to eat here. I hope I get to finish it without being ran out of town."

CIVIL WAR IN BENTON COUNTY

The Eagle Hotel as it looked in 1887, when Sigel came back. He said it looked almost this way his first time here. See picture of General Sigel on page 223.

"Why, what do you mean sir? We wouldn't run anyone out of town," she said.

"I was ran out of Bentonville in March of 1862. And I was eating breakfast at this very table," he stated.

The man having breakfast was Union Gen. Franz Sigel, who had come back to visit the Pea Ridge Battlefield. He was writing his memoirs of the Civil War.

When the Union Army moved into Benton County in February of 1862, Gen. Sigel made Bentonville headquarters for his first and second divisions. The commander took rooms at the old Eagle Hotel, which at that time was called the Eagle House.

On the morning of March 6, the general was eating a late breakfast in the dining room of the hotel. Most of his troops had been sent on to Sugar Creek where they were to form a battle line and wait for the Confederate Army.

Sigel himself was in no hurry to leave Bentonville. He had a small guard unit with him, and a small unit was coming in to Bentonville from Osage Mills. After the unit's arrival, the general planned to leave for Sugar Creek.

Then the general's breakfast was interrupted. Shouting was heard from the square where his troops were resting. A sergeant rushed into the dining room, saying the entire Confederate Army was coming into Bentonville.

Gen. Sigel quickly cut himself a large bite of ham, ran from the hotel and leaped on his horse, which was tied to a rail in front of the hotel. He shouted to the bugler to sound to arms.

The General hurriedly formed his calvary troop on the square, but before they could leave, the first of the Confederate scouts were sighted. But, the scouts stopped to wait for the cavalry unit following them.

Soon after Gen. Sigel and his guard rode out of Bentonville, the unit from Osage Mills caught up with them.

A running battle ensued between Sigel and the Confederates until part of the Union Army came to his aid. The Confederate forces were stopped at the banks of Sugar Creek.

Sigel was heard to remark as the Confederates were close to him, "I may get caught this time, and all because I wanted to have a good breakfast before I went into battle."

When Gen. Sigel returned to Bentonville in 1887, he stayed in the same room at the Eagle Hotel and ordered the same breakfast each day, taking his time at eating it.

He spent several days at the hotel and made several trips to the Pea Ridge Battlefield. He also visited with a few of the men who had fought in the Confederate Army.

He left Bentonville, feeling that he had made friends in the South.

Indian Raid In Benton County

In the early days in Benton County, the white man and the Indians got along good. They worked along side one another in making this a better place to live. And many were very close friends.

It was not until the Civil War that there was any trouble with Indians. Then it was the Pin Indians who would raid in the west part of the county, killing and stealing what they could.

There were not too many of these raids, but they did take their toll in lives; and made much hardship for the white people they raided.

The following letter tells of one such raid. It is hard to say if this was the last one, or if more followed it. The letter was taken from a story in the Record and Democrat, March 7th, 1929. This was a Bentonville newspaper.

"On my recent visit to the Ozarks I went to see a true and tried friend, S. H. Shelton who lives near Bentonville. We were boys together and comrades in the Confederate service when the Civil War closed.

On the 7th. Day of May, 1864, the "Pin" Indians made a raid in the west part of Benton County, killing old men and boys and robbing houses as their custom was. They were in our neighborhood before we knew about it. The women gave the alarm by blowing horns.

Sam heard his mother blowing the horn, and some parties

who were trying to get out of the way told him that the Indians would be there in a few minutes. Sam knew I was at home and would not get the word unless he brought it to me. They tried to keep him from taking such a fearful risk and told him he was sure to get killed.

He replied, "I'll save Nathan if I can." And then as fast as his horse could run he came and delivered the warning in time for me to hide in a thicket of buck brushes. He then made a dash for the Spavinaw hills and got away just in time to save himself from the bullets of the red-painted warriors.

Our folks who heard the shots that killed my father, thought that Sam and I both were killed. They laid out some clean clothes to dress us for the last time.

I remained in my hiding place until dark, when my sister brought me a dress and bonnet and told me what had been done. One Indian has passed within 20 steps of where I lay, and I counted eight gunshots not far away. After killing my father the Indians returned and robbed the house. As soon as they were gone the women went in search of us, expecting to find us dead. They carried father's mutilated body to the house, wrapped it in a blanket and buried it in the garden. The next morning Sam Shelton came, with a dress and a bonnet on. To help the women dig a grave in the grave yard. Where father was laid to rest until after the war was over, then he was removed to Bethel Cemetery.

Now I want to say a word for Sam, which his modesty will not allow him to say for himself. As I see it, what he did for me was nothing less than a brave deed, prompted by that kind of friendship which should always be remembered with heartfelt gratitude.

May God bless the dear old boy. On the 4th of July when I told him good bye as he held me by the hand he said, "Nathan I'm expecting to meet you in heaven."

Our race is nearly run, but as we live so far apart we are not likely to meet any more in this world but,

> Some where, some where, beyond the sky
> where there'll never be a tear nor sigh,
> Where friends will never say
> Good-bye, we hope to meet again.

> N. E. Fair
> Belleville, Ark."

Editors note: Mr. Shelton was a member of company D, Second Cherokee Cavalry Regiment, under General Stand Watie's command. His commanding officer was Captain Hendren. He was discharged May 29, 1865, at Boggy Depot in the Cherokee Nation.

With the end of the Civil War, came an end to the Indian raids in Benton County. The Pin Indians also had made many raids on the other Indians living in the Indian Territory. They mostly hit places where the young men were all off to the war.

The First Reunion Of The Blue And Gray

"Pea Ridge, Arkansas, March 7th, 1862. As daylight came, we could see just a little sun shining behind snow clouds. The hills were a pretty white, the camp areas were slush and mud. In a very short time we forgot the snow, and the mud, for we were in the middle of hell on a battle field. Those who walked off of it would never forget the battle. And many other brave men didn't walk off this bloody field that day."

This three-day engagement was written about far and wide at the time it took place. Since then, it has been told in the pages of history books and biographies of the men who lived through the battle.

It was because of this three-day battle that we remember Pea Ridge, and that is why a great national battlefield park has been built on the ground that the battle took place on.

But time and people have forgotten the events that took place there on the same ground 25 years and a few months later. Only two or three county newspapers printed stories on this at the time.

At that date, men from both armies met in a reunion and asked that each forget and forgive. Then they honored all the dead, who died so bravely on the battlefield. This was by far a greater victory for those present than the Federal Army had when they won the battle of Pea Ridge.

Here on this ground at Pea Ridge, the men formed the first Reunion Association of the Blue and the Gray. This was the first group to meet annually to honor the dead of both the Blue and the Gray. Also, here on this battlefield was placed the first monument in honor of both sides.

On July 9th, 1887, a meeting was held in Bentonville to plan for a reunion at Pea Ridge, and also to make plans for a monument to be erected there in honor of the Confederate dead.

The first reunion to be held at this battlefield was on Sept. 1st, 1887. It was called a Confederate Reunion, and was held for the purpose of unveiling a monument in honor of the three Confederate generals, and all the Confederate soldiers who died so bravely on this battlefield.

As the people gathered for this great event, it was noticed that many former Union soldiers were present, and they asked to be allowed to pay their respect to the Confederate dead, as did the people of the South.

One speaker said that day, "The white dove seemed to spread her wings alike over all. And harmony reigned supreme as men from both armies honored the dead at this battlefield."

Confederate Dead - This monument, honoring all Confederates who fell at Pea Ridge, was placed on the Battlefield in September of 1887, near Elkhorn Tavern.

253

The absence of the cannon's roar and the bugle call were no doubt gratefully noted by soldiers and citizens alike.

On this great day, a monument was unveiled on the battlefield about a hundred yards from the then famous Elk Horn Tavern. The monument was paid for by the people of Benton County, and part of it came from former Union soldiers. It was in honor of the Confederate dead of this battle.

The square pedestal that rises from the base has an inscription on each side, as follows:

"On the north, Gen. W. Y. Slack, of Missouri, on the west Gen. Ben McCulloch, of Texas, and on the south, Gen. James McIntosh, of Arkansas, and on the east, The Confederate dead, who fell on this field March 7 & 8, 1862." The top is plain shaft of marble that does credit to the donors.

Below the pedestal and about the sandstone base is a marble block, upon which the following verses are inscribed:

O give me a land where the rains are spread
And the living tread lightly on the hearts of the dead:
Yes, give me a land that is blest by the dust
And bright with the deeds of the down trodden just.

O give me a land with a grave in each spot,
And names in the graves that shall not be forgot,
Yes, give me the land of the wreck and the tomb:
There's a grandeur in graves, there's glory in gloom.

The graves of our dead, with green overgrown,
May yet form the footstool of liberty's throne,
And each single wreck in the war-path of might,
Shall yet be a rock in the temple of right.

The welcome address was delivered by Col. Sam W. Peel, a member of Congress from the district; the response was made by Judge C. A. DeFrance. He spoke of the contrast between the welcome given the large number of former federal soldiers present, and the terrible reception given them twenty-five years before. They were welcomed then with rifle and cannon shot, and now they were welcomed as friends and neighbors, and were happy to accept this friendship and give theirs in return.

Former Governor Lubock, of Texas, delivered the general address, concluding it by commending both the "Blue and Gray for their bravery and by asking his hearers to stand by the old constitution, as it now is, be a loyal people."

He was followed by Senator James H. Berry, Judge DeFrance, Col. T. J. Patton and others who all made appropriate short speeches.

This was said to be the first reunion ever held, that every speaker praised both the Blue and the Gray, and asked that everyone clasp in friendship the hand of his former foe.

Several thousand people attended this reunion. Many of them traveled many miles to get there.

At the end of the day, a committee was appointed to form a Reunion Asso. of the Blue and the Gray. Those on the committee were Capt. Lewis Puckett, Garfield; Capt. G. T. Lincoln, of Bentonville; Capt. C. L. Pickens, of Pea Ridge; E. S. Morgan, of Pea Ridge; Capt. J. B. Steele, of Rogers, and H. M. McGaughey, of Rogers.

These men met at Pea Ridge, October 18, 1887, and organized the Reunion Asso. of the Blue and the Gray. They elected Capt. G. T. Lincoln as chairman and H. M. McGaughey, secretary. They then made plans for the reunion the next year.

On Sept. 24, 1888, a meeting of the Blue and the Gray was held in Rogers to plan in full for the reunion to be held that year. This was the first reunion held by the Asso. of the Blue and Gray. Capt. Lewis Puckett was elected as chairman, and Capt. J. B. Lankin as secretary.

The following men were named to the committees to take care of the reunion: Capt. John F. Shepherd, Peter Roberts, Capt. C. L. Pickens, Jim Smith, S Robottom, Capt. W. J. Price, I. B. Gilmore, Capt. R. A. Hickman, Capt. J. B. Steel, Geo. Raupp, Rev. E. T. Russell, Capt. J. B. Lankin, Capt. L. Puckett, J. W. Fry, and J. H. McClinton.

Of these men, half were Federal and half Confederate. But they were all listed just as members of the Asso. of the Blue and Gray.

The reunion of the Blue and the Gray was held at the Pea Ridge Battlefield on Oct. 16, 17, 18, 1888. Camping areas were set at the best springs not far from Elk Horn Tavern. The main program was held in the field where the monument had been placed the year before.

Over 2,500 people came to the reunion; many of these camped on the ground they had fought over in years gone by. Men came from seven states to attend the reunion.

The highlight of the program was held the afternoon of Oct. 17th. This was a drama called Secession and Reunion. It was a dance routine put on by 35 beautiful girls, all dressed to look their prettiest. One was dressed all in white and reigned as Miss Goddess of Liberty. The other girls, each with a banner telling the state she represented, came on the stage and all danced around the goddess. Then, they fell out, part went to the south side of the stage, the rest to the north.

This was to represent the breaking up of the union. After a while, they made up and all danced once more around the goddess. The people, both young and old alike, said this was the best part of the reunion.

255

Speeches were made by Col. Sam W. Peel, Senator James H. Berry, Judge DeFrance, Capt. Puckett and many others in the three days. But much time was spent visiting. Every evening, the men sat around campfires and told tales of the battles.

The next reunion was held Sept. 3rd to 7th, 1889. Even though it rained out one day of it, they had a record attendance of over 7,000 people; and they all seemed to have a good time. The first speech was made by Gen. Fagan; he said that the forming of the association of the Blue and Gray here at Pea Ridge had made history.

He was followed by Col. Sam W. Peel, Senator James H. Berry, and Judge Campbell, after which there was a gathering around the campfires.

A heavy rain came the next morning, but it cleared that afternoon and Rev. Peter Trone of Clinton, Mo., made a speech.

He was followed by Miss Annie Kerr, age 11, of Missouri, who recited, "The American Flag," in a way that was very pleasing.

The next day, Col. Sam W. Peel spoke on the history of the Civil War. Then, Miss Annie Kerr recited "Patrick Henry." This little girl won the hearts of all who heard her.

In the afternoon came the unveiling of the monument to the goddess of Liberty, and was dedicated by appropriate ceremonies. The monument was presented to the Blue and Gray by Miss Daniels. This was the sculptress' first work. It was placed just a few yards from the other monument.

Capt. Lamkin made the reception speech, followed by Gov. Eagle of Arkansas.

The top of the monument is a figure of a woman, the next piece is a plain slab of marble, on the front of which is an index pointing upward, surrounded by the words, "Angel Aloft". On the left side of this block is inscribed: Blue, Maj. Gen. S. R. Curtis, Commander of the Army of the Southwest. On the opposite side is: Gray, Maj. Gen. E. Van Dorn, Commander of the Army of the Southwest.

The next piece is a shaft-like slab, with the following on the front:

"Spirit of eternal light,
Keep silent vigil o'er the brave
The untarnished Blue
The unsullied Gray
In peace and love unite.

Proud heroes have fallen,
And over their grave,
Our hearts are united,
Our country to save.

A United Soldiery - This monument to "A United Soldiery" was unveiled near Elkhorn Tavern during the reunion of the Blue and Gray on the battlefield in 1889.

257

Over the dead the living bend,
And up to their God their voices send
That in Liberty's crown of eternity's day,
The Blue and the Gray.

Under this is clasped hands, under the inscription "A United Soldiery."

The inscription on the monument was composed by Capts. Puckett and Lamkin, and Prof. John R. Roberts. It was the very first monument to the Blue and Gray ever erected.

The drama, Secession and Reunion, was again put on by a group of pretty girls. This was always a big event at all of the reunions of the Blue and Gray.

The reunion that drew the most attention nationally was the one held September 8-9-10th, of 1890. There weren't as many people attending this as there had been in past years, but there was a lot more soldiers. By this time, it was called Reunion of the Western National Reunion Association of the Blue and Gray.

There were twenty bands here in the three days. One of the best liked out-of-state bands was the Summit City Cornet Band from Aurora, Mo. They could play all the old songs that both armies had sung.

As well as the speakers who had spoken here in past years, this time they had the governors from three states, and Gen. W. L. Cabell, and Col. A. S. Cabell, so there was a lot of speech making in the three days.

Gen. Cabell's speech was the best liked one made. He said that the people of Northwest Arkansas were first to erect on their noted battlefield a reunion for universal peace and fraternal friendship. Their motto, he said, was "One Flag and One Country."

Senator Berry said, "The object in starting the Reunion Assn. had been to wipe out the ghastly bloodstains of the past." And this he thought was happening here in northwest Arkansas more than on any other battle field.

In war, the fields on Pea Ridge were dedicated to both the Blue and the Gray, as a place to kill or be killed. And many men from both sides were killed here.

In peace, the fields on Pea Ridge were dedicated to the reunion and friendship of the soldiers of both the Blue and the Gray.

In dedicating the fields of Pea Ridge as a National Battlefield Park, we not only honor the dead of the Blue and the Gray who died so bravely on this field, but we honor those who in later years brought about the friendship of those who survived the Civil War.

The motto of the men who started the Reunion Assn. of the Blue and the Gray, could best be told in the following verse.

Then let us clasp in friendship true
The hand that once we sought to slay

CIVIL WAR IN BENTON COUNTY

> One flag for all, Red White and Blue
> One Country for the Blue and Gray.

This quote from the first reunion at Pea Ridge tells a lot: "Only God will ever know who was right, but the men on both sides were brave, and should be honored for their bravery."

Confederate Reunions

For many years the biggest happening in Northwest Arkansas was the Annual Confederate Reunion at Bentonville. Here, to the tune of Dixie played by the men who fought to that song, was held parades and programs of a type that will never be seen again.

The parades for the most part had a mixed theme; part of the floats would class as military, the rest were farm equipment with a few with girls on them. Every band in the area would come and play. They always had 25 to 30 bands, with anywhere from 4 to 34 players.

The big parade was always held on the first day of the reunion. Then, after that, each morning the men had a parade from the campgrounds, up town and back.

The Northwest Arkansas Confederate Reunion Assn. was formed in 1891 and they held their first reunion in Bentonville Sept. 3 and 4th that year. Several Confederate reunions had been held before this one, but they were small and unorganized.

This organization was named Camp Cabell, in honor of "The Old Tiger," as Gen. W. L. Cabell was called. He attended this reunion and made the main speech.

There were only about 2,000 people attending this reunion, and the papers of that date told very little about it. They did list the speakers as Sen. James H. Berry, Gen. W. L. Cabell, Col. M. E. Benton, Col. T. M. Gunter, Col. Bob Crockett, and Hon. Hugh Dinsmore.

They had a parade with twelve bands, a few floats and about 350 veterans of the Confederate Army. About 500 people followed the parade on horseback or in buggies, and many more on foot.

The program was held at the Old Spring Park in the north part of town. They set up a campground and many of the men and their families camped overnight here.

The biggest reunion ever held in Benton County was the Confederate Reunion of 1893. That year, Bentonville and the Camp Cabell Confederate post was host to the National United Confederate Veterans Assn.

Camp Cabell served a barbecue meal to all the soldiers who came. A campground was fixed to bed down 2,000 men, and their teams. Each night the men gathered around the campfires and told tales of the war.

259

First Day Parade—Part of the first day parade of the Confederate Reunion in Bentonville in 1893. Stevenson Hose Company of Bentonville is in the foreground.

Confederate Reunion—These young ladies rode on a float in the parade for the Confederate Reunion in Bentonville, Sept. 27-28-29, 1893. The parade was held each day at 10:30. There was a girl for each of the Confederate States.

Back row, left to right - Mabel Clark, Texas - Etta Jackson, Louisiana - Effie Morris, Kentucky - Kitty Smartt, Alabama - Nannie Whayne, Georgia - Mary Woods, Florida.

Front row, left to right - Miss Hines, Tennessee - Katherine Watson, Mississippi - Carrie Henry, Virginia - Jennie Berry, Arkansas - Minnie Robinson, Missouri - Ophelia Bates, North Carolina - Olive Suggs, South Carolina.

Miss Arkansas always ruled over these girls.

The reunion was held Sept. 27-28-29, 1893. The parade was also the biggest ever held.

The parade, the first day, started out with the Rogers band leading, followed by the float with the girls representing the Confederate States; then, the troops of Camp Cabell, the speakers for the program. There were 15 floats of military, many of these had bands and flags; 7 fire carts with men pulling them; and many of the newest farm wagons and equipment. Then, all the rest of the soldiers on foot, and many on horseback and in wagons. All this was followed by thousands of people. It is said to have been the longest parade ever held in Bentonville at that date.

The First Regiment Band, led by Alex Black, was playing at the park when the parade and crowd arrived there. It was reported at that time that they had a crowd of 15,000 people and soldiers.

The prayer was said by Dr. R. Y. Dabney, chaplain to Stonewall Jackson. He also gave the closing prayer at the end of the reunion, at which time he asked the Lord to show us all a way to live in this great country, with peace among us all, and friendship for our fellowman.

The welcome address was given by Senator James H. Berry, and in the following three days these noted men all made speeches: Hon. J. M. Harrell, Gen. W. F. Cabell, Gen. B. T. Duvall, Hon. Jno. H. Rogers, Judge Edgar C. Bryan, Dr. John M. Allen, and Judge J. E. Cravens.

Gen. W. F. Cabell told the people that more had been done in Northwest Arkansas to help to heal the wounds of the War than in any other State. He said he hoped they would all attend the reunion of the Blue and Gray at Pea Ridge the next month.

Confederate soldiers came from seventeen states to this reunion, and it was by far the biggest one.

Confederate reunions were held here for a number of years. And as the soldiers died out, it turned into just a reunion. And then they just stopped.

The Lost Cause

I found the following poem in a December, 1887, issue of the Benton County Democrat. Like the editor, I feel that it shows the feeling of the "Lost Cause" more than many longer-written articles.

He stated that it had been written on the back of a $500 Confederate note, which was presented to Miss Ann Ruch of Philadelphia by the author, Major B. A. Jones, Editor of the Aberdeen Mississippi Examiner.

LOST CAUSE.

Representing nothing on God's earth now,
    And naught in the waters below it:
As the pledge of a Nation that passed away,
    Keep it, dear friend, and show it,
Show it to those who will lend an ear,
    To the tale this trifle will tell,
Of liberty born of a patriot's dream,
    A storm cradled Nation that fell.

Too poor to possess the precious ores,
    And too much of a stranger to borrow;
We issued today our "promise to pay",
    And hoped to redeem on the morrow,
The days rolled on, and weeks became years,
    But our coffers were empty still,
Gold was so scarce, the Treasury quaked,
    If a dollar should drop in the till.

But the faith that was in us was strong indeed,
    Though our poverty we well discerned,
And this little note represented the pay,
    That our suffering veterans earned,
They knew it had hardly a value in gold,
    But as gold our soldiers received it,
It gazed in our eyes with a promise to pay,
    And every true soldier believed it,

But our boys thought little of price or pay,
    Or of bills that were overdue,
We know if it bought our bread today,
    T'was the best our poor country could do.
Keep it, it tells all our history o'er,
    From the birth of the dream to its last,
Modest, and born of the Angel Hope,
    Like our hope of success, IT PASSED.

Chapter Twenty Two
Unveiling the Monument

Saturday, August 8th, 1908, was a delightful day in Bentonville. The weather was just right. The immense crowds in town had a feeling of friendship and the spirit of a carnival. There was a big program for all to enjoy.

The event was the unveiling of the monument erected by the Jas. H. Berry chapter of the United Daughters of the Confederacy to the memory of the Confederate Veterans of Benton County. The U.D.C.'s were ably assisted in this great work by Hon. James H. Berry, Mr. A. J. Bates and other friends.

The occasion and the friendly crowd must have made the old veterans feel that, though years had gone by since those dark days of blood and war, they are still dear to the hearts of the people of our Southland.

Early in the morning you could hear Dixie being played, and the singing of Bonnie Blue Flag on the square. The first part of the program was a band concert on the courthouse yard. (This was the old courthouse on the corner of NW 2nd. and North Main. Now a parking lot.) Then the people walked or rode to Park Springs where the remainder of the morning program was held. A band played America, followed with the invocation by Rev. Peter Carahan. Mayor Morris gave the welcome address, followed by a solo by Miss Emma McAndrew. Then a speech by Hon. Hugh A. Dinsmore.

After this, under a canopy of forest trees, a sumptuous old-fashioned basket dinner was served with Park Spring water — cold, clear and sparkling and the only beverage. Everybody was invited to the feast.

At 1:30, the parade started led by the Marshal of the day assisted by a number of the Sons of The Confederacy. Then a beautiful white float that looked like a moving bank of red and white roses. It was drawn by four horses, covered with red and white trappings and mounted by 4 little boys in red and white

UNVEILING THE MONUMENT

This was part of the parade from the park to town.

uniforms. The whole guarded by outriders in the same uniforms.

The freight of this beautiful float was fourteen pretty girls in white representing the seceded states. In the center of the float and elevated above the others sat Miss Berry Hyatt, representing Grand old Arkansas.

In beautifully decorated carriages came the orators of the day, Hon. Clifton R. Breckenridge of Fort Smith. Hon. H. A. Dinsmore, Wn. F. Patton, President of the James II. Berry chapter. Miss Emma McAndrew, state sponsor of the reunion at Birmingham. James H. Berry, Mayor A. W. Morris and Felix Lindsey, Master of Ceremonies.

Then followed the veterans, and as they passed with that old time "tramp, tramp," a loyal friend to the lost cause said with tearful eyes and choking, trembling voice, "Bless their old hearts."

Next, a rose covered float with members of the S.M.A. of Fayetteville and the Sterling Price chapter of Rogers. Then a large rose float with members of the U.D.C. of Bentonville, followed by many decorated carriages. One of the prettiest was a tiny white throne drawn by a tiny ebony pony with white trappings, and a fairy like passenger in white.

"The Monument"

UNVEILING THE MONUMENT

Then a red throne drawn by a pony with red trappings was graced with four bright little fairies in red. Following these came the Sons of the Confederacy and the citizens.

The parade went to the city park on the square where more people waited for them.

From the platform, invocation was given by Rev. R. E. L. Bearden. Next, the great song of the South, Bonnie Blue Flag, was sung by a chorus of ladies.

As the last note faded away on the breeze, the young ladies representing the states took their place around the base of the veiled monument, each taking a cord in her hand.

After a few words by Mrs. W. F. Patton, Miss Ruth Terry pulled the cord and the veil of red and white, which shrouded the entire monument, slowly left the figure that crowned it and fell gracefully to the base. As the battle flag and the flag of the Confederacy unfurled and floated out from the shoulders of the figure, the band played Dixie and the larger crowd cheered.

Mrs. Rex Peel then sang that song loved by every southerner, and was followed by Mr. Breckenridge, who was introduced by Sen. Berry.

"The war," he said, "was to be viewed with respect to the conduct and achievements of the soldiers and people and the object for which it was all done."

One side of the base reads, "To The Southern Soldiers— Erected by A. J. Bates and The James H. Berry Chapter United Daughters of The Confederacy Aug., 8, 1908." Another, "Their Names Are Borne On Honors Shield. Their Record Is With God. They Fought For Home and Fatherland."

All in all this was a great day for Bentonville. Special coaches were put on trains from Fort Smith, Fayetteville, and out of Missouri to bring people here for the program. It was said to be one of the most colorful programs ever held in Benton County.

For some years before this, some people wished to have the new courthouse built in the square. This talk was stopped by an order of the Benton County Court, issued on petition of W. S. Floyd, then County Judge, deeded to the Daughters of the Confederacy for its preservation of the area known as the Public Square Park.

Chapter Twenty Three
Bella Vista Resort

Since just after the Civil War, summer and health resorts started up all over the county. Most were at some big spring with water said to do some special good.

Sulphur Springs lasted as a resort for years, because they had the railroad to bring the people there. Siloam Springs started as a resort, but didn't make it on that. But it did leave us a good town in the county.

Based on popularity and out-of-state interest, I would say that Bella Vista was the best known of any resort in Benton County.

This resort, four and one-half miles northeast of Bentonville, was laid out in 1916 by Dr. Cotton and Lou Smith; later that year they sold it to the three Linebarger brothers, C.C., F. W. and C. A. They built one of the best known and most popular resorts in the midwest.

During the years that they ran the resort, they had the best accommodations in the area, with top grade hotels or cabins for rent. Top bands to dance to, swimming, fishing, hunting, golf, tennis and a large cave and big spring, plus many special programs going on throughout the season.

Many people owned their own cabins here, and at least a part of the family would spend the full summer there.

When the Linebarger's bought this land, the road didn't run through it at all. They had to build roads, as well as the Rustic Lodge, dance pavilion and other buildings in 1917. It didn't take them long to have a resort going and start selling homesites.

Dr. Dick Atkinson bought the first lot and had the first one-room cottage built here as a homesite.

The Sunset Hotel was built in 1929, and at the time was said to be one of the best of this type hotels in the State. The Wonderland Cave nightclub was opened in May of 1930. For opening night, they had a top name band and over 800 people came. This

BELLA VISTA RESORT

These cabins were built in the heyday of Bella Vista. At that time most of the hillsides were filled with cabins like these.

This boxing match was part of the special program at Bella Vista in 1919.

cave became very famous as a top nightspot in the state. Many of the top bands and singers were here over the years.

One could write a book on Bella Vista, but there is not space so I will let the Linebarger brothers tell you a little about what they had here.

The following is taken from booklets that the Linebargers wrote to sell people on Bella Vista. This part was from their booklet for 1918. It was full of pictures and maps, showing what they had to offer:

"To you who love the great out of doors, the open spaces, the peaceful, the quiet, the restful, the pure fresh air, the nearness to nature, the shady nook, the clear cool stream, and the deep blue holes, the pleasure of bathing, rowing, hunting, fishing, dancing, tennis, golfing, exploring, riding, hiking, motoring, climbing, or any other clean sport or recreation, Bella Vista is forever dedicated.

Water system—A great hydraulic ram said to be the largest in the State, pumps pure fresh water from Big Spring into a concrete reservoir; it is then run into the mains. Water for domestic purposes is furnished free. Summer homesite owners are at liberty to tap the mains and pipe this water directly into their cottages or secure their supply from hydrants located about the property.

BELLA VISTA RESORT

Bella Vista heyday — This was one of the better cabins built here.

Electric Light Plant— Generated by water power, furnishes electric lights to Lake, Big Cave, buildings and surrounding grounds.

Refreshment Booths—At the Dining Lodge and Bath House.

Edibles—An abundance of milk, butter, eggs, chicken, all kinds of fruits, berries, vegetables, an endless variety of good things to eat, fresh daily from the rich valley farms nearby and cheaper than any other place we know. Arrangements are being made for grocery stores at Bella Vista. Grocery delivery daily from Bentonville now.

Dining Lodge—Among the great oaks, upon the rock faced bluff overlooking the lake and commanding a view of the magnificent valley below, has been erected a large combination dining lodge, rest rooms and general headquarters; constructed in rustic fashion of native oak and surrounded with wide screened porches, modernly equipped for serving first class meals. This feature is especially attractive for those who do not care to prepare their own meals.

Bath House and Pavilion—A combination boat pier, bath house and dancing pavilion affords endless water sports and pleasure. The bathing is especially delightful, the water is clear, pure and warm, the beach is graveled and the diving tower, rafts and spring boards add much to the sport.

Public Auto Sheds—Have been constructed to accommodate

a number of cars.

Communications—Local and long distance telephone, mail delivered daily.

The Lake—This beautiful lake of spring fed waters affords unbounded sport, recreation, diversion, happiness and genuine pleasure to every member of the family of the Bella Vista Summer Home Owner. By day, a jewel of limpid blue and by night, bathed in the soft radiance of the moon, a silver effulgence of glory that draws the soul of man close to the heart of Nature. The Lake is the scene of many happy parties throughout the summer, its tranquility and charm leave the cares of the world forgotten and make the hours of the vacation all too short.

Spring Park—Delightful and interesting Spring Park is located near the center of Bella Vista. The Park is a wonderful valley or glen so densely shaded by the native forest that at places, only a sunbeam penetrates here and there. It is surrounded by tree-covered mountains. At one end is the towering semi-circular cliff from the bottom of which gushes the waters of Big Spring and the mysterious blast of cold air. Spring Park is another rich endowment bestowed by the hand of Nature upon every member of the Bella Vista summer home owner's family.

Big Cave—This marvelous subterranean wonder has been brilliantly lighted by electricity to the "Mile Post." Tis said it has never been fully explored, although one can travel miles into it. The mammoth rooms, grotesque freaks of nature, crystallized specimens, enormous crevices and the great variety of formations distinguish it as one of the geological wonders of the Ozarks— a cool place to spend many interesting hours and a fascinating diversion for exploring parties. In addition to Big Cave there is also Hidden Cave and Cold Cave on the Bella Vista Tract. Crystal Cave, noted for its rare and magnificent specimens of crystallized formation, is one mile distant. Devil's Hole, a great hole straight down into the rocky cliff at Inspiration Point, is another interesting wonder and freak of Nature.

Bella Vista is rich in exceptional natural attractions, all of which add spice, pleasure and interest to the life of the Summer Homeowner.

Drives—The Mount Pisgah Loop Drive commands a view from the brow of Mount Pisgah rarely equaled. Mountain Crest Loop winds in and out among the giant shady oaks, granting snatches of thrilling scenery.

The Sky Line Drive,—which almost completely skirts the property, presents view of fascinating scenery and reaches its climax at Inspiration Point, where your car stands on the brink of a great semi-circled cliff. From an immense cavern far below flows Big Spring and Spring Brook and spread out before you is a panorama of entrancing beauty.

Advertising folder from the 1930's.

Size of Homesites—The majority are fifty by one hundred feet, some a few feet less, and others run to one hundred by two hundred feet or more, according to location and lay of the ground.

To further the rapid development of Bella Vista we are offering a limited number of Summer Homesites at the following Special Prices and Easy Terms. Prices $100 to $300 each. Terms $300 or $250 Summer Homesite, $15.00 cash, $15.00 per month. $200, $150 or $100 Summer Homesite, $10.00 cash, $10.00 per month. No interest. Discount 8% for all cash.

We will build for you a neat, attractive Summer Cottage of from one to three rooms for from $100.00 to $400.00. Native oak can be had very cheaply from nearby sawmills; our buildings except the pine floors, are constructed from this material. If you prefer to plan or build your own Summer Cottage, Bungalow or more pretentious Summer Home, we will gladly co-operate with you to the fullest extent."

One can tell by the above that the Linebarger brothers started out to build a resort that would last, as well as one that people would be proud to own a summer homesite at. Very few people ever forgot the time they spent here.

Every year new buildings were added, new attractions and entertainment. Many local people spent Saturday or Sunday at Bella Vista to picnic, swim or take in some of the other special entertainment.

In a brochure they put out in the late 1930's, Linebarger Brothers were offering: The Ozarks finest all expense vacation. One glorious week, seven full days, Hotel Room, Meals, Golf, Dancing, Swimming, all for $26.50. The following is what you got for your money;

Delightful room, and excellent meals at the Rustic Bella Vista Lodge Hotel, also one week of unlimited free admission to the following Bella Vista amusements and recreations.

Golfing on the Ozarks sportiest course, from daylight to dark if it suits your pleasure, the course is yours.

Swimming in the Ozarks' largest concrete, spring-fed swimming pool as often as you like, a favorite rendezvous for the refreshment and invigoration of everyone.

Wonderland night club, dancing and entertainment underground in nature's most uniquely sculptured ballroom, with an unvarying temperature of 62 degrees. America's Night Club in the depth of a Big Cave. Our congenial staff hostesses will be in attendance here to assist you in every way possible to enjoy yourself.

A sightseeing trip and exploring in Wonderland Cave, a marvel of the underground world.

Dancing in the New Lake Pavillion, High Class orchestra.

Moonlight Gardens, over Bella Vista Lake. Best music in

BELLA VISTA RESORT

the Ozarks by popular orchestras.

Tennis—Double courts adjoining swimming pool. If you desire, play tennis in your bathing suit.

Fishing, in the Bella Vista Lake and nearby streams.

Hiking and Picnic Parties in the fascinating mountains and forests of the extensive Bella Vista property and surrounding Ozarks.

Saddle Horses, not owned by the management, but a special rate of only 50 cents per hour will be available to you.

I am sure that everyone felt they had their money's worth when they left and started home after this $26.50 week of fun.

Like all the other businesses in the county, they had very slow business during the depression, but they weathered it and went right on giving people a lot of fun every summer.

Anyone who spent a week or a summer at Bella Vista left there with memories they never forgot.

Chapter Twenty Four
Towns and Villages

In writing these articles about the towns and villages of the county, I tried to just show the highlights of the history. Some of the towns were very hard to find out much about. Many I couldn't even find out when the post office opened. I have listed the postmasters for the towns that had a complete record.

I used the list of business places from Goodspeed's history of 1889 in most of the towns. These lists were made for 1888. I also used the business list from the R. G. Dun & Co. rating book for January, 1915.

Avoca

Early in 1881, when Albert Peel moved his store to the Frisco main line to start a new town, he also took the town's name with him. His wife then renamed the town they were leaving.

Some time after the Civil War, date unknown, Albert Peel started a store at what was later named Brightwater. This store, and the little village that grew up around it, was named Avoca by Mrs. Peel.

I have an 1878 map listing Avoca and showing it on Sugar Creek. I cannot say for sure if there was a post office here at that time or not. But most of the towns listed on this map did have post offices.

Some time in the late 1870's, Mr. Peel laid out the town of Avoca here. It never did do too much growing.

When the Frisco railroad started into Benton County, Albert Peel gave the right-of-way across all of his land. He also gave land for a depot, siding space for loading cars, stockyards and a tie yard.

Some time in the spring of 1881, he moved his store to his new town of Avoca. He also built the first house in Avoca. I have not been able to find out how long it was until there was a post office here.

TOWNS AND VILLAGES

By 1888, the town was listed as having a railroad depot; two general stores, those of A. Peel and J. R. Dunagin; a blacksmith shop; grain warehouse; and a district school. Fruit, cattle and hogs; grain, railroad ties, and fence posts, were the main items shipped from here.

By 1900, they had a post office, two or three apple evaporators, a large stockyards, tie yard and a very important station in that part of the county.

In 1912, they had three general stores, a drug store, produce house where the farmers could sell all their goods, two apple evaporators; one cooperage house where barrels were made; a vinegar plant, where they made apple juice to ship to where it could be made into vinegar; also a lime plant. At this time, Avoca was more than likely at its best. Over the years there have been two canning factories here.

As the years passed and the fruit went out, so did Avoca.

Beaty

The first public building I find in the area of what was later the town of Beaty, was the Beaty school which was started in 1873 on land donated by Mr. J. W. Teel. Later, the name was changed to Liberty Hill. In 1878, W. H. Williams was the teacher; he was paid $79.35 for a three-month term. They also held church and Sunday school in this same building.

Late in 1887, Jasper Parks started the first general store here. A post office was opened in Dec., 1888, at the home of Theodore Matthews, who was the first postmaster. On Nov. 28, 1890, Jasper Parks was named postmaster and he moved the office to his store.

In 1895, a man named Fishburn opened the second store in Beaty, In May, 1896, B. A. Gravett bought out Jasper Parks and put in a larger and complete general merchandise line. Ben was just 21 and was said to be very young for the job.

Later in 1896, Gravett built a two-story business and lodge building; it was 24 x 36. His store was downstairs and the Odd Fellow Lodge was up. This building was at what was then called new Beaty; it was a short ways from the old town, but was where the railroad later built through.

The lodge was established in Aug. of 1896 with 25 members. The officers were M. F. Leonard, Jasper Parks, B. A. Gravett, B. Shirley and E. Meek.

Late in 1896, Gravett sold his store to Mr. Hess who ran it for several years.

In April, 1897, Jasper Parks started the task of laying out the townsite of Beaty. A newspaper in Nov., 1897, stated that Jasper Parks has suddenly become a full fledged lawyer and had put up a shingle at Beaty.

277

Store and Post Office building at old Beaty about 1896. The man in the buggy is Jacob Lewis, his wife Lucy is standing inside the store and her son Earnest Brown is holding mail sack.

In May, 1897, Steven H. Kimsey (may have been Lindsey) became post master. He moved the post office 1½ miles southwest of Beaty. It later was moved back.

In 1898, the Arkansas Oklahoma railroad made its way through Beaty.

At the beginning of 1900, Beaty had two stores, Parks & Co General Merchandise and Perry Marshall Co; a post office, hotel, depot, blacksmith shop, charcoal kiln, apple evaporator, and school. Later, Perry Marshall Co. became Perry Hanna Co., when Sterling Hanna bought in.

In 1902, Frisco Railroad Co. purchased land from the Rark Roark farm and laid out town lots.

G. P. Beavers and J. W. Jordan ran a sawmill at Miller Springs on Honey Creek west of Beaty.

In July, 1907, Jacob Lewis became postmaster; he was also mail carrier, storekeeper and village blacksmith.

B. F. Frantz of Maysville moved his grocery stock into the lower floor of the Odd Fellow building in 1908. He later ran the hotel and for some time was Mayor of the town.

Perry-Hanna & Co. Charcoal Oven Kilns at Beaty were the largest in the state. There were four of these huge airtight brick kilns, which had a combined capacity of 180 cords of four foot wood.

A large part of the charcoal went to powder manufacturers. Several carloads were shipped each week.

These kilns were of the beehive-type, similar to the ones used in early coking of coal. The kilns were on the south side of the railroad track, a short distance from the store and post office.

The process known technically as destructive distillation was used. The beehive kiln was filled with hard wood: red oak, black-jack, chinquapin, and post oak. The wood charge was then fired and allowed to burn until it was well ignited. The combustion of oxygen (air) was then limited by closing off most of the draft openings. The wood then burns slowly until the volatiles are burned off; the combustion is then stopped. The resulting product, charcoal, is almost pure carbon.

About 1922, Perry Humes sold his store to Joseph C. Brisby and Mrs. Brisby ran the hotel and served family-style meals.

In May, 1931, Dr. J. S. Thompson, postmaster of Gravette, announced that the Beaty post office would close June 1. From then on, Gravette route 4 carried the mail for people at Beaty. John Loghry was the first carrier.

In 1934, Perry Hanna's store closed and the area was hit hard by the depression; many of the people left, looking for work. That was the end to Beaty.

Beaty Postmasters

Theodore Matthews	Dec. 15, 1888
Jasper Parks	Nov. 28, 1890
Steven H. Kimsey (or Lindsey)	May 5, 1897
Carl M. Parks	May 2, 1898
Jasper Parks	April 20, 1903
Estella F. Parks	May 2, 1904
William J. Reese	Mar. 10, 1906
Nellie C. Bagley	Dec. 13, 1906
Jacob Lewis	July 19, 1907
Henry L. Wilson	Feb. 15, 1910
Perry V. Hume	Apr. 15, 1911
Joseph C. Brisby	Mar. 31, 1922

Bentonville

Bentonville was started as the county seat by an act of the General Assembly on Sept. 30, 1836. It was Nov. 7, 1837, before the site was picked and recorded, then the town was laid out.

Just after the town was laid out, Dr. Nicholas Spring opened the first general store under the name Blythe & Spring. This stood somewhere on the east side of the square where the courthouse is today.

The second store was started a year or so later by John G. and William T. Walker. The town was so far away from everything, that it grew very slowly. Because this was the county seat, the town did become the center of all goings-on in the county.

In digging in early court records, I have found a hint that showed we may have had an early bank. The record showed that the Bank of The State of Arkansas bought lot number 53 from James H. Wallace for $353.99. This is on the west side of the square. It was dated Feb. 22, 1845. About the same time, they bought 160 acres from Nicholas Spring for $600.00. I haven't been able to prove if they got a bank open or not. If they did, it didn't last long I know.

By 1861, Bentonville had the following businesses: five general stores, A. W. Dinsmore, James Woolsey, Greenwood & Hobbs, J. M. Vestal and James A. Dickson; Henry Baumeister, furniture; J. W. Clark, saddle and harness shop; The Eagle House, J. W. Clark; Vestal Hotel, W. R. Vestal.

There were a few other small businesses, plus the County buildings downtown. There was a Cumberland Presbyterian Church, a Methodist Episopal South and the Masonic building and school. The population was about 500.

The Masonic Lodge was organized and chartered on the 4th of Nov., 1852, with J. A. Dickson, W. M., J. H. Hobbs, S. W., James M. Rogers, J. W. The Royal Arch Chapter was chartered Oct. 23, 1874.

Early doctors were C. D. Talliaferro, H. D. Hobbs, William Wilson and John Gray.

One of the first two-story buildings built in Benton County before the war, was built for James T. Craig for a general store. It is still standing.

Many of the buildings in Bentonville was burned during the Civil War; this included the county courthouse. It took several years for the town to be rebuilt after the war. By 1888, the town had made a good growth.

The Bentonville Mill, erected 1869, had two sets of buhr stones running full time, using 100 bushels of wheat and 200 bushels of corn a day. The Bentonville Canning and Evaporating Company had its evaporator going, using 800 bushels of apples a day. Arkansas Tobacco Company was manufacturing several brands of plug and smoking tobacco. The Eagle Mills had a new roller process and was running 60 barrels of flour a day. At that time, they were running day and night.

Barney & Ferqusson Cigar manufacturers were making the following line: Havana Star, Leader, Standard, Pearl, Flora, De Castillo and Barneys Bouquet. Their factory was on the south

A street scene made in Bentonville in 1882. The large building to the left is the old courthouse. It was finished in 1874 and used until 1927. The park on the right, where the old courthouse had stood, was fenced to keep the cattle out. There was a stile at each side to go in and out.

side of the square, upstairs.

Bentonville was incorporated as a town by the county court at its Jan. term in 1873. By 1900, they had a city-owned light and water plant, and were working on a sewer program. There was also a telephone company. Plus a very good school system.

The first Ford car agency was opened in Bentonville in 1912 by Charles Hess, a livery barn owner, and J. M. McAllister of Gravette. A Ford touring car that year cost just over $600.

The first filling station, if you could call it that, was run by Benton County Hardware Co. They had a 500-gallon tank buried in the alley alongside their building. This had a hand pump that brought up one gallon at a time. Most people bought 5 gallons at a time. If they had a tank filled, it would take from 10 to 12 gallons. Most of the time they used this, gas sold for 20 cents a gallon, but it did get down to 13 cents at one time.

This gas was brought up from Rogers in 50-gallon drums to fill the big tank. At first, the gas company was named Pierce Oil Co. Later it was Barnsdal.

Some time in 1919, a filling station was put in on South Main and Henry. This became known as the first filling station. After that, many more were opened in that town.

Businesswise, Bentonville was hurt bad by the loss of the apples, but because it was the County Seat and a very strong business town, it was able to withstand this loss and the hardships of the great depression that followed so close. So, the town kept on slowly growing.

The Goodspeed history listed the following businesses in Bentonville in 1888:

Benton County Bank; The Peoples Bank; W. A. Terry & Co.; Craig & Sons, Woods & Claypool, George Jackson, all dry goods; W. E. Goodwin, auction store; J. C. Knott, Morris & Co., J. H. & J. P. Burns, Wagner & Jefferson, G. M. Bates & Co. and P. S. Powell, all had grocery stores; Drugs Dr. C. D. Taliaferro, E. H. Looney, and W. S. Black; confectioneries, Inson & Larick, W. R. Hoffman, M. M. Harkins and P. McBride; T. C. Barney, J. L. Pluck, furniture; hardware, Hobbs & Co., Maxwell & Hickman; harness and saddles, H. A. Rogers, Stahl & Crough.

Lincoln & Arthur, clothing; Laughlin & Brashear, boots and shoes; R. J. Laughlin, M. M. Hawkins, watchmakers and jewelers; J. Huffman & Son, undertakers; Marble works, McWhirter & Robbins, J. K. Putman; candy factory, H. C. Turner; agricultural implements, C. W. Clapp, F. C. Hawkins; millinery, Wakefield & Deming, J. A. Sanderson & Co, Miss Julia Loomis; Roberts & Thomas, D. R. Thompson, boot and shoemakers; produce dealers, McHenry & Bryan, R. Y. Nance, blacksmiths, W. H. Ferguson, W. A. Smith, A. Marcum.

Corley, & Son, feed store; S. N. Price, J. H. Houston, meat markets; livery, Smartt & Brown, Faircloe & Brim; brickyards, J. Haney, Z. Mitchell, M. T. Carroll; contractors, J. Haney, C. A. Blanck, A. W. Duffie, J. Cook, Carney & Dodson, Robert Carley; Eagle Mills, H. W. Schrader, proprietor; Bentonville Mill. John Curtis, proprietor; Arkansas Tobacco Co.; Bentonville Canning and Evaporation Co.; wagon factory, McGruder, McAdams & Co.; lumber yard Hall, Guthrie & Co.; copperage, Dungie & Hunter; hotels, Rogers House, Western Hotel, Eagle Hotel, Eclipse Hotel; Physicians, T. W. Hurley, J. M. Thompson, John Smartt, C. D. Taliaferro, B. F. Smith, J. R. Lucas, W. R. Davis, J. M. Hobbs, J. A. Gill, N. B. Cotton; dentists, D. A. Watson, S. H. Petit, M. B. Vaughter; insurance C. E. Bruce, Cotton & Craig.

Bentonville Railroad Co., which at this time ran just from Bentonville to Rogers. This later was extended to Grove, Okla.

Bentonville Business 1915

In 1915, the Dun rating book listed the following for Bentonville, population 1,958.

Lee Allen, shoemaker; Arkansas Spray Co.; Atkinson &

Ammons, wholesale grocery; Beck Tailoring Co.; Benton County Hardware Co.; Benton County Lumber Co.; Bentonville Cash Store, dry goods & shoes; Bentonville Coal Co.; Bentonville Ice & Cold Storage Co.; Bentonville Plumbing & Supply Co.; Bentonville Steam Laundry; J. H. Blevins, blacksmith; J. W. Blocker, apple evaporator; Bohart Hardware Co.; Boon Bro. dry goods; J. T. Browne, grocery; M. Brown, drugs; W. F. Burns, grocery; C. O. Butler, general store; E. Carnahan, jeweler; Chandler Cash Grocery; City Meat Market; R. R. Cook, grocery; J. G. Crawford, blacksmith.

H. L. Cross, publisher; L. C. Crouch, harness; M. C. Cunningham, livery; P. P. Curtis, builders supplies; Eagle Milling Co.; Ferguson Lumber Co.; F. F. Floyd, grocery; D. S. Foster & son meats; Four S Fly Trap Co.; A. F. Frey, grocery; Gardiner & Gardiner, grocery; Miss Laura Harris, photographer; W. T. Haxton, drugs; G. E. Hildebrandt, tailor; Aug Hulbrock, fuel & feed; H. S. Jackson, grocery; Jackson Dry Goods Co.; Geo. H. Jefferson, grocery; Geo. A. Johnson, electrician; Z. E. Keck, racket store; Ray D. Keith, grocery; Kerr & Orr, furniture & undertaker; J. C. Knott, grocery; E. Latham, hotel; McDaniels & Matkins, hotel; McHenry & Bryan, wool buyers; and fruit; Macon & Carson Distilling Co.; Massey hotel; S. C. Mayhall, hotel; E. E. Menasco, fuel; C. O. Mitchell Co., marble; A. T. Moody, shoemaker; Mrs. M. Moore, millinery; Elay Morgan, furniture.

F. Novitzky, baker; J. W. blacksmith; Ohl Julius Co. meat; E. T. Peck Cooperage Co.; A. B. Phinney, jeweler; Strode-Long Mercantile Co. L. C. Sultzer, second hand goods; J. H. Sweeney tinsmith; Ben Terry, publisher; M. B. Tisdale, drug; Webb & Miller, plumbers; E. J. Worthington, undertaker; Worthington News Co.

Banks listed, Benton County National Bank, First National Bank, First State Bank.

Town of Bentonville

Ordinance No. 1

An ordinance to better secure the peace and quiet of the town of Bentonville, Ark.

Be it ordained by the council of the town of Bentonville, Ark.

Section 1

It is hereby made unlawful for any person or persons, either by day or by night, to disturb the peace and quiet of the incorporated town of Bentonville, or any neighborhood or family within said corporated limits, by loud and unusual noise, or by violent, profane or obcene language, whether addressed to the parties disturbed or not, or by the singing of indecent songs, or by fighting quarreling, or threating to fight, or challenging others to fight or by discharging any firecrackers or firearms, or by casting or throwing any stones, brick, brick-bats, or other mineral, metallic, wooden or vegetable substances at any building within the intent to inflict an injury upon the person or disturb the peace and quiet of any individual or family, or by riding or driving any horse or horses at an unusual speed along any of the streets, alleys or other public highways with in the said corporate limits.

Section 2

Any person or persons violating any of the provisions of this ordinance, shall upon conviction thereof be punished by a fine of not less than one Dollar or exceeding Twenty-five dollars.

Section 3

That this ordinance take effect from and after its publication.

Feb. 17, 1886

> E. S. McDaniel, Mayor
> J. W. Talliferrio
> Recorder Pro Tem

The town was incorporated in 1873, but this was the first ordinance on record.

City of Bentonville

Ordinance 97

Section 1

It is hereby declared unlawful to skate on roller skates or roll hoops of any kind upon any of the side walks of the city of Bentonville.

Section 2

Any person violating the provisions of this ordinance shall be fined in any sum not exceeding Five dollars.

June 23rd. 1908

> A. W. Morris, Mayor

City of Bentonville

Ordinance No. 104

An ordinance prescribing the speed of automobiles in the city of Bentonville, and for other purposes be it ordained by the council of the city of Bentonville.

Section 1

It shall be unlawful to drive any automobile at a speed greater than eight miles per hour on the public square of the city of Bentonville, or with in 200 feet of said square on any street leading into said square, and it shall be unlawful to drive any automobile at any greater speed than ten miles per hour on any other public street or alley in said city of Bentonville.

Section 2

Any person operating or driving any automobile on the public streets, square or alleys of the city of Bentonville, is required to slacken the speed of such machine at all street corners or crossings and to give a signal by sounding a bell or horn suffuciently loud to be heard distinctly at a distance of 150 feet, and in case it is apparent that any horse, mule or team is frightened or becoming frightened at such automobile, the person in charge there of shall bring said machine to a stop unless requested by the person in charge of such horse, mule or team to continue moving the same, and remain standing until such horse, mule or team shall have safely passed such machine.

Section 3

Any person violating the provisions of this ordinance shall be fined in any sum not exceeding Twenty-five dollars.

Section 4

This ordinance shall take effect and be in force from and after its passage and publication.

Passed July 20, 1909

A. W. Morris, Mayor

Town of Bentonville

Ordinance No. 26

An ordinance to regulate the fire department within the incorporated Town of Bentonville.

Section 1

The council, of the Incorporated Town of Bentonville shall elect a Fire Department Inspector who shall inspect the Engine, Hose, Reels and all things there to belonging, once in every month.

Section 2

The inspector of the Fire Department shall cause the Fire Company to turn out for inspection once in every month at which time he (the said inspector) shall inspect to, and report the condition of said Fire Company in writing to the council.

Section 3

The failure of the Fire Company to comply with section two (2) of this ordinance, by the council, be deemed sufficient cause for depriving the Fire Company of Engine, Hose, Reel, Elc.

Section 4

That this Ordinance take effect from and after it's publication.

285

Passed June 7th, 1888.

W. D. Mauch, Mayor
W. H. Cown, Recorder

It seems very odd to pass an ordinance about a fire engine that year in Bentonville, as all they had was a hose cart and hose.

Bloomfield

Bloomfield was a small village on the west side of the county and six miles north of Siloam Springs. There is no date as to when it was started, but it must have been several years before it was plotted and recorded at the courthouse. That was done Nov. 12, 1873. They did lay out a nice-sized town with a big town square.

R. B. Mitchell was the original proprietor and owner of the whole town. He put in the first general store, and Dr. J. H. Neagle built the first house. A year later, a post office was put in the general store of R. B. Wilson, with Wilson as postmaster. His had been the second store in the village. For several years, other merchants just came and went.

The Bloomfield Lodge No. 243, A. F. & A. M. was chartered in 1871 with William Kellum as first W. M.

By 1888, the following businesses were in the town. General stores of R. B. Wilson and W. I. Richardson; Mitchell & Bro. drugs and groceries; hotel, David Chandler; J. Johnson, blacksmith; J. E. Stewart, woodworker; J. R. Floyd, physician.

Three-fourths of a mile south of the village was the Bloomfield Steam Roller Mills, which was one of the bigger mills on the west side of the county at that time.

The Rogers Academy was in a two-story brick building with a seating capacity for 150 pupils. Prof. A. B. Marbury was the principal. He had all the classes taught in high school, as well as having the public school.

This was more than likely as big as Bloomfield had ever been. When the railroad came near, but missed the town, its business began to slow down. In time, several from here moved to Gentry. The Roller Mill being one.

In 1915, the general story of A. R. Wilson was the only business that was rated by Dun rating book.

In time, the town just faded away.

Brightwater

This was a village of many names, but today only the last one is used. In about 1840, Enoch Trott built the first store here. It was a general store and tavern. There was a campground here where travelers could stay to rest. The selling of liquor was the big business. From this it took the name Trott's Stand.

When the Civil War started, Judge Long was keeping the only store here. During the war, this and the other buildings were all burned down.

Some time just after the end of the Civil War, Albert Peel bought the land and put up a house and general store. His wife then named the place Avoca. In 1881, they moved to a new location on the Frisco main line. They then named it Avoca; at this time, Mrs. Peel renamed the old Avoca, Brightwater. These towns were both in the northeast part of the county.

After the railroad came through Brightwater, the town grew some. In 1888, the town consisted of a general store of Joe Dickson and Son; drug store of Dr's T. M. & R. S. Rice; a grocery of Hill & Lynch; one blacksmith shop, and the apple evaporator of Kimmons & Son. This had a capacity of 200 bushels a day, and employed about 25 hands.

They had a schoolhouse but no churchhouse at that time. The members of the Christian Church met at the schoolhouse. The Pea Ridge Lodge No. 119 A. F. & A. M. was located here also.

The Dun rating book of 1915 listed just the general store of J. H. Buttram in the town. There could easily have been more, but they were very small.

At one time, the post office department changed the name of this town to Bestwater, and it has been on the map that way for years. But to the people in that part of the county, it was still Brightwater.

Cave Springs

Cave Springs was best known for its cave and spring. Yet, it was first known for the gristmill built here by George Robbins just after statehood. This mill was sold to Elijah Allen in 1852, who ran it as the Allen mill for many years.

John Sandusky had the first general store. The first school was a one-room log house called "Stick in the Mud". It was named this because the chimney was made of mud and sticks.

At a very early date, James Dickson built a gristmill a mile north of Cave Springs. He later sold this mill to Mr. Finncannon, who got a post office put in. He was the first postmaster and ran the office in one room of his mill. The post office was named Cannon, so the area took that name. For several years, the post office was moved back and forth from the Finncannon mill to the Allen mill as the two men changed as postmasters.

The Finncannon mill was one of the few mills in the county to run throughout the Civil War. Buck Phillips later bought and ran the mill. Many people still think of it as the Phillips Mill. He sold it to J. L. Martin of Purcell, Mo., in 1912. In later years, it was moved somewhere else.

After the Allen mill ceased to operate, W. M. Bartlett bought

Main street of Cave Springs about 1910.

the spring and farm around it. He built a dam and made a lake, then built a new mill.

It is said that the name of Cave Springs was started in 1902 or 1903. But the post office was called Cannon until 1908.

In 1906, the Kansas City and Memphis Railroad was built through here and that gave Cave Springs its first big start. Later, a line was run from here to Fayetteville. These lines were a great boost for the lake and playground here.

For several years people had been driving out to Cave Springs for an outing. But with a horse and buggy, they spent more time in the buggy than at the lake. After the train came, it was very easy for anyone to go there and have almost a full day of pleasure at the lake and cave.

Mr. Bartlett had the town laid out after the railroad came. Yet, he didn't record the plot until 1909. This plot was for a good-sized town. It showed the lake as being named Loch Lono.

With the coming of the railroad, this little village became a good businesstown fast. There soon were several stores and businesses. Bill Zirenberg built a canning plant and Bob Sikes and Bill Rozer put up an apple evaporator. The railroad had a large loading area here, and many a carload of apples were shipped from Cave Springs.

At this time, most of the land around Cave Springs was planted to apples.

A bank was founded in Cave Springs about 1908. In 1911, Dr. Highfill fitted up an office upstairs in the bank building. Dr. Fausset was also in the same building.

In 1915, we find the following business in Cave Springs: hotel, D. J. Beard; Bohart Hardware Co., branch of Bentonville store; Cave Springs Lumber Co., branch Ferguson Bentonville; Cave Springs Milling Co., H. C. Stroud; Cave Springs Telephone Co.; C. Chastain, groceries; Coger & Bardwell, drugs; O. E. Culp, harness; W. T. Ellston, flour & feed; L. J. Haire, hardware; H. B. Livington, general store; J. D. Peace, restaurant; C. Stanared, racket store, this was a 5 & 10 cent; J. M. Stewart & Co., general store; City Barber Shop; Jepson and Tabor, blacksmith; Bohart Land Co.

This was the very peak of their heyday. The railroad was taken out in 1918. The bank closed in 1929. Later, the apples were gone and the town became a small village again.

Cave Spring Postoffice

The postmasters for Cave Springs have been:

Hugh C. Stroud	Mar. 2, 1908
Isaac W. Chastain	May 2, 1914
John P. Allison	Jan. 7, 1919
Cyril Flack	Jan. 8, 1920
George A. Stroud	Nov. 16, 1925
B. H. Fagala	Dec. 10, 1926

Fagala was still postmaster in 1936.

Centerton

Years before the town of Centerton started, there was a Methodist Episcopal Church South at this place named Centerpoint. When the Rogers to Grove railroad was built through here, a station and shipping yard was put in.

Since there was a Centerpoint in some other part of Arkansas, this town was named Centerton in 1898 when it got its start. For several years there had been a post office named Seba just north of here. After a few years, the name was changed and the post office moved to Centerton.

At that time, Miss Mittie Lee was the Station mistress for the railroad in Centerton and she was also made the first postmistress. She stayed in Centerton until some time in 1906.

For a time there was just one general store here, but others soon came. In 1905, a bank was started as a branch of one in Bentonville.

By 1907, this was a nice-sized shopping and shipping center. Mitchell & Sammons general store had a large stock of every need

Looking south on Main Street in Centerton about 1906 or 1907.

for the home, farm or orchard. A Corley general store said they sold a little of everything. Thomas Richards had a blacksmith shop; E. C. Rozar, a drugstore; A. M. Black, lumberyard; the Bank, and E. H. Fair & Co., land agents.

There were four apple evaporators; a large new vinegar plant where they made apple juice to be tanked to the Rogers Vinegar plant; There were also several places buying apples with storage sheds.

A school was started here almost as soon as the town was formed and at one time they had a two-year high school.

The town kept growing until, in 1915, they had the following listed by the Dun rating: Population 300; one good Bank; Bohart Hardware Co, (branch of Bentonville); W. L. Boon groceries; J. A. Carley, general store; Jones Bros & Co. Vinegar, (branch of Rogers); Ed Rich, general store; E. C. Rozer drugs; St. Louis Commission Co., (branch of St. Louis Mo.); J. W. Wall, general store. There were several smaller businesses that were not listed in this.

Centerton was more than likely as big right then as it ever got. First, the apples gave out; then the railroad was taken up. After that, this was just a small village.

Cherokee City

Hogeye was the name of the little village that stood on Hogeye Creek before the Civil War. There was a still kept here and since it was just three-fourths of a mile from the Indian Territory, most of the business was selling whiskey to Indians. There must have also been a general store and blacksmith here.

A Frenchman, Samuel Hoag, moved here in 1876 and built the hotel which he operated until his death in 1892.

In 1880, James Ingle, David Chandler and M. D. Cunningham plotted a village across the creek from Hogeye. They had planned to name their town Hogeye, but since there was a Hogeye in Washington County the post office department had them pick a new name.

In 1881 and 82 they had a boom as a summer resort; due to this, there was a fast growth that didn't last long. M. D. Cunningham opened the first general store in Cherokee City.

By 1888, there was his store plus the general stores of J. M. Tucker, Crawford Brothers; J. M. Norris and the drug stores of Eurial Farmin; plus Mr. Baxter, a furniture store; the blacksmiths were A. E. Funk and a Mr. Cook. The hotel was the "Cherokee House," owned and ran by Samuel Hoag. Dr. O. M. Dodson was the only doctor.

The churches included Baptist, Christian, Methodist, Episcopal-South and the Congregational. Population 200.

The orchard of T. A. Fleener, with over 2,200 apple trees, was close by.

There was a large spring on the Hampton B. Wooldridge farm just across Hogeye creek. The village water was pumped from here uphill with a ram. There was a large watering trough near the spring for the livestock. This also was a favorite meeting place for the young men.

At one time, Uncle Will Shaw ran a sawmill and gristmill along the creek with a Case steam engine.

John M. Norris arrived in Cherokee City with a wagonload of fixtures and drug supplies in 1887, and set up a drug store in a small building. Some time later he moved into a large building with the I. O. O. F. Hall upstairs. As well as selling drugs to the people, he bandaged skinned heads, or other parts, and set bones.

Hamp Wooldridge ran a hardware and harness store on spring street across Hogeye creek. It was said that he also had a still back in the timber as he sold whiskey too.

About 1890, a Mrs. Haxon bought a large house and added onto it and ran what was known for years as Haxon Hotel.

In 1915, the Dun rating book gave Cherokee City with a population of 79, and having the hardware of W. H. Alvey; general E. H. Raymond; and the mill of W. O. Shaw.

Some time in the 1920's there was a canning factory here run by A. S. Bailey.

For many years, this was a town of just one or two stores.

Decatur

The early history of Decatur is not easy to follow, as I can find no written report of when the first store went in or who opened it. I can not find when the name was first used.

We do know that John B. Allensworth had one of the early general stores here; he opened it some time in 1882. There could already have been a general store and blacksmith shop here at that time.

When the first post office opened on Feb. 12, 1883, John Cotton was made the Postmaster, but the records don't show if this was in his home or a business that he had.

In 1893, the Kansas City, Pittsburg and Gulf Railroad started building their line through Decatur, on land that was given by John W. Leslie. The same year he laid out a new town called Cornor Springs, but this town never took the place of Decatur. The railroad did make the town grow some.

I found some records for 1903 that showed S. P. Londagin and two other people as having hotels here. It also listed a blacksmith, livery barn, post office, sawmill, depot, stockyard, two churches, a school, and a large shipping yard. This said there were several stores, but gave no list of what kind.

The State Bank of Decatur was opened in 1906. At this time they had three general stores, one dry goods, one drug store, a blacksmith and a livery barn. At one time they had as many as three apple evaporators. In 1912, there was also a canning plant here.

By 1915, Decatur was a good business town; the Dun rating book listed the following: Population 246. The State Bank of Decatur; John L. Buckner, publisher; W. L. Cato & Co., general store; Decatur Hardware Store; Decatur Lumber Co.; Edmiston & Whitaker, grocery; C. S. Hedges, general store; Holland American Fruits & Products Co.; Ihmels & Ihmels, grocery; D. C. Loudigan, hotel; Mrs. J. McCrady, restaurant; W. S. McGaugh, general store; Mount Zion Farmers Mutual Tel. Co.; B. P. Northcutt, second hand good; R. E. Stephens, general store; C. Wilkins, hotel.

This would show that in 1915 Decatur was at its very best. It more than likely stayed this way until the apple industry started to fail; then it, too, slowly died out.

Decatur

The first post office was opened in Decatur on Feb. 12, 1883. The following is the list of postmasters.

John Cotton	Feb. 12, 1883
Riley J. Mathis	Jan. 17, 1884
John B. Allensworth	Nov. 2, 1886

Henry P. Lovell	Feb. 8, 1889
Eliza J. Allensworth	Sept. 11, 1890
Green L. P. Sugg	Jan. 15, 1894
William F. Hines	Nov. 30, 1897
Floyd Blaney	Sept. 29, 1898
Thomas Trammell	Aug. 10, 1906
Frederick M. Priestly	July 7, 1913
Addie Gilbert Murphy	March 1, 1922
Addie Murphy	May 2, 1930
Clinton H. Northcutt	Dec. 1, 1934

Eldorado

Eldorado was the first health resort town in the county and it boomed fast, but in a few years it washed away. The town was just seventeen miles west of Bentonville. I have not been able to find out who laid it out, or what year. It must have been some time in the early 1870's.

At one time there many houses here; stores, a three-story hotel, school, post office and whatever else it took to have a first class resort.

It all layed along Spavinaw creek; the springs they used for water is said to have had a curing power and many medicinal claims were made about them. Many people came here to be cured of almost anything. Others just spent their time resting in a good hotel and playing along the stream, or doing whatever else there was to do.

When the post office was put in, it was named Pactolous as there was an Eldorado elsewhere in the state. But the town still was called Eldorado.

In the spring of 1883, the spavinaw went on a real rampage and a wall of water came down on Eldorado and washed most of the buildings away.

The town was never rebuilt. For many years there was a store there and the post office. There was also a mill a short way off at the spring known as Pactolous Spring. This was one of the older mills in the county.

The next new life along this part of the Spavinaw was when Frank and Bertha Root bought the property in 1918. They repaired the dam and started the mill running again. They divided about 100 acres west of the creek into city lots and started Root's Playground. There was a county store, a big dance pavilion, and cabins to rent and sell.

There must have been some kind of an eating house, as I find a report that Mrs. Root served chicken and dumplings and went swimming between times.

In 1924, the mill was running good, grinding corn and wheat as well as making electricity. The dam washed out in 1928, so the

The Arkansas Store—The Arkansas store in Garfield, operated by Harry C. Baker, became famous throughout this section because of its unusual sign. They used the letter R, and a picture of an oil can and a bucksaw.

mill was closed.

In a few short years, all of Root's Playground was gone too.

Garfield

Garfield is one of the towns in the county that no one is sure of when it started or how it started. At one time it was listed on the Maps as Blansett, and I have been told that it also has been called Blansett station.

I have an 1878 map of the State of Arkansas which listed Avoca, but it didn't show any town where Garfield is. But it could have been there and been too small to mark. Goodspeeds History gave it as starting in 1881.

We do know that Archbald Blansett owned the farm here for a number of years before the railroad came in. He could very easily have had a small store here at an earlier date.

By 1875, there would have been enough people living in this area to have supported a store. I feel sure that Mr. Blansett already had a store here by the time the railroad came. If so, they more than likely named this stop Blansett station, after the man who had given them the right-of-way as he had. They could very easily have had a work camp here for a short time.

Goodspeeds History gives the following account of the town. The first store was opened by Archbald Blansett in 1881. The next year, Albert Peel opened one. Following this, Thomas R. Marshall opened a drug store.

For 1888, they listed the following business: General stores— A. Peel, G. P. Rogers & Son, and J. A. Wilks; hardware, L. Ellison; groceries, J. W. Cundiff; confectionery, H. Wilks; post office; jewelry, etc., A. J. Wilks; hotel, J. N. Wilks; drugs and jewelry, M. J. Walters.

There also was two blacksmith shops, a barber shop, the Arkansas Lime Works, the fruit evaporator of D. D. Ames and the lumber yard of A. L. Ricketts.

The Arkansas Lime Works manufactured 200 barrels of lime per day, they made their own barrels and employed about seventy-five men. The fruit evaporator had a capacity for from 100 to 150 bushels of apples a day, and employed fifteen people, mostly girls.

There was a large two-story building that housed the school downstairs and the Masonic hall up. A great quantity of fruit, timber, railroad ties, and fence posts were shipped from here then.

Some people have said that the first post office date not known was called Blansett; this has never been proven. But a marriage license that was issued in 1882 to a young couple living there gave the mailing address as Crowell.

In the early days, the students went to a school a little ways from here that was called Head of the Creek.

Peter McKinlay, who owned the lime company, later bought one of the general stores. It is said everyone who worked for him had to buy part of their goods there. He also ran the lime company office at the store.

The 1915 Dun rating book listed the following business in Garfield: H. C. Baker, general store, W. A. Galyan, general store; P. McKinlay Jr. had the Garfield Lime works and Garfield Mercantile Co.; Garfield Lumber Co; Garfield Milling Co.; Garfield Mutual Telephone Co.; H. K. Legg, drugs; J. W. Reddich, groceries. Of course there could have been some small businesses not listed.

By the 1920's, Jess Whitney had the largest peach and apple orchard in the area. He shipped 8 to 10 carloads of fruit a year. About this time, the apple evaporators in the area were paying 15 to 20 cents a 100 lb. for apples to dry. At one time there was a canning factory that bought fruit, beans and sweet potatoes.

By the late 1920's and early 1930's, this town was on its way out, like so many others in the county.

William Steele, who owned the first Drug Store in Gentry, stands by their first water works—A public well along the main street of the town. The building in back was a store downstairs and the Lodge up.

Gentry

Gentry is one of several towns that started along the Kansas City, Fort Smith and Southern Railroad Line. It was named in honor of the president of the railroad line that gave the town its start.

The town was started some time in the summer of 1893. At about that time, William Steele started the first drug store, and A. G. Wasson and Bro. opened the first general store.

On May 21, 1894, the Gentry post office was first opened with William Steele postmaster. He put this in his drug store.

In Sept. of 1897 the name was changed to Orchard because of all the apple orchards in the area. After all, most of the money in the area came from apples in some way.

The town was incorporated in 1898, with the name back as Gentry but using Orchard as their mailing address. They used this until Feb. 2, 1900, when the post office name was changed back to Gentry.

John H. Johnson was made postmaster in Sept., on the day the name was changed to Orchard. He was still postmaster when it was changed back to Gentry.

TOWNS AND VILLAGES

The Benton county Sun said in 1907 that Gentry was a fast growing town with 1,200 people. They were laying cement sidewalks throughout the city. They listed the following businesses: State Bank of Gentry, W. D. Wasson, President, $10,000 capital; Wasson & McGaugh & Co., general merchandise; J. W. Carpenter, staple & fancy groceries, furniture and undertaking; J. T. Mitchell, dry goods, groceries, boots, shoes and country produce; C. D. Highfill, City Drug, cool lemonade and ice cream; McKinney & Bennett, hardware, full line carriages; A. J. Miller, full line ranges, stoves, tin ware, granite ware; Sugg & Hanshaw, blacksmith; The Elberta Hotel, first class rooms and dining area; Geo. Chapman, restaurant and cold drinks; Gentry Lumber, D. W. Feemaster; McNeil Scott, meat market; D. C. Londagin, liveryman; W. V. Steele, first class pharmacy, drugs and herbs; S. M. Sheldon, harness maker; J. J. and T. M. Carl, Gentry hardware; P. D. Chastain, jewelry and watch repair.

Many of these stores had been moved from one of the other small towns nearby. Right from the start, Gentry was a good business town. The Roller Mill moved here from Bloomfield.

There were three or four apple evaporators running here for a number of years. Some time in the early 1900's, a group of Seven Day Baptists moved here and they built a very good canning plant that they ran for several years. This one closed and later a second canning plant was put in.

The Benton County Sun may have overrated the population of Gentry in 1907. The Dun rating book of 1915 gave the population as just 668. They listed it as a banking town and having its own post office, plus the following business: Baker & Scott evaporators; J. R. Baver Co., prod. & fruits; Mrs. Marie Carpenter, millinery; Carpenter Bros., furniture & groceries; Cox & Co., groceries and produce; D. A. Crandall, meat; Fristoe & Feemster, Racket store; Gentry Electric Light, Heat & Power; Gentry Independent Telephone; Gentry Hardware Co; Gentry Lumber Co.; Gentry Milling Co.; J. L. Greenlee, general store; Paul Isaacson, dry goods; Mrs. J. H. Johnson, millinery; G. W. Late, distillery; S. Laurse, restaurant; R. E. McClurg, shoemaker; C. S. McKinney, grocery; J. L. Middletyn hotel; A. J. Moller, stoves & tinware; J. F. Mitchell, general store; New York Racket, Fristoe & Feemster (this was a 5 & 10 cent store); W. V. Steele, Red Front Drug Store; J. E. Richardson, pumps; Ricketts & Watts, livery; J. P. Roush, lumber; H. W. Russell, jeweler; J. L. Stout, harness; A. Tallman & Co, publisher; Walk & Talk Cash Store; Wasson McGaugh & Co., general store; F. E. Willmer & Co., bakery.

Like all of the towns in Benton County, Gentry was hurt bad by both the depression and losing the apple industry. But they were able to overcome both of these and stay a good business town.

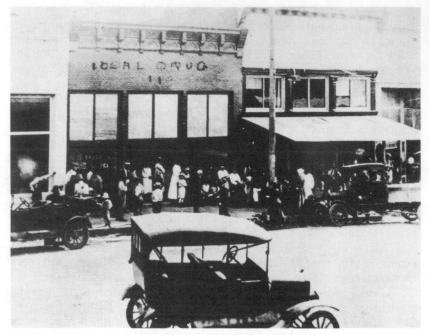

Main Street of Gravette about 1920. The store in the foreground is still the Ideal Drug, but has a new owner.

Nebo and Gravette

The village of Nebo started some time in the mid 1880's. By 1888, it was listed as having two or three businesses and a post office. Also there was a G.A.R. no. 62, post. Sometime about 1890, or just after, the Chalk Valley Distillery was opened. I haven't been able to find out just who started this.

In 1891 or 92, E. T. Gravett bought this and ran it for a short time until the railroad built a line through about a mile from Nebo. Then Gravett went up on the rail line and built a store and laid out the town of Gravett.

The following article on Gravett was written by A. C. Veach, editor of the Gravett News, on Sept. 29, 1894.

The post office was moved here from Nebo on Sept. 1st and the name was changed to Gravette. G. L. Bates, who has been postmaster at Nebo for some time, was here as postmaster too.

The biggest business in Nebo was the Chalk Valley Distillery, which was making 30 gallons of corn whiskey a day. This soon will be increased to 50 gallons a day.

A good size town has been laid out and the following are all doing a good business here. Chalk Valley Distillery; Gravette Roller Mills, who turns out 50 barrels of flour a day; Grain

Elevator, 5,000 bushels capacity.

Gravette has a new town look, main street, modern building, hotel, blacksmith shop, new school building, nine stores, a brick yard and lumber yard. A tannery was soon to be added. 25 new buildings were put up that season.

There is a Methodist, Missionary Baptist and Adventists church all in town. Also a Holiness preacher. Bethel Lodge No. 232 F & A.M.; Nebo Lodge No. 118 O.O.F.; Rebecia Lodge; and Eastern Star.

E. T. Gravett the founder of the town, came to this region in 1877 from Kentucky. A. O. Young and W. T. Webb, who succeeded him in mercantile business, came from Pea Ridge.

W. C. Croxdale, of Croxdale & Elderkin, is from Tenn. J. W. Rhamy from Ohio; R. Adkins, Ill. Dr. W. D. Foster was born in Benton County and studied in Iowa. W. H. Myers from Indiana; and Editor Veach is from Kansas.

One of the finest homes in town is that of E. M. Gravett the distiller. He was E. T.'s son, and had taken over the Chalk Valley Distillery from his dad.

Last month the railroad took in $1,175 for freight. People had shipped wheat, cattle, produce and railroad ties. L. B. Anderson was agent. He was also a noted artist.

Gravett Mercantile house has $45,000 goods in value on hand. Young & Webb will enter their new brick and stone building in November. They are shipping 1,000 dozen eggs a week.

Mr. G. L. Bates, postmaster, also has a first class pharmacy; this is where the post office is.

R. Adkins, of Foster & Adkins Pharmacy, is also in J. W. McAlister and Adkin's Lumber yard.

Dr. Foster, I think that his jovial, genial manner does about as much good as his medicine.

T. J. Plater & Son is doing a good business, and so is J. R. Dunagin. L. C. Schoonover left the plow for the grocery counter.

J. W. Rhamy, one of the popular men of the day, and J. A. Ragsdale do a lot of hardware business. J. W. McAlister House feeds with quality and quantity.

Lots are selling all over town from $50 to $100 each.

Editor Veach's article may sound a bit odd. But that was his way of trying to put the name of every business man in the article.

John Wesley Cromwell donated land for the first school in Gravette. This was a two-room frame building known as Cromwell school district No. 23. In 1899, there were 105 students enrolled, with an average attendance of 88.

A few years later Gravette built a larger school.

In Aug., 1907, the Benton County Sun ran a short article on Gravette and they listed the following businesses:

One large canning factory; three apple evaporators; a Vinegar factory; one flouring mill; a stave and barrel plant; five churches; two banks, a First National Bank and the Bank of Gravett; Gravette Milling Co.; C. W. Witty's Department store; David T. Roseboro Hardware; Robt. Laughlin Livery & Feed stable; Harry Allsman Blacksmith; J. A. Steward Grocery store; Laughlin House Hotel; J. W. Oglesby Drug; W. L. Spyres General Store; J. M. Grimsley Gravett Drugs; Cato & Dorsett General Store, they also buy all farm goods; McAlister & Co. General Merchandise; McAlister Bros. also Lumber and all building material. Buy farm products.

J. W. McAlister had one of the first cars in Gravette. It was a 1912 Ford touring car which cost just over $600. He had to pick the car up at Bentonville. In 1917, he bought a Model T. Ford for $385.85. It was a hand crank starting model.

The first filling station, or should we just say place to buy gas, was at the McAlister Lumber yard. Here they got the gas in 50 gallon drums. They were turned on their side with a spigot in them. The gas was run into a one-gallon spout can, then put in the gas tank.

For years now there have been several stories going around as to why the town of Gravette had a "e" on the end of the name; but over the years many businesses, the Bank of Gravett being the only one today, didn't have the "e" on the end. Mr. Mark Ernst, a grandson of E. T. Gravett told this fact about it.

When E. T. Gravett left Kentucky he had a falling out with his family, who used the "e" on the end of their name. He dropped the "e" and changed the sound of the name. But when the railroad sent the name in to go on their records as a station, a clerk who knew how it should be spelled put the "e" back on the end of the name. The bank was named for Mr. Gravett and it has stayed that way.

For many years now there has been very little change in the size of the town of Gravette.

Healing Springs

Healing Springs was a small village four miles west of Cave Springs. It was started when the Arkansas, Oklahoma & Western Railroad was built.

This town was never too big, and I have found out very little about it. In 1915, they had the general stores of C. A. Gorum, A. M. McClure, J. T. Salyer, Thomas Tate; and Mitchell & Burch grocery. There was also a post office and a few small businesses.

Highfill

Highfill was started in 1906 when the Arkansas, Oklahoma & Western railroad was built from Rogers to Siloam Springs. The post office was opened later that year.

In 1907, they had the general store of J. A. Mason; W. H. Mason, hardware; H. C. Childs, grocery; a blacksmith shop; a depot and loading yards. From these, many a carload of apples were shipped.

A two-story hotel was built soon after the town was started. In 1915, they had the general stores of W. W. Black, A. E. Story, and J. W. Thurman. T. B. Leach was the blacksmith. There may have been one or more small businesses, but not much.

In 1920, the post office closed, and some more of the town was gone.

This town was eight miles west of Cave Springs.

Hiwasse

Hiwasse was started in 1898 when the Rogers to Grove, Okla. Railroad was started. There had been a post office and store just north of there called Dickson. But in a short time this was all moved to Hiwasse.

This was a big shipping point for apples for many years. In 1907, they had three large apple evaporators; Henry Banks, Hiwasse mercantile Co.; Joseph Croxdale, general store, Lambeath Hudson, drugs; one blacksmith.

In 1915, they had a population of 150; Elmo Ballew, store; Jos. Croxdale, general store; A. H. Duncan, blacksmith; W. B. Hart, general store; Hiwasse Mercantile Co.; J. E. Holloway, general store; Walthall Bros, grocery; Hudson, Drugs.

There would have been a few small businesses. This was more than likely as big as Hiwasse ever got. After the apples were gone, the town dried up a lot.

Lowell

Lowell is in the south central part of the county very near to the Washington County line. The town was founded on the present site, after the completion of the Frisco Railroad. Until that time, there was a village located a mile east of this present site on the old wire road. It was known as Bloomington. It also was nicknamed Mudtown; there were three stores and a saloon here. Close by, there were several stills where corn whiskey was made. Some were legal, some were not.

The present townsite was homesteaded by Mr. Withrow; and later owned by J. H. McClure, who donated some of his lots to the Frisco Railroad for founding of a town.

Lowell's first store belonged to J. W. Main, and Wolf Otey and Captain Eaton had the first drug store.

The first school was built in 1884 on the present site of the A. C. Mayes home. It was a two-story, two-room brick building erected through the cooperation of the Masonic Lodge and used as a meeting place by Masons and the I.O.O.F. Until this building was put up, the school children of Lowell had to attend school at Goad Springs. L. P. Davis of Springdale taught the first school term in the new building.

In 1915, a larger brick structure was erected on a big campus in the eastern part of town. By 1936, just the first through sixth grade students went to school here; they had three teachers. The school had been consolidated with Rogers and the other grades went there.

Lowell's first church, a union or community church in which all denominations worshipped, was built in 1888 by donated labor. The land was donated by J. H. McClure. In 1892, the Presbyterian church was built and dedicated by Rev. Peter Carnahan. Before these churches, the people had gone to a Sunday School services, which were held at Goad Springs west of town, with John Cowan as superintendent.

Lowell was never a very big town, but it had all of the businesses that it took to make a good little town.

It is in the center of a rich fruit and garden district; and the Steele canning factory, built in 1936, supplies work in season to many of the townspeople. In 1936, there were five stores, a post office, two churches and a modern school.

Mason Valley

Mason Valley was started in 1883 by Joshua Mason. He got a post office opened here that year and was made the first post-master. He had it in his home for a short time as he was building his store building. He opened a big general store there that year.

There was no railroad here, so the village never was very big. For years there was just the one store and a blacksmith shop. At the best, there were just two stores.

In the late 1890's, Robert Coffelt started an apple evaporator. The first year he had just one peeler running. In a few years, he had eight. This ran for several years.

In 1914, he and his son Walter built a canning plant. They canned tomatoes, beans, sweet potatos and peaches. The first year, they shipped three carloads all under their own label. As time went on, they canned under the labels of some wholesale houses. This plant was closed in 1931. After this, there was a small store here for a few years.

Maysville

Maysville is one of the older towns in the county. It lies in the west part of the county, almost on the State line. It was the first town in the county to be built on the old military or line road, as this early road was called.

In 1839, an Englishman by the name of Tigret opened the first store in Maysville. Like many of these early general stores, his best selling item was whiskey. He did a real good business with the Indians. About ten years later, he returned to England.

One good business will draw others, so by the mid-1840's Maysville had six or seven stores. It is said that in 1846 this village was bigger than Bentonville.

The Civil War was very hard on the town, what with one battle there and troops and outlaws running up and down the border.

Maysville had the following business in 1888: General stores of Freeman & Dumas, Henry Coats, and Mrs. E. J. Tinnin; Thomas Keith had groceries and hardware; Samuel Ward and M. Harmon each had a grocery store; Isaac Harrouff, harness and saddlers; Alex McDonald ran the Line House hotel; Spencer Taylor, a grist mill; Mrs. Mary Linch was Postmistress; physicians, C. F. Baker, E. N. Freeman, J. L. Larue, and A. B. Bills.

There was also a Union church and a public school house.

The 1915 Dun rating book listed the following for Maysville: Population, 271; J. M. Abercrombie, milling Co; Ballard & Beaman, drugs; T. C. Cawood, hardware and groceries; R. D. Moore, printer and stationery; S. N. Thomason, general store; G. B. Tinnin, general store; J. E. Wells, blacksmith.

For a few years, Maysville had a sister town named Rome City. It was founded by Thomas R. Kieth, who had ran a hardware store in Maysville for some time. He then went one mile south of there and built a large two-story brick building with brick from his own brickyard.

He laid out a good size town, but it never did grow very much. When the railroad came in to the west part of the county and the town of Gravette started, he took down his building brick by brick and moved it to Gravette. For several years, he ran a hardware store there. The building was later used as the Buffington Hotel.

As the car became more usable, and the roads better, people went to bigger towns to shop and Maysville became more of a town with a past.

Maysville Fire

Maysville is the only town in Benton County to lose most of its business in one fire.

The fire was discovered by Hugh and John Jackson at a little past midnight on Wed., March 12th, 1891. They had been sleeping in the store of N. S. Jackson and Son. The fire started in the general merchandise store of Henry Coats.

The fire had such a big start that the people could do nothing to put it out. There was no fire department of any kind. All the storeowners could do was stand by and watch all they owned burn up.

The fire was a loss of over $40,000; and only $3,000 of this was covered by insurance. That was on the stock of N. S. Jackson, and paid less than half his losses.

Losses were as follows: N. S. Jackson General merchandise stock $7,000.00; building owned by E. J. Tinnin $2,500.00; Mrs. E. J. Tinnin General merchandise $6,000.00, building $1,000.00; Henry Coats, cash $125.00, stock $5,000.00, building $2,000.00; Freeman and Dumas General Merchandise, stock $6,000.00, building $2,000.00; Thos. Keith Hardware, stock $2,000.00, he saved part of the stock; W. E. Sellers Drug $2,000; Sam Ward grocery and dry goods, $6,000.00; Dr. Wilkerson, Drugs $400.00; Wills and Gibson, Blacksmith tools and shop $250.00; J. T. Peck, $75.00.

All of the storeowners were able to save their account books. A few other houses burned in the fire too.

Pea Ridge

The town of Pea Ridge uses the date Aug. 6 as their birthday, as the first post office opened here on that day in 1850. No one knows who had the first store here or when it was opened.

I don't know just why it was that so little was written on early businessmen of Pea Ridge, but I was unable to find any listings of business here until after 1900. In 1889, Goodspeeds History didn't list it with the towns, so they must have found it too small to write about, as they did several other villages.

In 1915, the Dun rating book showed them as a nice-sized business town. The population was 302, and they had one bank and the following business: O. F. Anderson, general store; C. E. Foster, grocery & hardware; J. D. Lasater, grocery; Miss Kate Lasater, millinery; W. M. Martin & sons, grocery and milling; Pea Ridge Barrel Co., W. T. Patterson; Pea Ridge Canning Co., L. E. Watson; Pea Ridge Drug Co.; Pea Ridge Milling Co.; Price & Watson, Telephone; J. J. Puttman & Son, general store; Stewart & Howe, general store.

In the early days, anyone wanting to ship by rail had to take their items to Avoca, as this was the closest shipping station. Also, anything they got by train had to be picked up there.

Like many small towns in Benton County, there were many changes in Pea Ridge over the last 50 years, but very little real growth.

Pea Ridge's first post office was open on August 6, 1850. The postmasters have been:

Robert H. Wallace	Aug. 6, 1850
William Martin	June 30, 1852
Miss Martha Martin	Apr. 18, 1866
Elijah H. Buttram	Mar. 21, 1867

Mrs. Mary J. Rice	Dec. 4, 1867
W. T. Lasater	Sept. 25, 1868
David Massey	Feb. 2, 1869
John M. Carter	June 15, 1871
H. K. T. Lasater	Apr. 17, 1872
E. H. Buttram	Dec. 12, 1872
Allen B. Stroud	July 3, 1879
Jacob R. Wheat	May 28, 1883
Martin L. Stroud	Sept. 18, 1884
Jacob R. Wheat	Feb. 2, 1886
Adora B. Wallis	Oct. 21, 1889
Robert S. Hill	Dec. 7, 1893
Newton L. Wallis	Nov. 20, 1897
Daniel L. Estle	Oct. 16, 1907
Charles E. Foster	June 14, 1912
Isaac T. Sharp	June 24, 1914
Joseph S. Ottinger	Mar. 17, 1924
Alvin J. Armstrong	Oct. 31, 1933

Pea Ridge was incorporated as a town some time in 1936. Their first ordinances all were against fighting or making noise within the town. This one on speeding gives the idea that all the driving wasn't done on the roads.

Ordinance No. 6

An ordinance prohibiting speed of animals and vehicles.

Be it enacted by the Town council of the incorporated town of Pea Ridge.

Sect. 1. Any person or persons who shall ride or drive a horse or other animal, or who shall drive a motor vehicle along a public or private road street or highway or across any public grounds, within this town at an unusual and unreasonable rate of speed shall upon conviction be fined not more than $25 dollars.

Sect. 2. A speed of fifteen miles per hour in case of motor vehicles shall be prima facie evidence of violation of this ordinance.

> Approvie this 31st. day January 1936
> Mayor F. F. Wood

Rogers

Rogers got its start in life on May 10, 1881, when the first Frisco train pulled into the station there. This was a big day for Benton County, too, for many of the people there from all over the county had not seen a train before, so this was a big happening in their life.

A note to history should be made here, that the following men gave the Frisco Railroad Co. $600 to help build the first depot in

Rogers: Henderson B., William B., and Simeon S. Horsley, George E. Wilson, Ben T. Oakley, Clark Brixey, J. R. Swafford.

The real start was in February of 1881 when the town's first lots were plotted, 180 in all. The town was laid out on what had been part of the B. F. Sikes farm. It is said that Sikes gave the railroad 30 acres of land free.

At the time the railroad came in, B. F. Sikes was postmaster of Cross Hollows and had the post office in his home. So, the first mail that came to Rogers was delivered and called for at the Cross Hollows post office. This was soon changed.

John A. Pertle was the first postmaster when Rogers got a post office of their own. That was in late 1881, and Pertle put it in his drug store.

Dr. R. D. Cogswell is credited with having built the first business building on Walnut street. I can't find out who built the first one on first street. Among the very first businessmen in Rogers were, J. H. Rackerby's Hardware, Capt. Blue's saloon, Raupp's furniture store, C. C. Davis general mercantile, Will and Charles Aid's tin shop.

The town was named for Capt. C. W. Rogers, general manager of the Frisco Railroad. He was a New England man who did more to help this southern town than almost anyone else.

Mrs. Rogers, who visited here many times, helped to form the first church here in 1881. It was the Congregational Church. She was a member of the Congregational Church in St. Louis, and it was entirely through her activities that the Roger's church was started.

Soon after this, several other churches were started.

Some of the many firsts in the history of Rogers were: The first Bank was established by W. E. Felker in 1883. The water works was started in 1888, with Joe Braden manager. A brick water tower was built then, and replaced in 1900.

Wn. Jennings Bryan spoke at the old Chautauqua in 1894. It was on the hill above Electric Springs. Roy Hooker, first male child born in Rogers in 1882. The largest apple evaporator in the county was built in Rogers in 1896.

In 1898, the Rogers to Grove, Oklahoma, railroad was built. April the same year, the Harvey Dining Hall was opened. 1902, the Bank of Rogers installed the first adding machine in town.

Electric lights were first seen in Rogers on Feb. 5th, 1895. There were some troubles before the town had lights all of the time. In May of 1905, arc street lights were put up in town, four of them.

In 1903, Rogers became a second class city; and in May of the same year, they held their first city election. Sept., 1903, W. H. McMullin brought the first auto to town. June 4, 1904, the public library opened.

Long Time Ago—The business district of Rogers as it appeared in 1882. These were the first business buildings in the town. The picture looks south from Walnut Street down First Street.

Carrie Nation paid Rogers a visit in 1906, but she found no saloons to smash.

In 1907, Rogers shipped 191 cars of green apples, 80 cars in cold storage here, 40 cars evaporated apples, 20 cars of strawberries and 48 cars of peaches.

Contract for the first sewer system was let in 1909. The first movie theatre opened in 1910. City mail delivery started in Aug., 1911. In Dec. that year, the telephone came.

One could go on and on, for Rogers has been a fast growing town ever since the day the first train came in. By the end of their first year the population was 600.

One of the big unanswered questions about Rogers is, would the Frisco have built the railroad into Bentonville if the people there had raised the $15,000 to help them like they asked for. Some people think they would have, others say no. The Frisco Railroad would never say a word about it after Rogers was laid out. So this will go unanswered forevermore.

Rogers Business Firms late in 1881

Rogers had a fast business growth in the first year. The following is a list of the business firms there in late 1881.

Drygoods and clothing, W. A. Miller and C. S. Bell.

Clothing, C. C. Davis.

Furniture, George Raupp.

Restaurant, J. L. Merritt.

General merchandise, J. W. Brite, Berryhill and Durham, J. Beasley, Mitchell and Dunnagin, and George Marshall.

Hardware, Pratt and Gibbs, J. H. Rackerby, C. T. Aid and Brother.

Grocery, Stokes and Bowman, Scogin, Lowry and Robertson, and O. F. Beasley.

Millinery, Mrs. Alice Johnson.

Meat market, J. F. Kelley, W. L. Pruiette and Company, George Marquette.

Lumber, Van Winkle and Blackburn, Redington and Chester, (C. H. Sheppard manager), Hardesty and Lunsford, a few miles east of Rogers.

Grain and livestock, McCubbins and Peck, Hall, Huffman and Company, Huffman and Williams.

Saloons, John Cox, A. Greenstreet, and Captain Blue.

Livery barn, H. L. and S. T. Stokes, and Kathon and Fant.

Real estate, B. F. Sikes.

Watchmakers, J. Watkins.

Drugstore, John A. Pirtle, and Drs. Pennington and McNee.

Auctioneer, W. E. Trone.

Barbershop, G. W. Hinkle.

Commission house, Van Winkles.

J. E. Applegate and his brother A. R. Applegate bought the Pennington and McNee drugstore on Dec. 1st, 1881. A short time later, A. R. sold to his brother, J. E.

In running ads, the stores all pointed out that they were either on the east or west side of the railroad tracks.

Rogers' Business 1915

By 1915, Rogers had made a great growth as is shown by the Dun rating book. They list:

E. E. Adams, tinners; J. E. Applegate, drugs & books; Bennett Lumber Co.; Benton County Hardware; Benton County Produce Co.; G. H. Bingham, photographer; W. S. Boyd, ice cream; G. W. Brewer, general store; John W. Bryant, hardware & furniture; W. R. Cady & son, cooperage; A. D. Calson, undertaker; Mrs. A. G. Carse, millinery; J. D. Cole, transfer & fuel; C. M. Compton, meat; A. S. Daniels, racket store; Roy Davis, hotel; Virgil Davis, grocery.

J. T. Dean, livery; Deason Grocery; S. L. Dickover, clothing; W. L. Edwards, grocery; J. S. Elder, grocery; C. C. Ernest, tea & coffee; The Fair., dry goods; Fashion Clothing Co.; Ferguson lumber Co.; A. T. Fisher, second hand furniture; Ford & Johnson, grocery; Fraser Grocery Co.; Frunk & Son, publishers; J. M.

Griffith, hotel; Roy Hamilton, restaurant; J. D. Hartley, second hand goods; J. A. Hathaway, photographer; Mrs. R. L. Hays, restaurant; Herring Dry Goods Co.; J. H. Heverly, racket store; A. B. Hunter, portrait co.

Jones Bros & Co., preserves & vinegar; Johns & Milligan, feed; Chas. Juhre, meat; W. E. Kefauver, grocery; Kennan Shoe Co; P. M. Kokanour, publisher; D. E. Latto, grocery; W. S. Layman, hotel; Lewis grocery Co.; Theo Logus, confectioner; W. G. Luker, tailor; McHenry Drug Co.; McNeil's Pharmacy; Maddox & Oakley, grocery; W. F. May, blacksmith; A. M. Merrill, publisher; Mitchell Bros. second hand goods; T. P. Morgan, news and books; Morgan Evaporator; E. E. Mussleman, bakery; S. H. Nail, meat; F. B. Nash, grocery; E. R. Oakley, fuel; O. A. P. Oakley, produce; J. H. Owens, grocery; Ozark Garage; Palace Drug Co.; Parks Dry Goods Co.; J. R. Peach, second hand goods; Plain Price Variety Store.

J. A. Pollock, contractor; Mrs. Ina Pollock, millinery; J. P. Proudfit, notions; Quisenberry Rice Drug; J. O. Rand, feed; Robinson Planing Mill, Lee A. Robinson, contractor; Rogers Bottling Works; Rogers Building Supply Co.; Rogers Commission Co.; Rogers Hardware Co.; Rogers Ice & Cold Storage Co; Rogers Light & Water Co.; Rogers Marble & Granite Works; Rogers Pressed Stone Co.; Rogers White Lime Co.; Rogers Wholesale grocery Co.

Saunders Bros & Millsap, furniture, Shook Hoover Music Co.; W. R. Spikes, general store; H. L. Stroud Mercantile Co.; F. H. Taylor, plumbing; Teasdale Fruit & Nut Product Co.; R. J. Terrill, general store; Trotter & Edwards, general store; Victor Creamery Co.; E. W. Vinson, printer; Lee H. Williams, Restaurant; I. H. Young, restaurant.

Farmers State Bank, and First National Bank. The population was 2,820.

Rogers Post Office

Before Rogers was started, the post office for the area was at Cross Hollows. B. F. Sikes was made postmaster here in 1877. Mail for the men who built the Frisco railroad was all handled at Cross Hollows. And for several months, all of Rogers' mail was taken care of at Cross Hollows too.

After Rogers was incorporated in June of 1881, B. F. Sikes moved the Cross Hollows post office to Rogers and for several months still used the old name.

The date of the change to Rogers for the post office is unknown, but it was some time in mid 1881, John A. Pertle, owner of a drugstore, was the first postmaster. Yet, before the year was out, J. H. Rackerby held this post.

Next was D. W. Hinman; then came Campbell Stroud who

served until 1886. As the postmaster changed, so did the location of the office. At that time, the postmaster could move the office to his business building, or any other he wanted to.

The years that the early postmasters served are not known for sure, but from 1886 it ran as follows: D. A. Oakley, 1886-1890; W. C. Chynowerth, 1890-1894; John W. Puckett, 1894-1898; Leo K. Fesler, 1898-1902; W. R. Cady, 1902-1906; W. C. Roberts, 1906-1914; John W. Puclett, 1914-1922; Byron Cady, 1922-1925; Claude Williams, 1925-1936.

The Rogers' post office became an office of the second class in July, 1895. The first rural mail delivery was inaugurated April 1, 1904, and Rogers had three routes; No. 1 Jube Lee; No. 2 J. T. Milligan; No. 3 J. R. Threet. A month later they added No. 4, Schyler Evans, No. 5, J. M. Keeth.

Free city delivery in Rogers began August 1, 1911, with two carriers, Algie Burns and C. T. Kirkwood.

Johnny Rhoads, carrier on Route 5 out of Rogers, was the first rural mail carrier in Northwest Arkansas to use a car. He used a Buick car from March, 1911, until some time in May that year, and then had to go back to a team as there were no bridges over the creeks.

On February 22, 1919, under postmaster Puckett, this office moved into their new building on the corner of Second and Poplar. Where they were to stay for many years.

The Rogers of Erwin Funk

Mr. Erwin Funk was not one of the very first comers to Rogers, yet at the time I met him in the late 1950's he was a walking history of the town. After all, Rogers was only 15 years-old when he came with his father to help run the newspaper. So, you might say he grew up with the town.

Being a newspaper man, he paid close attention to everything that went on around him. For some years he kept notes on the happenings in Rogers and the world. For some reason he stopped this in 1919, or the books after this time were all lost.

This chapter is made up of notes of Mr. Funk's. Some I got from him, others I have taken from the Rogers newspaper.

An ad in Rogers Champion fall of 1881, Kelley Meat Market was advertising choice roast beef for 7 cents a pound and boiling beef for 5 cents. Liver was free for cat food. Eggs 8 to 10 cents a dozen, butter 12 to 15 cents a pound. Wood was 50 to 75 cents a rick delivered.

Roy H. Hooker, son of Mr. and Mrs. L. C. Hooker, was born February 19, 1882 and the newspaper credited him with being the first child born in Rogers.

In 1889, the Rogers Milling Co. shipped 222 cars of flour,

meal and feed. The Rogers Canning Co. shipped 20 cars of tomatoes, corn and blackberries. D. Wing & Bros. shipped 80,000 lbs. evaporated apples and 10,000 lbs. evaporated peaches. (this was dried fruit). J. A. C. Blackburn, the lumber king of N. W. Arkansas, sold over 3 million feet of lumber, besides larger amounts of sash, doors, shingles and lath.

In 1890, when manager J. B. Steele of the Rogers Roller Mills discovered kerosene on the floor of a railroad car he was to load with flour, he decided to burn out the oil. He succeeded beyond his most sanguine expectations. The car was destroyed and the mill badly scorched.

Turkey for your Thanksgiving dinner cost six cents a pound in 1896. The greatest need for Rogers in the spring of 1897 was for better streets and sidewalks. The first car came into Rogers that year. He didn't say what make it was.

Mr. E. M. Funk, father of Erwin Funk, bought the Rogers Democrat in 1896. They moved from Springdale to Rogers that year.

In 1897, 197 ricks of wood sold for $90. A meal at the Iowa House was 15 cents for "all you want." Sugar sold for 5 cents a pound in 1898, and ham was nine cents a pound. Rogers tax was nineteen mills, for city, county and schools.

Clothing was as necessary in 1899 as today, but it didn't cost as much. From an advertisement of the H. L. Stroud Mercantile Co. that year, one finds men's suits priced at $3 to $7.50; overcoats, $1.50 to $7.50; shoes, $1.50 to $2.50; dress shirts, 75¢; workshirts, 19¢ to 38¢; flannel shirts, 75¢; 2-pc all-wool underwear, 75¢. This was a January 1, 1899, clearing sale; prices a month or two later were not much higher. Baby carriages at John Bryant's Hardware were $3.75 to $15.00, not so low, but from the illustrations, they were elaborate. In the grocery advertisements one finds 7 pounds navy beans, 25¢; 8 lbs oatmeal for 25¢; 10 bars laundry soap, 25¢; 18 pounds granulated sugar for $1.00. Clover seed was $5 a bushel. Eggs were 15 cents. Butter 15 to 20¢. Wheat sold for 60¢ to 80¢ a bushel.

From a Garfield correspondent came an item recording the death of Samuel Bayless in 1901; his age and the exact date of death were not given. The item said Bayless came to Benton County in 1851, but had never been in Bentonville. There was a reason. In 1869, when he was around twenty years of age, he weighed over 400 pounds and traveled with a circus as the fat man in the sideshow. During a year of sickness in his later years, he lost much weight but was still too heavy to enjoy travel.

1901, the apple blossom was made the state emblem and Blind Dutton won the Monte Ne fiddlers contest. On Sept. 6, President McKinley was shot; he died eight days later and Teddy Roosevelt was made President.

Food prices in 1901 were: eggs, eight cents a dozen; butter, 15 cents a pound, wheat, 65 cents a bushel; strawberries, a 24 qt. crate $1.60.

An elephant once held up a train in Benton County. A Frisco passenger train had a small elephant in the baggage car, enroute to a Minnesota zoo from some point in Texas. The train crew was puzzled when their train was stopped by the emergency air brakes. They soon discovered that the air brake control had been jerked by the elephant. The train was delayed until the trainmen induced their passenger to shift its position so they could release the brake. It allowed the local editors to claim the Frisco had loaded one trunk too many.

William Jennings Bryan was at Monte Ne on June 19, 1902. The first adding machine in Rogers was put in the Bank of Rogers that year.

In 1903, the mayor of Rogers was paid $1 a meeting plus fees. The city marshall $25 a month, and the aldermen a dollar a meeting. March special census gave Rogers as 2,563. "A Noble Outcast" was the last performance in the old Opera House. Too many horses were being scared by W. H. McMullin's car. First locally owned one.

May 2, 1904, the McMullin barn burned with his car in it.

Carrie Nation was in Rogers Feb. 9, 1906. At a library benefit on Sept. 4, Bettie Blake and Funk sang a duet.

Rogers had its first introduction to an Eastern fad when Carnahon & Bradford's drugstore placed "Teddy Bears" on sale for the Christmas trade in December, 1906. It was thought worthy of an extended newspaper notice, and while it was admitted that most Rogers people would think one crazy if seen on the street with a bear under one's arm, it was thought to be the correct thing if one's aim in life was to ape an Eastern fad. They were not cheap; the cheapest sold for $2.50.

Court attendants in April, 1907, had a good laugh at the expense of Attorney Claude Fuller. A witness was testifying in an assault case and Claude insisted he be more exact in his explanation as to just what did happen. The witness was willing, and as a result of his demonstration Claude went home minus a coat sleeve.

Milk sold for five cents a quart in 1908, and the Lyric Theater had five cent movies for a month. Building in Rogers was $160,000 for the year.

1909, first auto agency opened in Rogers that summer. A report listed eight automobiles in Bentonville. The Army tested the Wright plane in Washington at a cost of $30,000 for 75 minutes of air time. A contract was awarded for $23,084 for a Rogers sewer system.

Morgan McMichael owned the first motorcycle in Rogers,

that was 1910. Fare on the railroad was just three cents a mile.

In 1911 one could board at the Rogers Academy for three dollars a week.

E. A. Zanders from Buchanan, Michigan, sold $4,000 worth of stock in a glove factory to local people and the plant was moved to Rogers from his hometown May 1, 1911. J. A. C. Blackburn donated a site in the southeast part of town. The building was a two-story concrete block of fair size. At its height, it employed 15 to 25 women and girls paying from $4 to 7 a week. Zanders and his family supplied the skilled labor. There was trouble over the stock subscriptions and Zanders brought suit against 16 of the local holders. The building burned August 12, 1912, and Zanders claimed a loss of $15,000. It was not rebuilt and Zanders and family left Rogers after effecting some sort of settlement with the insurance company and stockholders out of court.

Woodrow Wilson carried the nation and Rogers in the November election in 1912. The Louis Groshong peanut stand was the official gossip center of Rogers. In October, Avoca prayed for rain and better phone service.

May 28, 1913, was the last graduating class from the Rogers Academy. The state auto tax raised from five dollars to $10 a year.

1913—Phone rates were $2.50 for business and $1.75 for residential.

1916—The Rogers Democrat sold for $1.50 a year.

Football ties happened in 1917 too. Rogers 0, Bentonville 0.

1919—The tax levy in Rogers was 32 5/8 mills.

Siloam Springs

Siloam Springs has been a town of many names. It started out as Hico, then Siloam City, and then Siloam Springs, which name it kept. The town is along Sager creek. It is said that there were 27 springs in the area of the town, with the one right downtown being the biggest.

Simon Sager was the first white man to live near these springs, and the creek along which he built his first log cabin was named after him. In interviews with members of the Sager family, the newspapers have used dates from 1835 to 1840 as the year he came here.

In 1844, C. D. Gunter moved here from Tennessee. He bought an 160-acre farm lying on both sides of Sager creek and near some of the springs. Later, he started a general store. At that time the Hico post office was two miles away, but it was moved to his store in time and the town of Hico was started. The name is said to have been a Cherokee name.

In 1853, Key Lodge No. 7 was started. They built a two-story frame building at Hico. The lodge met upstairs, the church down. The first school was also held here.

By the time the Civil War started, this was a good little business town as well as having some 15 or 20 families living here.

When the war started, Mr. Gunter and his family left, as well as most of the other people, so for several years the town was dead. After the war, he came back and opened his store in 1865.

By 1879, there were several businesses in Hico, also a big mill, a school, churches, and the lodge. Just two blocks from the main part of town was a set of seven springs. Here they had set up a picnic area and a camping grounds to be used by the people for an outing or to camp in. Many people moving west stopped here for a few days rest.

By 1879, the stories of the cures at some of the healing springs in the area had people talking of what a great place it would be for a health resort.

In 1880, John V. Hargrave, a resident of Hico and owner of the land around one of the biggest springs, had a survey made and laid out the town of Siloam City. He built the first store, which was a large general store. Other businesses soon followed.

The spring was called Siloam after the Biblical pool of the same name in Jerusalem. Hargrove donated every odd lot to anyone who would build, and sold each even lot for prices ranging from $25 to $50. This made the town grow fast; when it was incorporated in 1881, there were over 2,000 people here.

On June 24, 1880, the Key Lodge No. 7 had a celebration for St. John's Day. In the morning the members met at the lodge in Hico, and their families met in the park nearby. Then, the rest of the day was a picnic and games. The next year, the program was held at a spring in downtown Siloam, where it has been held ever since.

In 1886, the post office was moved from Hico to Siloam Springs. But, by this time, the town looked more like a ghost town. For most of the people who came in 1881 left when they found out there would be no railroad. There were less than 1,000 people here at that time.

The town made no growth from 1883 to 1894. But that year the Kansas City, Pittsburg and Gulf Railroad built through. In two years the population doubled.

The first church in Siloam was the M. E. Church erected 1882. A Baptist church soon followed. By 1922, the papers listed seven churches.

The first school started almost as soon as the town was laid out. It was a three-month school, held in a vacant store building. The Congregational Academy was started in the mid 1880's. The Siloam Springs Academy a few years later. In 1898, the Arkansas Conference College was started. Out of these, the Siloam Springs school system has grown.

The Farmer's State Bank was incorporated June 1st, 1895, as

the first bank. There have been several since then. A telephone franchise was granted on Nov. 24, 1904. A town-owned electric and waterworks had been set up some years before this.

The first great catastrophe was a flood on the evening of May 13, 1892. Three people were drowned and a loss of $20,000 was listed. There have been several floods to follow this one.

One almost-forgotten Siloam industry was the Siloam to Rogers Stage Line which was started in late 1881, after the railroad had been built into the county. They carried people, small freight, and the mail to the train and back. They changed horses each way at a half-way stop, as it was too hard a run for one team.

From the time they got their own railroad, Siloam has made a very good growth and, by 1936, it was a busy little town.

Siloam Springs Business 1915

By 1915, the Dun rating book listed the following for Siloam Springs. Population 2,405;

J. R. Abercrombe, hardware; Alfrey & Alfrey Co., dry goods; Andrews & Son, grocery; Anthony Pharmacy; Arkansas Auto. Co; J. W. Baker, feed & fuel; Bartell Stores Co. dry goods; Bass Bros., produce; Clem E. Bates, hardware; Beaird Auto Co.; Benton County Hardware Co.; J. A. Bloomfield, machine shop; J. A. Britt, meat; W. W. Brown, dry goods; J. W. Butler, general store; A. A. Carl, produce; Central Drug Store; Chandler C. D. Drugs; Clyde Chew, restaurant; L. E. Collins, racket store; E. C. Cooper, shoemaker; J. H. Cooper, tailor & restaurant; M. Cravens, laundry;

A. B. Current, feed and flour; D. A. Daniel, grocery; C. H. Dunham, racket store; W. F. Duskin, plumber; Patrick Egan, furniture; J. W. Elrod, billiard; J. H. Eno & son, shoes; The Fair, dry goods; Fenno Bros, grocery and meat; J. C. Fisher, livery; Frank Flanders, grocery; C. A. Ford, fruit & seed; Fountain City Lumber Co.; W. H. Frame, tinner; M. E. Gaither, flour & feed; Gamble Co., general store; General Electrical Supply Co.; R. F. Guilliams, photographer; F. M. Hadaway, livery; C. Harvey, grocery;

Wm. Haynes, jeweler; L. W. Helmrick, grocery and dry goods; R. C. Henry, second hand goods; Mrs. J. Z. Jahn, millinery; J. A. Johnson, restaurant; Jones Plumbing & Supply; Dan Lafollette, grocery; Lindsey Shoe Co.; W. P. Little, restaurant; T. C. McArthur, furniture; McClesky Book & Music store; H. I. McCoy, confectioners; McCulloch, & Son, furniture; E. C. McCulloch, grocery; John McNair & Son, garage; F. L. Main, grocery;

B. L. Miller, lumber; W. L. Miller & Co, racket store; W. P. Neely, jewelry; J. B. O'Neal, grocery & meat; Sam B. Ogg, publisher; Ozark Auto & Supply Co.; Ozark Cider & Vinegar; Ozark Electric Co.; Ozark Harness Co; Peat & Flickinger, tailors;

R. B. Pegues, drugs; A. W. Perrine, publisher; C. J. Phillips, painter; Post Office Drug Store; E. C. Ragsdale, hotel; Red Star Cider Co.; Revival Publishing Co.; Paul Reynolds, bakery; Rich Hardware Co.; T. E. Ritchie, grocery; H. Rosen, shoemaker; L. B. Russell, grocery; W. C. Schiede, restaurant; A. Shipman, restaurant; Siloam Lumber Co. .

Siloam Springs Ice & Water Co.; Siloam Springs Millinery Co.; Siloam Springs Telephone Co.; C. T. Smith, racket store; Sussman & Marshall general store; J. H. Suttle, photos; S. H. Thompson, marble; T. A. Trowbridge, laundry; B. O. Walker, bakery; L. W. Walton, hotel; Weaver Bros, grocery; J. W. Webster, drugs; C. P. Westerfield, grocery; G. Westerfield, hotel.

Banks listed: Bank of Commerce; First National Bank; State Bank.

There may have been several small businesses not listed, but this was most of what there was.

The Siloam Celebration

This article was taken from the July 2nd, 1887, Benton County Democrat. The editor, J. B. Thompson, went to this program.

"Friday last was the 7th anniversary or birthday of the city of Siloam Springs, in this county, and according to their custom of celebrating annually the event that day was observed there with the usual ceremony of a picnic and a gathering together of the people to make merry. We accepted an invitation to attend, and in the good company of Gov. Berry, we enjoyed a delightful ride on Thursday over a long reach of magnificent country. We stopped at Hico, a village just this side of the Springs where we enjoyed the hospitality of Mr. Sam Box and his excellent wife, and lodged during the night with our friend N. M. Thompson.

On Friday morning our expectations of a crowd were disappointed when the rain commenced falling, continuing at intervals throughout the day. We were again disappointed at the people coming in during the day in great crowds despite the rain, until several thousand had assembled in the park 'by cool Siloam's shady rill.' And right here commenced the disappointment of the people. Senator Berry had written the committee that it would be impossible for him to make an out of doors speech, and Col. Gunter failed to come as he was detained by business in court at Fayetteville, Senator Berry stated these facts to the audience, and then flashed on this writer, who had thought that he was put on the programme just to full things up, that he was expected to do the speaking. The Senator in spite of the admonition of the doctors made a good little patriotic talk. The editor of the Democrat was then introduced and spoke for 40 minutes. Subject; The essential elements in building a city. The speech was made wholly without preparation and without any merit except for the practical suggestions that should be axioms with all who give the subject consideration.

Siloam Springs has evidently witnessed a boom in her day. The houses look like they were all built about the same time, and many of them are now vacant, though the people are indulging themselves in the hope that they will have a railroad at an early day, and then their town will attract the attention it deserves as a great watering place and health resort. There is up and down the valley upon which the town is situate, 27 springs, Siloam Springs, proper leading the van. This is the only water we have seen in Arkansas that tastes like medicine. The city is in the midst of a fine agricultural region. There are large, fine prairie farms, of rich, black land on the east and north of the town, and with a good railroad it would be bound to prosper.

We came home by way of Bloomfield, spending the night at the hotel of Uncle Davy Chandler. This old gentleman is 83, yet he is as active in his business as a man of 50, and his good wife knows how to put a meal upon a table in better shape than you will find at the grandest hotel in a large city.

At least that is the way it unanimously struck our party, which was now augmented by Dr. Davis and his son, Sam. Bloomfield is located in one of the richest farming sections of our county, and the farmers are rejoicing in abundant harvests and prospects of good crops. The business of the town is carried on by Mitchell Bros., drugs, R. B. Wilson & Co. and W. I. Richardson, who have general stores. Dr. J. R. Floyd one of our Bentonville boys, heals the sick, and we were glad to hear of his success. We are indebted to all these gentlemen for courtesies, and will treasure as a happy memory our visit to Bloomfield. Mitchell's mill is one of the prosperous adjuncts of the town, and the proprietor is seriously considering the propriety of putting in the roller process."

From Benton County Democrat, Saturday, January 15, 1887

A Siberian Exile

Prince Dolgorouki's escape from the tomb of political prisoners in Russia. Banished to the mines, plotting for liberty, flight to America, and settlement in Benton County.

"The subject of this sketch is a citizen of Siloam Springs, in this county, and was the founder of the Chatauqua Society in this State. But few of our people know that royalty dwells with us." Editor Democrat.

Special Dispatch to the Globe-Democrat, St. Louis.

"Tahlequah, I. T. January 9. Angels are sometimes said to be entertained unawares, but the entertaining of a live Prince at the unpretentious capital of the Cherokee Nation has not been heretofore thought of. We have noticed for some time past a stranger in our midst of whom no one seemed to know but little. This stranger is a small, neat, trim man, some 45 years of age. His manner and deportment indicated a gentleman of more than ordinary culture. His appearance induced us to believe that he was not an American, but an importation from some country beyond the sea. We approached the stranger to-day and asked him something of his history.

He told us that he was a native of Russia, and that he was a brother of the Princess Dolgorouki, the wife of the late Czar. On pressing him for further particulars, he said in explanation of his absence from his native land, that he had, when quite young, incurred the displeasure of the Czar on account of his nihilistic proclivities, and consequently was banished to Siberia with about 176,000 others. Said he to your reporter:

'A large majority of the American people do not understand what nihilism means. They think it means everything bad, but I'll tell you it does not; it simply means democracy, or republicanism. That is, a large lot of us were in favor of a government by the people and for the people, and were getting tired of anarchy.

Having The Same Experience

In 1861-62, when your people over here were having your little unpleasantness we, too, in Russia were having the same thing, and my word for it, we nihilists would have gained the day and a republican form of government would have been existing there to-day, to the delight of an overwhelming majority of the Russians, had not other powers interfered. Nihil in Latin, you know, means nothing, and that is what they called us Republicans, to make us as insignificant as possible.'

'Mr. Dolgoronuki, how long were you in Siberia, and how did you escape.'

'Aye, that's what I thought you would want to know, and I'll tell you some of it.'

'As soon as I landed in Siberia I was put to work in the mines about 2,500 feet under the ground, where I could not see day light. I began at once to plan some means by which I could make my escape, and being especially educated in the art of engraving, by this art I accomplished my purpose. Upon small blocks of stone I engraved characters, till I had the requisite number to forge the facsimile of genuine passports. I was five years in accomplishing my object. I took no one into my confidence. Armed with my passport, I made my way with great difficulty to the sea-coast, got aboard a vessel bound for China, which country I ultimately reached, and among these almond eyed people I remained nine years. From there I went to South America, and after staying there awhile, not liking that semi-civilized country, I shipped for the shores of the North American continent, which I first touched at San Francisco, and drifted here.'

Here he says he has realized the dreams of his early youth, a government by the people, for the people, and he believes that all Russia will in his day and time see the same thing and realize this great blessing. He says he hears from his sister, the Princess Dolgorouki often; that she is now in France; that a little cloud is hanging over her, and that she is what might be termed in plain English half-way exiled. Her predicament, he says is caused from the fact that her oldest son is really entitled to the Czardom, or will be ere a great while, hence she does not stand in great favor just now with the Russian nihilists and those in power. She is wealthy, though, and is living in France in fine style, but she or her children will some day be called back to Russia by the people to take their proper places at the head of the Government.

. For a livelihood Mr. Dolgorouki teaches music, and is well qualified for the pression, so his patrons say. He has good letters from the Chautauqua Society of New York, where he taught music awhile and from others of equal note, stating that he is a gentleman and a scholar. Rev. W. L. Miller, Presbyterian minister here vouches for the correctness of Prince Dolgorouki's statements."

Springtown

This little village is 18 miles southwest of Bentonville. It started out with just one general store, then became a good-size business town with a railroad and shipping yards.

In 1868, Manning Richardson built the first general store and home in what later became the town. Thomason & Northcut were next, but they didn't stay long. In 1871, the town was laid out and named because of the big spring here.

By 1888, it had outgrown a village and was a town, Good-speed listed the following business: W. D. Wasson, McGaugh Bros, both general stores; W. Collins & Co. had hardware, drugs and groceries; Sewell & Enterkine, drugs; Hotel, J. L. Allen; steam grist and sawmill, Mitchell & Loy; Collins & Holland, Collins & Brown, blacksmiths; boot and shoemakers, R. D. Morland, A. T. Moodey; post office and telephone office both ran by William J. Collins; physicians, N. Sewell, James Hall, T. H. Roughton; churches, Baptist, Methodist, Episcopal, Methodist Episcopal South. There was also a two-story building that was school downstairs and lodge up.

The Springtown Lodge No. 222 A.F. & A.M. was chartered about 1868. They had 35 members. Springtown Chapter No. 70, R. A. Masons was chartered about 1873; it then had 30 members.

Some time in the summer of 1907, the Benton County Sun ran the following article on Springtown. "This town lays on the Rogers Southwestern railroad line. It has one of the largest springs in the state. They have just struck natural gas, and have organized the Spring Town Oil - Gas & Mineral Development Co.

They have a good public school, two churches, a flouring mill, five stores, one blacksmith. There are seven good roads coming into the town and they have two beautiful parks. The area around the town is full of fruit.

Mr. C. M. Scott was then organizing a Bank to have a capital $20,000. A. A. Hazle is selling lots in the new town site and insurance.

W. L. Wasson has a large general store and is helped by E. C. King. The Springtown Roller Mill operated by Geo. W. Rouse is three story high, and has a 40 horse engine.

R. J. Hawk's, Sam D. Reynolds also have general stores, A. S. Huls & Sons are blacksmiths. W. J. Collins, grocery and drugs. Misses Maggie and Phena Crokett run the hotel. Dr. J. L. Clemmer cares for the sick."

Springtown must have been at its biggest at that time. By 1915, the Dun rating book shows that the bank was closed. They list Springtown Mercantile, general store; A. M. Ottinger, Drugs; S. D. Reynolds, J. M. Richardson, and G. A. Stephenson, all general stores. This book didn't list the real small business.

From then on, the town just kept getting smaller 'til there was just a store or two and the post office.

Sulphur Springs

The town of Sulphur Springs won its fame as a resort town, and many people came there because of the water. Many were the claims made about the water here. There is a group of springs here, each one different; one white sulphur, one potash sulphur, one magnesia, one chalybeate, one nitre, and one intermittent freestone spring.

When the Kansas City, Fort Smith & Southern Railroad was built to Split Log, Missouri, the owner of the land here had it surveyed and laid out the town. That was the year, 1885, and it was laid out for Hibler & Cox. Very soon, others added additions to this.

A large hotel and several cottages were built and run by Charles Hibler and his wife. They also had an excellent bath-house. The promenade grounds reserved around the springs contained several acres, beautifully ornamented and shaded with natural forest.

Goodspeed told much about the resort, but very little of the business when they wrote of it in 1888. They spoke of a first class

The Kilburn Hotel as it looked when it was opened in May of 1909. At that time this was the biggest hotel in northwest Arkansas.

livery stable, several stores, a post office, school, and all it took to make a first class village. The village was reached by hack line from Bentonville; from Southwest City, Mo.; and from Split Log, Mo.

The train line was built down from Split Log, Mo., in 1889. Then this became a real boom town. Then they were listed as Sulphur Springs, the City of Delight.

By 1907, it was listed as a summer resort town at the intersection of the Kansas City Southern and Frisco railroad, with a beautiful park with large skating and dancing pavillion, baseball lawn, tennis grounds and bath houses.

Also, a new State Normal College; The bank of Sulphur Springs, which had started Sept, 1906, with a capital of $10,000; E. B. Guthery, Prest. A. M. Counterman, hardware & lumber; Barnhill & Roberts, meat market; C. F. Church, livery man, feed, sell-rent horses and buggie, also sell real estate;

W. B. Hart, cash Store, dry goods and shoes; John I. Dunn, Furniture & funerals and burials; L. M. Stout in downstairs of the opera block, general store and buys eggs, butter, and poultry; J. H. Edgerton, Grocery, whose motto was "live and let live"; Wood & Cobb, large general store, anything and everything; Cass

321

Hamilton, restaurant and ice cream parlor; Lee Abercrombe, blacksmith; also there were several hotels.

The Kilburn hotel opened on May 9th, 1909. At that time it was by far the biggest hotel in northwest Arkansas. The town was a busy place every summer for so many people came and just stayed for several weeks.

In 1915, Dun rating book listed Sulphur Springs as having 500 people and being a banking town with the following business: J. T. Dunn, furniture & undertaking; M. A. Edgerton, grocery; L. E. Edwars, grocery; W. B. Hart, general store; C. H. Hibler, restaurant; Laura C. Hutton, stationery; A. K. Johnson, plumbing; Mrs. F. D. Lazenby, millinery; McGee & Sons, grocery; Geo. L. Marney, hotel; Char. H. Palm, tinner; G. C. Ralston, hotel; Star Baking Co; L. M. Stout, general store; Sulphur Springs Pool Hall; Sulphur Springs Press Co.; Sulphur Springs Telephone Co; J. B. Thompson, drugs; Western States Lumber Co; D. C. Wilson, grocery & restaurant; S. D. Woods & Co., general store.

During World War I, business fell off bad at this town, and stayed that way for a few years. But along in the 1920's things picked up for some years. Then, in the 1930's, it was all gone again and this time didn't come back at all.

The Sulphur Springs post office first opened on April 26, 1878. This is the list of all the postmasters.

Lewis Phillips	April 26, 1878
James E. Calvin	Aug. 15, 1878
Frank M. Phillips	Oct. 16, 1879
John G. Abercrombie	Feb. 16, 1880
Flavious Lindsey	May 1880

On July 21, 1885, the post office was moved and took the name Round Top; but on Nov. 11, 1885, it was changed back to Sulphur Springs.

Charles H. Hibler	Nov. 11, 1885
John Parker	May 9, 1889
David N. Kennedy	Sept. 11, 1890
William A. Gammill	Sept. 22, 1892
William A. Blàir	April 17, 1893
William A. Gammill	May 5, 1897
Laura C. Hutton	April 11, 1902
John B. Thompson	Feb. 4, 1915
Storm O. Whaley	Feb. 8, 1919
William N. Stranahan	Sept. 30, 1923
Lena Hodges	Dec. 11, 1928

Vaughn

This small village was started in about 1895 by T. Turner, who had the first general store and was also the first postmaster.

TOWNS AND VILLAGES

The Post Office was opened in October 1895. He ran the office in his store. The next business here was Andy Smith's blacksmith shop. Then, next came an apple evaporator.

Some time very early, they built a church and school. The first school was a one-room building. Some time later, a two-story building was built and this housed the school with the Masonic hall upstairs. At this school they had all the grades, plus a four year high school. The Masonic Lodge was moved here from Hazel Valley.

T. Turner sold his store to W. D. Hoback in 1905 or 6. Some years later, he sold to a Mr. Milligan.

Some time in the 1920's, Andy Smith closed his blacksmith shop and opened a general store. After the evaporator was closed, Henderson's put in a canning plant.

Late in the 1920's, Bright's had a general store and filling station.

The post office had closed some time around 1905 or so. By the 1930's, there was just one store and the filling station which ran for several years more.

Small Villages

There have been many small villages over the county in the last 100 years; several of these died out during the Civil War, and their history has been lost.

After the war, and on until about 1910 or so, many new villages started. Most of these were at some small post office, or were built along the railroads as they crossed the county. Here are a few that I have been able to check on.

BUTTREY, post office, general store, and apple evaporator; GALLATIN, post office, general store, blacksmith, Flitt distillery; HERD, also called OSBORNE STATION, post office, school, distillery, blacksmith, two grocery stores, Baker Bros, general store and shippers of tie's, lumber, mining timbers and fruit; HOOVER, post office, school, general store, apple evaporator, blacksmith; LARUE, post office, general store; LOGAN, post office, general store, blacksmith; OSAGE MILLS, post office, school, blacksmith, mill, three general stores; PACTOLUS, post office, general store; PARN, post office, general store; PIPPIN, post office, general store, blacksmith; SEBA, post office, blacksmith, two general stores; RAGO, post office, general store; ROBINSON, post office, school, church, blacksmith, general store; SEDIALIA, post office, general store, feedstore, blacksmith, gristmill; WAGER, post office, school, general store, blacksmith, mill.

As I haven't been able to get hold of a post office record for the county, I am unable to say when these post offices opened or closed.

Chapter Twenty Five
Benton County's Last Pioneer

Benton County's Last Pioneer

On the 12th of Nov., 1905, there were still several people living in Bentonville who thought that they were the last of the pioneers. This because they had ridden on or walked behind the wagons that brought their families here just after Arkansas statehood.

If anyone that day would have told them that the little girl just born at the Roy McPhetridge's would grow up to be a pioneer, they would have laughed at them. Too, if you had said she would fly an airplane, win several handfuls of awards and trophies, and some day land a plane just out of Bentonville, they would have sided away from you as if you had just gone crazy.

Yet that baby, Louise McPhetridge, was one of the leading flying pioneers. She attended grade and high school in Bentonville where her parents were in business. The years 1921 to 1925 found her in classes at the University of Arkansas. As she said in her book, she and school didn't get along too good, as she changed her mind too many times as to what she wanted to be.

In 1924, she worked in Wichita, Kansas, for J. H. Turner Coal Co. All her spare time was spent at the Travel Air factory where Walter Beech was making a name for himself building three place biplanes.

By the time she went back for her third year at the University in 1925, she had made up her mind that she could and would learn to fly. So, at the close of school, 1926, she went back to Wichita.

Here she met Walter Beech, who hired her to go to San Francisco to work for D. C. Warren, who was the new Pacific Coast distributor. He told her the pay wouldn't be high, but she would learn the aviation business and how to fly.

So, our little Bentonville girl was off to make her name in flying, and she did. It was in California that she started breaking records and winning trophies.

December, 1928—Louise McPhetridge sets new altitude record of 20,260 feet in a Travel Air plane with a 180 hp. Hisso engine.

Louise, just after landing when she set a new solo duration record in March, 1929. The plane was a Travel Air with Hisso engine.

Louise with the Travel Air plane with a Wright J-5 engine that she flew in the 1929 Women's Air Derby.

The first was in December, 1928, altitude flying to a altitude of 20,260 ft. in a Travel Air plane with a 180 hp. "Hisso" engine. Next solo duration, March, 1929, she flew around and around for just over 22 hours. Speed record in April 1929, 156 mph in the same type plane as the above two records.

August, 1929, was the first real chance for women to prove they could fly as well as men. That was when the first Women's Air Derby was run from Santa Monica, California, to Cleveland, Ohio. Louise came in first out of a field of ten, including famed Amelia Earhart. Her plane was a Travel Air with an Wright J-5 engine.

In August, 1932, Louise and Frances Marsalis broke the refueling duration record by staying in the air 196 hours in a Curtiss Thrush with an 220 hp Wright J-6 engine.

In July, 1934, she set a light plane speed record, 100 km, in a 90 hp Porterfield.

August of 1936, Louise again made and remade the headlines in the newspapers around the world. First, she set a new East-West speed record in a Beech Staggerwing C17 R with an Wright 420 hp engine. Then she was the first place winner in the Bendix Transcontinental Air Race, in the same plane. She was also the first woman to win a Bendix Race.

In August, 1938, she won the 100 km speed in a Beech Staggerwing D17 with a Wright 420 hp engine.

1929—First women's air derby, Santa Monica, Calif., to Cleveland, Ohio, National Air Race. Louise came in first in a Travel Air. Picture made in Cleveland.

The above were the big records set and races won, but Louise has flown thousands and thousands of air miles and had many hair raising experiences to tell about. Many of these are related in her book, "High, Wide, and Frightened," republished in 1973 by Air Press.

She tells of having an engine kill out at 3,000 feet and landing dead stick. Three forced landings in one day, after many hours of overhauling the engine. They found out it was killing out because of stopped up vents on the gasoline tank.

For the altitude record, she had to make up her own oxygen outfit using a small metal cylinder of oxygen from a machine shop, ether mask from the hospital, and a rubber hose and pair of pliers to complete the outfit.

She tells of having to land in pastures, golf fields or any other open spots when trouble arose. In these early days, there were no marked routes to fly, so sometimes a pilot would have to land to find out where they were.

She worked for several airplane companies and schools, as well as helping run her husband's several engineering companies.

With Phoebe Omlie, she developed and organized the Marking Program 1934-1936.

In October, 1932, in honor of her refueling duration, Louise and Frances Marsalis spent several days in Washington, D. C., where they met President and Mrs. Hoover. They made about 10 engagements a day, rode in the President's car from place to place with a motorcycle escort, and were presented the keys of the city.

Hoover told her, "I wouldn't like to make an endurance flight." She said, "Nor would I like to be president." His reply was, "Well, at least I can walk around."

She married Herbert von Thaden on June 19, 1928. They had two children, William and Patricia. Herb was a flyer and engineer and spent most of his life running Thaden Engineering Co.

Since his death in 1969, Mrs. Louise Thaden has been running the company.

Her books and many pictures of her planes are on display at the Bentonville City Library.

Chapter Twenty Six
Small Talk

This chapter I am calling small talk. It was all copied out of the newspapers of the date that I used. I feel this shows a lot about the life at that time.

Dec. 12, 1883 — The Hibler Hotel, Bentonville has reduced fare to 25 cents per meal.

∞∞∞∞

Dec. 12, 1883 — Dickson and vicinity have raised money for the purpose of building a school house which will be 24 x 34. Their teams started for the lumber the first of the week.

∞∞∞∞

Dec. 19, 1883 — Albert Peel of Avoca and E. M. Dinsmore of Bentonville returned off their hunting trip yesterday. They had killed 3 deer and 19 turkeys.

∞∞∞∞

Sept. 1, 1884 — A Rogers apple buyer in 1884 was offering to pay $1 a barrel for No. 1 Shannon Pippins, and 25 cents a bushel for Ben Davis, Willow Twigs, Pippins and Winesaps.

∞∞∞∞

Jan. 8, 1887 — Money to loan in sums of $200 or more for 3 to 5 years on well improved farms at 10% interest. Brand and Brand.

∞∞∞∞

Jan. 8, 1887 — Our wealthy neighbor of the Journal managed to get together sufficient lucre to buy a whole quarter of beef and in the goodness of his heart, brought us a large roast. Thanks. (The Journal was the other newspaper in Bentonville then).

∞∞∞∞

Jan. 8, 1887—Dr. Smartt informs us that some kind of an epidemic is prevalent in this community caused, he thinks by the people using water out of their wells that are so low. He says there is something very unhealthy in the sediment at the bottoms of these wells, and advises people to clean them out, and haul water from the springs and fill them up. There is a water famine in many sections of the country and the question of water supply is becoming a serious one in more places than Bentonville.

∞∞∞∞

Feb. 5, 1887—Trotter & Wilkes are putting up a fine article of smoking tobacco called the "Trotter". It has a gilt illustrated label with a picture of a fine trotting horse at his best speed. This tobacco is of the Hico variety that grows successfully only in this county and in Durham County North Carolina. It is superior to anything that ever filled our pipe. Its color is as bright as gold.

∞∞∞∞

Feb. 5, 1887—J. C. Knott has a lamp of 400 candle power in his store. It lights up all the large store room, so that you can see to read in any part of it. It holds 1½ gallons of oil, and costs two cents per hour.

∞∞∞∞

Feb. 5, 1887—Mr. Jim Parker, a merchant of Siloam Springs, called to see us this week. He has engaged extensively in the pigeon trade this winter, there being a large roost of wild pigeons in the territory tributary to Siloam. He says two Indian boys killed 1,100 pigeons in one night. Mr. Parker ships to St. Louis where his birds are in cold storage. He has been paying 50 cents per dozen.

∞∞∞∞

Feb. 12, 1887—Paid Ad—Oil in paying quantities in Bentonville, at all our grocery houses at 25 cents a gallon.

∞∞∞∞

Feb. 12, 1887—The new mill at Rogers can make 100 barrels of flour per day. They have been paying 70 cents per bus. for wheat.

∞∞∞∞

Feb. 19, 1887—The Sunday bill has passed both houses of the Legislature. It repeals the law of 1885, which required every one in this state to observe Sunday as the Sabbath. Now every man can select his own Sabbath day, provided he observes one day in the week as such.

∞∞∞∞

SMALL TALK

March 5, 1887—Uncle John Black has just received an addition of 100 volumes to his library. These books were bought of the Alden Publishing Co. and the express charges on them amounted to nearly as much as the cost of the books. Mr. Black is a public benefactor in this building up a library to which every citizen has access for he invites all his friends to come and read his books, but under no circumstances can they be taken from the library. It is not a circulating library.

∞∞∞∞

March 5, 1887—Glover School House. News is rather scarce this week. Health good. Everybody is busy sowing oats, some are done. J. Williscraft, an old miner from the west has gone down to Southwest City to see what kind of mineral they have there.

∞∞∞∞

Prof. Smith of the Indian Territory is teaching a class in instrumental music at Mr. A. E. Bright's. The school at this place is progressing rapidly.

∞∞∞∞

Some of our farmers are improving their places. Messrs. C. Middleton and E. F. Rife have new gates, hung on good post, but what puzzles us is the way they are fastened. Middleton has got his tied to a tree with a 20 pound log chain, and Rife has a heavy stake driven on each side. We think they lay down the fence and go around.

∞∞∞∞

March 23, 1887—The Rogers Mill will give 36 pounds of good family flour, as good as any mill in the county can turn out and 10 pounds of feed for one bushel of good wheat. We make this explanation to correct an erroneous impression that prevails that the Rogers mill does not give any bran with their flour.

∞∞∞∞

April 9, 1887—School Report, Springtown, April 2, I commenced teaching here on the 7th of March. The average attendance for the first week was 31; second week, 39; third week, 46; fourth week, 51. The school is progressing nicely, and there is more interest manifested both by students and parents, than I ever witnessed before. I wish to thus publicly return my thanks to the people of Springtown for their kindness to me, and invite them to visit my school often. D. M. Setser, Teacher.

∞∞∞∞

April 9, 1887—The Bentonville waterworks will soon be completed. Mr. Clapp has placed the windmill in the depot well, and the contract for laying the pipe to the public square has been let to James Haney, who will complete the work at once.

∞∞∞∞

April 9, 1887 — From this date on the following prices will be maintained on fresh meats; Steak 10 cents per pound; Roast from 5 to 8 cents; sausage, 10 cents; (signed) W. R. Clark and Z. Mitchell.

∞∞∞∞

May 7, 1887 — The strawberry excitement is quite lively this week at Garfield and Avoca. Berries have been worth $8 per 6 gal. crate in Kansas City. Buyers are paying $4 per crate at these two places.

∞∞∞∞

May 7, 1887 — The Bentonville Mining Co. struck ore in their mine on Pea Ridge that indicates exceeding richness. It is mineral of some kind, as it melts readily and has every appearance of silver. Specimens have been sent to different points, and a report of its value is daily expected.

∞∞∞∞

May 7, 1887 — The rains will enable the farmers to handle their tobacco and prepare it for market, so that the tobacco factory can resume work. There has scarcely been a time in the past year suitable for handling tobacco. We hope now that it has commenced that the rain will continue.

∞∞∞∞

May 16, 1887 — Frank Seitz, the painter for the Bentonville Wagon works, gave a good display of his skill on the drummer wagon this firm turned out for Smartt & Jefferson's livery stable. It is a fine piece of painting and a credit to our town.

∞∞∞∞

May 16, 1887 — L. B. Mallory has delivered several loads of tobacco to Trotter & Wilkes, it is of the crop of 1885.

∞∞∞∞

May 21, 1887 — S. N. Williams of the Nebo neighborhood called on us last Saturday. He is 51 years old, born in Bentonville, and is likely the oldest native of the county. His father, Rev. Ambrose Williams, built the first cabin in Bentonville. It was built for Singleton Langston. Mr. Williams says the first store in Bentonville was on the lot now occupied by Pluck's furniture store (where the court house is today).

∞∞∞∞

SMALL TALK

May 21, 1887 — The city council has made an order for the erection of eight street lamps, to be erected on the corners of the public square. The lamps of the Rochester kind, 65 candle power. If they prove satisfactory, other lamps will be put up.

∞∞∞∞

May 28, 1887 — A five mill school tax was voted in this past week for Bentonville.

∞∞∞∞

May 28, 1887 — A baseball club was organized in Bentonville last week with John E. Sykes, president, Geo. M. Craig, secretary, Charlie Citsworth, field captain, Geo. Backus, assistant. The club will be known as the Bentonville Reds and number twelve members with three substitutes. They are now ready for business.

∞∞∞∞

May 28, 1887 — I am now selling the Arkansas semi-anthracite coal, the best coal ever brought to this county. Free from sulphur. Only 25 cents per bushel, in ten bushel lots 22½ cents per bushel. G. W. Backus, Bentonville.

∞∞∞∞

May 28, 1887 — Farmers, we want one hundred thousand pounds of broom corn at the Bentonville Broom Factory.

∞∞∞∞

June 4, 1887 — Benton County Surveyor Robertson has made a map of the county for Gen. Sigel, especially noting that part of it covered by the Pea Ridge Battleground. It is likely that Gen. Sigel is preparing a sketch of that battle for Century Magazine.

∞∞∞∞

June 4, 1887 — The new oil street lamps are a success. Score one for the new council.

∞∞∞∞

July 7, 1887 — E . B . Fuqua has rented the Whayne tobacco barn. He is paying from $2 to $20, and has already bought about 50,000 pounds.

∞∞∞∞

July 7, 1887 — W. A. Cash & Co. threshed for Alex Oakes of Sugar Creek 200 bushels of wheat in two hours. Their machine is a horse powered and they have threshed this season 4,000 bu.

∞∞∞∞

July 14, 1887—Last week some parties put giant powder in a hole of water 14 feet deep in the Illinois river to kill fish. When the powder exploded one young man jumped into the pool of water to save an extra fine fish that came to the surface but showed signs of life. The young man went in with arms extended as is natural in making such a plunge. He uttered a shriek as he struck the water, but sunk like lead to the bottom. He was fished out and found to be in the same position as when last seen, his limbs being stiff and rigid in death. The shock of electricity by the giant powder killed him almost instantly. His friends tried to make it appear that his death was caused by cramps, because it is a violation of the law to kill fish with giant powder.

∞∞∞∞

Sept. 8, 1887—Fifty wagon loads of wheat were delivered to the Rogers mill last Saturday.

∞∞∞∞

Sept. 8, 1887—Merrill Pratz saw a black bear a few days ago while camped near White River.

∞∞∞∞

Sept. 15, 1887—Good apples in Washington and Benton countys are selling from 50 to 65 cents a bushel. The celebrated Shannon Pippin retails 75 cents a bushel. These prices at the farm. At these prices an apple orchard in full bearing with a good crop will yield its owner from $350 to $500 per acre.

∞∞∞∞

Oct. 1, 1887—Removal Ad—We have removed our undertaking establishment to the new Haney Building, which we will occupy in connection with Mr. Barney. We will keep a full stock of coffins, burial caskets, burial robes & etc. And invite the patronage of those who are so unfortunate as to have to have to buy such articles. We will also continue to do job work, repair furniture & etc. Jos. Huffman & Son.

∞∞∞∞

Oct. 22, 1887—The total Benton county school fund for 1887, including $8,885.91 from the state, was $13,218.93. There were 11,002 children enumerated; and the per capita apportionment was $1.20. There were 129 school districts. Bentonville school population was 636, and apportionment, $764.14. Rogers had 312 school children and received $374.36, Siloam Springs 317 children and received $380.87.

∞∞∞∞

Oct. 18, 1888—J. A. C. Blackburn sent some of the apples that were on exhibit at the Rogers fair to President Cleveland. It is hardly probable that Grover will send them back like he did that whiskey from Kentucky.

∞∞∞∞

Aug. 19, 1893 — New apple & peach brandy distillery just completed by E. J. Macon & Co. no fruit will go to waste it makes no difference how little are your peaches and apples or how rough they look just bring them in and get cash.

∞∞∞∞

Sept. 29, 1894 — Ad — Old Chalk, a pure sour mash whiskey. Covey & Company. R. W. Covey & E. M. Gravett.

∞∞∞∞

Nov. 3, 1894 — Coal in Benton county, on the farm of C. L. Fields 5 miles west of Bentonville and near Seba, while digging a well last week. Parties at a depth of only 26 feet struck a splendid vein of coal and also struck a fine vein of water, which ran in so rapidly that the parties could not determine the thickness of the coal vein. But Mr. Fields with several enterprising citizens over there will form a stock company for the purpose of sinking a shaft.

. ∞∞∞∞

Nov. 3, 1894 — For sale 92 acres, 70 acres in cultivation, 80 tillable, log house small orchard, good well, 4½ miles east of Gravett, $800. cash.

∞∞∞∞

Nov. 3, 1894 — Good paying restaurant furniture and fixtures building on main street near depot, stock of goods will invoice about $100. A money maker $500.

∞∞∞∞

Nov. 17, 1894 — Ott McAllister came near meeting a fatal accident with a run away team west of Gravett Saturday last. He was driving a horse which became frightened and jumped in to the buggy turning it over throwing him out and the team ran away and completely demolished the buggy and harness. Fortunately Ott received no serious injuries.

∞∞∞∞

May 25, 1895 — Ad — I have opened up a brick yard in this city and am prepared to burn brick and do contract work. If you are thinking of building a brick house come to me for estimates. G. N. Gribble, of Gravett.

∞∞∞∞

Nov. 13, 1897—E. M. Gravett Chalk Valley Distillery, started in Monday for the fall run and expects to make about 10,000 gallons during this season's run. Mr. Gravett makes a pure sour mash corn whisky which has won a wide reputation for his house and his sales are increasing every year. He now has on hand several hundred gallons of three and four year old whisky of which he supplies his customers. He has an extensive trade in Missouri, Kansas and Oklahoma.

∞∞∞∞

Nov. 27, 1897—A physician observing a barrister about to drink a glass of brandy said, "Don't drink that filthy stuff, brandy is the worst enemy you have."

"I know that, was the answer, "but you know, we are commanded by scriptures to love our enemies."

∞∞∞∞

Dec. 18, 1897—Ad—About this season of the year most people suffer more or less with "that tired feeling." For a sure and reliable cure write to the Chalk Valley Distillery—Gravett, Ark.

∞∞∞∞

Dec. 25, 1897—The editor enjoyed a nice little sleigh ride Thursday with Mr. L. S. Hewitt. Sleigh riding in this country is something very uncommon, but highly agreeable when the opportunity presents.

∞∞∞∞

April 28, 1898—War with Spain was declared April 21, 1898, and Garfield was the first town or community in the county to erect a flag pole and hold a public patriotic rally.

∞∞∞∞

Aug. 3, 1899—On the 10th of July, 1899 there came unexpectedly and in a quite unobtrusive way to the home of the pastor of the M. E. Church in this city. Mr. John Morris and Mrs. Rachel Miller, and requested the preacher to unite them in the bonds of Holy Matrimony, which he did in the presence of several witnesses. After a little impromptu repast the happy pair drove away and the preacher found himself in the possession of a new $5.00 bill which greatly added to the interest of the occasion. (signed) J. H. Maddox, pastor. M. E. Church South.

∞∞∞∞

Jan. 18, 1899—Robbins & Stephens will ship two cars of mules next week to Pine Bluff. This will make four carloads this firm has shipped since the first of the year.

∞∞∞∞

SMALL TALK

Feb. 16, 1899—Wanted 25,000 railroad ties at Bentonville, Seba and Dickson.

∞∞∞∞

Feb. 16, 1899—Ad—"Are you still going to ride to town or church this year in the farm wagon or muleback? Don't you really think you should gladden the hearts of your wife, sons and daughters by buying a nice buggy or carriage, and allowing them to enjoy some of the comforts of this life?" This was part of a full page ad showing buggys and carriages.

∞∞∞∞

March 10, 1899—Considerable interest was taken in the sale of delinquent town lots for water works taxes Tuesday at Bentonville.

∞∞∞∞

March 17, 1899—J. B. Keeth was tried before U. S. Commissioner Petty yesterday on the charge of selling liquor in less than five gallon lots, and after a hot trial was acquitted.

∞∞∞∞

April 11, 1899—City Marshal Baker gives warning that hereafter the ordinance against riding bicycles on sidewalks will be rigidly enforced. Wheelmen who wish to avoid a fine should keep off the sidewalks.

∞∞∞∞

April 11, 1899—Prices are unusually good for eggs this time of year, ranging from nine to 11 cents a doz.

∞∞∞∞

June 14, 1899—Charley Cunningham has purchased a new street sprinkler of the Winkler patent for service on our streets. It is a good one and Charley should be complimented for his progressiveness.

∞∞∞∞

July 11, 1899—Morris & Company have just completed a cooperage house where they will manufacture apple barrels during the season. They are also building an apple house at the old depot, where they will purchase and ship apples.

∞∞∞∞

Sept. 18, 1899—The Macon and Carson distillery has up to the present date used something over 30,000 bushels of apples in the manufacture of brandy. They expect before the season is over to use over a quarter million bushels.

∞∞∞∞

Oct. 17, 1899 — Good corn is selling on our streets for 27 cents a bu.

∞∞∞∞

Oct. 17, 1899 — Irish potatoes sold for 20 cents a bushel the first week in Sept. But now that the home grown are all sold they are being shipped in to sell at 75 cents a bushel.

∞∞∞∞

Nov. 7, 1899 — Ad — We have suits beginning at $2 and going to $7, and they are about the finest made. Tery and Burks.

∞∞∞∞

Dec. 18, 1899 — Football, Springdale vs Bentonville, score, 5 to 13. The football game between Springdale College and Bentonville College was an interesting game with the exception of a little dispute over the rules. First touchdown by Thurman Bohart, Bentonville.

∞∞∞∞

May 11, 1901 — It will require about 400 pickers ten days to pick the strawberry crop, to be marketed at Rogers. Most of these will be furnished by the town and immediate neighborhood.

∞∞∞∞

May 11, 1901 — Rogers is to have a new depot soon, that is partly new, as the old one will be remodeled and made several feet longer. The colored waiting room will be made longer and we suppose seated, if not it ought to be.

∞∞∞∞

Dec. 30, 1901 — R. L. Nance shipped 1,367,000 eggs from Rogers this year. The eggs were bought from farmers at 10 cents a dozen.

∞∞∞∞

Jan. 10, 1903 — Joshua Wright was awarded a contract to care for the county's paupers for this year on his bid of 33 cents per day per person.

∞∞∞∞

1904 — In the winter of 1903-04 meetings were held in Rogers and Siloam Springs to plan ways and means of slitting Benton County into east and west divisions with the county seats at Rogers and Siloam Springs. A lot of newspaper space and a lot of time were wasted on meetings and discussions and editorials that got nowhere. Bentonville refused to get very much worried over the fight inasmuch as Gentry, Decatur, Gravette and Sulphur Springs did not enthuse over having Siloam Springs gain prestige at what they thought would be their loss.

∞∞∞∞

July 6, 1906—The Rogers Christian Church installed an electric motor to pump its organ. It was not a pipe organ, but was too large to be manipulated by hand or foot power.

∞∞∞∞

July 10, 1907—The Gentry Fruit Association has built an evaporator at Highfill with a capacity of 500 bushels of apples a day.

∞∞∞∞

Sept. 26, 1907—Girls strike at Gentry. Sixteen ladies who operate the peeling machines at the Gentry Fruit growers association evaporator struck Monday for a raise of a cent a bushel. They had been receiving 3 cents per bushel up to that time. The manager of the evaporator has since offered them 3½ cents, but the girls are still contending for 4 cents.

∞∞∞∞

June 28, 1907—In an ad, Terry Dry Goods Co. ran the copy of a letter from the Spool Cotton Co., W. P. Neel, sec. dated June 20, 1907. Stating that unless Terry raised the price of thread from 5 cents to 6 cents a spool, they would not sell him more thread and had so notified Atkinson & Huffman Grocery Wholesale. Terry said he would always sell at 5 cents and would go to court to do so.

∞∞∞∞

July 8, 1907—The leaders for the Chautauqua program July 9th to 21st 1907, W. J. Bryan, Rev, Anna H. Shaw, M. Flowers, Hon C. B. Landis, Lieut. Baldwin, R. M. LaFollette, plus many other programs.

∞∞∞∞

Sept. 26, 1907—Pick them up, you can sell your cider apples to the Southern Fruit Product Co. at its Springdale, Centerton or Rogers mill, for 30 cents per 100 pounds.

∞∞∞∞

Sept. 26, 1907—Will commence to receive sorghum cane at its Rogers Vinegar factory Monday Oct. 7th. $3.25 per ton delivered stripped and headed.

∞∞∞∞

Dec. 3, 1907—The Ozark farm wagon from factory to farmer. If you want one of the best farm wagons made, write for prices to the Ozark Wagon Co. Fayetteville.

∞∞∞∞

Aug. 6, 1908—"Now that we are married," he said, "we are one, and I must insist that this be the last time that you appear in public in a low-necked gown." "We may be one," she responded with asperity, "But you are only half of us, and I shall dress my half as I please."

∞∞∞∞

April 22, 1909—First ad for a car I found in a Benton county paper. Pullman Motor Car Company, Kansas city Mo. Model "L" toy tonneau, seats 4, 20 horse power, four cylinders, cylinder arranged vertical under the hood. Cooling system, water centrifugal pump. Ignition jump spark, weight 1850. Equipment: gas head lights, generator, oil side and tail lamps, horn. Price $1,600.

∞∞∞∞

Feb. 6, 1909—From Hotel Annex—there was a big convention going on in a small town and the hotel proprietor of the only hotel had leased a church across the street from the hotel and put beds in there to accommodate the overflow. Two drummers, who had been imbibing quite freely, were given beds in the church. About 2 o'clock in the morning the church bell, which was also the town's fire alarm began to ring. It brought out the fire department and all the natives. When the proprietor of the hotel rushed across the street and into the church, he called out, "Who's ringing that bell." "I am," responded one of the drummers. "Send over two scotch highballs and a pitcher of ice water to pew 17".

∞∞∞∞

July 8, 1909—There was gloom in Rogers Tuesday, so dense that you could drive "railroad spikes in it". The cause was that Bentonville beat them on their own grounds by a score of 3 to 1. The Rogers rooters got sore and most of them left before the game was out.

∞∞∞∞

Jan. 3, 1911—Luther Fletcher and father sold 60 turkeys here for $115.

∞∞∞∞

Jan. 6, 1913—J. T. Greenfield mailed the first parcel post package sent from the Rogers post office January 1, 1913. It was a six-pound baby carriage and cost 32 cents to mail.

∞∞∞∞

Aug. 8, 1922—J. W. Null was in from west of town Saturday and states that he has been busy making brooms all summer at his factory on the farm. He also has two acres of broom corn planted on his farm and some of the neighbors have out a little for next year's use. He is now buying most of his broom corn from Kansas City at fifteen cents a pound. Since starting up he has turned out over 1200 brooms.

∞∞∞∞

Oct. 12, 1923—From commissioner Jim G. Ferguson's annual report of the State Department of Agriculture. Benton County was first in the following: livestock, dairy cattle, poultry, apples, acreage and production, dairy products, number of horses; second in wheat production.

∞∞∞∞

March 23, 1923—Gravette Produce Co. was paying for the following: Eggs 20¢ a doz.; springs 19¢ lb.; old cox 6¢ lb.; butterfat 44¢ lb.; hides 6¢ lb.; hens 19¢ lb. young cox 8¢ lb.; butter 20¢ lb.

∞∞∞∞

April 27, 1923—Electric Theatre Decatur, showing "The Sheik" with Agnes Ayers & Rudolph Valentino. Admission 25 and 35 cents.

∞∞∞∞

Oct. 5, 1923—Maybe it was a record, but the hog that L. H. Easley killed was one big lot of pork. It dressed out over 800 pounds of meat and lard.

∞∞∞∞

April 2, 1924—The March sales day held by Bentonville merchants last Saturday with 11 settings of fancy hatching eggs given away attracted a large crowd with much interest among the poultry fanciers of the county. The eggs are from the finest flocks of the county and special prizes are to be given at the Benton County fair next fall for pens of chickens hatched from the eggs given away on sales days.

∞∞∞∞

April 5th, 1924—Miss Anna Patton, who has been clerk of Benton County since last October on appointment of Governor McRae, has announced her candidacy for the Democratic nomination, Miss Patton is well known in local business circles, having served a number of terms as deputy county clerk. Though women have appeared as independent candidates in previous elections, Miss Patton is said to be the first woman candidate for a democratic nomination.

∞∞∞

April 12, 1924—The contract has been awarded for the summer camping lodge to be erected on the Swift farm between Bella Vista and Bentonville, for the Camp Fire Girls of Oklahoma, and work will begin at once.

∞∞∞

The first unit will accommodate 50 girls and will include a large living room, sleeping porches enclosed on three sides with windows, sleeping and dressing rooms, servants quarters and garage. The camp, which is located near abundant springs, will have running water in the buildings, and the girls will have the fishing, boating and bathing facilities of Sugar creek. Located near Bella Vista, the visitors at the camp will be able to take advantage of all the conveniences and recreation of that large resort.

The camp will be formally opened on June 3, when the first contingent of 45 Camp Fire Girls are expected. It will be used in groups of about fifty girls for 10 day periods throughout the summer.

∞∞∞

April 23, 1924—A Bentonville schoolgirl, suggests that Siloam Springs, whose city park possesses the only buffaloes in the State of Arkansas, name its baby buffalo, "Rebecca." The city of Siloam Springs secured its buffalo, "Ivanho," from the U. S. Government and the cow was secured later from the buffalo herd of the Pawnee Bill show aggregation, and was promptly named "Rowena." The baby buffalo has attracted wide interest.

∞∞∞

Oct. 20, 1924—Mrs. Farmer, an elder in the Church of the Nazarene at Siloam Springs, was credited this month with being the first woman to perform a wedding ceremony in Benton County, when she officiated at the marriage of Albert F. Robbins and Mrs. E. G. Robinson, both of Siloam Springs. As the license was issued by a woman, County Clerk Anna Patton, it was a sort of woman's affair.

∞∞∞

April 30, 1926—Pathe News showing pictures of the Apple Blossom Festival at Rogers, at the Royal Theatre, Bentonville, Thursday night, May 6.

∞∞∞

April 30, 1926—The Benton County Utilities Corporation, which recently purchased the Gravette light and water plant, will have its office in the Ed. Gravett building.

∞∞∞∞

April 30, 1926—Clarence Burg of Fort Smith was in Sulphur Springs last week arranging to open his summer school of music. A school of expression will also be added this year. Mr. Burg's piano playing at the Chautauqua last summer was greatly enjoyed.

∞∞∞∞

April 30, 1926—Baseball fans at Sulphur Springs are building a ball park on the site given by Axel Johnson just over the line in Missouri. As Missouri allows playing ball on Sunday is the reason for building it a mile or so from town.

∞∞∞∞

April 30, 1926—S. M. Smith, who bought Mr. Flack's business and moved to Cave Springs a short time ago, has rented the Haase Hotel there and is having it wired for lights and will take charge of it and be ready to accommodate the public by the first of May.

∞∞∞∞

April 30, 1926—An added attraction that will be at the Royal Theatre Bentonville next Monday and Tuesday nights will be Bouvier the Great, the world's youngest hypnotist. See the young lady put to sleep at 9 o'clock Monday morning in the show window of Kerr & Callison's store. She will be awakened on the stage of the Royal Theatre at the end of the picture that evening.

∞∞∞∞

May 20, 1927—The lecture of Rev. Marion Nelson Waldrip of Kansas City at the auditorium Monday night was well attended. Dr. Waldrip's subject was "Arkansas Hill Billie." The doctor ought to know his subject well, since he is a Benton County boy himself.

∞∞∞∞

May 20, 1927—The Leonard Stock Company opened a week's engagement at Gentry Monday night in their tent theatre. The company has 20 people with the show.

∞∞∞∞

May 20, 1927—While the berry crop has been light, yet most of our growers have profited as the price has never been below $3.25 and has ranged as high as $3.90. The above prices were paid shipping and expect still better prices. Most berries grown in this and the Centerton communities have been shipped from Hiwasse.

∞∞∞∞

May 20, 1927—The Cline Electric Moving Picture Company of Missouri is showing at Vaughn two nights this week. Wednesday and Thursday, in their tent which is located on the vacant lot in the rear of J. A. Milligan's store.

∞∞∞∞

May 20, 1927—S. P. Boling, city electrician, turned on the new White Way lighting system Friday night. The old light poles and fixtures will come down as soon as electrician Boling and his helpers can do it.

The new lights are as attractive as could be wished and compare favorably with those in use in larger cities. The lights are 400 candle power and covered with opaque globes, and give out a bright clear light. The city council is to be congratulated upon giving the town such a splendid lighting system with a few cents cost to tax payers. The entire cost of the system will reach over $4,000 and all will be paid from the revenue of municipal light and water plant. This was Bentonville.

∞∞∞∞

Nov. 15, 1928—Will Rogers says, "Arkansas voted last Tuesday against Evolution and Republicans. They don't want anything taught about either subject in their schools."

∞∞∞∞

June 13, 1929—Over 500 licenses for automobiles and trucks have been issued in Benton county so far this year, according to E. R. Berry, who is acting as collector for Sheriff Edgar Fields. After the first of July, when a license for six months may be taken out, he expects to issue several hundred more before the close of the year.

∞∞∞∞

Sept. 30, 1929—The first sound motion pictures in Rogers were shown at the Victory Theatre on Sept. 30, 1929.

∞∞∞∞

Dec. 31, 1930—Benton County, with 13 state and seven national banks, led all other counties in the state of Arkansas this year in the number of Banks.

∞∞∞∞

Nov. 10, 1932—Otto Carlson's 3 quarts for 5 cents, ends milk war. Milk as low as two and two-thirds cents a quart was enjoyed for a little while just recently by dairy patrons of Rogers as the result of a milk price war waged for a month by the five Rogers dairies, and a price of one and two-thirds cents was reached when milk from the Otto Carlson dairy was sold at one store as low as three quarts for a nickel. On the same day, however, the five warring dairymen got together and compromised on a price of five cents per quart. It was reported that this "Stabilized" milk price of a nickel a quart would be maintained in Rogers indefinitely.

∞∞∞

Nov. 10, 1932—Sam Henry, well known farmer of near Bentonville, also is establishing a reputation for the manufacturing and marketing of good old sorghum molasses in a big way. As a long haul shipper of this delicious and symphonious accompaniment to good old southern made hot biscuits, Mr. Henry already has rung the bell. Just recently he shipped one barrel of his high-grade Arkansas Ozarks "long-sweetening" to Elmer Berschy at Wheeling, West Virginia, and another barrel to M. R. C. Smith at Missoula, Montana.

∞∞∞

March 6, 1936—On February 29th, Mrs. W. H. Sears of Cave Springs observed her twenty-first birthday, although the family Bible showed her to be 84. She missed a lot of birthday cake due to leap-year.

∞∞∞

April 17, 1936—Notice is hereby given that the ordinances prohibiting chickens and stock from running at large in the City of Bentonville, Arkansas, will be strictly enforced by the City Marshall and all persons are hereby warned to keep chickens penned up, and notice is hereby given that the grazing of cattle in streets and alleys by running at large or by staking same out is prohibited. Witness my hand as Mayor of the City of Bentonville, Ark., this 13th day of April, 1936. Sam Beasley, Mayor.

∞∞∞

A reprint from the past. "The devil has settled in Benton county," bemourned a Baptist Minister upon observing a "Bloomer Girl" in 1861.

∞∞∞

Early Politicians were gifted in verbosity; Arkansas political spellbinders of the good old days pulled no punches when they talked about their home state.

A former secretary of State visiting in Tennessee is quoted as saying. "My home is in Arkansas where the mountains are so

345

high one can stand on their peaks and tickle the feet of the Democrat angels in heaven, and the swamps are so low one can stand flat footed and pat the bald heads of the Republicans in Hell."

∞∞∞∞

All of the following was taken from letters people sent me telling of life in early years in Benton county.

Letter from Mr. Don Roller

I was born and raised around the Gateway area and I can remember the first steam thresher machine around there. It burned wood. It belonged to Bill Vandagriff. He would come to my grandfathers place each year to thresh for him and would also thresh for all the neighbors around. He would leave our place and would go to the Geo. Schnitzer farm to thresh for him. He would have to go up north to cross the Frisco railroad tracks and one time the separator hung up between the rails on the track. He sent one man each way to stop a train if any came and one did. The man flagged it down and it stopped. The brakeman and fireman came down off the engine and helped get the separator on across the track. This was about 1918.

I know there was another threshing machine around there before I was born, for my father and mother lived down on Spider creek south of Clantonville and a machine came down there to thresh and the steam engine turned over on the Spider Hill and the boiler burst and scalded the engineer to death. My father helped pick the body up. I guess it was an awful sight in those days.

Marion Clanton had a steam engine. His boys Jake, Edgar and Bill made a merry go round out of lumber and would run it with their steam engine and had a 4th of July celebration at Clantonville.

It cost a nickel to ride it. It did a lot of squeaking and puffing but was a good ride in those days. Old Jake would pull that old whistle and you were already scared but when that whistle blowed you got more scared. That was in the year of about 1920.

I can also remember the first air plane that landed around there. It landed in my grandfather Bill Roller's wheat field. A hose had busted and it had run out of water. Us boys carried water from the spring at my grandfathers to refill the radiator. In landing and taking off the plane tore up about two acres of wheat which made my grandfather pretty upset. That was about 1915.

There at Herd Switch, which was listed on the railroad as Osborne Ark. there was a little building called the depot. There was a spur track that branched off of the main line that Frisco spotted off cars to be loaded with ties, minning props and my uncle Keen Roller unloaded car loads of shelled corn to feed hogs.

He also would load car loads of apples he raised to be shipped out.

There was a mercantile store there, it belonged to Harry Baker and was operated by Bill Hecky. We would buy kerosene to burn in our lamps and lanterns. He would put a big piece of gum drop candy on the spout so it wouldn't spill out. As soon as we left the store, I would take the gum drop off and eat it.

At one time when the railroad work crew was laying new rails and ties on the Devils Eyebrow Hill, the crew lived in cars that were parked on the spur.

The grocery store had a barber shop on the south side operated by Bill Lombard, haircut 25 cents.

The store had a big block of wood with about 2 feet diameter with a block of cheese on it that was covered with cheese cloth. They kept a big knife on the block and would cut off the amount you wanted and then you weighed it. We didn't have to go to Seligman or Garfield for very much, we sold our eggs and other commodities to the store, received 8 cents per dozen for eggs and a penny bought a pretty good size sack of candy. This was during the year 1912 to 15.

From Mrs. Don Roller (Lena Hays).

My father, James P. Hays, was born July 10, 1857, in eastern Tennessee. When he was a very small boy, the family migrated to Benton County, Ark. They were living at Lee Town during the Battle of Pea Ridge. The family had to leave their home for a time while the battle was being fought.

He took up blacksmithing at an early age. Around 1875, he built his first shop. It was located across the road from the Winton Springs. He was at that location for a good many years, later having shops at Corinth and Garfield. He had a small shop at the Charlie Cox place just south of Elk Horn when he passed away in 1925.

He made most of the tools he used. He specialized in horse shoeing; he was known for miles around for being one of the best horse shoers.

He said that one time the Jesse James gang came to our house in the night and had him go to the shop and shoe their horses. They hung their coats and blankets over the windows so no light would shine out. There were nine horses, but he got them all shod and the men were on their way before daylight.

Letter from Joan C. Jorgenson:

My great grandmother, (wife of James Dickson, general store owner) trained to be a mid-wife and delivered many, many babies around Bentonville. She usually went on her horse (side saddle) and stayed one or two weeks with the family or they came for her and brought her home. She got $10, which was good money in those days.

Letter from Louise McPhetridge Thaden, telling about flying over Bentonville;

The first time I flew over it, I remember being impressed with how small it looked from the air and how beautiful.

Letter from Percy R. Cheney:

In 1924, we moved to Decatur and my father R. V. Cheney opened a blacksmith shop at the north end of main street. I went to school in Decatur.

In 1928, I joined the business with my father, we added a gasoline service station and auto repair shop.

Decatur was a very active town at that time, exporting fruit and vegetables during the strawberry season. One day there were 7 refrigerator train cars shipped from there. During the year, many apples were also shipped. One evening during the summer, there were 952 different pieces loaded on the south bound passenger train and sent by express, most of them were hampers of green beans and flats of tomatoes.

Along about then J. C. Scott was constable and Frank Finch was Mayor.

In 1931, my father and I bought a feed hammer mill. It would pulverize all types of feed and grain from corn fodder to corn meal and whole wheat flour. During the early 30's, it became nearly a lifesaver for all the people in the area.

Early in 1936, the top half of the school building blew off.

∞∞∞∞

Chapter Twenty Seven
Pictures from the Past

Rogers White Lime Works—Production of industrial lime from the abundant limestone in the area once was one of the leading industries of the area. The picture shows one of the plants of the Rogers Lime Works at Cross Hollows.

349

First Rural Carrier—Jube Lee, the first mail carrier out of the Rogers post office, is pictured above with the one-horse mail cart with which he served his patrons for many years. Mr. Lee received the appointment as rural carrier April 1, 1904, and retired from the postal service October 31, 1916, because of ill health.

Old Big Four Tavern—The first building erected on the site of what later was Monte Ne. In its day it was a place of merriment for the boys on Saturday night, as well as a place for a drink and a bit of rest if you were riding by. The building was built in 1856. During the Civil War it was used as headquarters by the Union and Confederate armies.

Monte Ne mill was built by a Mr. Pettigrew some time before the Civil War, and was operated by him during the war. In 1890 a stock company bought it and put in new machinery. John Puckett was the miller.

Later, Rev. J. G. Bailey bought the mill and named it Silver Springs Milling Co. He in turn sold it to Coin Harvey in 1900, who had it taken down in 1905.

Benton County built its first steel bridge of importance over the White River, east of Rogers. The contract was let in Nov., 1903, for $11,695. It was done by Nov., 1904.

Prior to the erection of this bridge, White River was impasable in high water. It was one of the first high water bridges in the county.

The Joe S. Stevenson Hose Co. of Bentonville. The picture was made in 1904. This was a contest day when hose companies came from Arkansas and Missouri to have a race to see who could set up and throw water the fastest.

From alongside the old courthouse, they ran to the bank corner and climbed a 12-foot tower with a hose as other members of the company hooked it up and turned on the water.

Joe S. Stevenson was editor of the Benton County Democrat. He bought the hose cart for the town in 1888.

Many a fire has been fought with this old fire cart.

Wheat harvest in 1894. This was one of the early day steam engines and thrasher. The picture was made on the Bryan Miller farm near Pea Ridge.

Hands who ran this outfit brought their own shack where they lived and did their cooking.

At that date, wheat was only making about 12 bushels to the acre. An article in the paper that year told of a farmer who made 18½ bushels to the acre. It asked who could beat that.

Rogers Academy football team about 1900. At that time there were a lot of small academies in the three-state area and they played all of them. They beat both the University of Arkansas and Drury College in the early days.

A few of the leading merchants of Bentonville in the early 1890's.
Standing left to right, Jim Lankford, Jim Alfrey, Alex Hall, Asa Lankford. Sitting left to right, Geo. Jackson, Col. Terry, Bob Brasher, Bennet Burks.
The mustaches were not for some show, they were the dress of the day.

Bentonville Base Ball Club, 1910
Back row left to right—Dr. C. E. Hurley, Nap Covey, Frank Hamilton, Grover Lindsey, Bill Cloe, Harry Sweeny, Dave Peel. Front row left to right—Lloyd Woods, Earl Austin, Glover Orrick, Walter Wright, Jack Hutchinson, Red Dunley.

Laying a cornerstone—A large crowd of Masons and other people were on hand in Bentonville at about 10:30 the first Saturday in July, 1909, for the laying of the cornerstone of the new Masonic Temple.
Chief Justice E. A. McCulloch of Little Rock, the Grand Master of the Masonic Grand Lodge of Arkansas, participated in the laying of the stone.
The music for the day was played by Prof. Stewart and band.
The Bentonville Lodge was founded Nov. 4, 1852.

354

On July 1, 1900, Rogers celebrated completion of this new 100,000 gallon elevated water storage tank. It replaced an old brick tower. Some of the old bricks can be seen in the picture.

The Tally Ho—This odd looking wagon was called a Tally Ho.
It was built special by Fred Cunningham of Bentonville. He used
it to haul groups of people to special programs or picnics. It was
made so the luggage was carried under the seats.

This group was Gus Hurley's baseball team from Pawhuska,
Okla. They came to play Bentonville in 1909. Gus is standing.

Fred is in the driver's seat.

Jeff Davis Democrats—The picture was made in 1904 and shows
the political idol of the Arkansas hill folks surrounded by a group
of the faithful in front of the Monte Ne Hotel. Left to right, front
row, Alex Sigmon, Gov. Davis, P. B. Hummel, and Lewis Archer
standing.

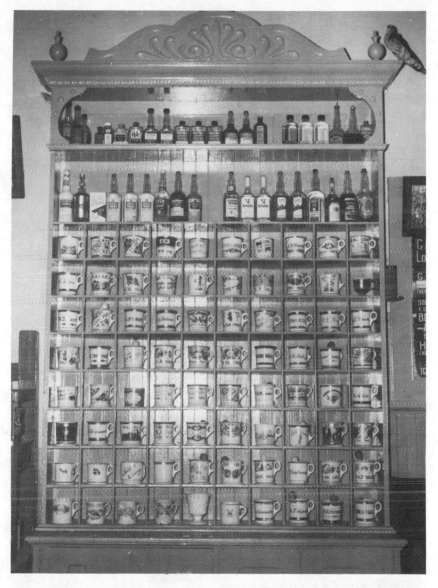

This display of old shaving mugs in the Elk Horn Barber Shop in Bentonville is a memorial to the days gone by when men kept their shaving mugs at whatever barber shop they used.

The collection was started by Mr. A. J. Bates. He gave it to Kit Campbell in 1918. Kit is the founder of the Elk Horn Barber shop.

The mugs had belonged to the prominent men of Bentonville.

Cooling meat in Bentonville—Charles W. Foster eyes the slabs of meat hanging to cool in the D. S. Foster and Son Meat Market. Big iceboxes were located in the rear. Photo was taken about 1905.

Frisco Station—The Rogers Frisco passenger and freight stations and the Fred Harvey dining room as they appeared when they were located between Elm and Poplar Street. These were destroyed by fire. The station was then moved, and the new one opened April 26, 1914.

Hoover Store—This is the general store at Hoover, which existed two miles southeast of Highfill in Benton County. Left to right, Edwin Flynt, Sam Flynt, Sandy Flynt, Annie Flynt, Mollie Jones Flynt. On the porch is Samuel Jones, or Mexican Sam as he was called after returning from the Mexican War. The picture was made about 1891. There was a store here for 50 years or more.

Ozark Hotel—One of Rogers' first hostelries was the Ozark Hotel, which was operated by Mr. and Mrs. Robert P. Pace, the couple shown seated in the picture. The hotel was located at Arkansas and Walnut Street, and was destroyed by fire in 1909.

*Benton County's
First Circuit Judge*

*Joseph H. Hogue was a circuit
judge in northwest Arkansas
from 1837 to 1845, serving in
Benton, Washington and Madison Counties. He lived in
Bentonville and also in Fayetteville, moving to Texas in
1845.*

*A War Eagle Gathering—A visit by candidates for office always
was the occasion for a gathering of leading citizens of a com-
munity. One such group is pictured above in front of Ledbetter's
store at War Eagle about 1904. Identified in the picture are F. M.
Hemphill, Rev. Isaac Shenks, Jack Hegwood, W. L. Frost, Jasper
Denney, Ray Hemphill, Samuel Garvin, Dr. Morgan, Miss Addie
Rutherford, Ebbie Key, Geoger DeGoff, Doss Denney, Mr. Arch-
er, Magnolia Rutherford, Ona Ledbetter, Gene Denney, H. L.
Ledbetter, Mrs. Ledbetter and children, Sam Burks, Mrs. Celia
Burks, J. Rutherford, Ollie Blackburn, Arlie Frost, and Mose
Cook. The building was built by J. A. C. Blackburn.*

No history of Bentonville could be complete without a picture of one of the music classes of Miss Fannie Lockhart. She taught music in Bentonville for many years and her students gave many programs at the churches and in the opera house.

In the above picture, back row, left to right, Lily Stahl, Etta Jackson, Effie Morris, Ethel Sedwick, Lucy Boggs. Second row, left to right, Eve Dickson, Myrtle Hickman, Kitty Smartt, Miss Fannie Lockhart, Josie McClinton, Amy Looney. Front row, left to right, Ethel Craig, Clara Frye, Ebe Laughlin, Olive Suggs.

The picture was taken in 1893.

Walnut Street, looking west from First Street in Rogers.

South First Street, looking north from Poplar Street in Rogers as it looked in the early days. Except for modernization, there has been little change in this street.

A history making train—It was the arrival of the above Frisco passenger train on May 10, 1881, that gave Rogers a birthday. Old No. 17 was the first to run over the new tracks into Rogers. The town began with that trip.

These next six pictures were taken from a booklet of The Southern Fruit Product Company, manufacturers of pure apple cider vinegar, apple cider, cider syrup and jellies, and sorghum vinegar. The main plant was at Rogers and a branch plant was at Centerton.

Oaken casks for clarifying cider, with a capacity of 5,000 gallons each. The juice is racked from one cask to another until every particle of sediment has disappeared.

Gasoline engines at Centerton—forty horse power.

PICTURES FROM THE PAST

Press and engine rooms at Centerton. This factory was completed just in time for the 1907 crop. The town of Centerton is practically in the geographical center of Benton County, which contains more apple trees than any other county in the world. From the top of this building the landscape forms a veritable orchard as far as the eye can reach.

Grinding sorghum cane at Rogers. Vinegar fermented and generated from the raw juice has a piquant, fruity flavor. Our individual process is now beyond the experimental stage. Next season we intend to plant large quantities of cane on our own farms, and hope to have a very considerable supply of this product to offer the trade.

Apple packing sheds at Centerton. The fruit is hauled here from the orchards, and after being culled and packed, is shipped to our customers or placed in cold storage.

Receiving bins at Rogers. The contents of wagons are dumped from the driveway into a large hopper, and then conveyed into the different bins by an endless chain elevator. No shoveling. A wagon can be unloaded in two minutes with practically no labor. Six hundred wagon loads are often consumed in a day at our mills.

Workers at the Blocker Evaporator—This plant was built in 1888 as the Bentonville Evaporating Company, and later was sold to Jim Blocker who ran it for many years. When first built, it used 800 bushels of apples a day.

Wagons waiting to unload apples at the Blocker Evaporator.

This picture of Bentonville was made some time in the early 1900's. This is one of few pictures showing the peanut and popcorn stand. Today the address is Main and Central.

This picture was made just before World War I. It was called Spring Street looking West, Bentonville. Today this is Central Street.

PICTURES FROM THE PAST

Carl Starck moved to Benton County in 1888 and bought a large farm near what was later Monte Ne. He soon started experimenting with grapes. He wanted to raise the best wine grapes that would grow.

For many years he grafted and cross bred cynthia grape vines. He always dreamed of the day when this would be a wine country.

He won several medals at the Chicago World Fair in 1893. In later years his wine won prizes all over the world. He took a first place in Vienna, Austria.

Very little of his wine was sold in Benton County, but it was shipped to many states.

In 1915, when Arkansas voted dry, Starck stopped making wine. He lost all interest in the grapes and let them die out.

Carl Starck is best remembered for the weather records that he kept for over 40 years in Benton County. He died in 1939.

Grecian Theater program in the early 1920's in Sulphur Springs. At this time there were many summer theater programs here.

Mr. & Mrs. Buck Phillips in front of the Phillips Mill north of Cave Springs. At one time this was also known as the Dickson Mill. Picture made about 1900.

The Allen Mill at what was later Cave Springs. It was built on the north side of the lake in about 1890. Left to right in the picture, Jones Scoggins, Frank Goodrich, Nate Maxwell, Lige Allen and Henry Gaston.

This picture of Cave Springs was made by Hansard of Bentonville in about 1890. At that time this was a free picnic ground; people came here from over a large part of the county for a day off and a picnic.

These two pictures were made at one of the old Benton County Poor Farms. They are said to have been made in the early 1900's.

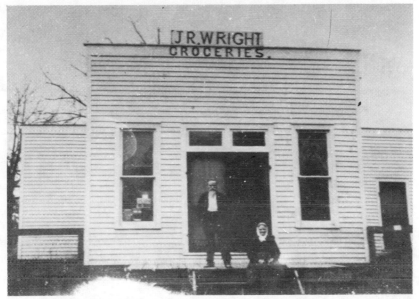

Mr. & Mrs. J. R. Wright in front of their grocery store in early day Rogers.

"Whoopee" Jack Lanye of near Siloam Springs. He was called Whoopee because every time he went into any store he would yell out, "Whoopee!"

Grocery store in Bentonville some time in the late 1890's.

First Street in Rogers as it looked in the early 1900's.

Eagle Hotel Bentonville—For several years in the early 1900's there was a monument plant in the hotel.

A train work crew somewhere in Benton County about 1900.

The Maroon Band of Rogers about 1905.

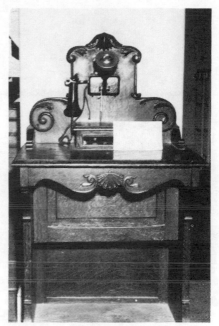

This was one of the first telephones installed in Benton County. It is a Stromberg Carlson Telephone, with 1900 as the last pat. date. It was used in Siloam Springs and was given by John C. Haney to the Museum at the U of A in Fayetteville.

A. W. Cadman's Photographic Gallery—Mr. Cadman was Rogers' first commercial photographer and he made almost all of the early pictures of Rogers.

This train engine made many runs into Sulphur Springs in the early 1900's.

Passengers unloading at Sulphur Springs in the summer of 1909. They were all going to one of the resort hotels there. The next year a new station was built, so they didn't have to walk along the tracks.

The Terry block in Bentonville, as it looked in 1889. At that time it housed the Benton County Bank, which at that time was the richest bank in the county. There also was a dry goods store in the building.

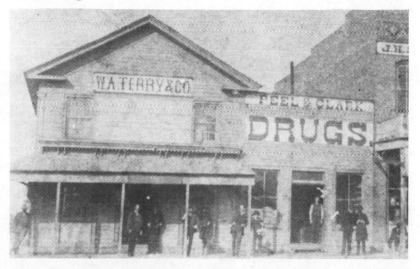

These buildings were built just after the Civil War for the dry goods store of W. A. Terry. When the Terry block was built, these were moved around the corner and up the block on Spring Street. They can be seen in the background of the top picture on this page.

The Bank of Centerton, built in 1905.

The square in Bentonville about 1912. Note watering tank in foreground for stock to drink from.

A water mill somewhere in Benton County.

Shop of the past—This picture of Tony Back at the right was taken at the largest blacksmith shop in Bentonville in 1910. Tony ran the shop for many years and his blacksmith shop was the last in town.

These four prints were printed from glass plate negatives. All that I know about them is that the box was marked Benton County about 1890.

Benton County Courthouse, built in 1874 and used until 1928. It is said to have cost the county $60,000.00. It was on the corner of North Main and N W 2nd.

The picture was made in the late 1880's.

Benton County Courthouse opened in Nov., 1928. It is on the east side of the square in Bentonville. It cost the county just over $200,000.00.

This dirt road was north of Bentonville, and is now part of Highway 71. The picture was made in the early 1920's.

A parade in Bentonville, said to be part of the program for the Confederate reunion, 1893. In the foreground is the Stevenson Hose Company of Bentonville. In back is Alex Black's Band of Bentonville.

This is the drill team of Oakland Camp No. 22, Woodmen of the World. The camp was organized in 1896 in Bentonville. The drill team was at the famous Crystal Springs near Bentonville. It was under the management of Capt. John A. Sheffield. At that time, Woodmen of the World was one of the strongest fraternal insurance organizations in the world.

The charcoal kiln owned by Perry-Hanns & Co. at Beaty, built in early 1900's. The brick work was done by Ben Locke. The kilns were torn down during the early 1930's.

9563 Apple Jack Factory, Bentonville, Ark.

The above picture was made of the Macon & Carson's Brandy Distillery at Bentonville about 1900.

It was opened in Aug., 1893, and at that time it was said to be the biggest Brandy distillery west of the Mississippi River. They had thirty fermenters with a total capacity of 215,000 gallons.

One of their first ads read, "New apple and peach brandy distillery opened in Bentonville. Bring your fruit in by the wagon load or less. No fruit will go to waste, it makes no difference how little your peaches and apples are, or how rough they look. Just bring them in and get cash."

This was a big business in Bentonville until 1915 when the state was voted dry and they had to close down.

This was a big help to the fruit growers as it got cash out of fruit that couldn't be sold for anything else. Many are the stories that were told about this distillery and the brandy they made.

These two cars belonging to Emma Maxwell Meade were driven over most of Benton County in their day. And at that time we had only dirt roads.

Spring in the park at Park Springs Hotel. A sign stated, "Stomach Springs, it's radio active."

These ladies are at Lithia Springs, in Sulphur Springs some time in the early 1920's.

Electric Springs sanitarium building—In the mid-1880's, Electric Springs near the northeast city limits of Rogers were known far and wide for the curative properties. They had a large first class resort hotel here and a very good and well known sanitarium. Many were the claims made about the water here.

Other building at Electric Springs, in late 1880's.

PICTURES FROM THE PAST

The above picture of the Electric Springs and the one below of the picnic grounds at the Electric Springs Resort were made from glass plate negatives in about 1890.

Early day gas stations at Sulphur Springs.

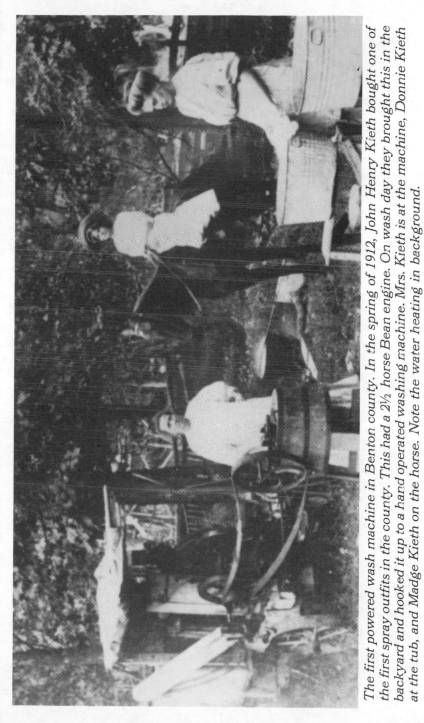

The first powered wash machine in Benton county. In the spring of 1912, John Henry Kieth bought one of the first spray outfits in the county. This had a 2½ horse Bean engine. On wash day they brought this in the backyard and hooked it up to a hand operated washing machine. Mrs. Kieth is at the machine, Donnie Kieth at the tub, and Madge Kieth on the horse. Note the water heating in background.

Baptizing in the lake at Cave Springs in the 1920's.

Ice wagon in Rogers in the early 1900's.

This picture shows the students of the Orchard Hendrix Academy at Gentry in 1909-1910.

This picture was copied from a postcard of Gentry made in 1911 or 1912.

Chautauqua crowd at the tent in Bentonville in the early 1900's. The summer meets were always held in a tent; the winter program was held at the opera house.

Wonderland Cave, Bella Vista, was the only underground nightclub in the county. Many were the programs that were held here in this underground wonderland.

Pea Ridge in the early 1900's. This shows the business section at that time. J. J. Putman general merchandise on right; J. R. Wheat on left.

Cave Springs Water Mill—This mill was near Cave Springs and its imported millstones ground grain for about 100 years. The above picture shows the mill in a dilapidated state. It was later rebuilt and continued in operation until it was destroyed by fire.

Post office at War Eagle—The post office was opened in this building in 1883. Over the years it was moved to other store buildings as the postmasters changed. But before it was closed it moved back to its first home.

The first railway depot in Bentonville.

Hot air balloon flight over Bentonville in the early 1900's.

OPPOSITE PAGE:
The east side of the square of Bentonville in 1886 left to right—
Ed. Graves; Livery Barn and Feed Stables; Post Office; G. C.
Davis, postmaster; John Galbreaith's grocery store; Dry Goods;
Claypool & Woods; Joe Plucks Furniture; N. S. Henry's Hard-
ware and Implement House. The photographs would have been
made by Hansard Studio.

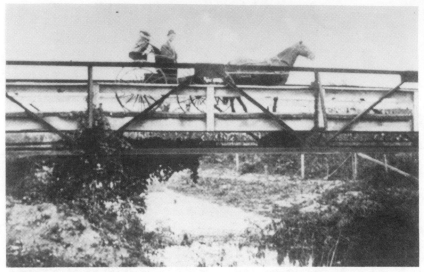

Buggy on bridge north of Bentonville.

Dr. Elisha J. Highfill and wife in the buggy they were married in. Picture made in 1903 in front of their first house. Doc. was a great hound dog lover and had many hounds around at all times.

Flood in Twin Springs Park in Siloam Springs in 1928.

Buggy fixed as a float for some long forgotten program at Siloam Springs.

The flag in this picture is one of the Confederate battle flags carried in the Battle of Pea Ridge. The rifles also were used there and for many years were in the museum at Elk Horn Tavern run by the Scott family.

Elk Horn Tavern as it looked about the time of the Battle of Pea Ridge.

The Union flag in this picture was carried at Leetown and Elk Horn Tavern, then on to the end of the war in many other battles. For many years this hung in the Scott museum in the Elk Horn Tavern.

Pictures of floats in the Apple Blossom Festival Parades held in Rogers in the mid-1920's.

Fayetteville

Hiwasse

Hiwasse

Green Forest

Pea Ridge

Springdale

Rogers

Looking west on Main Street in Gravette in about 1910.

Looking east on Main Street in Gravette in about 1910.

This picture was made in the county judge's office in the old courthouse, sometime between 1908-1910. In the picture are Ed Hill, Judge Norris, Sheriff Andy Russell, and Deputy Ed Young.

Providence School in 1912. This was in the east part of the county.

R. J. Allen Hardware and Groceries at Brightwater. Bob Allen with mail sack, man getting mail unknown. Other man sitting on porch is Albert Peel Jr; on the step left are John Pitts and Hugh Rice.

Vren Rife putting the head in an apple barrel after it was filled.

413

Jim VanHook sawmill at Pine Top in the late 1930's.

Second crew on a hand car some place in Benton County.

PICTURES FROM THE PAST

Brightwater Wreck on Nov. 29, 1907—The second section of a Frisco freight train piled into Sugar Creek when it rammed into the rear of the first section on the railroad bridge at Brightwater. The accident occurred at the time the railroad was replacing the original wooden trestle with steel beams. The wreck was said to have been due to failure of the second section to comply with an order to reduce speed over the bridge to four miles an hour while the construction was in progress. The engineer on the second train alerted the train crews with the whistle and the trainmen on both freights leaped to safety.

Dot Brammer and J. Calvin Evans at Sedalia in the east part of the county. Mr. Evans had the general store, post office, feed store, blacksmith shop and saw mill. This made the town.

Apple Maid—At one of the Apple Blossom Festival programs at Rogers in the mid-1920's.

416

The log building at the left in this picture was a tobacco barn.
In the late 1870's and early 1880's many of the farms in the county
had this size tobacco barn or larger.

This whiskey still was found north of Bentonville near the
Missouri and Arkansas State lines in the 1920's. Men in the picture are, left to right, Willie Graham, special deputy; Sheriff Joe
Gailey; and Chief Deputy Edgar Fields. At that time many stills
were found every year in the county.

417

Rogers Hose Company, or fire department as they are called to-day. Picture made some time in the 1890's.

Rake's Water Mill, north of Bentonville, as pictures on an early day colored postcard published by Keck's Variety Store, Benton-ville. The mill was built in 1858 and was known for many years as the Steele Mill.

418

This was the carnival part of the Fruit Fair in Bentonville about 1910. The tent is standing on part of the lot where the Courthouse is today.

This was one of the many general stores in Rogers in the late 1890's.

419

For many years there was a colored baseball team in Bentonville that played other colored teams from Fort Smith to Joplin. This picture was made about 1912, and shows just part of the team. Top row, left to right— Thad Whayne, Marion Finney, Lyod Troutt. Bottom row— Yates Claypool, Virg Black, John Barker. Part of the time there were two teams called the Old Heads and the Young Heads.

This is said to be Gus Hurley. At one time he was a part owner of the Benton County Democrat. Isn't that some team and buggy. Just think how it would look rounding the square.

This is one of many pictures that Capt. Field Kindley sent home when he was in the Army Flying Corps. It is not known if he flew this one or not. His unit had this type in Europe. It is a Sopwith Camel, with Clerget rotary engine that developed 130 HP. and the cylinders revolved with the prop. They had two Vickers machine guns with about 300 rounds each.

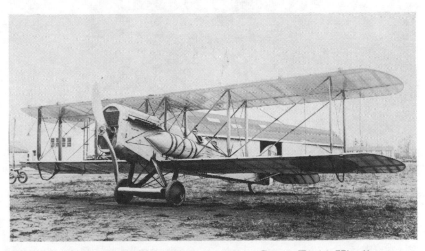

This is another of many pictures that Capt. Field Kindley sent home when he was in the Army Flying Corps. It is not known if he flew this one or not. It is said to be a J. N. Y., U. S. Trainer, about 1918. His unit used this type plane.

This picture of Capt. Field Kindley was made at the end of World War I.

Pea Ridge junior - senior girls in Bentonville in 1928, playing at flagging a freight train. Girls, left to right are—Frances Cable, Ernestine Ricketts, Sue Caldwell, and Lillian Hickman. On ground are Mary Childs and Marie Mitchell.

All ready to go and the car won't run. The senior girls of Pea Ridge, 1928.

College Band—This photograph, taken from an old postcard, shows the Pea Ridge College Band probably around 1900.

This sign was for one of the very early radio repair shops in Pea Ridge.

This was a new sign for Putman & Son General Store in Pea Ridge. Left to Right are—Alma Woods, Cleva Lee, Bill Putman, Edna Swift.

This right hand drive Ford was seen for several years at Sulphur Springs. No one knows who the people are.

A well dressed young lady in Benton County about 1890.

This was a Detroit 2 cycle engine. It ran both directions and also burned kerosene. The large tank at the left was a 30-gallon cooling tank. The engine was used on a buzz saw to cut fire wood. The boy is Herbert Rakes.

Beaty School, 1911. Miss Sarah Bale was the teacher. The students from here had to go to high school at Southwest City, Mo.

This picture was taken from a drawing of the spring at Sulphur Springs as it looked in 1874.

This is an early day picture of the Sulphur Springs Mineral Water bottling works. Millions of gallons of water were shipped from here in years gone by.

From a painting of the Cave Springs Rail Road Station.

Clyde (Pea Ridge) Day at the high point of his pitching career.

Clyde (Pea Ridge) Day was one of Benton County's great baseball players. He was as well known for his hog calling as he was for his fast ball and screw ball. He would give out with a loud hog call that would unnerve the batter, then come across with a fast ball when they weren't looking for it.

Pea Ridge Day took his name from his home town of Pea Ridge, where he grew up on a farm and learned how to call hogs.

He was on the pitching staff of the Fort Smith Twins in 1922. Day won four and lost 13 games that season and the following year was released, immediately catching on with Joplin. He went back that year with the Joplin club and beat the Twins twice in the series.

The champion "hog caller" of baseball was with Wichita in the Western league in 1927 when he won 13 games and lost 11.

He also played with Omaha of the Western league, and the Pacific Coast league. He served with Kansas City in 1929 when the Blues won the American Association pennant. He later was drafted by Brooklyn and then returned to the American Association with Minneapolis.

His hog calling unnerved the opposition and caused him no end of trouble. The entire Kansas City team was once compelled to leave a fashionable Milwaukee hotel because Day went to the central part of the lobby while an orchestra was playing and emitted his piercing yell.

His fast ball and screw ball made his delivery at times baffling to the batters.

Pea Ridge Day died in March of 1934 in Kansas City, Mo., at the age of 32. He was looking for a new pitching job at the time.

429

This log cabin in Benton county has sure seen better days.

This house was built in 1832 by Robert Dickson, who came to Benton County in 1831 with his twin brother Joseph, and his brother Ezekiel. This was the first home which Robert Dickson and his wife, Esther Moore, built after coming here and in which they lived. It stood in Bentonville until the late 1950's.

Baseball has been the leading sport in Benton County for many years. Bentonville had teams just after the Civil War.

Bentonville baseball team of 1905. Back row, left to right—Fred Berry, Thurman Bohart, Lloyd Woods. Second row, left to right—Charles Trone, Charles Hopkins, Roland Trone, Morgan McMichastian. Front row, left to right—Frank Hamilton, Frank Thone, Charles Robinson.

Back in 1890—Sale Day in Bentonville, about 1890. This was on the east side of the square where the courthouse is today. Many a horse and mule trade was made here. The stories that were told would make several books.

Twenty five years after the Battle of Pea Ridge these men met there for a reunion of the Blue and the Gray. They were a part of the five hundred men who met at Pea Ridge in 1888.

Co. F, 15th Northwest Arkansas Infantry
Top row, left to right—
Bob Heckman, Jim Lee, Newt Harris, Bill Lee, Bob Webb.
2nd row, left to right—
John Grogory, Jack Maxwill, Capt. Etris, Jack Goad, Robt. M. Phillips, Pomp Patterson, Cotton.
3rd row, left to right—
Jim Cavness, Tom Kendericks, Bill Carden.

Carl & Oakley evaporator, 1901. This was near Siloam Springs.
They dried apples here.

Hay baling on the west side of the county in an early day.

When this building was built in 1887, it housed The Peoples Bank. As far as design and beauty goes, this building topped all others in the county. For years this was the most photographed building in the county.

Decatur freight building with station in the background to the right, 1907.

This is an early day lumberyard in Bentonville. Dr. Hobbs is standing in front.

In this picture the Benton County Democrat was backing Grover Cleveland for his second term as President, in 1888.

Early picture of the K. C. S. Depot, Siloam Springs.

Siloam Springs—Floodwater at Twin Springs, 1892.

Siloam Springs—This building was almost washed away in the flood of 1892. It was the Nobby Clothing House.

437

*This building was built for E. C. Bartell in 1894 at Siloam Springs.
It held a dry goods store named The Right Place.*

*Wagons in front of the Good Luck Grocery in Siloam Springs in
about 1910.*

The Jasper Parks family at Beaty in 1903. Mr. Parks started the town of Beaty.

An early day parade in Siloam Springs.

The home of D. K. and Martha Wetzel at Maysville.

This house was built in Bentonville for Mr. W. B. Deming in 1887, at a cost of $3,000. Next to live there was Dwight Dickson and family. Then it became the home of Dr. Charles Hurley. It is on North Main and Second Street.

These two pictures are of the Bentonville Steam Laundry in the early 1900's. The man standing by the horses is Roy McPhetridge.

This was a special sale by Doke Motor Co. Bentonville, in about 1920. The Doke Motor Co. was operated by the Benton County Hardware Co. They sold Fords in every town they had a hardware store.

The early home of Mr. and Mrs. Char. Juhre, Rogers. Mr. Juhre is holding the horse.

The Bentonville Mills—located on the spring branch below town, was erected in 1869 by T. K. Blake and J. Claypool. It was supplied with two runs of buhr stones, with a capacity of 100 bushels of wheat and 200 bushels of corn per day. A carding machine was operated in connection with the mill.

White Sulphur Sanitarium
Sulphur Springs, Arkansas

Architect's drawing of the Kihlberg Hotel in Sulphur Springs. At the time it opened in 1909, this was the biggest hotel in northwest Arkansas.

Officers in the Centerton Masonic Lodge 19

Building of a railroad grade some place in Benton County about 1900.

School at Hiwasse in an early day.

Looking north on South Main Street in Bentonville about 1890.

445

The dry cleaning and pressing shop of P. A. (Dot) Brammer, Rogers.

One side of the street was in Arkansas; the other, the west side, was in Indian Territory, later Oklahoma. Picture made about 1910.

446

THE NEIGHBORS

"I don't know what my parents are thinking about—letting me stay up listening to the radio all hours of the night!"

George Clark is another Bentonville boy who made good. When he was in school all he could think about was drawing pictures. He went on to make a great name as a cartoonist. When he was 17 he was receiving regular pay for drawings sold to an Oklahoma newspaper.

He was the creator of Side Glances, which appeared in The Oklahoma News. From there he went to New York where he had his own studio.

On April 17, 1939, his cartoon "The Neighbors" first appeared in The New York News. Shortly after, it was running in over a hundred newspapers.

The above cartoon was taken from his book, The Neighbors. A collection of cartoons by George Clark. Copyrighted by News Syndicate Co. Inc., New York 17, N.Y.

Gravette, 1903

Coats House, Henry Coats, Prop.,
Gravette.

Livery Barn of R. E. Laughlin, Gravette.

Witty Bro.'s General Merchandise

H. P. Lewis, Gravette.

Siloam Springs 1903

Photograph Gallery of R. F. Guilliams.

Port Arthur Hotel, J. W. Miller, Prop.,
Siloam Springs

Livery Stable of J. A. Jordan,
Siloam Springs.

"The Republican" on upper floor,
Siloam Springs.

Gentry 1903

Elberta Hotel, C. C. Lale, Prop.,
Gentry.

Journal-Advance Office, Arthur Tallman,
Editor, Gentry.

Office of Maxon & Severance, Real Estate
Agents, Gentry.

Postoffice, H. D. Lefors,
Postmaster, Gentry.

Residence of J. P. Milliken.
Sec. 28-19-32.

Residence of A. L. Hays, Bright Water,
Ark.

Store of Baker Bros., Osborne Station
(Herd P. O.)

Residence of W. L. Turman.
Sec. 2-17-32.

Homes in Siloam Springs 1903

Residence of C. D. Gunter,
Siloam Springs.

Residence of Judge C. Cooley,
Siloam Springs,

Residence of Dr. H. H. Canfield,
Siloam Springs.

Residence of L. W. Wallace,
Siloam Springs.

Award for 1936 Bendix Transcontinental Speed Race.

Louise McPhetridge Thaden with the first place award she won in the 1936 Bendix Transcontinental Speed Race. She was the first woman to win a Bendix air race.

4th—July—4ht

Bella Vista

Reunion of Soldier Boys---Big Day of Fun---Bathing Free to Soldiers---Music All Day---Cash Prizes Water Contests---Boating, Bathing and Dancing

Famous 142nd F. A. Band

Provided They Are Discharged With Their Instruments

Regular Old Time Rally and Picnic ·

Everybody Come

June 23, 1919

January 11, 1924

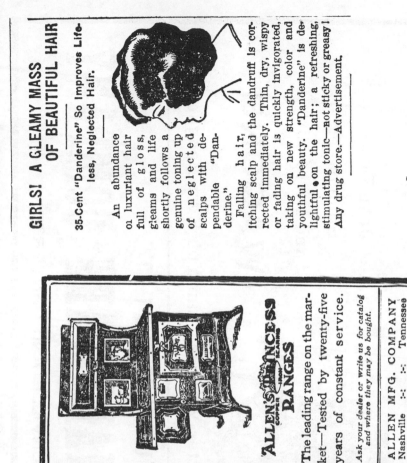

John Deere
Studebaker
and Fort Smith

WAGONS

Better Values and Better Wagons Than You Ever Bought Before

"WE'VE GOT IT"

BOHART HARDWARE COMPANY

BENTONVILLE AND CENTERTON

October 1, 1915

March 29, 1923

A Double Treat For The Ladies
ROYAL AIRDOME
Monday Night, June 25th

At **8:10** "The Social Key" BY ESSANY FILM CO.
(For Women Only)

At **8:30** "The Combat" Featuring Anita Stewart
For Everybody

We will give all ladies calling at Our Store
Free Tickets for Both Performances

Provided they are presented at the Royal Airdome Not later than 8:10
Monday Night June 25th

"THE SOCIAL KEY"

Is an Artistic and Intensely Interesting and Instructive Production; very human in its mixture of Romance, Fun and Facts, Demonstrating by the living models carrying out the plot of the story, how any woman no matter how homely her figure, may obtain a most charming grace of figure and carriage through

Get your tickets early **GOSSARD CORSETS**

Jackson Dry Goods Co.
"The One Price Store"

1917

for Economical Transportation

CHEVROLET

The Economical Quality Car

Chevrolet prices are not the lowest on the market, yet Chevrolet economical transportation averages lowest in cost. This average cost considers the purchase price, interest on investment, depreciation and all operating and maintenance costs.

A detailed comparison with any other car in the low priced field will convince you that Chevrolet is the best buy because of its superior quality and because the purchase price includes full equipment.

More than a million Chevrolets are now in use. Twelve huge plants are now building them at the rate of twenty-five hundred per working day. Nearly one-half million Chevrolets were bought in 1923 —far exceeding in number the sales of any other quality car.

Thus, our statements have the strongest possible backing, namely, the faith and patronage of the American people who know automobiles and know practical values better than any other people on earth.

Let any one of our seven thousand dealers show you our seven types of cars and explain how easy it is to get one and enjoy its use.

Prices f. o. b. Flint, Michigan

SUPERIOR Roadster - - -	$490
SUPERIOR Touring - - -	495
SUPERIOR Utility Coupe - -	640
SUPERIOR Sedan - - -	795
SUPERIOR Commercial Chassis -	395
SUPERIOR Light Delivery - -	495
Utility Express Truck Chassis -	550

Chevrolet Motor Company

Division of General Motors Corporation

Detroit, Michigan

January 17, 1924

1912

September 6, 1913

1911

DAVID BENJAMIN MORGAN, V, S,, M, D, V,

Graduate of Ontario Veterinary College, Toronto, Canada, and McKillip Veterinary College, Chicago. Twenty-three years active traveling service as Veterinary in America.

ASSISTED BY HIS BROTHER

DR. HENRY BOWEN MORGAN

REGISTERED VETERINARY

Surgeons, Dentists and Horse Educators

Late of Swansea, Wales.   Permanent Home, Fayetteville, Ark.

OUR DEPENDENT FRIENDS.

Successfully treats all diseases of horses, mules and cattle. Makes specialty of operations on ridgling horses and old stallions. Best to keep horses off feed for a day when they have to be thrown for an operation.

Special Attention Given to Horse Dentistry. How to know when your horse's teeth are not right: He will turn his head to one side while chewing, spill food from his mouth and slobber, have swellings, lumps or running sores on the jaw. All big head or big jaw comes from bad teeth. Tossing the head, fighting the bit, champing the teeth, lolling the tongue, starts suddenly, stopping short, shying, driving sideways, lunging and running away, are some of the bad habits caused by the mouth being out of condition, with colic, indigestion and hide-bound. Cure all these habits and prevent diseases by putting the teeth in perfect order.

It is not the amount of food a horse eats that makes him fat, but what he digests.

Bad and irregular teeth kill many horses and cause many bad habits and diseases. The horse suffers death often from his teeth; they are hid back in his mouth so his master can't see them, **and he can't talk** and tell his sufferings. **He is a silent sufferer.**

"WE SPEAK FOR THOSE THAT CANNOT SPEAK FOR THEMSELVES."

We should remember that all the horse gets for his services is **what little he eats.** He has few friends. **Examination free at my office.**

I carry with me the most complete set of instruments on the road, and have some of the finest specimens in existence. Special invitation extended to stockmen and all interested in horses. I also have for sale a new system on the education and treatment of the horse. Price during this advertisement, $1.00.

Wednesday, November 6, for one week at Chastain's Stable.

1907

1907

January 17, 1924

March 8, 1934

October 21, 1932

Thursday, October 20, 1932

* * * * * * * * * * * * *

I.G.A. STORES

I.G.A. Toasted Whole Wheat, Pkg..... **18c**
1 Hallowe'en Mask—Free with each Pkg.

1 No. 2 1-2 I.G.A. Pumpkin, Fancy
1 Package I.G.A. Pumpkin Pie Spice
    Both for.. **19c**
Palmolive Soap .... Bar..... **7c**
Camay Toilet Soap................ 3 Bars..... **17c**
P. & G. Laundry Soap................ 5 Bars..... **13c**
I.G.A. Preserves, 25c size................ 2 for..... **35c**
I.G.A. Mayonnaise................ 8 oz. Jar..... **15c**
I.G.A. Salad Dressing................ 8 oz. Jar..... **10c**
I.G.A. Green Beans................ 2 No. 2 Cans..... **19c**
I.G.A. Pumpkin................ 2 Large Cans..... **25c**
I.G.A. Pumpkin................ 3 No. 2 Cans..... **25c**
I.G.A. Royal Anne Cherries..No. 1 tall..... **15c**
I.G.A. Pink Salmon................ 2 Tall Cans..... **25c**
I.G.A. Red Salmon, Fancy 2 Tall Cans..... **35c**
I.G.A. Corned Beef................ 25c size..... **19c**
I.G.A. Spaghetti................ 2 Cans..... **19c**
"I" Blend Coffee................ Pound..... **35c**
"G" Blend Coffee................ Pound..... **30c**
"A" Blend Coffee................ Pound..... **25c**
Hersheys Cocoa................ 1 lb. Can..... **22c**
I.G.A. Cocoa................ 1 lb. Can..... **17c**
Butter Corn Candy................ 10 oz. Pkg..... **10c**

SMITH'S I.G.A. GROCERY
JACKSON'S I.G.A. GROCERY

* * * * * * * * * * * * *

October 20, 1932

PICTURES FROM THE PAST

CORN PLANTERS

International—Latest Improved
Sale Price.................................... **$57.50**

ENTIRE STOCK

Cook Stoves and Ranges

WEBER WAGONS

The WEBER WAGON has long been the most popular wagon of the Southwest. Built of first-class materials throughout and designed especially for the needs of this territory, it is known today as "the wagon that always stands up."

OUR SALE PRICE ON WEBER WAGONS IS

$115.00

Benton County Hardware Co.
ADV. January 11, 1924

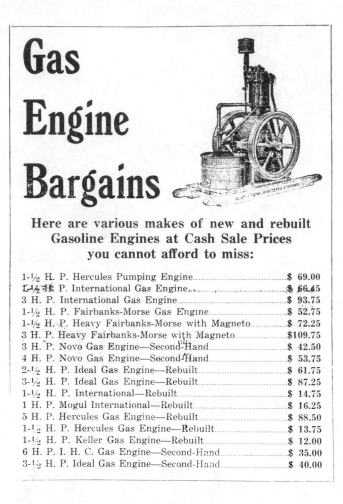

Gas Engine Bargains

**Here are various makes of new and rebuilt
Gasoline Engines at Cash Sale Prices
you cannot afford to miss:**

1-½ H. P. Hercules Pumping Engine	$ 69.00
1-½ H. P. International Gas Engine	$ 66.45
3 H. P. International Gas Engine	$ 93.75
1-½ H. P. Fairbanks-Morse Gas Engine	$ 52.75
1-½ H. P. Heavy Fairbanks-Morse with Magneto	$ 72.25
3 H. P. Heavy Fairbanks-Morse with Magneto	$109.75
3 H. P. Novo Gas Engine—Second-Hand	$ 42.50
4 H. P. Novo Gas Engine—Second-Hand	$ 53.75
2-½ H. P. Ideal Gas Engine—Rebuilt	$ 61.75
3-½ H. P. Ideal Gas Engine—Rebuilt	$ 87.25
1-½ H. P. International—Rebuilt	$ 14.75
1 H. P. Mogul International—Rebuilt	$ 16.25
5 H. P. Hercules Gas Engine—Rebuilt	$ 88.50
1-½ H. P. Hercules Gas Engine—Rebuilt	$ 13.75
1-½ H. P. Keller Gas Engine—Rebuilt	$ 12.00
6 H. P. I. H. C. Gas Engine—Second-Hand	$ 35.00
3-½ H. P. Ideal Gas Engine—Second-Hand	$ 40.00

Benton County Hardware Co.
ADV. January 11, 1924

470

Walking Plows and Plow Shares

Oliver Walking Plows

No. 0 Wood Beam, Cash Sale Price	$ 4.85
No. 10 Steel Beam Chilled M. Board	$10.90
No. 13 Steel Beam Steel M. Board	$14.60
No. 19 Steel Beam Chilled M. Board	$15.25
No. 20 Steel Beam Chilled M. Board	$14.50
No. 20 Steel Beam Steel M. Board	$15.75
No. 40 Steel Beam Chilled M. Board	$14.50
No. 82 Steel Beam Steel M. Board—12-inch	$14.75
No. G-12 Steel Beam—All Steel—12-inch	$17.65

Cream Separators

International Primrose

No. 1—Latest Model Sale Price	**$49.25**
No. 2—Latest Model Sale Price	**$56.75**

Sharples

No. 2—Latest Model Sale Price	**$64.75**
No. 3—Latest Model Sale Price	**$70.85**

Benton County Hardware Co.
ADV. January 11, 1924

April 30, 1926

FORD BRAKES
ARE UNUSUALLY
EFFECTIVE

Reliability and safety
due to simple design and
careful construction

ONE OF the first things you will notice when you drive the Ford is the quick, effective action of its four-wheel brakes.

They are unusually safe and reliable because they are mechanical, internal expanding, with all braking surfaces fully enclosed. This prevents mud, water, sand, etc., from getting between the band and drum and interfering with brake action.

Other outstanding features of the Ford are the Triplex shatter-proof glass windshield, four Houdaille double-acting hydraulic shock absorbers, aluminum pistons, torque-tube drive, more than twenty ball and roller bearings, Rustless Steel, reliability, economy, and long life.

You save when you buy the Ford and you save every mile you drive.

THE FORD DE LUXE PHAETON

THIRTEEN BODY TYPES

$430 to $630

(F. o. b. Detroit, plus freight and delivery. Bumpers and spare tire extra at low cost. You can purchase a Ford on economical terms, through the Authorized Ford Finance Plans of the Universal Credit Company.)

Ford

May 8, 1931

October 13, 1932

Shop Friday and Saturday at the

A. B. C. STORE

Rogers, Ark.

Special values await you. . . Investigate before you invest.

New Dresses
$4.95

Marvelous values, in the season's latest styles and newest materials; wines, blacks, browns; travel prints. One- and two-piece models.

Fall and Winter Coats
Two Special Groups—
$8.75 and $22.45

Here you will find the greatest coat values. Fine rough woolens, heavy all-silk linings, inner lined, trimmed with fine quality rich furs; also tailored sports coats, the newest materials and styles. Investigate! . . . See these real values.

New Prints
15c

36-inch, heavy, closely woven, 80-square count, plaids, diagonal stripes and hundreds of other new patterns. All guaranteed fast. No better 80-square print made; no better selection of patterns to be found.

Curtain Marquisette
10c yard

40 inches wide, fine quality pastel colors, ecru, cream and white. Outstanding value.

Men's Union Suits
59c
2 pair $1

Fine ribbed knit, winter weight, long sleeve and ankle length. Sizes 36 to 46.

Muslin
6c

36-inch brown muslin, heavy quality, closely woven, smooth finish. You save by buying now.

Outing Flannel
10c yard

36-inch, good quality, solid colors, white, light and dark fancies.

Boys' Sheep Lined Coats
$2.95

Leatherette and corduroy, sheep lined. Sizes 8 to 18. An outstanding value.

Boys' Union Suits
39c
3 suits $1

Fine ribbed, winter weight, long sleeve and ankle length. Sizes 6 to 16.

Men's Handkerchiefs
2 for 5c

Regular 5c values. Excellent quality, full size.

Silk Hose
59c
2 pair $1

Full fashion, pure thread silk, fine sheer chiffon, lace tops. All the new Fall shades.

Ladies' Union Suits
49c

Fine knit, rayon stripe, built-up tops, tight knee.

Misses' Union Suits
35c
3 suits $1

Fine ribbed, tape waist, long sleeve and ankle length. Sizes 2 to 12 years.

Misses' Hose
10c pair

Derby ribbed, excellent quality, new Fall shades. Sizes 5 to 9½. These sell for 15c most everywhere.

Ladies' Hose
19c

Fine quality rayon silk, new Fall shades. Sell most places for 29c. Outstanding value.

New Prints
10c yard

36 inches wide, fine count, wide range of new patterns; guaranteed colors.

Ladies' Handkerchiefs
6 for 10c

Former 5c value in a special purchase, passing to the consumer at a most ridiculous price. See these.

Ladies' Handkerchiefs
All Pure Linen
2 for 15c

All pure linen, fancy handkerchiefs. An unusual value.

October 13, 1932

1898

1898

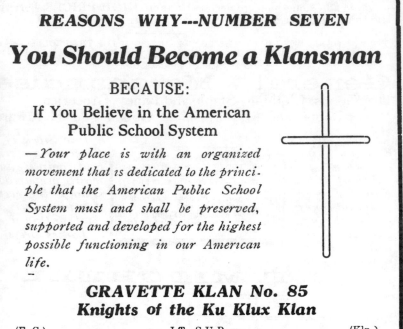

REASONS WHY---NUMBER SEVEN

You Should Become a Klansman

BECAUSE:

If You Believe in the American Public School System

—Your place is with an organized movement that is dedicated to the principle that the American Public School System must and shall be preserved, supported and developed for the highest possible functioning in our American life.

GRAVETTE KLAN No. 85
Knights of the Ku Klux Klan

(E. C.)   IT SUB   (Klp.)

1925

478

November 4, 1887

November, 1887

November 4, 1887

OSAGE VALLEY HIGH SCHOOL.

This institution was organized in 1885, and begins its third annual session, Monday, September 5, 1887, to continue for 10 months.

The success which has attended the school, and the growing interest manifested during the past year have demonstrated the fact that a permanent High School, at home, is now recognized by the community as a necessity; enabling the youth to obtain a practical and thorough education at the least expense.

The Osage Valley High School is situated in Benton County, Arkansas, the extreme northwestern county of the State, in a valley of the Ozark Mountains, at an elevation of about 1,500 feet, in a region noted for its healthfulness, crystal water and bracing atmosphere; in a community peaceable, prosperous, and intelligent.

The building is new, pleasantly located in a native grove, and furnished with the best of school furniture, improved seats and desks, slated black-boards, reading charts, &c.

The Principal is a graduate, has had several years' experience as teacher in the schools of the East, and having had control of the Osage Valley High School during the past year, he can enter upon the year's work intelligently and in a manner beneficial to all who may attend.

Our course of instruction will be thorough, and above all, practical, embracing all those studies properly belonging to a High School or Academy, in addition to the common school branches, being admirably suited to the wants of the young gentlemen and ladies of this practical age.

While we have a regular course of study, and would advise a student to follow the course strictly when it is at all possible, yet the school realizes that there are many young people who have neither the time nor the means to take a complete course, but wish to pursue special subjects and must attend school at such times as are convenient for them. To those who may be so situated we say, "Come and take such part of the whole course as best meets your requirements."

Expenses here are less than at any other school of equal rank. Good board costs from $1.50 to $2.00 per week, with private families, and the principal and friends of the school will secure good places for those desiring to attend.

Tuition, from $1.00 to $2.00 per month, due monthly, without deduction for irregular attendance, excepting in case of sickness of two weeks duration. Contingent fee for term, 25 cents, due on entering.

Students may enter at any time, but will find it to their advantage to enter at the beginning of the term.

The school is open to males and females alike. All acceptable white students, over six years of age, will be received and instructed alike.

The text books can be purchased here of the dealer. A union Sabbath school meets weekly. Daily mails.

For further information, call on or address

A. W. STARCK, Principal,
Osage Mills, Benton Co., Ark.

PEA RIDGE ACADEMY.

Programme of Commencement Exercises.

TUESDAY, MAY 24, 1887.

9:45 A. M.—Music—Prayer—Music—Declamations.

Pompii—Julian Blake, Bentonville, Ark.

What a Little Boy Says—Orville Wood, Pea Ridge, Ark.

The Dead Soldier Boy—Minnie Prather, Vinita, I. T.

Better than Gold—Lula Hall, Pea Ridge, Ark.

A Love Letter—Junius Crick, Bentonville, Ark.

A Vision—Josie Roberts, Pea Ridge, Ark.

The Golden Ladder—Stella Maris, Pea Ridge.

A Plea vs. Facts, (A Western Lawyer)—Willie Roberts, Pea Ridge, Ark.

MUSIC.

Essays:

Like a Dream—Miss Ida Pascoe, Southwest City, Mo.

Intelligence at the Ballot Box our only National Safety—J. A. Steward, Mason Valley, Ark.

MUSIC.

Declamations:

The Pilot's Story—Miss Rattie Foster, Pea Ridge, Ark.

Death of a Reveler—Miss Viola Comax, Pea Ridge, Ark.

The National Flag—R. E. L. Rogers, Garfield, Ark.

Infidelity Tested—Miss Mary Inman, Nixa, Mo.

The Losses of Chicago—Preston Davis, Bentonville, Ark.

Strong Drink—D. L. Wheat, Pea Ridge, Ark.

MUSIC.

Debate—Resolved, that the war between the United States and Mexico, in 1846, the cause of the Mexicans was right.

Affirmative W. O. Young, Colville, Ark.; J. P. McClure, Exeter, Mo.

Negative J. W. Osborn, Pea Ridge, Ark.; Ed. Foster, Pea Ridge, Ark.

2:30 P. M. MUSIC.

Alumni address—Ed. G. Lee, Frisco, Kansas.

MUSIC.

Graduating address—God, Country and Truth—Miss Ida Speaker, Bright water.

Annual address, by Principal of Academy.

MUSIC.

Delivering Diplomas.

Conferring degree of A. B. upon Class of 1886.

MUSIC.

Benediction.

September 9, 1899

December 27, 1900

GEO. D. PARKS.   GEO. D. PARKS.

BARGAINS EVERY DAY
⋙→FOR←⋘
PEOPLE NOW ON EARTH!

SPECIAL BARGAIN PRICES
On Men's and Boy's Clothing.

Men's Tan Herringbone Stripe Satinet sack
suit, $3 50; special Holiday price.... 2 50
Men's Black Fancy Cotton Worsted sack
suit, $4; special Holiday price...... 3 00
Men's Navy Blue Cheviot sack suits, $4 50
special Holiday price............. 3 50
Men's Black Cotton Twill Worsted sack
suits, $4.50; special Holiday price... 3 50
Men's Fine Black Diagonal Worsted sack
suits, $6.50; special Holiday price... 5 00
Men's Grey Stripe Worsted, fast color, latest style sack suit, $9 00; special Hol-
iday price 7 50
Nobby Tan Check Cassimere, double
breasted vest, sack suit, $11,00; spec-
ial Holiday price................. 8 50

Men's and Boy's Overcoats.

Grey Beaver Overcoat, velvet collar, 5.00;
special price............... 4 00
Black, brown and blue Beaver Overcoats,
large sizes only, $6.00; special price . 5 00
Heavy Wool-lined, grey storm coat, large
collar, $6.00; special price......... 5 00
Heavy, Black, Irish Frieze, storm, good
value at $8 50; special price....... 7 00
Our finest block, raw edge Kersey Overcoat, lined with Italian serge, satin
sleeve lining, as good in appearance
and wearing qualities as money will
buy, was $12.50; special price.... 11 00
Good Black Diagonal Cape Mackintosh,
not the short skimpy kind, our regular $1 50 grade for.............. 1 15

BOY'S LONG PANT SUITS.
Age 14 to 19 Years.

Good Heavy Black Cheviot suit, 3.50; special price.......................... 2 50
Same goods in neat brown check.......... 2 50
Good Quality Cassimere Suit, grey and
brown check, will wear well and keep
its color, $4 50; special price......... 3 50
Brown and tan stripe, fine Scotch Cheviot,
double breasted vest, neat and stylish,
7 50, special price.................. 6 00
Finer quality same goods, in check, with
double breasted vest, the best and nob-
biest young man's suit we carry, $10.00
special price........................ 8 00

Children's Suits.

Two piece suits, age 8 to 15 years; Vestee suits,
age 3 to 8 years.
Grey check Satinet suits, 8 to 15, $1, special
price 75
Two piece stripe, cotton worsted, $1.25, spec-
ial price.......................... 1 00
Two piece suit, neat brown check worsted
$2.00, special price.................. 1 50
Two piece suit, small grey check worsted,
$2.50, special price.................. 2 00
Two piece suits, heavy weight, grey Cheviot,
$3, special price.................... 2 50
Two piece suits in several patterns, grey and
brown Cheviots and fancy worsteds, the
best suits we carry, $5, special price... 4 00
Three piece vestee suit of heavy navy blue
Cheviot, splendid suit for service, has
sold well at $2.50, special price 2 00

GEO. D. PARKS, ROGERS, ARK

February 21, 1901

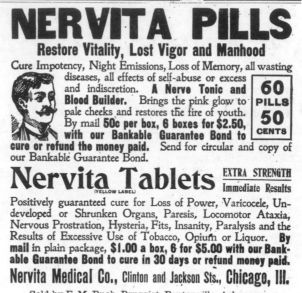
February 21, 1901

July 11, 1902

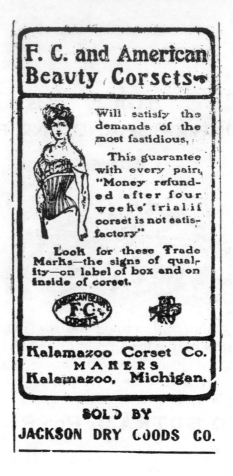
July 11, 1902

July 11, 1902

HOUSE CLEANING TIME.

You may want some nice pieces of **Furniture** to fill up odd corners. New goods are now being arranged for the biggest Furniture Sale of the season.

Will Commence at Our Store on April 25th.

Each and every value is double tripple the sale price.

➤FURNITURE, MATTINGS AND STOVES.◄

ROCKERS.

Ladies' Rockers, good solid oak, sale price
$1 25

Ladies' Rockers, worth 2.00, our sale price
$1.40

Good substantial oak arm cobler seat Rockers, sale price
$1.80

Fine polished golden oak Rockers in all the latest designs, all beauties,
$5.00 to $8.50

In this sale you can find just the Rocker to suit you and at the right prices.

SIDEBOARDS

No one can touch us on quality and prices on

SIDEBOARDS.

We have good oak Sideboards For $9.50 and $12.00

Our Best Ones which are the prettiest we have had, quartered oak, big swell fronts, the very latest Sale prices, $22.50, $25, $26, $32.50 and $35.

CHIFFONIERS.

Our $18.50 and $20.00 ones are Bargains

Iron Beds, Dressers, Leather Couches, Book Cases, will all be on sale for **RIGHT PRICES.**

MANTEL ➤➤➤BEDS.

Our Cheap Ones

Are nice solid goods,
Sale price $12.50

Better Ones

Nicely engraved,
Sale price $14.50

Our Best Ones

Have nice French bevel mirrors, good size, in golden oak and swell fronts, sale price
$20, 21.50, 22.50.

Nothing Only
BARGAINS

J. W. BRYANT,
ROGERS, ARKANSAS.

October 16, 1902

July 31, 1902

October 16, 1902

THE STUDEBAKER.

THE SORT THAT SELL AND WEAR.

We are unloading a **BIG CAR** of **STUDEBAKER** latest
ring specialties in Road Wagons, Gentlemen's Driving wag-
s, Buggies, Open Top, stick seat surreys and Driving wagons.
y kind from a $37.00 Studebaker road wagon to a $135.00
rey. $60 buggies to the prettiest $90 vehicle you ever
ked at.

TUDEBAKER HARNESS

Like their entire line have no defects.

od single buggy harness for - - - -		$8.50
1e " " " " - -		$10.00 to $13.00
1e single surrey harness, good and heavy		$11.00 to $14.00

OUR FURNITURE DEPARTMENT is at its best. Special
es for bargain hunters in all lines.

. W. BRYANT, ROGERS, ARK.

March 6, 1902

—→ ESTABLISHED 1872. ←—

GEO. H. JEFFERSON.

Northwest Corner Square, Bentonville, Arkansas,

The LEADER in LOW PRICES of GROCERIES

14 lbs best Eastern granulated sugar for.. $1.00
Early Breakfast Coffee per lb.............. .15
Extra fancy Carolina Rice per lb.......... .08
Extra fancy California Peaches per lb..... .10
3 packages Squirrel Rolled Oats for....... .25
12 boxes good Matches for................. .05
6 oz. bottle Scotch Snuff for.............. .15

Late Burbank seed Potatoes per bu....... .75
3 cans fancy Maine Corn for............. .25
4 cans good string Beans for............ .25
4 cans good Blackberries for............ .25
8 lbs Lion Coffee for.................... 1.00
Best German Millet Seed per bu......... 1.25
A dandy good Broom for only............ .25

Get your Yeast Foam from me and you will get it fresh.

Bring your Butter and Eggs to me if you want the top price.

Yours Respectfully,   GEORGE H. JEFFERSON.

1901

November 21, 1932

December 4, 1902